Leaders of the Lost Cause

Leaders of the Lost Cause

New Perspectives on the Confederate High Command

Edited by
Gary W. Gallagher and Joseph T. Glatthaar

STACKPOLE
BOOKS

Published by
STACKPOLE BOOKS
5067 Ritter Road
Mechanicsburg, PA 17055
www.stackpolebooks.com

Printed in the United States of America

10 9 8 7 6 5 4 3 2 1

FIRST EDITION

Library of Congress Cataloging-in-Publication Data

Leaders of the lost cause : reflections on eight generals of the Confederacy / edited
by Gary W. Gallagher and Joseph T. Glatthaar.— 1st ed.
    p. cm.
  Includes index.
  ISBN 0-8117-0087-9
  1. Generals—Confederate States of America—Biography. 2. Confederate States of
America. Army—Biography. 3. United States—History—Civil War, 1861–1865—
Campaigns. I. Gallagher, Gary W. II. Glatthaar, Joseph T., 1956–
E467.L436 2004
973.7'42'0922—dc22

                                                                    2004004160

CONTENTS

INTRODUCTION

Gary W. Gallagher and Joseph T. Glatthaar

Among the many concerns of the fledgling Confederate Government in early 1861, national defense took center stage. Initially, seven states, later joined by four more, seceded from the United States to form the Confederate States of America, and most citizens assumed that their former country would not allow them to exit peacefully. War was on the horizon, and Confederate politicians and voters alike looked for a leader around whom they could rally.

Fortunately, the new government had selected Jefferson Davis as its provisional president. Davis had graduated from the U.S. Military Academy at West Point in 1828 and joined the Regular Army. After several years, he left the service and eventually found his way into politics. Davis represented his constituents of Mississippi in the U.S. House of Representatives and the U.S. Senate, serving on the Military Affairs Committees in both chambers. When war erupted in Mexico, Davis raised a regiment of infantry and commanded it heroically, suffering a painful wound for his country. During Franklin Pierce's administration, from 1853–57, Davis not only elevated the post of secretary of war to the height of influence within the cabinet, but he also expanded and reformed the U.S. Army to meet the needs of the country's ever expanding empire. By virtually all accounts, Davis proved himself a brilliant secretary of war, perhaps the best in the nineteenth century. He later returned to the Senate and its Military Affairs Committee, until he resigned his seat in 1861. Rarely has such an experienced leader assumed the helm of a democratic republic in wartime.

Davis immediately began doling out military commissions to qualified soldiers to meet the emergency. At the same time, he worked with the Provisional Congress to formulate a sensible command structure for its new army. On March 6, 1861, Congress authorized Davis to appoint four brigadier generals in the Army of the Confederate States, and eight days later, it legislated a fifth position, which the president could use for an adjutant and inspector general of the army. All commissions, so Congress specified, should reflect the rank that the individual held in the U.S. Army prior to secession. But Secretary of War Leroy Pope Walker perceived problems when militiamen held commissions as major generals. As a solution, he proposed the creation of the rank of general in the Confederate army. Davis adopted the suggestion and recommended it to Congress, and by mid-May, Congress had established the rank of general. With proper foresight, Davis and the Congress had forged a much more sensible command structure than the one they had left behind. A general could command an army; lieutenant generals would serve as corps commanders; the rank for division commanders would be major general; and brigadier generals would lead brigades.[1]

Prior to the first battle of the war, Davis had filled four of the vacancies at the general rank. Albert Sidney Johnston, Davis's *beau ideal* during his own days as a cadet at West Point, received one of the positions. So, too, did Samuel Cooper, the adjutant general of the U.S. Army since 1852, who took over the duties of the adjutant and inspector general for the Confederacy. Robert E. Lee, who emerged from the Mexican War as the finest officer on Winfield Scott's handpicked staff of elite officers, was awarded a third position. Lee had turned down command of the principal field army of the United States to serve his home state of Virginia and the Confederacy, and many people viewed him as the finest officer in either country's service. The fourth went to Joseph E. Johnston, a fellow Virginian and classmate of Lee's at West Point. Johnston had exhibited great courage on several battlefields and held the staff position of quartermaster general in the U.S. Army prior to his resignation. At the end of August, when Davis placed them in rank order, he also elevated Pierre Gustave Toutant Beauregard to general. Beauregard had performed valiantly on Scott's staff in Mexico, and had been a key figure in the capture of Fort Sumter and the Confederate victory at 1st Manassas.

In his appointment to the rank of general, Davis followed what he believed to be both the spirit and the letter of the law. He dated the commissions based on their permanent U.S. Army rank. Because Cooper held the position of adjutant general and ranked as colonel since 1852, he would date first. Sidney Johnston, promoted to the rank of colonel in 1855 in the U.S. Army, received the second highest date. Lee, elevated to colonel just prior to his resignation, came next. Fourth in rank among the full generals was Joe Johnston. Although Johnston held the rank of brigadier general of staff, his permanent rank was lieutenant colonel. Beauregard, a major prior to secession, stood fifth. The various dates of rank satisfied all of the men except Joe Johnston. Extremely sensitive to rank and prerogatives, as Robert K. Krick explains in his essay, Johnston erupted in an indiscreet, 2,000-word complaint to his commander in chief, insisting that as a brigadier general, he should have ranked first. Davis exhibited unusual depths of self-restraint when he replied that Johnston's diatribe was "one-sided, and its insinuations as unfounded as they are unbecoming." The relationship never recovered.[2]

Throughout the war years, Davis elevated three other individuals to the rank of general. When Sidney Johnston was killed in action at the battle of Shiloh in April 1862, Braxton Bragg, Johnston's chief of staff and corps commander, replaced him. In February 1864, Edmund Kirby Smith, the commander of the Trans-Mississippi Department, received a promotion to the rank of general. And the last to hold the rank of general, John Bell Hood, assumed the promotion temporarily when he supplanted Joe Johnston as commander of the Army of Tennessee in July 1864.

The common thread among these officers was Jefferson Davis, to whom they were beholden for their appointment. Davis entered West Point in 1824 and graduated four years later. Among those who attended during his years were Sidney Johnston, Lee, and Joe Johnston. Two years ahead in class, Sidney Johnston, a fellow Kentuckian, impressed Davis and many others as the Academy's outstanding cadet. Powerfully built, Johnston exhibited extraordinary leadership skills and proved adept academically, graduating near the top of his class. In the years afterward, Johnston did nothing to diminish his reputation in the eyes of Davis. Many knowledgeable individuals, who respected Johnston's record in the U.S. Army, would have concurred with Davis when he said, "If [Sidney Johnston] is not general, we had better give up the war, for we have no generals."[3]

In the class behind Davis were Lee and Joe Johnston. While neither of them associated closely with Davis during their West Point years, at a small school like West Point both cadets certainly knew the future Confederate president. As the son of the Revolutionary War hero Light-Horse Harry Lee, Lee's reputation preceded him. His academic prowess and gentlemanly cultivation reinforced the uniform, high opinion that fellow cadets had of Lee. Heroics in the Mexican War marked Lee as a very special officer, perhaps the best in the entire army. During Lee's days as superintendent of West Point, he communicated frequently with Secretary of War Jefferson Davis. When Davis convinced Congress to expand the Regular Army by four regiments, the secretary of war personally selected the officers, and chose them not on seniority but on merit. He appointed Sidney Johnston to command the 2nd U.S. Cavalry Regiment, and Lee to serve as its lieutenant colonel.

Davis also knew Joe Johnston at West Point, perhaps better than he did Lee. In the Regular Army, Johnston exhibited conspicuous courage on several battlefields, which kept his name in high standing with fellow officers and those who were knowledgeable about military affairs. Like Lee, his unusual bravery in Mexico earned him universal acclaim, no doubt paving his way to Davis's selection of him as lieutenant colonel in the 1st U.S. Cavalry Regiment. Although Johnston owed his appointment to quartermaster general, with the rank of brigadier general of staff, to his distant cousin, Secretary of War John B. Floyd, his assignment to Washington, D.C., for the previous two years, and his duties there as the army's chief quartermaster surely brought him into frequent contact with Senator Davis.

Unlike the other initial selections as general, Cooper did not graduate high in his West Point class. Fortunately for Cooper, that did not reflect his intellectual prowess. Cooper attended West Point in the days before academic standing, when class rank depended on length of attendance at the school before graduation rather than scholastic achievements. Cooper did not know Davis at the Academy, graduating nearly a decade before Davis entered. His relationship with the Confederate president stemmed from his service as adjutant general during Davis's tenure as secretary of war. When Davis engaged in a legendary dispute with commanding general Winfield Scott, which reached such a pique that Scott shifted his headquarters from Washington to New York City, Davis had to rely even more on Adjutant General Cooper, who handled all the army paperwork. Over four years, they built a strong relationship of trust and respect, which extended into the secession crisis. Cooper also benefited from his marriage to the powerful Mason family of Virginia. His brother-in-law served with Davis in the U.S. Congress and functioned in the diplomatic corps for the Confederacy.

Beauregard graduated second in his West Point class, ten years after Davis. Beauregard's exceptional service on Scott's staff—his heroism and two wounds—marked him as a rising star in the army. His appointment to the position of superintendent of the U.S. Military Academy in 1861 came most likely with Davis's knowledge and perhaps his support. Beauregard's successes at Fort Sumter and 1st Manassas offered convincing evidence that he merited both Davis's confidence and the rank of general.

Although Bragg graduated near the top of his West Point class (fifth) in 1837, he was the only one of the full generals who had returned to civilian life when the secession crisis erupted. But Bragg had other merits that ensured his high standing with the Confederate president. In the Mexican War at the desperate battle of Buena Vista, Bragg emerged along with Davis as the great heroes. At critical moments, the service of both men helped to save the army of Zachary Taylor, Davis's former father-in-law, from defeat. Nor did it hurt his promotion cause that Bragg's brother served in the U.S. Senate with Davis and for a time held a cabinet post in Davis's Confederate White House. Early in the war, Bragg's skills as a troop organizer and trainer once again elevated his stock with Davis. Shortly after the battle of Shiloh, when the Confederacy needed a hero among its high-ranking officers, Bragg was probably the best choice, and Davis rewarded him with a fourth star.

The final two generals whom Davis appointed were Smith and Hood. Neither had a particularly stellar academic record—Smith ranked 25 of 41 in the Class of 1845, and Hood stood 44 of 52 in the class of 1853—nor did they have much direct contact with Davis before the secession crisis. Smith's older brother Ephraim, who was killed in action in the Mexican War, graduated in Sidney Johnston's class and doubtless knew Davis. Hood may have come to Davis's attention simply because he graduated while Davis was secretary of war and both men had received their appointment from Kentucky. As a young officer, Smith earned an excellent reputation in Mexico, and Davis promoted him to serve in the 2nd U.S. Cavalry Regiment. The large and powerful Hood, whose only outstanding grades at West

Point were in cavalry tactics, also received an assignment as second lieutenant to the 2nd Cavalry. For several years, Smith and Hood served alongside each other, and Smith even considered Hood his protégé. Davis appointed Smith as general largely because of his duties as the head of the Trans-Mississippi Department. Once the Federals gained control of the Mississippi River, Smith's command functioned in relative isolation from Richmond authorities, and Davis felt he needed the rank to oversee the war effort there. Hood, the last of the full generals, received the rank temporarily when Davis selected him to replace Joe Johnston, with Federal forces at the doorstep of Atlanta. After Hood lost Atlanta and then suffered crushing defeats at Franklin and Nashville, Tennessee, he resigned as army commander and reverted to his previous rank of lieutenant general.

Aside from their military service and contacts with Davis, the background and experiences of the full generals varied widely. Cooper, the oldest person and the youngest graduate from the Academy at seventeen, hailed from the North. His connection to the South and the Confederacy stemmed from his wife's family. Hood, the youngest of the generals, also graduated lowest in his class, among the bottom fifth. Upon graduation from West Point, the generals collectively entered three of the four branches of service—engineers, artillery, and infantry—but during their prewar military careers, five of them transferred to the cavalry. Two of them, Lee and Beauregard, returned to West Point as superintendents, and Smith taught there.

All of them except Cooper had combat experience. Six of them fought in the Mexican War, and all of those received recognition for gallantry. Hood, the youngest of the lot, graduated long after the War with Mexico. Instead, he battled Indians on the Texas frontier, as did several others from the group. Without doubt, Sidney Johnston possessed the most diverse combat service. He fought in the Black Hawk War, the Mexican War, and against Indians in Texas and Mormons in Utah. A wound in a duel prevented him from seeing action for the Texas Republic.

Because nearly all of the full generals either came from or married into wealthy families, all of them had a direct connection to slavery. Despite Cooper's Northern upbringing, he embraced all trappings of Southern high society with the fervency of a true convert. His wife's family were large slaveholders, and he personally owned them. The wealth of Lee's immediate family had declined considerably in his youth, but he married into the Custis family—in fact, Martha

Washington's great-granddaughter—and slave ownership came with matrimonial bonds. Likewise, Beauregard married twice, both times into well-heeled Louisiana families. Bragg personally owned a substantial plantation in Louisiana, and Hood came from a very wealthy Kentucky family with numerous slaves. Joe Johnston and his wife owned slaves, as did Smith, and Sidney Johnston owned a slave family.

President Davis once wrote his brother that great generals only come around once in every generation. Unfortunately, Davis explained, the Confederacy needed a half dozen. Other than the acclaimed Lee, who directed the Army of Northern Virginia to such stirring victories, and perhaps Cooper, who handled the army paperwork, it is difficult to say that any of the other full generals were successful. Sidney Johnston died before he could prove himself one way or the other. Joe Johnston held commands off and on until the very end, but he never lived up to the expectations of Davis or the Confederate people. Beauregard rode a roller coaster of successes and failures, with his finest achievements coming in the spring and early summer of 1864 in Virginia. Bragg built an army skillfully but never seemed to fight it well, even when the "Gods of War" shined on him, as they did at Chickamauga in September 1863. Smith commanded in the Trans-Mississippi Department, an area of little importance to the rebellion once Federals gained control of the Mississippi River and severed it from the rest of the Confederacy. Smith failed to offer inspired leadership, but even if he had, it is doubtful he could have affected any change in the outcome of the war. By contrast, Hood had an opportunity to influence the course of the war, yet he proved unequal to the task of army command. During the last half of 1864, his army suffered defeat after defeat at the hands of more experienced Federal commanders.

We decided to write a collection of essays on the eight Confederate generals for several reasons. As full generals, they had an enormous impact on the ultimate outcome of the war. No one has examined them collectively in article-length form, and with the huge outpouring of recent scholarship, we believe that individually they warranted a fresh appraisal.

In an effort to to obtain new perspectives, we assigned each general to a scholar who has never written on him before. Only when someone backed out were we compelled to juggle the assignments, and although Gary Gallagher had to take on Lee, a familiar subject, he has offered some fresh ideas about a familiar yet popular subject. It

was also our intention that authors draft both biographical and inter-
pretive essays. In order to achieve this, they devoted extensive space
to prewar careers. Those formative years, and even their early wartime
service, shaped the eight generals and influenced the way they
responded in crises during their tenure as generals.

Charles P. Roland, the author of a classic biography of Albert Sidney Johnston, tackles an old nemesis of Johnston in Beauregard. What
emerges is a fair-minded exploration of a tumultuous life and military
career: from Beauregard's meteoric rise as the first hero of the Confederacy to his precipitate fall from grace—to the revival of his reputation through excellent service in 1864. Regrettably, Roland
concludes, Beauregard undermined his achievements late in the war
with a divisive and misleading memoir and the misuse of his fame to
promote a lottery.

In his investigation of Bragg, James I. Robertson, Jr., the
acclaimed biographer of Thomas J. "Stonewall" Jackson, concludes
that Bragg's choleric personality nullified much of his military knowledge and skill. In doing so, Robertson reminds us just how important
leadership is in the management and guidance of military forces.

William C. Davis, whose vast publications include biographies of
Jefferson Davis and Secretary of War John C. Breckinridge, mines a
wide array of sources to present the first modern portrait of the seemingly invisible adjutant and inspector general of the Confederacy,
Cooper. Ultimately, Davis challenges the negative depiction of Cooper
by various War Department personnel, and what emerges is an effective manager of army correspondence whose limited influences in
high circles were largely the product of President Davis's decision-
making style.

The biographer of Federal generals Don Carlos Buell and Franz
Sigel, Stephen D. Engle argues that Sidney Johnston took on a more
complex and difficult job for the Confederacy than anyone anticipated
or, at the time, even understood. Yet if any soldier could achieve success out west, it was that powerful soldier with the towering reputation. In death, Engle insists, Johnston resuscitated his declining
reputation. Whether the historian wags have attributed greatness or
failure to him, Southerners at the time viewed his demise as a turning
point in the war in the West.

Likewise, Gary Gallagher emphasizes those same linkages
between the army and the home front in his essay on Lee. Although
Lee suffered heavy losses in those huge battles in the Virginia Theater,

he fought a kind of war that met public demands and more than fulfilled public expectations. Gallagher portrays him as a modern warrior who functioned as the only general upon whom the Confederate people could rely.

Robert K. Krick, whose extensive and meticulous studies have focused on Stonewall Jackson and his subordinates, shifts over to the world of Joe Johnston. Armed with some new research, Krick argues that Johnston's lifelong fixation with rank and prerogatives undermined his ability to function effectively in the Confederacy.

As Joseph T. Glatthaar explains, early in the war, Smith served as Joe Johnston's chief of staff. During that duty, he embraced Johnston's approach to warfare. Johnston believed that the Confederacy should employ a Fabian strategy: sacrifice territory to avoid giving battle and fight only under the most advantageous conditions. Although he commanded in a backwater region, the employment of his Fabian strategy aided the Confederate war effort not a whit.

Keith S. Bohannon, whose own meticulous scholarship has earned him an enviable reputation as a rising young historian, argues that Hood's service early in the war shaped his approach to army leadership. Hood commanded the renowned Texas Brigade and a division in Lee's army. There, he thought that he had studied at the feet of the two great Confederate masters—Lee and Thomas J. "Stonewall" Jackson. Unfortunately for Hood, he extracted the wrong lessons about combat aggressiveness, and this misapplied approach combined with his own shortcomings to injure the Rebel cause.

As a group, these essays offer a window on the highest level of command in the Confederacy. Designed to be suggestive as well as descriptive, they should provide students of the Civil War with material for explorations of the military history of the conflict, the ways in which generalship influenced affairs behind the lines, and the importance of politics and personality in shaping the Confederacy's war effort.

NOTES

1. See: An act for the establishment and organization of the Army of the Confederate States of America, March 6, 1861; An act amendatory of an act for the organization of the staff departments of the Army, March 14, 1861; Walker to Davis, April 27, 1861; Davis to Gentlemen of the Congress, April 29, 1861; An act to increase the military establishment of the

Confederate States, May 16, 1861, U.S. War Department, *War of the Rebellion: A Compilation of the Official Records of the Union and Confederate Armies* (Washington, D.C.: U.S. Government Printing Office, 1880–1901) , IV, 1:128, 163, 249, 267, 326 (hereafter cited as *OR*).

2. Davis to Johnston, September 14, 1864; also see Johnston to Davis, September 12, 1861, *OR*, IV, 1:611 and 605–8.

3. Quoted in Charles P. Roland, *Albert Sidney Johnston: Soldier of Three Republics* (Austin: University of Texas Press, 1964), 299.

"A Great General Is So Rare": Robert E. Lee and the Confederacy

Gary W. Gallagher

In early May 1863, Jefferson Davis wrote a brief letter to his brother Joseph concerning the Confederacy's desperate need for talented field commanders. Robert E. Lee's recent success at the battle of Chancellorsville was on Davis's mind. The president termed it "a great victory, in view of the thorough preparation of the Enemy and his superiority of numbers, not less than two to one." Lee's campaign against Joseph Hooker along the Rappahannock River contrasted sharply with Confederate efforts elsewhere. Davis alluded to the difficulty in finding other generals whose accomplishments would inspirit the nation. "A *General* in the full acceptation of the word is a rare product, scarcely more than one can be expected in a generation," observed Davis, "but in this mighty war in which we are engaged there is need for half a dozen." A few months earlier, the president had made this same point to Francis W. Pickens of South Carolina, remarking that "a great General is so rare that their names mark the arch of history." Among the eight officers who attained the rank of full general in Confederate service, seven of whom led armies in the field, only Lee could stake a persuasive claim to inclusion on such an arch—a circumstance that helps explain why the Confederacy did not establish itself as a long-term slaveholding republic.[1]

Lee began his journey toward Confederate renown as a member of a distinguished family.[2] Born on January 19, 1807, at "Stratford Hall" on Virginia's Northern Neck, he was the third son and fifth child of

Henry "Light-Horse Harry" Lee and Ann Hill Carter Lee. His father had been a military hero of the Revolutionary War who later served as governor of Virginia and as a member of the Continental Congress and the U.S. Congress. Various uncles and other relatives had signed the Declaration of Independence and otherwise achieved notable reputations. On his mother's side, Lee was tied to the Carters, another of Virginia's leading families.

What might have seemed a future of almost certain comfort and privilege for young Robert soon fell victim to his father's lack of fiscal responsibility. In 1811, awash in debt and hounded by creditors, Henry Lee moved his family from Stratford to Alexandria, Virginia. He remained in the household only a short time, leaving for the West Indies in the summer of 1813. Six-year-old Robert never again saw his father, whom he later viewed with mixed feelings. He unquestionably took pride in the gifted, audacious commander who had won the friendship of George Washington and served the colonial cause well. Yet much of Robert's later life can be read as an attempt to avoid the personal and fiscal irresponsibility that had plagued Light-Horse Harry.

With little money at hand, the family settled on a career in the U.S. Army for Robert. Family connections helped to secure an appointment to West Point, and Robert entered the Academy in July 1825. His time at West Point revealed patterns that would be evident during the remainder of his professional life. He worked hard, held himself to the most rigorous standards of performance and behavior, and usually won the admiration of peers and superiors. He ranked second in his class at graduation in 1829 and, along with five others, survived four grueling years at the Academy without a single demerit on his record. Lee's forty-five classmates included fellow Virginian Joseph E. Johnston, who like Lee would become a Confederate army commander. Jefferson Davis, the future president of the Confederacy, had preceded Lee and Johnston by one year in the class of 1828.

Apart from his exceptional academic record and conduct, Lee also exhibited qualities of leadership at West Point. Named a staff sergeant in the corps of cadets in 1825–26 and 1826–27, he advanced at the end of his third year to cadet adjutant, the highest rank to which he and his peers could aspire. Fellow cadets referred to him as the "Marble Model"—a nickname that probably reflected a combination of envy and admiration. Just under six feet tall, handsome, and with black hair and brown eyes, Lee cut a very striking figure.[3]

Lee's high class ranking entitled him to enter the Engineer Corps, in which he was commissioned a second lieutenant on July 1, 1829. Promotions to first lieutenant on September 21, 1836, and to captain on July 7, 1838, punctuated fifteen years of peacetime service during which Lee exhibited considerable skill as an engineer. He traveled to "Arlington," across the Potomac River from the national capital, on June 30, 1831, where he married Mary Ann Randolph Custis, the only daughter of Arlington's owner, George Washington Parke Custis, who was himself the grandson of Martha Washington. Lee thus gained family ties to George Washington, a personal hero the young officer sought to emulate as a man and a leader. Three decades later, the Confederate people often would compare Lee to Washington, looking to him and the Army of Northern Virginia as the bulwark of their struggle for independence much as the American colonists had looked to Washington and the Continental army.[4]

Lee first participated in military campaigning during the war with Mexico in 1846–47. Assigned initially to Gen. John E. Wool's command in northern Mexico, he received orders in mid-January 1847 to join Gen. Winfield Scott, then at the Brazos preparing a force to strike at Vera Cruz. Scott immediately formed a favorable impression of his new subordinate and added him to his "little cabinet," a group of staff officers who advised the general on a variety of tactical and engineering questions.

Two months after joining Scott, Lee went ashore at Vera Cruz with the invading American army. Between March and September, against a foe superior in numbers if not in quality, Scott conducted a remarkable campaign from Vera Cruz to Mexico City. Lee performed exemplary service throughout Scott's operations. At Vera Cruz, his placement of batteries and coolness under fire were equally meritorious. His reconnaissance of the Mexican left flank at Cerro Gordo, in the course of which he was forced to hide under a fallen tree for several hours to escape capture, made possible a decisive American flanking movement. During a thunderstorm on the night preceding the battle of Contreras, he made a daring three-hour crossing of the Pedregal—an exceedingly rugged lava field—to deliver a critical message to army headquarters. Lee's work at Churubusco the next afternoon did much to ensure American success and elicited praise from several officers. In the last stage of the campaign, Lee positioned artillery in front of Chapultepec, acted as aide-de-camp to Scott, and worked around the clock in preparation for the final attacks. Wounded slightly during the fighting on September 13, he collapsed late in the afternoon from a combination of profound fatigue, stress, and loss of blood. He recovered sufficiently to don a dress uniform and participate in the formal surrender of the city the next day.[5]

Superiors lavished praise on Lee's accomplishments. General Scott called his trip across the Pedregal "the greatest feat of physical and moral courage performed by any individual" during the entire campaign. Gen. Persifor S. Smith's official report similarly singled out Lee: "His reconnaissances, though pushed far beyond the bounds of prudence, were conducted with so much skill, that their fruits were of the utmost value—the soundness of his judgment and personal daring being equally conspicuous." Brevets for gallantry to the rank of major (Cerro Gordo), lieutenant colonel (Contreras and Churubusco), and colonel (Chapultepec) were Lee's reward. More important, he had impressed influential officers. A witness close to Winfield Scott later remarked that the general came away from Mexico with an "almost idolatrous fancy for Lee, whose military genius he estimated far above that of any other officer in the army."[6]

Lee offered his own appraisal of the campaign in a letter written from Mexico City in October 1847. "Since this Army landed at Vera Cruz," he wrote, "it has taken all the fortified places known in the Republic[,] . . . taken more prisoners than it numbers men, defeated every army that has been brought against it, captured the capital & dispersed the Government." He closed with a tribute to Winfield Scott. "Our Genl is our great reliance," he affirmed: "He is a great man on great occasions. . . . Confident in his powers & resources, his judgment is as sound as his heart is bold and daring."[7] For Lee, Scott's audacious offensive against the Mexican capital had taught lessons about how a smaller army can overcome numerical odds, how turning movements can discomfit a foe, and how frontal assaults sometimes can succeed. Fifteen years hence, when at the helm of a much larger and more famous army, Lee would apply these lessons (though he would lose a far higher percentage of his soldiers in battle) and would be described in much the same language he used to praise Scott in Mexico.

Lee returned from Mexico as one of the war's conspicuous heroes but soon fell into a familiar routine of peacetime engineering work. On May 28, 1852, orders directed him to assume the superintendency of the U.S. Military Academy, a post he took up on September 1. Despite initial misgivings about the assignment, Lee compiled an excellent record as an administrator at West Point. He oversaw changes in the curriculum and the addition of a fifth year to the traditional four-year course of studies.

Promotion and transfer to a line command ended Lee's time at West Point. On March 3, 1855, Congress acted on Secretary of War Jefferson Davis's recommendation to expand the army by two regiments each of infantry and cavalry. Lee was offered the lieutenant colonelcy of the new 2nd Cavalry, his commission to date from the day Congress created the units (Albert Sidney Johnston was named colonel of the regiment). Nearly six years with the 2nd Cavalry brought more tedium than moments of drama. From March 1856 to October 1857 and again from February 1860 to February 1861, Lee served with the regiment in Texas, where he periodically pursued Comanches. During the second of these stays, he commanded the Department of Texas.[8]

Serendipity thrust Lee briefly into the national limelight in late October 1859. He chanced to be at Arlington when John Brown mounted his raid on Harpers Ferry, Virginia. Summoned to the War Department on October 17, Lee received instructions to proceed to Harpers Ferry with a detachment of Marines. Discovering that the raiders had taken a number of prisoners and barricaded themselves in the fire-engine house at the U.S. Armory, Lee planned an assault for the next morning. He narrated what happened on the morning of the eighteenth immediately after the event: "Tuesday about sunrise, with twelve marines under the command of Lieutenant [Israel] Green, [the detachment] broke in the door of the engine-house, secured the robbers, and released the prisoners unhurt."[9]

Along with the rest of the country, Lee watched the Union drift toward disaster in 1860–61. Shortly after Texas seceded on February 1, 1861, he received orders to report to Winfield Scott in Washington. In early March, he met privately for several hours with Scott, who likely made it clear that he wanted his former staff officer to remain in the U.S. Army. Lee's promotion to colonel of the 1st Cavalry followed on March 16. In the meantime, Confederate secretary of war Leroy Pope Walker offered Lee a brigadier general's commission in the Confederate army (Walker's letter, dated March 15, would have reached Lee after word of the promotion to colonel of the 1st Cavalry). Lee apparently did not respond to Walker's letter, but on March 30 he accepted the colonelcy and assignment to the 1st Cavalry.[10]

The final storm broke in mid-April. Confederates fired on Fort Sumter on the twelfth, and Lincoln issued a call for 75,000 volunteers to suppress the rebellion on the fifteenth. On April 17, Lee received requests to meet separately with Winfield Scott and Francis Preston Blair, Sr. The meetings took place on the morning of the eighteenth. Empowered by Lincoln to "ascertain Lee's intentions and feelings" and by Secretary of War Simon Cameron to make an offer to the Virginian, Blair asked Lee to assume command of the army being raised to put down the rebellion. Lee later remarked that Blair "tried in every way to persuade him to take it," including a suggestion that the country looked to him as "the representative of the Washington family." But Lee declined, explaining that he opposed secession but could not take the field against the Southern states. Proceeding immediately to Scott's office, Lee recounted his conversation with Blair and reiterated that he would not lift his sword against fellow Southerners. Scott advised that if Lee could not accept the proffered appointment, he should resign his commission immediately.[11]

Powerful emotions must have pulled at Lee as he pondered his future that evening and the next day. Word of Virginia's secession appeared in the newspapers on April 19, and early on April 20 he composed a one-sentence letter of resignation to Secretary of War Cameron. Later that day he wrote a much longer letter to General Scott, observing that he would have resigned immediately (as the general had suggested on the eighteenth) "but for the struggle it has cost me to separate myself from a service to which I have devoted all the best years of my life & all the ability I possessed." There followed one of the most famous of Lee's statements: "Save in the defense of my native State, I never desire again to draw my sword."[12]

Lee's decision made sense for one of his class, place, and political views. His Whiggish political philosophy stood strikingly at odds with the virulent rhetoric of secessionist fire-eaters—yet, as he wrote on January 23, 1861, "The South, in my opinion, has been aggrieved by the acts of the North. . . . I feel the aggression, and am willing to take every proper step for redress." He rejected the idea of a country "that can only be maintained by swords and bayonets. . . . If the Union is dissolved, and the Government disrupted, I shall return to my native State and share the miseries of my people, and save in defense will draw my sword on none." Lee's undoubted affection for a Union that had sprung from the efforts of George Washington, Light-Horse Harry Lee, and other revolutionary figures gave way to stronger allegiances. He loved his country, but he loved his state and his section more. Often portrayed as an opponent of slavery, he in fact described the peculiar institution as the best means for ordering relations between the races and resented Northern attacks against the motives and character of slaveholders. "[T]here is no sacrifice I am not ready to make for the preservation of the Union," he averred in January 1861, "save that of honour." As a member of the slaveholding aristocracy of Virginia and the South, his sense of honor dictated that he stand with those who would sunder the United States. It is worth noting that many other prominent Virginia officers, including Winfield Scott, George Henry Thomas, and Philip St. George Cooke, remained loyal to the United States, and that more than a third of all Virginians who had graduated from West Point declined to emulate Lee's example in leaving U.S. service.[13]

The U.S. War Department took five days to process Lee's resignation, which became official on April 25. By then he had received an offer from Gov. John Letcher of Virginia to take command of all the state's military forces with the rank of major general. Lee traveled to Richmond on April 22, talked with Letcher, and on April 23 accepted his native state's call.[14]

The new major general spent a feverish six weeks organizing resources to defend Virginia. He oversaw mobilization of thousands of volunteers and the creation of camps of instruction, set up departments to carry out the duties of the general staff, ordered construction of fortifications at key points along rivers and the coast, and worked closely with the governor in selecting officers to lead Virginia's soldiers. More than forty thousand Virginians were under arms by the end of May.

Political developments kept pace with military preparations during May and June. The Confederate Congress voted on May 21 to move the newly proclaimed republic's capital from Montgomery, Alabama, to Richmond. Pres. Jefferson Davis relocated to Richmond by the end of May, and events in Virginia soon assumed a distinctly national character. On June 8, Governor Letcher transferred to the Confederacy all the volunteers who had been mustered into Virginia's service.

Lee then embarked on a year marked more by frustration and trial than by public acclaim. He had been appointed a Confederate brigadier general on May 14, and one month later Congress had authorized his advancement to full general (confirmed in the latter rank on August 31, 1861, he stood third behind Samuel Cooper and Albert Sidney Johnston in terms of Confederate seniority).[15] While Lee completed his work as head of Virginia's state forces, the major

Confederate field commands in the state had been given to P. G. T. Beauregard and Joseph E. Johnston. Lee remained in Richmond, functioning as a military adviser to the president and chafing at his relative inactivity. "My movements are very uncertain," he confessed to his wife on June 24, "& I wish to take the field as soon as certain arrangements can be made." Lee watched from a distance as Confederate soldiers under Beauregard and Johnston won the battle of 1st Manassas or Bull Run on July 21. "I almost wept for joy at the glorious victory achieved by our brave troops on the 21st," Lee wrote to Johnston, "& the feelings of my heart could hardly be expressed on learning the brilliant share you had in its achievement." Later in the war, when Lee won more famous victories than 1st Manassas, an envious Johnston would display no such comradely pleasure in his old friend's success.[16]

On July 28, 1861, President Davis directed Lee to coordinate the defense of western Virginia, a region of rugged mountains and predominantly unionist sentiment. Federals had established a menacing presence west of Staunton; farther southwest, they also stood poised to move through the Kanawha Valley, whence they might threaten the vital Virginia and Tennessee Railroad. Lee formulated a strategy— undoubtedly too optimistic considering the terrain and the modest abilities of lieutenants such as Henry A. Wise, John B. Floyd, and W. W. Loring—to push the Federals toward and perhaps beyond the Ohio River. Awful weather and poor subordinate leadership, together with Lee's overly complex plan, contributed to ignominious failure. On October 30, he departed from western Virginia with a considerably diminished military reputation. The best that could be said of his effort was that it prevented further Union advances in the region and protected the railroads. Such meager accomplishment failed to satisfy fellow Confederates who yearned for decisive success on the battlefield. Richmond newspaper editor Edward A. Pollard spoke for many others in dismissing the Lee of September and October 1861 as "a general who had never fought a battle . . . and whose extreme tenderness of blood induced him to depend exclusively upon the resources of strategy, to essay the achievement of victories without the cost of life."[17]

Another difficult assignment quickly came Lee's way. In early November, Davis named him to head a new department encompassing the coastal regions of South Carolina, Georgia, and eastern Florida. Lee arrived in Charleston on November 7 and spent the next four months constructing a viable defensive line along 300 miles of the Atlantic coast. Little applauded at the time, this work showed Lee's engineering and administrative skills and rendered the area much better able to resist Northern military power.

Lee by this time had developed an unwavering sense of Confederate nationalism. He had argued from the war's outset that the Confederate people should focus all of their energies and material resources on the national struggle for independence—a stance at odds with the common, and incorrect, notion that Lee acted as a Virginia localist who conceived of the war primarily in terms of its impact on his home state. Lee laid out his views about the relative importance of state and national concerns in a letter to Andrew G. McGrath of South Carolina in late December 1861. "The Confederate States have now but one great object in view, the successful issue of war and independence," Lee explained to McGrath: "Everything worth their possessing depends on that. Everything should yield to its accomplishment." At about the same time, Lee told his son Custis that Confederates should be prepared to "[m]ake every necessary sacrifice of comfort, money & labour to bring the war to a successful issue & then we will succeed."[18]

In early March 1862, Jefferson Davis summoned Lee to Richmond to act as his principal military adviser. Lee informed his wife that he saw no "pleasure or advantage in the duties." Without any real power, he nevertheless helped mold Southern military policy over the next ten weeks. He played an instrumental role in fashioning a national conscription act, a controversial measure he considered essential if the Confederacy were to make the most of its pool of manpower. As early as December 1861, he had argued for open-ended terms of service for all able-bodied, military-age white men. "The troops, in my opinion, should be organized for the war," stated Lee in the previously quoted letter to Andrew McGrath. "We cannot stop short of its termination, be it long or short." Typically, Lee dismissed arguments that states' rights should come before the central government's war-making needs. The legislation passed by Congress on April 16, 1862, failed to include every provision Lee favored but nonetheless marked a crucial step toward maintaining a protracted resistance against the United States. Charles Marshall of Lee's staff later commented about Lee's attitude toward national mobilization. "He thought that every other consideration should be regarded as subordinate to the great end of the public safety," wrote Marshall, "and that since the whole duty of the nation would be war until independence should be secured, the whole nation should for the time be converted into an army, the producers to feed and the soldiers to fight."[19]

Growing Federal threats in Virginia occupied much of Lee's attention. By mid-April, George B. McClellan had placed his 120,000-man Army of the Potomac on the Peninsula below Richmond. Another 60,000 Federals spread in a great arc from Fredericksburg, across the Shenandoah Valley, and into the Alleghenies. At Lee's suggestion, Davis instructed Joseph Johnston, who had abandoned the lines at Manassas in early March, to concentrate his strength opposite McClellan on the Peninsula. Lee then formulated a strategic offensive that would deny McClellan reinforcements from Federal forces north and northwest of Richmond. The execution of this strategy he entrusted to Stonewall Jackson, who responded with his famous Shenandoah Valley campaign of May and June 1862.

Meanwhile, McClellan's army moved inexorably closer to Richmond. On May 31, Johnston, whose constant retreating had prompted widespread unhappiness behind the lines in the Confederacy, ordered assaults against the Army of the Potomac at Seven Pines, just five miles from the capital. Indecisive tactically, this two-day battle nevertheless ranked with the most important engagements of the war because on the first day Johnston received a disabling wound. Command of the army passed briefly to Gustavus W. Smith and then, on June 1, to Lee.

Davis's choice of Lee to lead the Army of Northern Virginia provoked a mixed reaction. Some Confederates believed Lee was long overdue for a major field command. Others inside and outside the army, including many who had thrilled at the news of Lee's decision to accept Virginia's major generalcy in April 1861, took a far dimmer view. The campaign in western Virginia and service along the South Atlantic coast had created an impression that Lee lacked aggressiveness, preferred entrenching to fighting, and otherwise failed to meet popular conceptions of a strong general. A woman in North Carolina voiced a common attitude about Lee in early June: "I do not much like him," she wrote, "he 'falls back' too much. He failed in Western Va owing, it was said, to the weather, has done little in the eyes of outsiders in S C. His nick name last summer was *old-stick-in-the-mud'*[;] . . . pray God he may not fulfil the whole of his name."[20]

A staff officer recalled the hostility with which many Confederates viewed Lee at this juncture. Edward Porter Alexander, who served as chief of ordnance in the Army of Northern Virginia from June through September 1862, wrote that at the time Lee took command "some of the newspapers—particularly the Richmond *Exam-*

iner—pitched into him with extraordinary virulence, evidently trying to break him down with the troops & to force the president to remove him." The *Examiner* claimed that "henceforth our army would never be allowed to fight" but only to dig, "spades & shovels being the only implements Gen. Lee knew anything about."[21]

Lee spent just more than three weeks preparing to engage McClellan's army. John S. Mosby, the famous Confederate partisan officer, later wrote that Lee told him in early 1865 that he believed Johnston "should have never fallen back to Richmond from York-town" in May 1862 without giving battle to McClellan.[22] As he would do in all of his subsequent campaigns, Lee sought to take the initiative, to force the enemy to react to his moves rather than waiting to respond to theirs. In this way, he believed, Confederates could partially offset their opponent's advantage in numbers. Lee counted on the arrival of Jackson's troops from the Valley to provide vital support and eventually set June 26 as the day he would launch his offensive.

The Seven Days campaign commenced on the twenty-sixth with the battle of Mechanicsville. Jackson arrived late on the field, and Federal defenders sharply repulsed a series of Confederate frontal attacks. The next day at Gaines's Mill, massive Confederate assaults carried the Federal position but failed to inflict a crushing defeat. McClellan began to retreat southward toward the James River, opening an opportunity, believed Lee, for a telling blow against an Army of the Potomac in motion. At Savage's Station on June 29 and again at Frayser's Farm on the thirtieth, Federal defenders fended off clumsy Confederate offensives. July 1 found McClellan's troops well positioned at Malvern Hill, where a series of Confederate attacks during the afternoon and evening achieved nothing beyond littering the slopes of the hill with thousands of casualties. That evening McClellan retreated to safety at Harrison's Landing on the James.

Lee had won a victory that lifted spirits across the Confederacy. Just three weeks earlier, Southern prospects had looked exceedingly grim. Defeat marked Confederate efforts in the West, where much of Tennessee and key cities such as New Orleans, Nashville, and Memphis had fallen. In Virginia, McClellan had edged close to Richmond. Only Stonewall Jackson's little victories in the Shenandoah Valley had broken this gloomy spell. In the wake of the Seven Days, the Confederate people could glory in a spectacular offensive victory—the kind they most craved—that had saved their capital and driven the enemy's largest army into a turtlelike defensive posture. Grumblings about

Lee's lack of aggressiveness ceased immediately, a phenomenon that prompted comment from the *Richmond Dispatch*. "The rise which this officer has suddenly taken in the public confidence is without precedent," noted the paper eight days after Malvern Hill. With this one triumph, public morale in the Confederacy underwent a seismic shift, underscoring the direct relationship between events on the battlefield and attitudes and expectations behind the lines.[23]

In strictly military terms, Lee's victory had been far from a masterpiece. Working with an unwieldy collection of division commanders, Lee had attempted to execute complicated plans with woefully inadequate staff support. Indeed, in terms of complexity and poor coordination, his effort in the Seven Days somewhat resembled his failed efforts in western Virginia. Time and again units had taken the wrong roads, commanders had been late to reach their destinations, and attackers had advanced without adequate support. Lee's hewing to the tactical offensive also had resulted in more than 20,000 Confederate casualties, a full 22 percent of his 92,000 men. At Malvern Hill, the attacks had been especially ill considered. Yet none could dispute that Lee's first major campaign as a field commander increased Confederate prospects for independence. His congratulatory order to the army did not exaggerate in observing that the soldiers' "service rendered to the country in this short but eventful period can scarcely be estimated."[24]

Lee reorganized the Army of Northern Virginia in the wake of the Seven Days. He divided his command into two large pieces, entrusting the Right Wing of five divisions to James Longstreet, whom Lee recently had called "the staff of my right hand,"[25] and the Left Wing of three divisions to Stonewall Jackson, whose performance during the Seven Days had been problematical. James E. B. "Jeb" Stuart commanded the army's cavalry, now organized into a division containing three brigades. Lee also removed several of the weaker division leaders from the army.

The revamped Army of Northern Virginia and its commander confronted a daunting strategic situation in mid-July 1862. McClellan's army remained just below Richmond at Harrison's Landing, while in north-central Virginia a new Federal army under Gen. John Pope—more than 50,000 soldiers drawn from the commands that had been in the Shenandoah Valley and near Fredericksburg—advanced toward the vital rail center at Gordonsville. Although heavily outnumbered, Lee pondered how best to strike before Pope and McClellan could concentrate. The result was a dazzling series of maneuvers that not only protected Richmond and its rail connections to the Shenandoah Valley but also cleared Federal forces from most of the state.

Between mid- and late-July, Lee divided his army, sending Jackson with his wing to confront Pope near Gordonsville while he retained Longstreet's divisions near Richmond to watch McClellan. Jackson defeated Pope's advance guard at the battle of Cedar Mountain, fought north of Gordonsville near Culpeper on August 9. Four days later, Lee received intelligence that McClellan's army seemed to be shifting away from the Peninsula to join Pope in northern Virginia. He decided to concentrate against Pope before McClellan could reinforce him.

Lee and Pope maneuvered and skirmished along the Rapidan and Rappahannock Rivers from the fifteenth to the twenty-fifth of August. Convinced he could accomplish little along that line, Lee sent Jackson on a strategic flanking march around the Federal right. Jackson captured Pope's supply depot at Manassas Junction on the twenty-seventh, drew Pope's attention by provoking a fight at Groveton the next day, and took up a defensive position on the old Manassas battlefield. Pope hurried his army from the Rappahannock to Manassas and attacked Jackson's wing on August 29–30. Lee and the rest of the army reached the battlefield on the twenty-ninth. On the afternoon of August 30, Longstreet launched one of the most powerful assaults of the war, plowing into Pope's left flank and driving the enemy from the battlefield after brutal fighting. Pope's army soon withdrew into the formidable Washington defenses, and each side tallied another depressing harvest of casualties—more than 9,000 Confederates and 16,000 Federals. "This Army achieved today on the plains of Manassas a signal victory," Lee telegraphed Jefferson Davis at ten o'clock on the night of August 30, attributing the triumph to the Almighty and "to the valour of our troops."[26]

Lee had completely reoriented the war in Virginia, pushing the Confederacy's eastern military frontier back to the Potomac River. The butcher's bill for this accomplishment may have caused some of his troops to long for a return of the cautious Joe Johnston; thousands more probably agreed with a member of the 12th Georgia Infantry who had remarked on August 27 that the men thought Lee would "do very well" but still looked to "the gallant Stonewall Jackson" as "the idol of the army, as well as of the people." For many others, however, Lee's decisive leadership and the victories it had produced catapulted him to the top position among Confederate military figures. Col. Robert Jones of the 22nd Georgia Infantry reflected this attitude in a letter to his wife on September 5, 1862. "We have the best leader in the Civilized world—," observed Jones, "Genl Lee stands now above all Genls in Modern History. Our men will follow him to the end." In another eight months, Jones's opinion would be that of the majority of the Confederate people.[27]

Lee's thoughts after 2nd Manassas focused not on his reputation but on the war's strategic picture. He strongly opposed assuming a static defense, sharing his views with Jefferson Davis on September 3. "The present seems to be the most propitious time since the commencement of the war," began this detailed letter, "for the Confederate Army to enter Maryland." "[T]hough weaker than our opponents in men and military equipments," Lee explained, "[we] must endeavor to harass, if we cannot destroy them." Believing the armies of McClellan and Pope to be "much weakened and demoralized" in Washington, he thought a movement across the Potomac, though entailing a substantial risk, could prove successful.[28] Here, as throughout his Confederate career, Lee thought that awaiting the onset of more powerful U.S. armies would place Confederates in a weak position that might end in a siege. Movement and daring could offset Northern numbers, he insisted, and provide the type of aggressive battlefield success that would lift Confederate civilian spirits and dampen those of their Northern counterparts.

A Maryland campaign would draw the Federals northward, freeing Richmond from threat and giving the farmers of northern Virginia and the Shenandoah Valley a respite from the destructive presence of armies. The Army of Northern Virginia would remain north of the Potomac through most of the fall season, collecting desperately needed food and fodder from Maryland's (and perhaps Pennsylvania's) countryside and returning as winter approached. Apart from these logistical and military benefits, Lee, as was typical in his strategic thinking, also considered possible political advantage. He thought his invasion of the United States might fuel pro-Confederate sentiment in Maryland and deal a blow to Lincoln and the Republicans during the North's autumn elections.

The Army of Northern Virginia crossed the Potomac at White's Ford on September 4–7. A ragged assemblage, it numbered about 45,000 infantry, 5,500 cavalry, and 4,000 artillery—totals that immediately began to decline as Lee marched toward Frederick. From that city on September 8, Lee issued a proclamation to the people of Maryland announcing that the Confederate army had come among them as liberators. The next day he issued Special Orders No. 191, which directed three columns under Jackson's overall control to sever the Baltimore and Ohio Railroad and capture Harpers Ferry (thereby securing Lee's line of supply to the lower Shenandoah Valley) while the rest of the army moved across the South Mountain range toward Hagerstown and Boonsboro.

The campaign began to unravel over the next six days. In a stroke of spectacular bad luck for Lee, Federal soldiers found a copy of Special Orders No. 191 in the abandoned Confederate camps at Frederick on September 13. George B. McClellan, who had taken control of the Federal forces in Washington after Pope's defeat, thereby learned the positions of each component of Lee's army. Moving more quickly than usual on the fourteenth, "Little Mac" pushed Lee's rear guard westward out of the passes on South Mountain. That evening Lee decided to abandon Maryland, changing his mind the next morning when word arrived from Jackson that the 12,000 Federals at Harpers Ferry were to be surrendered.

Lee's decision to make a stand at Sharpsburg, just across the Potomac River from Shepherdstown, Virginia, revealed his combative temperament. He knew the Army of Northern Virginia had hemorrhaged badly since leaving White's Ferry. "Our great embarrassment," he had written Jefferson Davis on September 13, "is the reduction in our ranks by straggling. . . . Our ranks are very much diminished, I fear from a third to a half of the original numbers."[29] He knew as well that his own soldiers would face a far more numerous foe. Moreover, his lines at Sharpsburg did not benefit from superior terrain, and the army would fight with its back against the Potomac, with Boteler's Ford below Shepherdstown its only avenue of escape.

McClellan advanced tentatively on September 15–16, positioning his soldiers along Antietam Creek to mount a heavy offensive on the morning of the seventeenth. By then Jackson had arrived with most of his wing, but 37,000 Confederate defenders faced an enemy that eventually would number approximately 85,000. Federal attacks began at six o'clock that morning and continued for nearly ten hours. Lee performed well throughout a day of near catastrophes. Along with Jackson and Longstreet, he provided an active presence on the field, shifting troops to threatened sectors and pushing his army to its physical limits. Lee's best efforts would have come to nothing had A. P.

Hill's division, summoned early that morning from Harpers Ferry, not moved onto the field late in the afternoon. Striking the attacking Federals on their left flank, Hill's brigades ended the day's last crisis and brought the battle to a close.

Northern minié balls and artillery rounds had claimed more than 10,000 victims—between a quarter and a third of the Confederates who fought on the seventeenth. At least 12,500 Federals also had fallen. Had McClellan managed to coordinate his attacks or used the thousands of Federal soldiers who remained idle during the day, he probably would have shattered Lee's army. Lee remained on the field throughout the eighteenth, though he stood to gain nothing. This decision seemed to pass beyond audacity to recklessness. He believed the army's morale would have dropped following a more precipitate retreat, but the possibility of a truly staggering reverse certainly accompanied the decision to remain on the field another day. McClellan declined to renew the Federal assaults during the course of a tense September 18, permitting Lee to escape further harm and retreat toward the Potomac that night.[30]

What is a fair assessment of Lee's Maryland campaign? He accomplished his goals of taking the war out of Virginia and gathering supplies in Maryland. Because McClellan chose not to pursue him after Antietam, he was able to maintain a presence in northern and north central Virginia for several more weeks. The soldiers who fought at Antietam added luster to their already high reputation. Lee remarked in his official report that "nothing could surpass the determined valor" his men exhibited on September 17. One of his artillerists agreed: "We have done much more," wrote John Hampden Chamberlayne, "than a sane man could have expected." More than 12,000 prisoners and dozens of cannon captured at Harpers Ferry constituted an unexpected dividend from the campaign. On the debit side, Lee had lost thousands of troops in a battle he need not have fought. In choosing to confront McClellan at Sharpsburg, suggested the astute Edward Porter Alexander, Lee committed his "greatest military blunder."[31] The campaign also gained nothing on the political front, as Marylanders conspicuously did not flock to the Confederate colors. Moreover, Lee's retreat, together with Abraham Lincoln's preliminary proclamation of emancipation issued on September 22, persuaded the British and French to back away from what seemed in mid-September to be a position favoring some type of intervention to bring a mediated end to the conflict.

In all, the Maryland campaign served as a mixed finale to a massive three-month drama that had begun with the Seven Days. Lee had pressed his worn army too hard in the end, finding himself at the ultimate moment of danger near Antietam Creek with a much-diminished force. But the entire drama stood as a striking Confederate success. Lee's victories had driven major enemy forces from Virginia, raised Confederate civilian morale, sent tremors through the United States, and laid the foundation for a bond between Lee and his soldiers, and between them and the Confederate people, that would be a notable feature of the rest of the war. A newspaper correspondent who saw Lee in Winchester five weeks after Antietam left a memorable description. "In appearance he is tall, portly and commanding," wrote this man. "His dress is usually, a plain Brigadier's uniform, a black felt hat, with the brim turned down, and he wears a short grizzled beard all round his face. He has much of the Washingtonian dignity about him, and is much respected by all with whom he is thrown." Lee had, thought the reporter, "won the way to everybody's confidence."[32]

Public confidence increased before the end of 1862 when Lee won his easiest victory of the war at the battle of Fredericksburg. The Confederate army that gathered on the right bank of the Rappahannock River opposite Fredericksburg scarcely resembled that which had fought so desperately at Antietam. Organized into the I and II Corps, which Longstreet and Jackson commanded respectively, and a cavalry division under Jeb Stuart, it numbered 75,000 men of all arms. Many incompetent officers had departed or been eased out by Lee since the retreat from Maryland. Lee had made excellent progress toward shaping the Army of Northern Virginia into the force that soon would become the Confederacy's most important national institution.

The Army of the Potomac, commanded by Ambrose E. Burnside, laid pontoon bridges across the Rappahannock under fire on December 11 and crossed in great numbers the next day. By December 13, Lee had perfected his defensive deployment. He set up headquarters on an eminence (known thereafter as Lee's Hill) that afforded a view of much of the extensive Confederate position. From that high ground on December 13, Lee took in a grand spectacle of Confederate victory. Burnside mounted a day-long offensive that struck first at Jackson's corps on the Confederate right. An admiring Lee watched Jackson's veteran infantry punish the Federals. Turning to James Longstreet, Lee said in an even voice, "It is well this is so terrible! we should grow too fond of it!"[33] Those two sentences did much to define

Lee and his army for future generations of Americans: the brilliant commander, his combative nature aroused, quietly exulting as his army demonstrated martial prowess on one of its famous battlefields. The fighting soon shifted to the Confederate left, where waves of Federals sought to breach Longstreet's impregnable position. Thousands of Northern soldiers fell on a killing plain below Marye's Heights. As the sun dropped low on that winter's afternoon, Burnside ordered an end to the slaughter. The battle had claimed more than 12,500 Northern and 5,300 Southern casualties.

Lee hoped the Federals would renew their offensive on the fourteenth, expressing deep disappointment when Burnside recrossed the Rappahannock after dark on the fifteenth. He believed the victory, however dramatic, had been incomplete. "They went as they came, in the night," Lee said of the Federals on December 16: "They suffered heavily as far as the battle went, but it did not go far enough to satisfy me." The following summer Lee told an officer that after Fredericksburg "our people were greatly elated—I was much depressed. We had really accomplished nothing; we had not gained a foot of ground, and I knew the enemy could easily replace the men he had lost."[34]

Lee's pessimistic evaluation overlooked the battle's impact on northern civilian morale and on his own reputation. Lincoln faced a serious crisis after bad news from the Rappahannock spread across the United States. "If there is a worse place than Hell," the president told a friend, "I am in it." Behind the lines in the Confederacy, Fredericksburg spread optimism and heightened faith in Lee. Georgian Mary Jones expressed a widespread sentiment: "I have not the words to express the emotions I feel for this signal success." Turning to Lee specifically, Jones, like the reporter who saw Lee at Winchester after Antietam, compared him to George Washington. "[T]he head of our army is a noble son of Virginia," she wrote, "and worthy of the intimate relation in which he stands connected with our immortal Washington. What confidence his wisdom, integrity, and valor and undoubted piety inspire!"[35]

The winter and early spring of 1862–63 tested Lee professionally and personally. Shortages of food and other supplies plagued his army, and Federal movements in mid-February compelled him to detach for service in Southside Virginia two divisions of the I Corps under Longstreet. Lee himself experienced poor health as the winter gave way to spring, coping with a heart problem in early April. "I have not been so very sick," he wrote Mrs. Lee with somewhat forced cheerfulness on April 5, 1863, "though have suffered a good deal of pain in my chest, back, & arms." On April 10, a physician who had been attending Lee reported that the general "is every day getting better, and he will, I doubt not, soon be well again. . . . He is cheerful and we all feel hopeful and determined and expect to win more victories over our insolent and wicked foes."[36]

Those foes in April 1863 numbered more than 130,000 under the command of Joseph Hooker, who had succeeded Burnside as head of the Army of the Potomac. Reduced to fewer than 65,000 soldiers after Longstreet's departure, Lee's army nonetheless maintained a jaunty confidence. "It is thought that we will soon attack the Yankees," wrote a major in the 50th Georgia Infantry on April 20: "Genl Lee remarked yesterday at preaching to Genl Kershaw that we would run those *people* from over there."[37]

The armies remained along the Rappahannock River in essentially the same positions they had held since Burnside's retreat from Fredericksburg the preceding December. In late April, Hooker commenced an imaginative offensive. Leaving a strong force under John Sedgwick at Fredericksburg to hold Lee's attention, he marched the bulk of his army up the Rappahannock to get around the Confederate left flank. The turning column reached Chancellorsville, a crossroads some ten miles in Lee's rear, by April 30, prompting Hooker to proclaim that the Confederate enemy "must either ingloriously fly, or come out from behind his defenses and give us battle on our own ground, where certain destruction awaits him."[38]

Lee declined to follow Hooker's script, reacting instead with a series of characteristically daring moves. He left Jubal A. Early with 10,000 men to watch Sedgwick at Fredericksburg, while he and Stonewall Jackson hastened to confront Hooker at Chancellorsville with the rest of the army. The campaign's defining moment occurred on the morning of May 1, when the vanguards of Hooker's and Lee's forces collided near Zoan Church on the road between Chancellorsville and Fredericksburg. Hooker immediately seemed to lose all confidence and ordered a withdrawal to Chancellorsville. Lee and Jackson met on the night of May 1 to plan a bold flanking movement of their own, which Jackson executed with considerable success the next day. Jackson's II Corps routed the Federal XI Corps late on the afternoon of May 2, but the largest part of Hooker's army still lay between the two pieces of Lee's force at Chancellorsville (Early remained opposite Sedgwick at Fredericksburg with the third piece of the Army of Northern Virginia). Thinking only of the defense, Hooker did nothing to exploit this advantage on May 3. Lee readily took the initiative. Heavy assaults that morning drove the Federal army away from Chancellorsville crossroads, allowing the two wings of Lee's army to reunite.

The morning produced a memorable moment of triumph for Lee near Chancellorsville, the stately brick structure that had been Hooker's headquarters for most of the battle. Shortly after hearing that the Federals were withdrawing, Lee rode toward Chancellorsville and into a scene that no artist could improve. Confederate artillery sent deadly missiles into the ranks of retreating Federals. Smoke from woods set afire by musketry and shells drifted skyward. In a clearing that had been the center of Hooker's line stood Chancellorsville itself, ablaze with flames licking at its sides. Lee guided Traveller, his sturdy gray warhorse, through thousands of Confederate infantrymen, general and mount dominating a remarkable tableau of victory. Emotions flowed freely as the soldiers, nearly 9,000 of whose comrades had fallen in the morning's fighting, shouted their devotion to Lee, who acknowledged their cheers by removing his hat. Seldom has the bond between a successful commander and his troops achieved more dramatic display. Colonel Marshall of Lee's staff captured the moment in a famous postwar passage: "One long, unbroken cheer, in which the feeble cry of those who lay helpless on the earth blended with the strong voices of those who still fought, rose high above the roar of battle, and hailed the presence of the victorious chief." Straining for an image that would capture the drama of the event, Marshall added, "as I looked upon him in the complete fruition of the success which his genius, courage, and confidence in his army had won, I thought that it must have been from such a scene that men in ancient days rose to the dignity of gods."[39]

When Lee learned shortly thereafter that Sedgwick had broken Early's lines at Fredericksburg, he divided his army a third time. Leaving Jeb Stuart and 25,000 men to keep an eye on Hooker, he concentrated the rest of his strength several miles west of Fredericksburg at Salem Church, where the Confederates won an awkward victory against Sedgwick on May 3–4. By dawn on May 6, the Army of the Potomac had retreated to the north bank of the Rappahannock, leaving the field in Lee's control and restoring the strategic situation in place at the outset of the campaign.

Chancellorsville confirmed Lee's reputation as an unexcelled Confederate field commander. Utterly dominating Hooker psychologically, he had wrested victory from circumstances—and against odds—that would have undone most generals. He also lost nearly 22 percent of his army, a total of more than 12,750 casualties. Among the fallen was Stonewall Jackson, who died on May 10 after being shot accidentally by some of his own men on the evening of May 2.

Lee mourned the loss of his brilliant lieutenant and found little satisfaction in repulsing Hooker's offensive. "At Chancellorsville we gained another victory," he remarked later, "our people were wild with delight—I, on the contrary, was more depressed than after Fredericksburg; our loss was severe, and again we had gained not an inch of ground and the enemy could not be pursued." The size of Hooker's army especially troubled Lee. In a letter to his brother written shortly after the battle, he overestimated Federal strength in claiming that the enemy "exceeded us more than three to one." Lee went on to call for an all-out mobilization to counter U.S. numbers: "Tell all the boys to get their hoes and go to the cornfields—Labor is the thing to make soldiers, they will then be able to do their share when they become men—"[40]

As in his assessment of Fredericksburg, Lee's comments about Chancellorsville ignored the battle's impact on the Northern home front and on Confederate sentiment regarding his generalship. His victory had sent new waves of disappointment rippling across a North already torn by dissension over the draft, emancipation, and other highly charged issues. "My God! my God!" said an anguished Abraham Lincoln when he realized that Hooker had failed, "What will the country say?" The Confederate people, like Jefferson Davis in the letter to his brother that opened this essay, understandably welcomed news of the victory, and they made Lee their leading military idol. Lee and his army henceforth would function, in the minds of most of their fellow Confederates, as the preeminent national rallying point. Like Washington and the Continental army during the Revolution, Lee and the Army of Northern Virginia eclipsed their civilian government as a symbol of Confederate nationhood. In this vein, the *Lynchburg Virginian* observed on May 12, 1863: "The central figure of this war is, beyond all question, that of Robert E. Lee. . . . Lee is the exponent of Southern power of command."[41]

Chancellorsville also completed the process by which the Army of Northern Virginia became almost fanatically devoted to Lee. In language echoed by countless others, Lt. Lewis Battle of the 37th North Carolina Infantry illuminated the deep bond that had formed between

Lee and his men during eleven months of campaigning. "It is impossible for me to describe the emotions of my heart," wrote Lewis shortly after Lee reviewed the 37th in late May. "I felt proud that the Southern Confederacy could boast of such a man. In fact, I was almost too proud for the occasion for I could not open my mouth to give vent to the emotions that were struggling within." A Georgian also described the men's dedication to Lee: "Wherever he leads they will follow. Whatever he says do, can and must be done. Language is inadequate to convey the idea of the supreme confidence this army reposes in its great and good leader."[42]

The next test for the soldiers of the Army of Northern Virginia would come on U.S. soil. In mid-May, Lee met with political leaders in Richmond to discuss how best to deploy Confederate military resources. He spoke against weakening his army to reinforce the troops defending Vicksburg. Although a strong coalition of politicians and generals urged the president to shift strength to the Western theater, Davis declined to go against Lee's advice. This debate often is cited as evidence that Lee was unable to grasp the larger strategic picture and selfishly called for more men and material in Virginia. In fact, it demonstrated his excellent understanding of how best to achieve Confederate independence. He knew that his army had supplied the victories necessary to sustain national morale and that most people looked to the Eastern Theater to determine who was winning the war. He understandably thought it wise to give him—the Confederacy's only successful field commander—as many resources as possible.

Lee argued for a second invasion of the United States. He believed such an operation would compel the enemy along the Rappahannock to conform to his army's movements. This would thwart any Federal offensive plans, direct the focus of action away from Richmond and Virginia's hard-pressed agricultural areas, permit the Army of Northern Virginia to forage on the enemy's soil, and fuel political discontent among Northern civilians. Once in Pennsylvania, he believed he could maneuver in such a way as to force the Federals to attack him or to make a mistake that might invite a successful Confederate tactical offensive. Above all, Lee hoped to avoid a siege at Richmond, the result of which almost certainly would be Confederate surrender. On June 8, Lee assured Secretary of War James A. Seddon that he grasped the "difficulty & hazard" inherent in taking the strategic offensive with so large an army in his front. But unless Hooker's force could "be drawn out in a position to be assailed, it will take its own time to prepare and strengthen itself to renew its advance upon Richmond, and force this army back within the entrenchments of that city. This may be the result in any event, still I think it is worth a trial to prevent such a catastrophe."[43]

The Confederate army that prepared to march northward numbered 75,000 men. Longstreet and his two divisions had returned from Suffolk, and the government had sent a few other reinforcements. Two-thirds of the infantry would be under new leadership. Lee had reorganized the army after Jackson's death into three corps of three divisions each. Longstreet retained command of the I Corps; Richard S. Ewell succeeded Jackson at II Corps headquarters; and A. P. Hill took the helm of the III Corps, which Lee created by taking one division from each of the other corps and adding a new third division.

Lee's second invasion began smoothly. By June 27, Ewell's divisions were approaching the Susquehanna, and Lee was at Chambersburg with the bulk of Longstreet's and Hill's troops. The Confederates had gathered immense quantities of food and other supplies during the course of their advance and triggered a frenzy of fear in Pennsylvania. But Lee had maneuvered in Pennsylvania without firm intelligence from Jeb Stuart, who had sent no communications since the afternoon of June 23. Stuart had decided to ride around the Army of the Potomac and had been caught east of Hooker's force when it began moving north. He would remain out of touch with the army for more than a week, finally rejoining Lee on July 2.

Information that indirectly led to the battle of Gettysburg arrived at Lee's headquarters about ten o'clock on the night of June 28. In the absence of information from Stuart, Lee had assumed the enemy remained south of the Potomac. Interrogation of a scout working for Longstreet convinced Lee that the enemy had marched north and that George G. Meade had replaced Hooker as the Federal commander. Just as during the preceding autumn's Maryland campaign, Lee confronted an approaching foe with his own army scattered. He issued orders early on June 29 for his three corps to unite along the eastern slope of the South Mountain range. The concentration had not been completed when a division of Hill's corps engaged Federal cavalry west of Gettysburg on the morning of July 1. What began as a meeting engagement escalated rapidly into full-scale fighting and eventually into the largest battle of the war.

Lee made crucial decisions on each of the battle's three days. At first hoping to avoid a general engagement prior to concentrating his army, he changed his mind when he reached the battlefield on the afternoon of July 1. He found a favorable tactical situation, with Hill's infantry pressuring Federals from the west and Ewell's corps coming onto the field from the north, and instructed his corps commanders to press the enemy. The Confederates drove the Federal I and XI corps through Gettysburg and onto high ground south of town. Lee decided to continue the tactical offensive the next day with assaults against the Federal right and left by Ewell's and Longstreet's corps respectively. The attacks achieved no coordination but almost succeeded, which convinced Lee that one more effort might carry the field. He initially hoped to repeat the offensive pressure against both Northern flanks on July 3, settling in the end for the alternative of the Pickett-Pettigrew assault against the Federal center. When that fabled effort ended in bloody repulse, Lee abandoned all thoughts of further aggressive tactics in Pennsylvania.

High drama and unimaginable slaughter had marked three days of combat that produced more than 23,000 Federal and at least 25,000 Confederate casualties. A third of Lee's generals were killed, wounded, or captured, many of whom stood among the army's most talented officers. As friendly a critic as Edward Porter Alexander, whose artillery had attempted to clear the way for the climactic Confederate attack on July 3, judged Lee quite harshly: "I cannot believe that military critics will find any real difficulties in our abstaining from further assault on the following day [July 3], or in pointing out more than one alternative far more prudent than an assault upon a position of such evident & peculiar strength." Many critics have agreed with Alexander, pointing to Gettysburg as proof that Lee's aggressiveness sometimes overcame his better judgment. Others have argued that Ewell's failure to carry Cemetery Hill on July 1 and Longstreet's less than diligent performance on July 2 cost Lee an opportunity to win a decisive tactical victory. Lee himself stated in conversations with William Allen after the war that "Stuart's failure to carry out his instructions *forced the battle of Gettysburg, & the imperfect, halting way in which his corps commanders* (especially Ewell) *fought the battle, gave victory,* (which as he says trembled for 3 days in the balance) *finally to the foe* [asides by Allen]."[44]

In the immediate aftermath of the battle, Lee took full responsibility for what had happened. As the soldiers of George E. Pickett's shattered division staggered back to Seminary Ridge on July 3, he told Cadmus M. Wilcox, whose brigade had fought on Pickett's right and suffered heavily, "Never mind General, *all this has been* MY *fault*—it is I that have lost this fight, and you must help me out of it in the best way you can." In late July, Lee wrote Jefferson Davis that "No blame can be attached to the army for its failure to accomplish what was projected by me. . . . I am alone to blame, in perhaps expecting too much of its prowess & valour."[45]

There is no reason to doubt Lee's own explanation about why he pursued the tactical offensive at Gettysburg. Momentum and high morale count heavily in warfare, and he knew his army had both in ample quantity following Fredericksburg and Chancellorsville. The events of May 3, 1863, when Lee watched his heavily outnumbered infantry and artillery close in on Chancellorsville, probably contributed to his decision to ask them to accomplish even more at Gettysburg two months later. Aware in retrospect that he had erred regarding the Pickett-Pettigrew assault (and perhaps regarding other aspects of his leadership in the Pennsylvania campaign), Lee responded testily when some newspapers, most notably the *Charleston Mercury*, bitterly criticized the campaign. Observing on August 8 that the "general remedy for the want of success in a military commander is his removal," Lee offered to step down as chief of the Army of Northern Virginia. Jefferson Davis immediately assured his "dear friend" that isolated newspaper carping could not "detract from the achievements which will make you and your army the subject of history and object of the world's admiration for generations to come." With Davis's warm letter in hand, Lee dropped the subject of resigning and went about his tasks.[46]

This exchange between Lee and Davis highlights their generally cordial and effective working relationship. Unlike Joseph E. Johnston and P. G. T. Beauregard, who stood perpetually at odds with their commander in chief, Lee understood how best to deal with Davis. Lee emulated his idol George Washington in never losing sight of the fact that civilian authority held sway in a democratic republic. He kept the president informed and asked his opinion on many occasions. He never directly challenged Davis and never went to the press to make a point. He understood perfectly that the president faced enormous political pressures, and he shared the president's ardent Confederate nationalism. The two agreed that the war would require nearly total mobilization of Southern resources, and that states' rights sentiment would have to give way to national conscription, impressment of goods by the central government, and, eventually, even arming slaves if necessary to achieve independence. In short, Lee was a master military politician who worked very effectively with a sometimes prickly civilian superior.[47]

Most Confederate soldiers and civilians joined their president in choosing not to regard Gettysburg as a major blemish on Lee's record. Losses had been heavy, but Lee's army had withdrawn safely from Pennsylvania by the middle of July. Moreover, the Army of the Potomac seemed to be in no hurry to find another battleground. Emma Holmes, a diarist in South Carolina, expressed a typical reaction to Gettysburg: "Lee has recrossed the Potomac, in admirable order, and the army in splendid trim and spirits without loss. . . . His retreat from Gettysburg was strategic, to draw Meade's army from the high hills behind which they took refuge." Shortly after Gettysburg, Lee told Maj. John Seddon, the secretary of war's brother, that the Federals had suffered such damage at Gettysburg that "it will be seen for the next six months that *that army* will be as quiet as a sucking dove." In fact, it would not be until ten months later, when Ulysses S. Grant began his Overland campaign, that the Army of the Potomac opened another major offensive in Virginia.[48]

Before that storied confrontation between the two greatest soldiers of the Civil War, Lee and the Army of Northern Virginia kept watch along the Rappahannock and Rapidan rivers during the winter and spring of 1863-64. Severe shortages of food, fodder, medicine, and clothing plagued the Confederates. As late as April 12, Lee grimly informed Jefferson Davis: "I cannot see how we can operate with our present supplies. . . . There is nothing to be had in this section for man or animals." Despite physical hardships, morale remained high in the army. Most of the men looked to army headquarters with unqualified trust. "General Robt. E. Lee is regarded by his army as nearest approaching the character of the great & good Washington than any man living," wrote one brigadier in late January 1864. "He is the only man living in whom they would unreservedly trust all power for the preservation of their independence." A private in the 12th Virginia Cavalry used fewer words to make the same point in late March: "No army ever had such a leader General Lee."[49]

Grant took the field to test Lee's leadership as the campaigning season approached in April 1864. He brought to Virginia a dazzling record of success in the Western Theater. His presence with the Army of the Potomac raised hopes in the United States that Lee and his army soon would be vanquished. The Confederate people and soldiers in the Army of Northern Virginia held an equally firm belief that Lee would triumph against Grant. Walter H. Taylor of Lee's staff may have reflected the dominant feeling at army headquarters when he prophesied that Grant, who had faced such modestly talented generals as John C. Pemberton in the West, "will find, I trust, that General Lee is a very different man to deal with, & if I mistake not will shortly come to grief if he attempts to repeat the tactics in Virginia which proved so successful in Mississippi."[50]

Lee entered the campaign with doubts about his own physical capacity and an army only slightly more than half the size of Grant's. He had suffered from severe pains in his back during the autumn of 1863, and on April 9, 1864, admitted to his son Custis, "I want all the aid I can get now. I feel a marked change in my strength since my attack last spring at Fredericksburg, and am less competent for my duty than ever." On a more positive note, he welcomed James Longstreet's two divisions back to the army at an emotional review in late April. Those I Corps veterans, absent from Virginia since the preceding September, greeted their old commander with the same spirit that had prevailed when Lee rode into the clearing at Chancellorsville not quite a year earlier. One observer noted that "a wild and prolonged cheer, fraught with a feeling that thrilled all hearts, ran along the lines and rose to the heavens." An artillerist likened the event to "a military sacrament." With Longstreet's troops, the Army of Northern Virginia numbered about 65,000 to face Grant's 120,000.[51]

A month of unprecedented fury opened on May 4 when the Federals crossed the Rapidan River and moved into the Wilderness, a region of desolate, scrub forest where the armies had grappled during the Chancellorsville campaign. Grant sought to bring Lee to bay, tie him down in Virginia, and bleed the Confederate army as much as possible. Lee hoped to find an opening to strike back, fearful that a protracted defensive campaign would culminate in a siege at Richmond and U.S. victory. Unlike previous campaigns wherein the armies had fought, withdrawn to recover and refit, and then maneuvered to fight again, the 1864 Overland campaign witnessed almost constant fighting—large battles followed by skirmishing and smaller engagements and then other large battles. The toll in men set a chilling new standard for slaughter as the two armies, together with civilians behind the lines who followed their operations closely, sought to come to terms with the nature and results of the campaigning.

Lee and Grant first tested each other on May 5–6 in the battle of the Wilderness. Confederates inaugurated the action as Grant's troops marched southward through the gloomy woodlands. The first day's fighting ended in a stalemate, but early the next morning Federals routed most of A. P. Hill's corps, which held the Confederate right, and nearly won a decisive victory. Lee rode into the swirling action at the Widow Tapp field along the Orange Plank Road, seeking first to rally Hill's men and then urging the Texas Brigade, just arriving on the field with the vanguard of Longstreet's corps, to counterattack. In the earliest and most famous "Lee to the Rear" episode, the Texans and their Arkansan comrades made Lee go back to safety before they would advance. Later on May 6 the Confederates managed to turn both of Grant's flanks but failed to deliver a knockout punch. The two days of combat claimed as casualties more than 18,000 Federals and 11,000 Confederates, among the latter James Longstreet, who was mistakenly shot by his own troops in circumstances reminiscent of Stonewall Jackson's wounding a year earlier.[52]

Unlike previous Federal commanders who had retreated after being roughly handled by Lee, Grant ignored his losses and pressed southward to get around the Confederate right. The two armies clashed again during May 8–21 in the battles of Spotsylvania Court House. The heaviest combat of the Overland campaign took place on May 12, when Federals smashed through the Mule Shoe salient in Lee's lines and almost split the Confederate army into a pair of vulnerable pieces. Once again Lee rode to the front, placing himself at risk as he worked to rally soldiers and direct reinforcements to the point of danger. Stalwart fighting by several Confederate brigades stabilized the situation in the Mule Shoe and enabled the army to withdraw safely to another position. By May 21, when the armies marched away from Spotsylvania, 18,000 Federals and 12,000 Confederates had joined the spiraling list of casualties.[53]

The first two weeks of campaigning in 1864 ravaged the Confederate high command. A southern minié ball had cost Lee the invaluable services of Longstreet (a staff officer noted "the sadness in [Lee's] face, and the almost despairing movement of his hands, when he was told that Longstreet had fallen");[54] A. P. Hill had missed crucial action because of recurring ailments; and Richard S. Ewell had performed in a manner that prompted Lee to remove him from the army. The full cost of this breakdown of command stood out starkly on May 24–25. Grant maneuvered his army into an awkward position astride the North Anna River, offering a tempting target that Lee normally would have attacked. But the Confederate commander lay prostrate in his cot with severe dysentery, unable to oversee an assault and unwilling to commit such a task to any available lieutenant. A staff officer later described a frustrated Lee as saying, "We must strike them a blow—we must never let them pass us again—we must strike them a blow!"[55]

A week after the missed opportunity at the North Anna, the armies had shifted southeast to the vicinity of Cold Harbor. There Lee constructed a defensive line with his right flank resting near the old Gaines's Mill battlefield. On June 1, precisely two years after he had taken command of the Army of Northern Virginia, Lee tried to find a way to turn Grant's left near Old Cold Harbor. That attempt failed, another day of entrenching followed, and on June 3 approximately 3,500 Federals fell when a part of Grant's army struck the well-engineered southern positions (Grant's losses on June 3 have been greatly exaggerated in most of the literature on Cold Harbor). The victory on the third did little to raise Lee's spirits. He knew the inexorable progression of the campaign had taken the armies ever closer to Richmond and a possible siege. Just after Cold Harbor, he spoke with Jubal Early, who had replaced Ewell as head of the II Corps, about his deepest fear. "We must destroy this army of Grant's before he gets to [the] James River," said Lee, "if he gets there, it will become a siege, and then it will be a mere question of time."[56]

On June 12, U. S. Grant began a movement that set the stage for the scenario Lee most dreaded. Fooling Lee completely, the Federal chief disengaged from the Confederates at Cold Harbor and marched toward the James. Crossing that imposing barrier on pontoon bridges, U.S. soldiers hastened toward Petersburg, where on June 15–18 they mounted a series of disjointed assaults that failed to take the city. Once certain that Grant had crossed the river, Lee shuttled troops to the Petersburg defenses in time to participate in the repulse of Federal attacks on the sixteenth and seventeenth.

The Overland campaign ended on June 18 as the armies settled into their lines around Petersburg. Since crossing the Rapidan on May 4, the Federals had suffered more than 60,000 casualties and their Confederate opponents more than 30,000—a ratio of losses to strength on each side that placed a greater burden on Southern sources of manpower. Hundreds of officers had been killed or maimed, the ranks of noncommissioned officers decimated, and veteran units bled almost to extinction. In short, the two armies scarcely resembled the forces that had opened the campaign. For the rest of the conflict they would engage in a more static form of warfare, constructing a maze of works along the Richmond-Petersburg front while Grant applied growing pressure, extending his lines westward and working to cut Lee's lines of communication and supply.

The siege of Petersburg lasted more than nine months. Lee ordered the last major Confederate strategic diversion in Virginia during this period, sending Jubal Early to the Shenandoah Valley in mid-June. Over the next four months, Early won a number of small victories, crossed the Potomac River and marched to the outskirts of Washington, and tied down more than 40,000 Federal troops before losing three sharp battles to Philip H. Sheridan's forces between September 19 and October 19. The last of Early's defeats, at Cedar Creek, marked the end of a significant Confederate presence in the Shenandoah. Along with William Tecumseh Sherman's capture of Atlanta, U.S. successes in the Valley ensured Abraham Lincoln's re-election to a second term. That election depressed morale across the Confederacy, where soldiers and civilians alike understood that Lincoln would continue to prosecute the war vigorously.

The final months of the conflict offered scant good news to Lee and his army. Some Confederates took heart at Lee's appointment as general-in-chief of all Confederate forces on February 6, 1865, but the promotion had come too late to have any practical effect. In private, Lee had decided victory was impossible. He told William Cabell Rives on March 5 that it was his soldierly "duty to fight it out to the last extremity as long as the contest continues," but as "a patriot and citizen" he thought the government should try to "close the war on the best terms we could."[57]

Lee's public support for continued resistance extended to recommending that slaves be armed and placed in the army. He also suggested that any slaves who served faithfully in this capacity, together with their families, should be freed, invited to remain in the Confederacy, and perhaps given a bounty. This topic had generated hot debate during the last winter of the conflict, placing at odds those who insisted independence outweighed every other consideration and those who argued that arming slaves would undermine the foundation of the Confederate social system. Lee's statement, made public in late February by Richmond newspapers, promoted considerable support for arming and freeing slaves. "With the great mass of our people," noted the *Richmond Sentinel* with some hyperbole, "nothing more than this letter [from Lee] is needed to settle every doubt or silence every

objection." In March 1865, the Confederate Congress passed legislation permitting the enrollment of slaves as soldiers but refused to provide any guarantee of freedom.[58]

The siege of Petersburg neared its end during the last week of
March. Lee made a final desperate effort to break the Federal grip on
the city with an attack on Fort Stedman, hoping this offensive would
compel Grant to shorten his lines and thereby relieve pressure on the
Confederates. Launched on March 25, the attack achieved momentary
success before heavy counterattacks restored the Federal position. A
week later, on April 1, Philip H. Sheridan crushed George E. Pickett's
defending Confederates in the battle of Five Forks, turning Lee's right
and forcing the evacuation of Richmond on the night of April 2–3.

A weeklong retreat westward from Richmond and Petersburg
ensued. Lee hoped to find a way to join Joseph E. Johnston's army in
North Carolina, but Grant's pursuit denied him an opening. Under
relentless pressure, the Confederates fought at Sayler's Creek on April
6, losing thousands of prisoners and prompting Lee, who watched the
debacle from high ground west of the action, to mutter to himself,
"My God! has the army dissolved?" Two more days took the armies to
the vicinity of Appomattox Courthouse, where U.S. cavalry reached
the front of Lee's column, blocking its way to Lynchburg. Hemmed in
by powerful forces to the east, south, and west, Lee told a group of
officers, "[T]here is nothing left me but to go and see General Grant,
and I would rather die a thousand deaths."[59]

The generals met in the parlor of Wilmer McLean's home in
Appomattox Courthouse on April 9. Grant extended generous terms,
Lee accepted them, and they signed the document of surrender. The
Army of Northern Virginia, which together with miscellaneous units
from the Richmond defenses numbered at least 60,000 on April 2, had
suffered massive hemorrhaging during the retreat. Fewer than 30,000
soldiers, many of them without weapons, remained in the ranks on
April 9. Writing shortly after the surrender, a Federal officer spoke
eloquently about the rebel chieftain's stature among his enemies. "To
tell the truth, we none of us realize even yet that he has actually surrendered," averred Stephen Minot Weld: "I had a sort of impression
that we should fight him all our lives. He was like a ghost to children,
something that haunted us so long that we could not realize that he
and his army were really out of existence to us."[60]

The Confederate people received word of events at Appomattox
with resignation. Thousands of other Confederate soldiers remained

under arms, but Lee and his army personified the cause for most white Southerners. The surrender of the Army of Northern Virginia understandably signaled the end of the war. "[E]verybody feels ready to give up hope," was a Georgia woman's representative response to news of Appomattox. "'It is useless to struggle longer,' seems to be the common cry," she wrote, "and the poor wounded men go hobbling about the streets with despair on their faces."[61]

Lee returned to Richmond following the surrender as a paroled prisoner of war. After nearly thirty-six years as a professional soldier, he found himself out of work and facing an uncertain future. Arlington had been seized by the U.S. government and turned into a military cemetery, and he and Mrs. Lee owned no other residence. He had no immediate means of supporting his family. One thing was not in question—he would submit completely to Federal authority. Lee harbored deep resentments against the North but in public statements over the last five years of his life always counseled former Confederates to accept their defeat and obey the laws of the United States. On June 13, 1865, he formally requested a pardon from Pres. Andrew Johnson (the pardon would never be granted). Lee's attitude toward defeat can be summed up simply: the Confederate people had waged a bitter struggle for independence, had failed to achieve that goal, and now must abide by the rules of the victors. He said as much in a letter to P. G. T. Beauregard, wherein he explained his reasons for requesting a pardon. "I need not tell you that true patriotism sometimes requires of men to act exactly contrary, at one period, to that which it does at another," stated Lee, "and the motive which impels them—the desire to do right—is precisely the same. The circumstances which govern their actions change; and their conduct must conform to the new order of things." Lee closed with an allusion to George Washington's example, noting that he fought with the British and against the French in the Seven Years' War and with the French and against the British in the American Revolution.[62]

Nearly four months passed between Lee's surrender and the arrival of an offer that would define the work of his last years. In early August 1865, Washington College of Lexington, Virginia, offered him its presidency. The opportunity to work with young Southern men (many of whom would be Virginians) appealed to Lee, as did the prospect of achieving some measure of financial security. On August 24, he expressed a willingness to take up the post. The college's board of trustees made the appointment on the last day of that month.[63]

Lee proved to be an able educator who left an indelible mark on Washington College. When he assumed control in the autumn of 1865 the school was struggling to keep its doors open. Four years of Lee's leadership worked a remarkable change. The student body increased from a few dozen to more than 300, the physical condition of the institution improved dramatically, and the faculty grew in size and stability. Lee also revised the curriculum, adding courses in science and engineering to the traditional offerings in classical subjects. These changes, he believed, would help prepare students for the practical challenges of the postwar years.

As he strove to improve Washington College, Lee often reflected on the Confederate war effort and how it would be portrayed in the writings of participants and historians. He thought seriously about undertaking a history of the Army of Northern Virginia (a project many people urged on him), corresponding on the subject with a number of former lieutenants during the autumn of 1865. Many of his official papers had been lost or destroyed during the chaotic last phase of the war, and he hoped these officers would be able to supply details about events during 1864–65. He especially wanted information about the strengths of the opposing armies and the extent of Federal depredations against private property. "It will be difficult," he predicted to Jubal Early, "to get the world to understand the odds against which we fought." What did he hope to accomplish by offering his version of military events in Virginia? "My only object," he assured Early, "is to transmit, if possible, the truth to posterity, and do justice to our brave Soldiers."[64]

Lee regrettably never found time to complete this project. Neither did he publish anything else relating to his tenure as head of the Confederacy's most famous army. Consumed with duties at Washington College, he sought relief in long rides on Traveller through the beautiful Shenandoah countryside and in periodic visits to the White Sulphur Springs and other such places. Whenever he traveled in Virginia and the South, former Confederates offered ample evidence of their affection. Lee and his daughter Agnes toured several Southern states in the spring of 1870. Instead of finding relaxation, Lee endured a procession of dinners, receptions, and public appearances that taxed his waning strength. At about the midpoint of his Southern travels, he described his physical condition to his wife: "The warm weather has dispelled some of the rheumatic pains in my back, but I perceive no change in the stricture in my chest. If I attempt to walk beyond a very slow gait, the pain is always there."[65]

In 1870, Lee passed a final summer and watched autumn bring its colors to Lexington. On the rainy evening of September 28, he slowly walked home from a vestry meeting at his church. Once inside the house, he removed his wet cape and went into the dining room. Mrs. Lee greeted him, but he sat down at the table without answering. He had been stricken with an unusual stroke that inflicted no paralysis but left him largely incapacitated. He lingered for two weeks, uttering an average of just one word a day until on October 12, with family nearby, he died peacefully.[66]

Lee's Confederate generalship already had been the subject of enormous attention by the time of his death, a phenomenon that has continued without abatement. Much written about him has been adulatory, comparing him favorably to other great captains in American and world history. Another strain of analysis, the majority of it offered in the past twenty-five years, has found him wanting as an army commander.[67] A number of Lee's most vociferous critics have focused on the fact that he frequently pursued the strategic and tactical offensive, discussing at length how battles during his first thirteen months in command of the Army of Northern Virginia drained Confederate manpower. Some historians have suggested that the Confederacy would have been better off with an officer in Lee's place who husbanded precious human resources. There can be no denying the bloody toll of Lee's battles. In 1862, more than 20 percent of his soldiers became casualties during the Seven Days, nearly 18 percent at 2nd Manassas, and more than 27 percent at Antietam. In all, the army piled up nearly 50,000 battle casualties during the first four months under Lee's leadership. In the spring and summer of 1863, the army lost another 20 percent at Chancellorsville and at least 33 percent at Gettysburg. In terms of losses as a percentage of his command, Lee must rank as the Civil War's bloodiest general.

Did Lee's results justify such immense loss? Except for the easy repulse of Burnside's unimaginative assaults at Fredericksburg, each of the campaigns conveyed to the Confederate people a sense that Lee was taking the war to the enemy rather than simply awaiting the next Federal move. Even during the protracted defensive fighting of 1864–65, Lee retained his reputation as an audacious commander who would seize any opportunity to smite the enemy. This was precisely the type of effort the Southern populace demanded of their generals and government. Confederates mourned the thousands of killed and wounded soldiers in 1862–63 but leveled remarkably little criticism toward Lee as the officer responsible for the effusion of blood.

Civilians and soldiers alike saw in Lee a daring and resourceful general who gave them splendid offensive victories during his first year in command. He alone proved to be a reliable source for good news from the battlefield, and the Confederate people came to trust him almost blindly. John H. Claiborne, writing on July 30, 1864, from the office of the senior surgeon in Petersburg, captured the depth of feeling most Confederates felt for Lee: "No man on this continent or any other now fills so large and important a place to so many people. I verily believe, under God, our whole cause is in his hands; and if he goes down the hope of the nation is extinct. If there be genius elsewhere, there is no confidence—the people and the Government unite on him only." Similarly, a British visitor to Richmond wrote in March 1865 that *"Genl R. E. Lee* . . . [is] the idol of his soldiers & the Hope of His Country. . . . [T]he prestige which surrounds his person & the almost fanatical belief in his judgement & capacity . . . is the one idea of an entire people."[68]

Lee fully understood that the key to victory lay in the civilian sector. Well attuned to intersections between military and political affairs in a war between two democratic republics, he grasped the ways in which his campaigns and battles bolstered Confederate and depressed U.S. morale. Equally aware of the staggering toll his style of generalship exacted, he hoped to win enough victories to convince the Northern people that the war was too costly before Confederate manpower had been exhausted. More than once his generalship brought the Confederacy to a point where independence seemed possible, most especially in the late summer and autumn of 1862, the late spring and early summer of 1863, and the summer of 1864. Lee and his army became the most admired national institution in the nascent slaveholding republic, inspiring the Confederate people to resist long past the point at which they otherwise would have conceded their inability to overcome Northern numbers and power.

NOTES

1. Jefferson Davis to Joseph Davis, May 7, 1863, in Jefferson Davis, *The Papers of Jefferson Davis*, ed. Lynda Lasswell Crist and others, 11 vols. to date (Baton Rouge: Louisiana State University Press, 1971–2003), 9:166–67; Davis to Francis W. Pickens, August 1, 1862, summary in ibid., 8:318.

2. The following three paragraphs are drawn from Douglas Southall Freeman, *R. E. Lee: A Biography*, 4 vols. (New York: Scribners, 1934–35), 1: chaps. 1-6 (hereafter cited as Freeman, *R. E. Lee*).

3. Ibid., 1:68, 84–85; Emory M. Thomas, *Robert E. Lee: A Biography* (New York: Norton, 1995), 54–55 (hereafter cited as Thomas, *Robert E. Lee*).

4. Dates for all of Lee's ranks in the U.S. Army are taken from Francis B. Heitman, *Historical Register and Dictionary of the United States Army: From Its Organization, September 29, 1789, to March 2, 1903*, 2 vols. (1903; reprint, Urbana: University of Illinois Press, 1965), 1:625. On Lee and Washington, see Richard B. McCaslin, *Lee in the Shadow of Washington* (Baton Rouge: Louisiana State University Press, 2001).

5. The best discussion of Lee's service in Mexico is in Freeman, *R. E. Lee*, 1:203–300. On Scott's "Little Cabinet," see Winfield Scott, *Memoirs of Lieut.-General Scott, L.L.D.* 2 vols. (1864; reprint, Freeport, N.Y.: Books for Libraries, 1970), 2:423.

6. Freeman, *R. E. Lee*, 1:274, 291; Erasmus D. Keyes, *Fifty Years' Observations of Men and Events, Civil and Military* (New York: Scribner's, 1884), 206.

7. Gary W. Gallagher, ed., "'We Are Our Own Trumpeters': Robert E. Lee Describes Winfield Scott's Campaign to Mexico City," *Virginia Magazine of History and Biography* 95 (July 1987):372–74.

8. Freeman, *R. E. Lee*, 1: chaps. 19–20. Carl Coke Rister, *Robert E. Lee in Texas* (Norman: University of Oklahoma Press, 1946) is the best treatment of that phase of Lee's pre-Civil War career.

9. J. William Jones, *Life and Letters of Robert Edward Lee: Soldier and Man* (1906; reprint, Harrisonburg, Va.: Sprinkle, 1986), 105 (hereafter cited as Jones, *Life and Letters*).

10. Freeman, *R. E. Lee*, 1:432–34.

11. William Allen, "Memoranda of Conversations with General Robert E. Lee," in Gary W. Gallagher, ed., *Lee the Soldier* (Lincoln: University of Nebraska Press, 1996), 10, 20 n. 23 (hereafter cited as Allen, "Memoranda of Conversations with General Robert E. Lee," in Gallagher, ed., *Lee the Soldier*); Freeman, *R. E. Lee*, 1:436–37; William E. Smith, *The Francis Preston Blair Family in Politics*, 2 vols. (New York: Macmillan, 1933), 1:17–18.

12. Robert E. Lee, *The Wartime Papers of R. E. Lee*, ed. Clifford Dowdey and Louis H. Manarin (Boston: Little, Brown, 1961), 8–9 (hereafter cited as Lee, *Wartime Papers*).

13. Jones, *Life and Letters*, 120–21; Robert E. Lee, *"To Markie": The Letters of Robert E. Lee to Martha Custis Williams*, ed. Avery O. Craven (Cambridge, Mass.: Harvard University Press, 1933), 58. I am indebted to Wayne Wei-siang Hsieh for data regarding Virginians who remained loyal to the United States.

14. For a very negative interpretation of the chronology of Lee's resignation from the U.S. Army and his acceptance of a post with the state of Virginia, see Alan T. Nolan, *Lee Considered: General Robert E. Lee and*

Civil War History (Chapel Hill: University of North Carolina Press, 1991), 39–45 (hereafter cited as Nolan, *Lee Considered*).

15. For Lee's Confederate ranks, see John H. Eicher and David J. Eicher, *Civil War High Commands* (Stanford, Calif.: Stanford University Press, 2001), 787, 790.

16. Lee, *Wartime Papers*, 54; Robert E. Lee to Joseph E. Johnston, July 24, 1861, "Letters of Confederate Generals Robert E. Lee/Stonewall Jackson," mss11576, Special Collections, Alderman Library, University of Virginia, Charlottesville [repository hereafter cited as AL-UVA].

17. Edward A. Pollard, *Southern History of the War: The First Year of the War* (1862; reprint, New York: Charles B. Richardson, 1864), 168. For an overview of Lee's campaign in western Virginia, see Clayton R. Newell, *Lee vs. McClellan: The First Campaign* (Washington, D.C.: Regnery, 1996).

18. Lee, *Wartime Papers*, 95, 98.

19. Ibid., 127–28, 93; Charles Marshall, *An Aide-De-Camp of Lee: Being the Papers of Colonel Charles Marshall, Sometime Aide-De-Camp, Military Secretary, and Assistant Adjutant General on the Staff of Robert E. Lee, 1862–1865*, ed. Sir Frederick Maurice (Boston: Little Brown, 1927), 30–32.

20. Catherine Ann Devereux Edmondston, *"Journal of a Secesh Lady": The Diary of Catherine Ann Devereux Edmondston, 1860–1866*, ed. Beth Gilbert Crabtree and James W. Patton (Raleigh: North Carolina Division of Archives and History, 1979), 189.

21. Edward Porter Alexander, *Fighting for the Confederacy: The Personal Recollections of General Edward Porter Alexander*, ed. Gary W. Gallagher (Chapel Hill: University of North Carolina Press, 1989), 90 (hereafter cited as Alexander, *Fighting for the Confederacy*).

22. John S. Mosby, *The Letters of John S. Mosby*, ed. Adele H. Mitchell ([Richmond, Va.]: Stuart-Mosby Historical Society, 1986), 77.

23. *Richmond Dispatch*, July 9, 1862. The best narrative of the Seven Days campaign is Stephen W. Sears, *To the Gates of Richmond: The Peninsula Campaign* (New York: Ticknor & Fields, 1992). See also Gary W. Gallagher, ed., *The Richmond Campaign of 1862: The Peninsula and the Seven Days* (Chapel Hill: University of North Carolina Press, 2000).

24. Lee, *Wartime Papers*, 210.

25. Thomas Jewett Goree, *Longstreet's Aide: The Civil War Letters of Major Thomas J. Goree*, ed. Thomas W. Cutrer (Charlottesville: University Press of Virginia, 1995), 98.

26. Lee, *Wartime Papers*, 268. On Lee's campaigning in July and August, see Joseph L. Harsh, *Confederate Tide Rising: Robert E. Lee and the Making of Southern Strategy, 1861–1862* (Kent, Ohio: Kent State University Press, 1998), 98–174, and John J. Hennessy, *Return to Bull Run: The Campaign and Battle of Second Manassas* (New York: Simon and Schuster, 1993).

27. *Columbus (Ga.) Weekly Sun*, September 2, 1862 [from an unidentified member of the 12th Georgia]; Robert Jones to My Dear Wife, September 5, 1862, typescript provided to the author by Keith S. Bohannon.

28. Lee, *Wartime Papers*, 287–88.

29. Ibid., 306-07. The best treatment of Lee's strategic planning during the Maryland campaign is Joseph L. Harsh, *Taken at the Flood: Robert E. Lee and Confederate Strategy in the Maryland Campaign of 1862* (Kent, Ohio: Kent State University Press, 1999).

30. The best study of Antietam remains Stephen W. Sears, *Landscape Turned Red: The Battle of Antietam* (New York: Ticknor & Fields, 1983).

31. Lee, *Wartime Papers*, 322; John Hampden Chamberlayne to Lucy Parke Chamberlayne, September 22, 1862, in John Hampden Chamberlayne, *Ham Chamberlayne: Virginian: Letters and Papers of an Artillery Officer in the War for Southern Independence, 1861–1865*, ed. C. G. Chamberlayne (Richmond, Va.: Dietz, 1932), 110; Alexander, *Fighting for the Confederacy*, 145.

32. *Atlanta Southern Confederacy*, October 31, 1862.

33. John Esten Cooke, *A Life of Gen. Robert E. Lee* (New York: D. Appleton, 1871), 184. In *R. E. Lee*, 2:462, Douglas Southall Freeman cited Cooke's biography but changed the quotation to: "It is well that war is so terrible—we should grow too fond of it!" Freeman's more dramatic form of the statement is quoted far more often than Cooke's original version and has become one of the most famous of Lee's utterances.

34. Lee, *Wartime Papers*, 365; Henry Heth, "Letter from Major-General Henry Heth, of A. P. Hill's Corps, A. N. V.," in *Southern Historical Society Papers*, ed. J. William Jones and others, 52 vols. and 3-vol. index (1877–1959; reprint, Wilmington, N.C.: Broadfoot, 1990–92), 4:153–54 (set hereafter cited as *SHSP*). Lee made these comments, as well as those about Chancellorsville cited in n. 40 below, to Maj. John Seddon, who related them to Heth.

35. James M. McPherson, *Ordeal by Fire: The Civil War and Reconstruction*, 2nd ed. (New York: McGraw-Hill, 1992), 303; Robert Manson Myers, ed., *The Children of Pride: A True Story of Georgia and the Civil War* (New Haven, Conn.: Yale University Press, 1972), 1001.

36. Lee, *Wartime Papers*, 428; Samuel Merrifield Bemiss to My dear children, April 10, 1863, MSS 1B4255d23, Bemiss Family Papers, Virginia Historical Society, Richmond.

37. William O. Fleming letter, April 20, 1863, MS 2292, William O. Fleming Papers, Southern Historical Collection, Wilson Library, University of North Carolina, Chapel Hill (repository hereafter cited as SHC).

38. U.S. War Department, *The War of the Rebellion: A Compilation of the Official Records of the Union and Confederate Armies*, 127 vols., index, and atlas (Washington, D.C.: U.S. Government Printing Office, 1880–1901), 1, 25 (1):171.

39. Marshall, *An Aide-de-Camp of Lee*, 173. Stephen W. Sears, *Chancellorsville* (Houghton Mifflin, 1996) is a well-written overview of the campaign and battle.

40. Heth, "Letter from Major-General Henry Heth," 154; Lee to "My dear brother Carter," May 24, 1863, MSS 438, box 1, Lee Papers, AL-UVA.

41. James M. McPherson, *Battle Cry of Freedom: The Civil War Era* (New York: Oxford University Press, 1988), 645; *Lynchburg Virginian*, May 12, 1863.

42. Lewis Battle to his brother, May 29, 1863, Battle Family Papers, SHC; *Augusta (Ga.) Daily Constitutionalist*, June 18, 1863 [quoting a soldier in the 2nd Georgia Infantry Battalion].

43. Lee, *Wartime Papers*, 504–05.

44. Alexander, *Fighting for the Confederacy*, 277; Allan, "Memoranda of Conversations with General Robert E. Lee," in Gallagher, ed., *Lee the Soldier*, 11, 14. For a gracefully written overview of the Gettysburg campaign, see Stephen W. Sears, *Gettysburg* (Boston: Houghton Mifflin, 2003); on Lee's crucial decisions, see the essays by Alan T. Nolan and Gary W. Gallagher in Gallagher, ed., *Three Days at Gettysburg: Essays on Confederate and Union Leadership* (Kent, Ohio: Kent State University Press, 1999).

45. A. J. L. Fremantle, *Three Months in the Southern States: April–June, 1863* (1863; reprint, Lincoln: University of Nebraska Press, 1991), 269; Lee, *Wartime Papers*, 564–65.

46. Lee, *Wartime Papers*, 589–90; Dunbar Rowland, ed., *Jefferson Davis: Constitutionalist: His Life and Letters*, 10 vols. (Jackson: Mississippi Department of Archives and History, 1923), 5:588–90. For Lee's brief response to Davis's letter, see Lee, *Wartime Papers*, 593.

47. For a positive assessment of the relationship between Lee and Davis, see William C. Davis's essay titled "Lee and Jefferson Davis," in Gallagher, ed., *Lee the Soldier*. For an interpretation that finds more conflict in their relationship, see Steven E. Woodworth, *Davis and Lee at War* (Lawrence: University Press of Kansas, 1995).

48. Emma Holmes, *The Diary of Miss Emma Holmes, 1861–1866*, ed. John F. Marszalek (Baton Rouge: Louisiana State University Press, 1979), 281–83; Heth, "Letter from Major-General Henry Heth," 54–55.

49. Lee *Wartime Papers*, 698; Robert Grier Stephens Jr., ed., *Intrepid Warrior: Clement Anselm Evans: Confederate General from Georgia: Life, Letters, and Diaries of the War Years* (Dayton, Ohio: Morningside, 1992), 342–43; Festus P. Summers, ed., *A Borderland Confederate* (Pittsburgh: University of Pittsburgh Press, 1962), 78.

50. Walter H. Taylor, *Lee's Adjutant: The Wartime Letters of Colonel Walter Herron Taylor, 1862–1865*, ed. R. Lockwood Tower (Columbia: University of South Carolina Press, 1995), 139.

51. Lee, *Wartime Papers*, 695; Alexander, *Fighting for the Confederacy*, 346; *Columbia Daily South Carolinian*, May 10, 1864 [letter from a soldier in Kershaw's brigade].

52. On the Wilderness campaign, see Gordon C. Rhea, *The Battle of the Wilderness: May 5–6, 1864* (Baton Rouge: Louisiana State University Press, 1994). For the best treatment of the famous "Lee to the Rear" episode, see Robert K. Krick's essay in Gary W. Gallagher, ed., *The Wilderness Campaign* (Chapel Hill: University of North Carolina Press, 1997).

53. On the Spotsylvania campaign, see Gordon C. Rhea, *The Battles of Spotsylvania Court House and the Road to Yellow Tavern: May 7–12, 1864*, and *To the North Anna River: Grant and Lee, May 13-25, 1864* (Baton Rouge: Louisiana State University Press, 1997, 2000).

54. Francis W. Dawson, *Reminiscences of Confederate Service, 1861–1865*, ed. Bell I. Wiley (1882; Baton Rouge: Louisiana State University Press, 1980), 116

55. Charles S. Venable, "The Campaign from the Wilderness to Petersburg," in *SHSP* 14:532.

56. Jubal A. Early, *The Campaigns of Gen. Robert E. Lee: An Address by Lieut. General Jubal A. Early, before Washington and Lee University, January 19th, 1872* (Baltimore: John Murphy, 1872), 37. The best work on Cold Harbor is Gordon C. Rhea, *Cold Harbor: Grant and Lee, May 26-June 3, 1864* (Baton Rouge: Louisiana State University Press, 2002).

57. Rives's conversation with Lee is recounted in Accession 2313, folder titled "1865," box 2, AL-UVA. In ch. 6 of *Lee Considered*, Alan T. Nolan criticizes Lee severely for not encouraging Confederate surrender in 1864.

58. Robert F. Durden, *The Gray and the Black: The Confederate Debate on Emancipation* (Baton Rouge: Louisiana State University Press, 1972), 209–10.

59. James Longstreet, *From Manassas to Appomattox : Memoirs of the Civil War in America* (1896; reprint, New York: Da Capo, 1992), 614–15; Armistead L. Long, *Memoirs of Robert E. Lee: His Military and Personal History* (1886; reprint, Secaucus, N.J.: Blue and Grey, 1983), 421.

60. Stephen Minot Weld, *War Diary and Letters of Stephen Minot Weld, 1861–1865* (1912; reprint, Boston: Massachusetts Historical Society, 1979), 396.

61. Eliza Frances Andrews, *The War-Time Journal of a Georgia Girl, 1864–1865*, ed. Spencer Birdwell King (1908; reprint, Atlanta: Cherokee, 1976), 371.

62. Jones, *Life and Letters*, 390.

63. See Freeman, *R. E. Lee*, 4: chaps. 12–27, for the most detailed examination of Lee's tenure at Washington College.

64. Lee to Jubal Early, November 22, 1865, March 15, 1866, George H. and Katherine Davis Collection, Howard-Tilton Memorial Library, Tulane University, New Orleans.

65. Lee's letter quoted in Thomas, *Robert E. Lee*, 408

66. For decades, most authors ascribed to Lee the last words, "Strike the tent." Marvin P. Rozear, E. Wayne Massey, Jennifer Horner, Erin Foley, and Joseph C. Greenfield Jr., "R. E. Lee's Stroke," *Virginia Magazine of History and Biography* 98 (April 1990), demonstrates that Lee spoke no sentences after his stroke.

67. For a sampling of positive and negative interpretations of Lee as a general, see Gallagher, ed., *Lee the Soldier*.

68. John H. Claiborne to "My Dear wife," July 30, 1864, "Letters of John Herbert Claiborne," MS 3633 [boxed with 3621-a], AL-UVA; Thomas Conolly, *An Irishman in Dixie: Thomas Conolly's Diary of the Fall of the Confederacy*, ed. Nelson D. Lankford (Columbia: University of South Carolina Press, 1988), 52.

P. G. T. Beauregard

Charles P. Roland

Confederate general Pierre Gustave Toutant Beauregard was unquestionably one of the most colorful leaders of the Civil War. His preeminent biographer, Prof. T. Harry Williams, in a simile that is as colorful as its subject, wrote that among the Lees, Jacksons, and Johnstons of the Confederacy the Louisiana Creole stood out like pompano en papillote in a mess of turnip greens. His generalship stood out as strikingly; no other figure of the war experienced such vicissitudes of command.[1]

Son of a distinguished family, Beauregard was born May 28, 1818, a few miles below New Orleans. He received his elementary education in a nearby private school. French was the language spoken in school as well as home. When he was eleven his father sent him to New York to study in an institution run by two French brothers who had served as officers in Napoleon's army. Here he learned to speak and write English with fluency. Here also he came to idolize Napoléon Bonaparte whose campaigns he studied diligently. His ethnicity and his evocation of the military principles of his idol would one day cause him to be designated as the "Napoleon in Gray."

Not surprisingly, he yearned to become a soldier and persuaded his reluctant father to use his influence to get him appointed to the U.S. Military Academy. Upon the recommendation of Gov. A. B. Roman of Louisiana, he was accepted by Secretary of War Lewis Cass and was admitted to the academy in March 1834.

Bright and earnest, he was a superb cadet. Among his fellow cadets were many whose names would be on every tongue during the Civil War, including Confederates Braxton Bragg, William J. Hardee, Jubal Early, and Richard Ewell, and Federals Henry W. Halleck, William T. Sherman, and Joseph Hooker. Beauregard graduated second in the class of 1838, and emerged with a commission as a second lieutenant of engineers, the elite branch of the army.

Fortunately, most of his time for the five years following West Point was spent near his home in Louisiana, where he carried out a topographical and hydrographical survey of Barataria Bay and its islands, and supervised the construction of forts on the lower Mississippi River. In 1841 he was married to Marie Laure Villeré, the daughter of one of the state's most distinguished Creole families.

His apprenticeship in war occurred in the Mexican War, a struggle that has been called "rehearsal for conlict" because so many young officers who would later become either famous or notorious in the Civil War cut their professional teeth there. Because of his excellent record as an engineer, he was soon appointed to the staff of commanding general Winfield Scott. This was both a signal honor and an opportunity to gain invaluable experience in his métier, for Scott was a master of military strategy, operations, and tactics. Also, Beauregard as a member of the staff shared experiences with other outstanding members of it, including such figures as Capt. Robert E. Lee, Lt. George B. McClellan, and Lt. George G. Meade.

Beauregard participated in the daring reconnaissances that enabled Scott to turn the Mexican positions and win victories at Cerro Gordo and Contreras, and he recommended the approach adopted by Scott for his successful attack at Chapultepec. Fortunately for Beauregard, his arguments in favor of this route coincided with Scott's, though Beauregard said he had come to them even before learning the commanding general's preference. He accompanied Gen. John A. Quitman's division into Mexico City, the first unit to occupy the Mexican capital, and bore the news of the entry to General Scott.

Though Beauregard's superiors commended him highly, along with Lee and others, and though he received brevet promotions to the rank of major for his services in the campaign, he fumed in his memoir of the war that he was not sufficiently recognized. He wished to be singled out above the others for his work, a character trait that would swell within him as he grew older.

He did not fully appreciate Scott's strategic and operational boldness and brilliance. He later wrote: "Although I am a great admirer of our glorious Old Chief—whom I consider the best General of the present day—still he has not been faultless." He went on to say that if the Mexican general Santa Anna had been supported by better subordinates, Scott would have been forced to follow more closely the "true principles of the art of war" on those occasions when he ignored them.[2]

These lines indicate another persistent characteristic in Beauregard: his penchant for criticizing the decisions of his superiors even though, in this instance, he was a lowly lieutenant (and brevet major) commenting on the actions of a lieutenant general who had just completed an extraordinarily successful campaign. Beauregard's emphasis on "true principles" reveals still another of his traits: his insistence on going by the book instead of improvising measures to meet the shifting exigencies of war.

For twelve years after the Mexican War Beauregard labored in building or improving the fortifications in what the U.S. Army Engineer Department labeled "the Mississippi and Lake Defences in Louisiana," an expansible term that actually included Louisiana plus much of the Gulf coastal region east of the state. During this period his wife died in childbirth and he remarried the sister-in-law of one of the most influential political figures in the nation, U.S. senator John Slidell of Louisiana.

In 1853 Beauregard received an appointment as superintending engineer of the construction of the New Orleans customhouse, a job that he desired, and one in which he demonstrated fully his engineering talents in solving the problems of uneven sinking in the area's pliant soil. The building is still quite serviceable almost 150 years later and promises to remain so indefinitely. He held the position of construction engineer until 1860, when he was appointed, in part through Senator Slidell's support, to the superintendency of the U.S. Military Academy, the appointment to become effective on January 1, 1861.

He was hardly on the premises of the Academy when his orders were revoked because of the onrush of secession and his outspoken views in favor of it. Ironically, he protested his removal on the ground that he ought be permitted to hold the job until his own state of Louisiana withdrew from the Union and he resigned his commission. Louisiana seceded the day after he wrote his letter of grievance. He also demanded, but failed to receive, travel pay for his trip from West Point back to New Orleans. He promptly submitted his resignation from the U.S. Army.

He next enrolled as a private in the Orleans Guards, an elite Creole volunteer battalion in the state forces that was soon mustered into

Confederate service. His enlistment was a flamboyant gesture, because he of course fully expected to be elevated to a much higher duty and rank. The battalion responded with an equivalent gesture; it kept his name on the rolls as a private; when it was called, the sergeant replied, "Absent on duty."

Beauregard was not disappointed. Near the end of February Confederate president Jefferson Davis summoned him to Montgomery and assigned him to the command of Confederate forces at Charleston, with the rank of brigadier general, the only one in the Confederacy at the time. It was, indeed, an ironic turn of circumstance: a fiery Creole general at the fuse of a political, and potentially military, powder keg.

The people of Charleston took instantly to the handsome, haughty soldier from the bayous. But the situation soon outgrew the social amenities. The Union and Confederate governments were engaged in a contest of verbal maneuver over the fate of Fort Sumter and its Federal garrison located in the harbor. On April 10 Beauregard received orders from the Confederate government to demand the immediate surrender of the fort and attack and seize it if the demand should be rejected.

His emissaries to the fort, upon receiving a conditional reply from the garrison commander, Maj. Robert Anderson, issued the fateful order to open fire, and at about 4:30 in the morning of April 12 the first gun spoke. After a forty-eight hour bombardment of 2,500 shells in which no one was killed, Anderson lowered the U.S. flag in surrender. Beauregard instantly became a Confederate hero.

On May 28, after the revocation of orders to take command of Confederate defenses from Vicksburg, Mississippi, to the Kentucky-Tennessee border, he received orders to report to President Davis in Richmond, Virginia, now the capital of the Confederacy. He did so at once and was sent to Manassas as the commander of "the Alexandria line," an undefined area that was under the threat of a Federal army commanded by Brig. Gen. Irvin McDowell. In mid-June, in response to Beauregard's urgent plea for reinforcements, Davis ordered Gen. Joseph E. Johnston to bring his force of some 11,000 from the Shenandoah Valley to join the Confederates at Manassas. Johnston arrived by rail with a part of his troops on June 20; the remainder were on the way. The Confederates now numbered about 35,000.

Though Johnston actually ranked him, Beauregard more or less assumed the command and an exhausted Johnston acquiesced by allowing him to write an attack order, which he did. Before the planned attack could take place, the Confederates found themselves under assault by the Federals. The first true battle of the Civil War—1st Manassas—was under way.

General McDowell, urged on by the cry "Forward to Richmond," attacked the Confederates across Bull Run creek in an effort to turn their left flank and seize their line of communication, the Orange and Alexandria Railroad. Before dawn of July 21 his troops successfully crossed the stream but soon found their progress hotly contested by a Confederate brigade holding strong ground on the flank. Johnston and Beauregard, obeying a venerable military axiom, rode to the sound of the heavy fighting on the Confederate left.

Finding the Confederates severely pressed back on the key terrain feature of the battlefield—the Henry House hill—Beauregard urged Johnston to retire to the rear where he might direct the general course of the battle and leave Beauregard to command at the front. Johnston demurred, then retired. Beauregard rode along the front, exhorting the troops to a determined effort. For a while the lines surged back and forth; it was in this melee that Brig. Gen. Thomas J. Jackson earned his immortal sobriquet, "Stonewall."

In the late afternoon the Confederates were reinforced and their spirits rekindled by the arrival of the last brigade of Johnston's troops from the Valley. Beauregard now ordered a counterattack; the Union soldiers, panicked by the rumor that their own flank had been turned, fled back across Bull Run and ultimately all the way to Washington. The opening engagement of the war was a Confederate victory, and Beauregard was the hero of it.

But his conduct in the moment of victory displeased Jefferson Davis and darkened Beauregard's prospects for the future as a Confederate general. Neither he nor Johnston indicated any understanding of the magnitude of the victory. Neither made any serious effort to pursue the routed Union army. When Davis arrived upon the field that evening, he was disappointed to learn that there was no pursuit and none planned. He instructed Beauregard, or remembered that he did, to order a pursuit for the following morning; instead, Beauregard issued orders for a mere reconnaissance in force. In time Davis came to believe that Beauregard had thrown away the opportunity for a decisive triumph.

At the moment, Davis thanked him for the victory, praised him for his skill as a commander, gallantry as a soldier, and zeal as a patriot, and recommended him for promotion to the rank of full general. The Confederate Congress approved the recommendation, placing him at the bottom of the five men who originally held that rank. Temporarily, he was the most popular soldier in the Confederacy.

Beauregard quickly became his own worst enemy by writing statements that were by implication critical of Davis's leadership. He said the Confederate forces ought to be more completely concentrated, and that Washington should have been taken and Maryland occupied following the victory at Manassas. Patient at first, Davis eventually grew angry and wrote that Beauregard appeared to be seeking to exalt himself at the president's expense.

In January 1862, perhaps in part to get Beauregard from underfoot, Davis ordered him to the Western Department to serve as second-in-command to Gen. Albert Sidney Johnston, the ranking field commander of the Confederacy. An observer in the War Department wrote: "Beauregard has been ordered to the West. I knew the doom was upon him."[3] Brig. Gen. Robert Toombs was quoted as saying, "Urge General Beauregard to decline all proposals and solicitations. The Blade of Joab. *Verbum Sapientii.*"[4]

He arrived at Johnston's headquarters in Bowling Green, Kentucky, on February 4, at a moment of crisis. Federal army and naval forces under Gen. U. S. Grant and Flag Officer Andrew H. Foote were moving against the two forts (Fort Henry on the Tennessee River and Fort Donelson on the Cumberland) that guarded the water highways into the heart of the Western Department of the Confederacy. When Johnston outlined his strength (actually his weakness) and the disposition of his forces, Beauregard was appalled. He threw up his hands and exclaimed that he could do nothing of service and said he might as well leave Kentucky. Johnston persuaded him to stay.

The relationship between Beauregard and Johnston in the ensuing operations would lead to one of the most persistent controversies of the postwar years as Beauregard would say that he had proposed measures quite different from Johnston's. The records, however, reveal no discernible disagreement between the two at the time. Their personalities contrasted sharply. Johnston was reserved, grave, and deliberate; he appeared hesitant and indecisive in the presence of the impulsive and opinionated Creole, but he actually made all of the major decisions of the campaign and Beauregard accepted them without opposition.

Beauregard wrote after the war that he urged Johnston to concentrate his forces at Fort Henry and Fort Donelson in an attempt to crush

Grant, and that Johnston refused because of the threat of another large Federal army under Gen. Don Carlos Buell that was moving south from a position below Louisville. Beauregard may have made this proposal; he was an ardent advocate of concentration. But there is no contemporary evidence that he did make it, and he was strikingly inaccurate in his later years about his role in the conflict.

On February 6 Fort Henry fell to a Union gunboat fleet commanded by Foote. General Grant prepared to attack Fort Donelson at once. Nashville was indefensible against the powerful Union army marching from northern Kentucky; the Confederate line for the defense of Kentucky and Tennessee was irreparably breached because Union forces could be transported by water, landed, supplied, and reinforced at any chosen position as far south as northern Mississippi or Alabama. Confederate forces within the great curve of the Tennessee River were subject to encirclement and destruction or capture.

Believing Fort Donelson to be untenable, Johnston planned a withdrawal of all of his forces to some position below the Tennessee River and temporarily placed Beauregard in command of the western wing. Beauregard wrote years later that he opposed this move and again urged Johnston to concentrate at Fort Donelson and fight Grant there. But again, all contemporary evidence indicates that Beauregard fully endorsed Johnston's decision at the time and offered no counter-proposal.[5]

Beauregard withdrew his column from its original location, Columbus, Kentucky, to Corinth, Mississippi, a strategic point where the two most important railroads of the theater (the Mobile and Ohio and the Memphis and Charleston) intersected. Corinth was only one day's march from Pittsburg Landing, a steamboat landing on the Tennessee River where the Union army encamped on March 13.

Beauregard set about planning a grand counteroffensive and calling for reinforcements from throughout the Confederacy. Meanwhile, Johnston completed an extremely difficult march from Bowling Green with the eastern column of troops; by late March he had an army of between 40,000 and 50,000 troops, including 10,000 from the Gulf Coast and 5,000 from New Orleans, assembled at Corinth. After the war Beauregard claimed to have arranged this concentration on his own initiative and to have persuaded his reluctant and befogged commander to accept his plan. The documents show that the two independently came to the decision to combine their forces at Corinth.

Both Beauregard and Johnston hoped to attack and destroy the Union army now commanded by General Grant at Pittsburg Landing. Delegated by Johnston to organize the army for the attack, Beauregard did so, arranging it into a compact force of three corps with a reserve of detached brigades. Johnston also chivalrously offered Beauregard the command of the army in the attack; Beauregard chivalrously declined it.

The night of April 3, after learning that Buell was moving rapidly to join Grant, Johnston ordered the attack and delegated to Beauregard the preparation of the march and attack order. A combination of bad roads, torrential rainfall, and inexperience among subordinate commanders delayed the Confederate movement so that the various corps were not deployed for action until the late afternoon of April 5.

Dismayed by the delays and blunders and the conviction that a surprise was impossible and the Federals would be prepared for the attack, Beauregard now lost his nerve and urged that it be canceled. In what the great Prussian military analyst Carl von Clausewitz calls the "moment of truth" that precedes battle, Johnston overruled his shaken second-in-command and ordered the army forward. The Confederates struck at dawn of April 6 and took their opponents by surprise, vindicating Johnston's decision.

While Johnston directed his attack and inspired his troops at the front, he placed Beauregard in charge of affairs at the rear. Both efforts were vital to Confederate success. The formation planned by Beauregard and approved by Johnston while on the march required the Confederate main effort to be made on the right for the purpose of cutting the Federals away from their base at Pittsburg Landing and scattering or destroying them in a creek swale beyond. The formation was ill-designed to do this. It provided for an assault in successive waves by the two leading corps, each spread across the front. Inevitably, this resulted in a weakening of the initial shock and squandered much of the advantage of surprise. Also, it caused the scrambling of the units once they were in action.

Mysteriously, Beauregard's formation was completely at odds with Johnston's announced intention to commit his three corps abreast with the largest corps on the right. There is no conclusive explanation for this difference. Johnston's son speculated after the war that when his father learned of it, he felt that because the plan had already been distributed to the subordinate commanders, the time was too late to make a change. The plan was also at odds with Beauregard's earlier

Napoleonic tactical ideas, which emphasized the advantage of attacking in columns instead of lines. Shortly before the war he wrote a friend saying he been converted to the English mode of assault, in lines rather then columns. The Confederates attacked in lines at Shiloh.[6]

During the morning and early afternoon of the sixth Beauregard vigorously carried out his assigned duties. He exercised control over the rear, employed his staff to keep himself informed of the situation at the front, moved reserve units into positions that enabled Johnston to bring them into battle quickly, ordered needed ammunition forward, re-formed stragglers and sent them back into the line, and reactivated and redirected the attack of formations that had lost contact with the enemy.

He was engaged in these activities when he received word shortly before 3:00 P.M. that the Confederate commander had been killed at the front. Beauregard ordered that the battle be continued and Johnston's death kept from the troops. He also shifted some of his units in a renewed effort to knock out a pocket of fierce Federal resistance, which the soldiers referred to as a Hornet's Nest, on his right front.

Eventually, in the late afternoon, the Confederates surrounded and captured the surviving Federal troops in the Hornet's Nest and surged toward Pittsburg Landing less than a mile away. But a two-hour loss of momentum following Johnston's death had allowed the Federals to establish a final defense line around the landing; the afternoon was almost spent, as was much of the energy of the attack.

Beauregard now made one of the most controversial field decisions of the entire war. He ordered his troops to halt and retire to the captured enemy camps and rest for the night. His intention was to renew the attack the morning of the seventh. Under other circumstances this might have been a wise decision. Under the prevailing circumstances the decision to remain and renew the battle risked destroying the Confederate army. In the late afternoon a missing division of the Union army reached Pittsburg Landing, and during the night a force of about 20,000 troops under General Buell arrived from Nashville. The next morning Beauregard faced an opponent commanding twice his numbers, half of the Federals fresh, the others with restored morale.

Beauregard's explanation for his decision can neither be confirmed nor refuted. In his report written a few days after the battle he said he received a "special dispatch" during the afternoon of April 6 saying Buell had been delayed in his march to Pittsburg Landing and could not arrive in time to save Grant's army. Years after the war Beauregard's chief of staff Col. Thomas Jordan, wrote that a telegram had arrived from Athens, Alabama, saying Buell was marching for Decatur, Alabama, instead of Pittsburg Landing.

Beauregard in his narrative of his military operations during the war (published in 1884) repeated the account about the telegram but substituted Florence for Decatur as Buell's objective. Both towns are located several days' march to the east of Pittsburg Landing. Adding to the confusion, Colonel Jordan said in his article that he gave the message to Beauregard after dark and hence after the cease-fire order was issued. Professor Williams resolved the discrepancies of these accounts by suggesting that perhaps Beauregard received two messages concerning Buell's march and confused them in his report. Unfortunately for the historical record, neither message has been found.

The battle of Shiloh was renewed the morning of the seventh. By noon Beauregard could plainly see that his force was being defeated and was in danger of destruction. In midafternoon he ordered a withdrawal to Corinth. The following morning the Federals made a half-hearted attempt to pursue the beaten Confederates but were easily turned back by the cavalry under Col. Nathan Bedford Forrest.

Federal commanding general Henry Halleck now arrived from St. Louis and took command of the entire Federal force at Pittsburg Landing. So haltingly did he advance toward Corinth that Beauregard was able to delay his progress for six weeks. Possibly Beauregard, now reinforced by some 15,000 troops from across the Mississippi, could have driven Halleck back and saved the important rail junction as Lee soon would save Richmond from Gen. George B. McClellan's great army.

Beauregard did not attempt it. When the Federals approached Corinth he withdrew his army so skillfully that Halleck was unaware of its exodus until his columns actually entered the town. By this time the Confederates were well on their way to Tupelo, Mississippi, more than forty miles south of Corinth on the Mobile and Ohio Railroad.

A few days after arriving in Tupelo, Beauregard made a move that cost him the command of the army. Without consulting with Richmond, he left the army to go to a spa, Bladen Springs, Alabama, near Mobile for a few days of rest because of a throat ailment that had bothered him for years.

Davis had been unhappy with him since Manassas and more so since Shiloh. Beauregard, who had wired him of a "complete victory" at the end of the first day there, wrote later that he would defend Corinth "to the last extremity." In both instances the rhetoric far exceeded the performance. Referring to Beauregard, Mary Boykin Chesnut commented prophetically in her famed diary, "Cock Robin is as dead as he ever will be now."[7] When Davis learned of his leaving the army, he removed him from command and turned the army over to General Braxton Bragg, previously one of the corps commanders.

Beauregard was hurt and furious over this turn of events, his sensitive vanity badly wounded. He hated Jefferson Davis for it and looked upon him as an implacable enemy. In Mobile and Bladen Springs during the rest of the summer, he read accounts of the war, and especially of the battle of Shiloh, that intensified his pain. From Tupelo, Colonel Jordan wrote him that he was being blamed for the loss of the battle. Jordan also predicted that when he was restored to command he would be ordered to such a presumably static post as Charleston.

Beauregard replied in anger and indiscretion, though he was sufficiently cautious to sign his letter "G. T. Buenavista." Among other caustic remarks, he referred to Davis as "that living specimen of gall and hatred," and said he had the consolation of knowing that if Davis should die the entire country would rejoice at once, whereas if he (Beauregard) should die, the country would regret it.

Beauregard also revealed in his correspondence a latent hostility against, or envy of, Lee. Speaking of Lee's recent success in driving McClellan's force from the outskirts of Richmond, he said Lee would have been even more successful if he had not violated the rules of war by dividing his army. "I would have attacked differently," he said, demonstrating again his own dedication to the prevailing tactical rules and his limited notion of the importance of boldness in a commander.[8]

Beauregard yearned to be restored to the command of the western Confederate army. He wrote his brother-in-law Villeré that if this should occur, he would execute a plan that would regain the states of Tennessee and Kentucky. Again, he was playing the role of a visionary strategist with no regard for the practical realities of the situation.

Villeré mustered heavy support in the Congress for Beauregard's restoration to the army command. But Davis was adamant; he said he would not yield even if requested by the whole world. He did, however, yield to the degree that he approved an appointment of the Creole general to another command: that of the defense of Charleston as Jordan had foretold. Beauregard was back where he had played the dramatic role of beginning the war.

He would remain at Charleston for almost two years.[9] He enjoyed a lively social life there, and he commanded the city's defenses with imagination and skill; the job suited his talents as an engineer. He strengthened the fortifications and their armaments guarding the harbor and the approaches to it. He drilled the gunners and kept them in a high state of readiness. He experimented with torpedoes (mines), surface torpedo boats, and submarines; one of the submarines, the *Hunley*, converted into a surface torpedo boat, actually sank a Union warship, the *Housatonic*. His fortifications proved to be impervious to Union attacks whether by sea or land. In early April 1863, a powerful fleet commanded by Adm. Samuel F. Du Pont sailed into the harbor but was repelled by the heavy fire of the many guns at Fort Sumter and the other forts around the harbor's border.

After the initial Union failure, Gen. Quincy A. Gillmore, known as a master of artillery and siege warfare, took charge of the combined army-navy operations against Charleston. His naval colleague was Adm. John A. Dahlgren who replaced Du Pont on July 12. Together, throughout the summer and early fall they attacked Fort Sumter and other key positions with massive artillery bombardments and direct assaults by ships and troops. Gillmore also bombarded Charleston itself with a long-range gun known as the Swamp Angel, which shot its 200-pound shells from a distance of more than five miles away on Morris Island. All efforts were futile. The city would ultimately fall, but only with the collapse of the Confederacy.

The Charleston command had turned out to be not at all a static one. The city was extremely important to the Confederacy both for the support of morale and as a useful port for the blockade-runners. Beauregard redeemed himself at Charleston for whatever deficiencies he had shown earlier.

Notwithstanding the duties of his Charleston command, he had enough spare time in the palmetto city to devote himself to large-scale strategic planning. By now Confederate military fortunes were sharply in decline, especially in the West. He strongly believed that Confederate resources were too much concentrated in the Eastern theater of operations, particularly in Virginia, thus jeopardizing the defense of the West. Through correspondence with Villeré, General Joseph E. Johnston, and others who shared his views, he set forth a scheme for redressing the strategic balance.

He advocated that Lee assume a strict defensive in Virginia, and that some 30,000 troops be dispatched from there to join General

Bragg's army in Middle Tennessee; the aggregate force would be commanded by General Johnston. It would then attack and destroy the Union army facing it and move west to the Mississippi River to threaten General Grant's besieging army at Vicksburg from the north. Grant would be obliged to withdraw from Mississippi and might be trapped and destroyed, argued Beauregard.

Other Confederate leaders designed comparable plans; Secretary of War James A. Seddon wished to send a portion of Lee's army directly to Mississippi to relieve the siege of the river city. When Lee was approached with Seddon's proposal, he opposed it explicitly on two grounds: the distance was too great to make the move practicable, and the employment of the troops to be transferred was questionable. Upon reading Lee's reply, Davis said he expected it and concurred with it.

These rebuffs did not cause Beauregard to give up on his strategic planning. He scoffed that Lee's invasion of the North in the Gettysburg campaign would in no way benefit the Confederacy. Only by adopting his plan for Western concentration could the South hope to succeed, he wrote Johnston. In October 1863, three months after the Confederate defeats at Gettysburg and Vicksburg, and shortly following Bragg's victory at Chickamauga in northern Georgia, he wrote Bragg to say the Confederate authorities should send 35,000 troops from the East to support an invasion of Tennessee. Actually, by now Bragg had already received two divisions from Lee's army under his senior corps commander, Lt. Gen. James Longstreet, who had played a critical role at Chickamauga.

The following spring, Longstreet proposed a plan for combining troops under Beauregard with his own force, now in eastern Tennessee, for an invasion of Kentucky. Davis and Lee considered this proposal carefully and vetoed it because it made no adequate provision for the necessary transport and supply, nor could they come up with one. For all practical purposes, this would end the designs of both Longstreet and Beauregard for a movement of troops from Virginia to Tennessee. Shortly both would be ordered to Virginia, Longstreet to merge his corps back into Lee's army, Beauregard to take command of the defense of the southern approaches to Richmond.

Beauregard's plans demonstrate both the strength and weakness of his thinking. He was seeking a means of offsetting the superior numbers and resources of the Union by a resort to Napoleonic strategy: the employment of interior lines to concentrate a sufficient force in the West to defeat the separated Union armies there by turns. But the plans were unrealistic because they minimized the numerical and logistical weaknesses of the Confederacy and the vulnerability of Richmond and northern Virginia if Lee's army should be significantly weakened. They also exaggerated the skill and will of any Confederate general in the West who would have been in command of the troops sent from Virginia. Beauregard failed to recognize that the main hope of Confederate success lay in an intact army in the East commanded by Lee.

Despite his successful defense of Charleston, Beauregard felt that his talents were not being put to their best use there; he disdainfully referred to his department as "the Department of Refuge." He keenly desired to get away for another rest at Bladen Springs. He did not repeat his earlier mistake of leaving his command without permission, but in early April 1864, sent a request for leave to the War Department.

He received instead a message from Bragg, now in nominal command of Confederate forces, asking him to come to Virginia to serve in a field command. Beauregard expressed his agreement and left Charleston for Weldon, North Carolina, where a staff officer met him and explained his assignment. He was to command an area spreading south from the James River in Virginia to the Cape Fear River in North Carolina; he named it the Department of North Carolina and South Virginia.[10]

It was a department of vital importance to the Confederacy. One of the great disadvantages to Lee in his assignment of protecting northern Virginia and the Confederate capital was the vulnerability of his right flank and rear. It was subject to being turned through Union naval control of the Chesapeake Bay and the Atlantic to the immediate south. This control enabled Union forces by landing on the lower Virginia Peninsula or the Atlantic coast to threaten Richmond or its vital supply line with the southeastern portion of the Confederacy, the Weldon Railroad.

Gen. George B. McClellan's massive drive on Richmond in spring and summer 1862 had employed this very line of approach. General Grant, recently appointed general-in-chief of Union forces, had suggested a comparable move in which an army of 60,000 would be landed on the North Carolina coast for a thrust inland against the Weldon. Grant believed it would, if successful, cause Lee to abandon northern Virginia, and Lee admitted as much to his authorities. Lee wished to have Beauregard in command of this sensitive region.

Grant's plan was not tried. The previous Union general-in-chief, Halleck, vetoed it because it would require splitting the Army of the Potomac with Lee between the two wings. In Halleck's view, this would create too great a risk for the safety of Washington. Instead, the Army of the Potomac, nominally commanded by General Meade but accompanied by Grant and actually controlled by him, moved directly south against Lee's army. At the same time, Grant sent a supporting force of 39,000 under Gen. Benjamin F. Butler by water to land south of the James River and advance against Richmond and its communications.

Butler landed his force successfully and doubtless could have taken the town of Petersburg, a rail center on the Weldon line south of the Appomattox River thirty miles below Richmond, if he had moved promptly against it. Instead, he hesitated indecisively then took a position in an area known as the Bermuda Hundred, which lay in the angle formed by the confluence of the Appomattox River with the James, thus placing Petersburg beyond the Appomattox from him and Richmond beyond the James.

Beauregard hastily formed a defense for Petersburg. When Butler moved up the south side of the James toward Richmond, Beauregard was ordered by the secretary of war to join Confederate forces at Drewry's Bluff in an attack on the Federal column. Beauregard haltingly and complainingly reached his destination and did what he was accustomed to doing in such a situation: he formulated a grandiose scheme for winning the war.

Again he proposed to employ interior lines and the concentration of force to defeat the enemy armies by turns. Let Lee withdraw from northern Virginia into the Richmond defenses, he said, and send heavy reinforcements to Beauregard who would attack and destroy Butler's army below the James, then cross the river to strike Grant's flank in coordination with a frontal assault by Lee. When Bragg objected to the plan, he cried: "Bragg, circumstances have thrown the fate of the Confederacy into your hands and mine! Let us play our hands boldly and fearlessly! Issue those orders and I'll carry them out to the best of my ability. I'll guarantee success!"[11] Bragg was unmoved, but agreed to lay the proposal before the president.

Davis visited Beauregard's headquarters the next day to inform him that he disapproved the plan. He ordered Beauregard instead to attack and defeat Butler, then dispatch reinforcements to Lee's hard-pressed army above Richmond. Beauregard's plan represented a desperate gamble for a quick victory; it characteristically ignored Confederate weaknesses in numbers, supplies, and transport. Whether it would have worked cannot be known since it was not attempted, but by now the Confederate plight was virtually beyond hope.

On May 16, reinforced to approximately 18,000 with troops brought up from North Carolina, Beauregard attacked Butler's army at Drewry's Bluff and drove it back into the Bermuda Hundred Peninsula. Beauregard then had his troops construct a line of earthworks across the neck of the peninsula, effectively penning Butler there and causing Grant to repeat what he heard from one of his subordinates: "[Butler] is corked up like a cork in a bottle."

Because this line could be held with relatively few troops, Davis now ordered some 5,000 of Beauregard's troops to reinforce Lee. With Butler trapped and inert, the Creole general again turned to matters of grand strategy. He repeated his recommendation that Lee pull back toward Richmond; then Beauregard with virtually all of his force would cross the James and join him. Together, they would destroy Grant's army; then Beauregard would recross the James and destroy Butler's army. Again, Davis considered the plan hopeless and impractical, and ignored it.

But when toward the end of May Lee was forced by Grant to move to a point only a few miles from Richmond, he asked for Beauregard to join him with most of his troops, leaving a thin force to hold Butler within the Bermuda Hundred. Beauregard now abandoned his earlier recommendation and reported that he was too weak to be able to make the move and hold Butler off. Again, neither Davis nor Bragg had the will to order him to make the move.

Lee continued to ask for troops; Beauregard continued to withhold them until ordered by the War Department to send them. They were sent in driblets, never enough to do any significant good. Reviewing the interchange of messages among Lee, Davis, Beauregard, and Bragg, Professor Williams concluded: "Nothing illustrates better the fundamental weakness of the Confederate command system. . . . Beauregard evaded his responsibility for determining what help he could give Lee; Davis and Bragg shirked their responsibility to decide when he refused. The strangest feature of the whole affairs was that, in the face of Lee's repeated requests, nobody thought to order Beauregard to join Lee."[12]

During the lull in operations after Grant's disastrous assault on June 3 against Lee's line at Cold Harbor, Beauregard accurately divined Grant's next move; he said it would be around Lee's right flank to the James River. It was. On June 12 Grant began a bold and brilliantly executed movement of his army away from Lee's front and across the James River to seize Petersburg. For a day and a half Lee lost contact with the Union army.

Beauregard sensed its objective and began to call upon Davis and Bragg for reinforcements, but Lee demurred in sending them because of his fear of a drive north of the James directly against Richmond. Grant's advance corps, commanded by Gen. W. F. Smith, struck Beauregard's Petersburg line the morning of the fifteenth. Outnumbered several times but fighting from fortifications, the Confederates held off Smith's timid and uncoordinated attacks. During the day both sides grew stronger: the Confederates with troops ordered by Beauregard from Bermuda Hundred, the Federals with the arrival of an additional corps from north of the James. By nightfall, Beauregard had some 14,000 men in line against approximately 40,000 of the enemy.

For the next two days Beauregard continued to call for reinforcements while Lee continued to delay in sending them. Some of the most critical messages never got through to Lee; they were stuck in Bragg's headquarters. Fighting went on along the Petersburg front throughout the sixteenth and seventeenth. By midafternoon that day the Federals numbered some 60,000 against Beauregard's 14,000; by night the Federals numbered 90,000. Beauregard's defense was bold and brilliant. At times he even launched limited counterattacks, deceiving his opponents into believing he was much stronger than he actually was.

Late the afternoon of the seventeenth Beauregard notified Lee that Grant was south of the James; shortly he wired that he had captured prisoners from four corps of Grant's army. There could be no doubt that the Army of the Potomac was in front of Petersburg in full strength. The following morning Lee's army filed into the Petersburg trenches and the climactic siege of the war began. Beauregard's remarkable defense had saved the city. It was his shining hour as a field commander.

Lee's arrival at Petersburg sharply changed Beauregard's status. He had commanded only a small force there, but he had been in independent command, his own boss. Despite being a full general, he was now a direct subordinate to Lee, something of a corps commander—not to the liking of a man of his temperament. The situation was aggravated by his proximity to Richmond where Davis and Bragg were in position to keep him under surveillance.

When on July 13 the Federals exploded a large mine under the Confederate line and opened a wide breach, Beauregard went immediately to the spot and called upon Lee for reinforcements to close the line. Lee soon arrived also and quickly took charge of the operation.

A month later a strong Federal thrust captured a section of the Weldon Railroad south of Petersburg. Beauregard tried to dislodge them but failed. Lee tried later and failed, then devised a wagon route around the rupture. The administration looked upon the episode as a breakdown in Beauregard's leadership. Only when Lee intervened and explained that the Confederates lacked the strength to hold the line was the matter dropped. The Richmond authorities continued to find fault with Beauregard on a number of issues, and he grew increasingly restive with his present situation. Lee helped get him out of it.

What Beauregard ardently desired was an army command. He had hoped to be assigned to lead the Army of Tennessee when Davis removed Joseph E. Johnston in front of Atlanta. Instead, Davis had named Gen. John Bell Hood who immediately launched a series of attacks against Sherman's threatening army. Cognizant of Beauregard's talents and aware of his unhappiness in Virginia, Lee sought to have him given an independent command. Also, because of the widespread popularity of Beauregard within the Confederacy, Davis felt it expedient to find a suitable role for him.

Lee used his influence to have Beauregard sent to inspect the defenses of Wilmington, North Carolina, one of the few remaining port cities of the Confederacy. Lee believed this might lead to the Creole's being assigned to the command there. Though not as important a position as Beauregard believed he deserved, it was an important one, and he indicated his willingness to accept it.

>─┤─◆>─○─<◆─┤─<

While he was in Wilmington on his inspection, Atlanta fell to Sherman. This led Davis to ponder a new assignment for Beauregard. Curiously, instead of approaching him directly about it, Davis asked Lee to determine whether he would accept an appointment in Georgia. Under the impression the president was talking about Hood's command, Lee questioned Beauregard, who indicated his willingness, though, in an uncharacteristic display of modesty, he said he felt unequal to the task.

Davis had no intention of placing Beauregard in command of the Army of Tennessee. Instead, he proposed to make him commander of a new department named the Military Division of the West, a broad area embracing Georgia on the east and spreading west to the Mississippi River. It included the Army of Tennessee under Hood and a scattering of troops in the Department of Alabama and Mississippi under Lt. Gen. Richard Taylor. This sort of command was not what Beauregard wanted, but when he met on October 2 with Davis in Augusta, Georgia, and the president offered it, he accepted it.[13]

It was a particularly frustrating assignment. He probably carried it out as capably as anyone could have. It was a shadow command. He actually commanded no troops at all, though he bore the responsibility for what occurred in his division. In the past, Beauregard had exhibited a tendency to assert his authority, even to assume authority when it was in question. Now, atypically, he appeared not to wish to exert any real authority. He wrote Davis asking whether his assignment required him to take command of an army when present with it, "Shouldn't my orders merely pass through the commanding general?" Davis replied, "You are right, you are not to assume command of an army. If you did you might not be able to leave it."[14]

Beauregard either was unable or unwilling to exercise any real control over Hood, who appears to have looked upon him as more or less a figurehead. In a meeting at Cave Spring, Georgia, some seventy miles northwest of Atlanta, Hood outlined a plan for striking Sherman's rail line just below the Tennessee border, a move designed to draw the Union general back into that area. In a subsequent meeting in Gadsden, Alabama, Hood announced another and far more ambitious plan; he would invade Tennessee and possibly Kentucky, then, if Sherman moved south instead of following him north, Hood would cross into Virginia and join forces with Lee. This was the sort of panoramic strategy that appealed to Beauregard and he approved it.

As Hood prepared for his great venture, Sherman moved south out of Atlanta. Beauregard, deciding he was of no use with Hood, went south in the hope of designing measures to stop Sherman. He joined Gen. William J. Hardee who commanded a small force of about 10,000 in Savannah. He instructed Hardee to avoid being captured and had him begin constructing a pontoon bridge across the Savannah River to enable him to escape as Sherman's army approached the city. When that moment came, Beauregard instructed Hardee to refuse to surrender and instead to evacuate the town. He did so on December 20.

In a desperate effort to stop Sherman, who was about to turn north toward the Carolinas, Beauregard wired Davis requesting reinforcements from Lee's army until Hood should return from Tennessee. Davis replied with what should have been evident, that no troops could be spared from Lee's hard-pressed army. Beauregard would have to do the best he could with what force he had.

The situation was probably beyond any effort he could have made. Possibly, by concentrating every solider he could muster around Hardee's little force he could have launched a damaging attack on an isolated column of Sherman's army as it moved north. Curiously, this vehement advocate of concentration failed to attempt it now, quite likely because it would have meant abandoning Charleston. Sherman, by bypassing this city, was left free to sweep through South Carolina almost at will.

Beauregard now received from Hood, who had been out of touch with him for almost a month, a request for reinforcements. He replied that none were available. Soon he learned that Hood had been disastrously defeated by Gen. George Thomas at Nashville and was retreating southward; then he received from Hood a request that he visit Hood's army at Tupelo, Mississippi. Beauregard hastened there with the intention of bringing the army east to join it with Hardee's force. At Tupelo he found only the remnant of the Army of Tennessee. Hood submitted his resignation at once, and Beauregard replaced him with Gen. Richard Taylor, an officer who might have been a better choice than Hood in the first place.

Hastening back to Augusta, Georgia, Beauregard met with Hardee in attempting to create a strategy to stop Sherman. Without knowing whether the Union general would strike for Charleston or Columbia, the Confederates came up with a plan that actually protected neither city; it divided the meager Confederate forces between the two. Sherman feinted at each with a column, then reunited his force and headed for Columbia. Meanwhile, Beauregard, overruling Davis's instructions, ordered Hardee to abandon Charleston. But Columbia was doomed; it fell to Sherman on February 17.

Beauregard set about to withdraw all of his forces to Greensboro, North Carolina, near the northern border of that state. His messages to Davis and Lee, who eleven days earlier had become general in chief of all Confederate armies, sounded confused because in the face of Sherman's rapid and unstoppable advance he was in fact confused. Davis and Lee were even more confused by the situation south of them; Lee doubted Sherman's ability to move as fast as he was moving. On February 22, pressed by Lee, Davis replaced Beauregard with the other full general he disliked just as much: Joseph E. Johnston. Beauregard was given the alternatives of the command of the Department of Western Virginia and Eastern Tennessee (by now a nondepartment), or remaining as Johnston's subordinate. He chose to remain with Johnston.[15]

Though his feelings were wounded by the change, he served Johnston faithfully until the end. The end was not long in coming. The Confederate armies were in a state of collapse. Johnston's army, a composite force of troops from the Carolinas and the remnant of the Army of Tennessee, faced three times its number in Sherman's host. On March 19, before Beauregard joined him, Johnston struck Sherman's left wing in the battle of Bentonville, North Carolina. Initially successful, Johnston was forced to retreat when Sherman collected his full strength.

As Johnston and Beauregard strove desperately to concentrate enough troops to stop Sherman, the Confederacy suffered its death blow in Grant's triumph over Lee. On April 2 Lee abandoned his lines around Petersburg and Richmond and pressed west in a forlorn effort to escape the vise of the Union army and join his force with Johnston's. Davis and his cabinet fled by train to Danville, Virginia, where they were met by a cavalry escort dispatched by Beauregard who was now in Greensboro.

Davis met with Beauregard in Greensboro the morning of April 11; two days earlier Lee had surrendered to Grant at Appomattox Courthouse. Beauregard was fully aware that this event marked the true end of the Confederacy. To his astonishment, Davis said the war must continue; that the word of Lee's surrender was not confirmed, and that, if necessary, the war would be pursued west of the Mississippi. He called Johnston from the field to determine his feelings on the matter. Davis repeated to both generals his determination to continue the struggle.

The two generals met with Davis and his cabinet the morning of April 13. Though Lee's surrender had now been confirmed, Davis again expressed confidence in Confederate victory "if our people will turn out." He then asked Johnston his opinion of the situation. In short, Johnston said the war was lost; that a continuation of it would be hopeless. When Davis asked Beauregard his opinion, he said, "I concur in all General Johnston has said."[16] Davis now tacitly authorized Johnston to approach Sherman for terms, but indicated that he would not surrender. Johnston would have to do it.

Johnston was able to negotiate such extraordinarily generous terms from Sherman that Davis was persuaded to approve the document. But the Federal government now repudiated the terms because they granted political concessions beyond the authority of a military figure. Johnston, determined to avoid further bloodshed, met with Sherman again and accepted the revised terms. Davis and his party fled south, headed for the Trans-Mississippi.

The final terms of surrender paroled the Confederates and permitted them to return to their homes, and on May 1 Beauregard and his staff began their somber journey there. He arrived in New Orleans on the twenty-first, at home for the first time in four years.

As a former Confederate general, his legal status was uncertain. President Lincoln had adopted a policy of amnesty to former Confederates who would lay down their arms and take an oath of allegiance to the Federal government; Lincoln's successor, Andrew Johnson, promptly issued his own proclamation embodying similar terms. But high-ranking civil and military Confederates were not included in Johnson's general amnesty; they were required to request pardon individually in submitting their loyalty oaths.

In early September 1865, Beauregard wrote Lee and Joseph E. Johnston inquiring their advice on this business, which, he made clear, was extremely distasteful to him. "It is hard to ask pardon of an adversary you despise," he commented in his letter to Lee. Lee's reply was a classic of pragmatic wisdom. He advised Beauregard to apply for pardon and take the oath of Federal allegiance. Lee's reasoning went: "I need not tell you that true patriotism sometimes requires of men to act exactly contrary, at one period, to that which it does at another, and the motive which impels them-the desire to do right-is precisely the same. The circumstances which govern their actions, change, and their conduct must conform to the new order of things."[17]

Even before receiving replies from Lee and Johnston, Beauregard decided to seek pardon and take the prescribed oath of allegiance. In applying for amnesty he wrote:

> In taking up arms during the late struggle (after my native state, Louisiana, had seceded) I believed, in good faith, that I was defending the constitutional rights of the South against the encroachments of the North. Having appealed to the arbitration of the Sword, which has gone against us, I accept the decision as settling finally the question of secession &

slavery—& I offer now my allegiance to the Govt. of the United States, which I promise, truly and faithfully, to serve & uphold hereafter, against all external or internal foes.[18]

Almost three years later Beauregard was included in a general amnesty declared by President Johnson. Eight years later his right to hold public office was restored by Congress.[19]

For a number of years he remained undecided whether to accept a military position in a foreign military force, as a number of former Confederates were then doing. Notwithstanding his conciliatory words to President Johnson, Beauregard was greatly upset over the prevailing conditions in Louisiana. At one time he apparently accepted an offer of military command from the khedive of Egypt, but the negotiations fell through. Beauregard also considered taking a command in the army of Japan.

The political turmoil of the times brought him temporarily into politics. In an effort to counteract the influence of the Republican "carpetbaggers" and "scalawags" over the black voters of the state, he joined a group of conservative whites in 1873 in the Louisiana Unification Movement, a venture to create a party of local whites and blacks, which he and others believed the whites would be able to control. The Louisiana Unification Movement failed because the local whites could not match the Republicans in their incentives offered to the blacks.

In the end, nothing came of any of Beauregard's thoughts to leave the country; he remained at home and made the best of it. The best of it turned out to be pretty good for him financially. In October 1865, he accepted a job as chief engineer and general superintendent of the New Orleans, Jackson, and Great Northern Railroad at an annual salary of $3,500, which was soon raised to $5,000. The line ran from New Orleans to Canton, Mississippi; it would later be absorbed into the Illinois Central Railroad. His engineering skills combined with an apparently innate business acumen to help make the railroad a booming success. But in 1870 the state Reconstruction government seized the road and sold it to rival entrepreneurs.

Overlapping his work with the Jackson line, Beauregard was involved with a local street railway, the New Orleans and Carrollton Railroad Company, which he leased by taking in two capitalist backers. He built it into a successful line but lost it in 1876 to a handful of controlling stock owners who held visions of much greater profits through their own management.

Beauregard's most lucrative postwar enterprise was his most controversial one: his role in the proceedings of the Louisiana Lottery Company. The company was the largest gambling enterprise in the United States. A twenty-dollar ticket won a prize of $300,000. Theoretically, a forty-dollar ticket would win $600,000, though the magic number was never actually drawn.

The Lottery Company attracted money from all over the nation; the annual profits sometimes amounted to as much as $13,000,000, a significant figure in those days. The company used a part of its income to purchase political favors, especially that of keeping its activities legal in Louisiana. It was instrumental in the overthrow of the state's Reconstruction government in 1877; it put up the funds to buy off a sufficient number of Republicans to achieve a quorum in the Democrat-controlled legislature. The company bought popular support with donations to the Charity Hospital of New Orleans and with other philanthropic bribes. Nevertheless, eventually (in 1893) its Louisiana charter would be annulled.

The lottery tickets were drawn from a large glass wheel by a young boy wearing a blindfold; cards bearing the amount of the prizes were drawn from a similar but smaller wheel. To assure the honesty of the drawings, the tickets and cards were scrambled by rotating both wheels in the beginning and occasionally throughout the course of the proceedings.

Yet there were suspicions of fraud, and to allay them the manager hit upon the idea of engaging two Confederate generals to supervise the drawings. As the state's foremost military hero, Beauregard was a natural for one of the positions; he was offered it and took it. He was to choose a companion from among his fellow Confederate generals. He chose Wade Hampton of South Carolina who was willing but declined because he was victorious in his state's gubernatorial election that year. Beauregard then turned to General Jubal Early, the explosive, unreconstructed former corps commander in Lee's Army of Northern Virginia. Early accepted.

For sixteen years, until virtually the end of Beauregard's life, the two old soldiers, Early in a suit of Confederate gray and Beauregard in sober black, sat by and supervised the drawings. For these exertions they received compensation ranging from $10,000 to possibly as much as $20,000 annually. Their real service, of course, was the selling of their names, reputations, and influence to the company.

Beauregard's most passionate enterprise during the final years of his life was the defense of his record as a Confederate general. He had done this from time to time during the period immediately following the war, but his efforts along this line increased markedly in the decades of the 1870s and 1880s.

In a number of articles, speeches, and a book titled *The Military Operations of General Beauregard in the War between the States, 1861–1865*—which, although he wrote, appeared under the name of former staff officer Col. Alfred Roman—he contributed significantly to the body of information about the military campaigns of the war. He reinforced the public awareness that he had shared in many of them. In a very human way, he inflated his part in those actions. He also took occasion to air his animosity for Davis and his resentment of the credits paid to certain other Confederate generals.

Beauregard went to great pains to prove that he was the author and executor of the Confederate operations culminating in the battle of Shiloh. He became particularly determined to do so after the appearance in 1878 of a biography of Albert Sidney Johnston by Johnston's son, a work that not only claimed Shiloh as being the product of Johnston's strategy, but further argued that Beauregard threw away a victory there that Johnston had in effect already won.

In Beauregard's analysis of the Shiloh campaign, and of the operations at Fort Henry and Fort Donelson, he portrayed Johnston as a commander of admirable personal character but one almost void of any military capacity. In this version, all of Johnston's wise moves were suggested by Beauregard, all of his foolish moves made against Beauregard's advice—an interpretation belied by the contemporary records.[20]

In the publication *Battles and Leaders of the Civil War* (1887), Beauregard expanded an article on the first battle of Manassas into a discourse on the strategic mistakes of the Confederacy and the dysfunctions of Jefferson Davis. He introduced this discourse with a typically Beauregardian flourish: "No people ever warred for independence with more relative advantages than the Confederacy. . . . The South, with its great material resources, its defensive means of mountains, rivers, railroads, and telegraph, with the immense advantage of interior lines of war, would be open to discredit as a people if its failure could not be explained otherwise than by mere material contrast."[21]

Why then had the South not won its independence? He laid the defeat of the Confederacy to the "narrow military view" of its government. He repeated the strategic nostrums he had recommended during the war, along with the implicit assumption that had they been attempted they would have brought victory to the Confederacy. He attributed to shortsightedness and obstinacy Davis's refusal to adopt them.[22]

Beauregard lived out the rest of his life in New Orleans, the idol of his people as the peerless Creole warrior. He died on February 20, 1893, and was buried in the tomb of the Army of Tennessee in the Metairie Cemetery on the outskirts of his city. The symbolism of the sepulchre is as ironic as it is evocative; above him rides the heroic equestrian statue of Albert Sidney Johnston.[23]

⋗⋅⋖⋗⋅○⋅⋖⋗⋅⋖

To evaluate Beauregard as a general is difficult. He represented a mixture of outstanding ability and limiting weakness. Unquestionably, he was brilliant, bold, and energetic, capable of flashes of keen strategic insight, yet at the same time he was mercurial, erratic, and visionary; and he relied excessively on what he considered to be the eternal "principles of war" formulated by his model, Napoleon.

Finally, his hypersensitive pride, along with an urge to criticize his superiors, kindled the disfavor of his commander in chief, a man of equal sensitivity. The conflict of egos between the two deprived the Confederacy of the full talents of both.

Beauregard longed throughout the war for an army command; he doubtless should have been given the Army of Tennessee as the replacement of Joseph E. Johnston in summer 1864. But this would have required a different temperament in Jefferson Davis or in Beauregard, or possibly both. Beauregard's vagaries of mind and mood combined with his indiscretions of utterance to relegate him to a secondary role in the Confederate war effort and in the southern pantheon.

NOTES

1. T. Harry Williams, *P. G. T. Beauregard: Napoleon in Gray* (Baton Rouge: Louisiana State University Press, 1954), 3 (hereafter cited as Williams, *Beauregard*). The present work relies heavily on this biography for the details of Beauregard's career. Beauregard gave his own account of his Civil War career in Alfred Roman, *The Military Operations of General P. G. T. Beauregard in the War between the States, 1861–1865*, 2 vols. (New York: Harper & Brothers, 1884) (hereafter cited as Roman, *Military Operations of General Beauregard*).

2. T. Harry Williams, ed., *With Beauregard in Mexico: The Mexican War-Reminiscences of P. G. T. Beauregard* (Baton Rouge: Louisiana State University Press, 1956), 104–105. This is the edited and published version of Beauregard's reminiscences of his activities in the war with Mexico.

3. John B. Jones, *A Rebel War Clerk's Diary at the Confederate States Capital*, 2 vols. (Philadelphia: J. B. Lippincott & Company, 1866), 1:107.

4. Quotation in P. G. T. Beauregard, "The First Battle of Bull Run," in *Battles and Leaders of the Civil War*, eds. Robert U. Johnson and Clarence C. Buel, 4 vols. (New York: The Century Company, 1887–1888), 1:225 (hereafter cited as *Battles and Leaders of the Civil War*).

5. This interpretation of the relationship between Beauregard and Johnston, and of their roles in the operations that culminated in the loss of Forts Henry and Donelson followed by the Shiloh campaign, is drawn from Williams, *Beauregard*, 113–49; and Charles P. Roland, *Albert Sidney Johnston: Soldier of Three Republics* (Austin: University of Texas Press, 1964), 282–351.

6. So named because of a small Methodist church of that name near where the fighting had begun.

7. C. Vann Woodward, ed., *Mary Chesnut's Civil War* (New Haven and London: Yale University Press, 1981), 336.

8. Quoted in Williams, *Beauregard*, p. 161.

9. See ibid., 166–196, for a full account of Beauregard's command of the defenses of Charleston.

10. See ibid., 207–235, for a full account of Beauregard's command of the Department of North Carolina and Southern Virginia.

11. Ibid., 215.

12. Ibid., 225.

13. See ibid., 241–252, for a full account of Beauregard's command of the Military Division of the West.

14. Quoted in ibid., 242.

15. Quoted in ibid., 255.

16. Quoted in ibid., 257.

17. Quoted in Charles Bracelen Flood, *Lee: The Last Years* (Boston: Houghton Mifflin, 1981), 102.

18. Quoted in Williams, *Beauregard*, 258.

19. See ibid., 257–329, for a full account of Beauregard's life after the Civil War.

20. See Roman, *Military Operations of General Beauregard*, 1:213–351, for Beauregard's view of his role in the campaigns of the Tennessee forts and Shiloh.

21. Beauregard, "The First Battle of Bull Run," in *Battles and Leaders of the Civil War*, 1:222.

22. Ibid., 222–223.

23. Johnston is buried in the Texas State Cemetery in Austin.

Braxton Bragg:
The Lonely Patriot

James I. Robertson, Jr.

He was the most enigmatic and hated field commander in the Civil War. For eighteen critical months he built, rebuilt, and led the Confederacy's principal army in the Western theater. He became a victim of personal weaknesses, administrative indifference, and unruly subordinates who would have shattered the effectiveness of any army. Braxton Bragg alone incurred the scorn of his nation for failing in four consecutive military campaigns. Only a handful of friends stood by him. One of them was commander in chief Jefferson Davis.

Bragg was as singular a mixture of solid competence and bewildering ineptitude as appeared in the Civil War. Despite extraordinary skills in organization and discipline, Bragg could never tame the high-level unrest in the Army of Tennessee. Corps and division commanders undercut him repeatedly. Jefferson Davis, who at critical times could have removed him or supported him, did neither. Bragg steadily acquired an image of arrogance combined with failure. It was so pronounced then that it remains firmly established today.

One of the most oft-quoted critics of Bragg was Pvt. Sam Watkins of the 1st Tennessee. Watkins wrote a delightful postwar memoir. Unfortunately, he was an opinionated veteran whose judgments thickened with time and often became exaggerations. The army, Watkins asserted, "had no faith in [Bragg's] ability as a general. He was looked upon as a merciless tyrant. . . . He loved to crush the spirit of his men. The more of a hang-dog look they had about them the better was

General Bragg pleased. Not a single soldier in the whole army ever loved or respected him."[1]

Writers over the last half-century have formed a veritable firing squad. Bragg "created favorable situations but lacked the determination to carry through his purpose."—"A ferocious disciplinarian, he shot his own soldiers ruthlessly for violations of military law, and his army may have been the most rigidly controlled of any on either side."—"Given independent command, he displayed vacillation and a tendency to evade responsibility. He seemed to dread precipitating a great battle, and, above all, he never followed up his victories."—"With a mind too moody to dare and too administrative to deliver a lightning blow, Bragg . . . lost his nerve, and the ability to see a battle to the end slipped from his grasp."—"[He] has long been depicted as a sour-spirited, curmudgeonly man who alienated all those around him."[2]

Bragg's best biographer quit in despair after completing one of two planned volumes. Bragg proved too tactless and too irascible for ordinary patience. A former graduate student eventually completed the study.[3]

The indictment against Bragg seems overwhelming. However, evidence suggests that Bragg had a number of positive qualities. No better organizer or disciplinarian existed in the Confederate armies. After Lee, Bragg was the South's most audacious army commander. Bragg made repeated efforts to subordinate personal quarrels for the good of the Confederate cause. Dislike of the man was not unanimous, but it was so widespread at high levels that it destroyed his generalship.

Lack of personality always plagued Bragg. Born March 21, 1817, in the tobacco belt town of Warrenton, North Carolina, he was the son of yeomen parents. The lad grew up hating snobbish neighbors, resenting their superior ways, but envious of their success. His father scrimped and saved to give Braxton a solid preparatory education. An older brother in the state legislature was instrumental in gaining sixteen-year-old Braxton an appointment to the U.S. Military Academy

Tall, grim, and ungainly, the Carolina farmboy was a solid cadet academically from start to end. He prided himself in being "the ugliest man in the corps."[4] Possessing opinions on all occasions and all subjects, he acquired a lifelong reputation for brusque and humorless behavior. Education for Bragg seems to have been a requirement and not a challenge. He was dutiful with classroom assignments, but not once in four years as a cadet did he check out a book from the Academy's library.

Bragg scored high marks in Prof. Dennis Mahan's course on military engineering. Two basic principles of the famous teacher imbedded deeply into Bragg: the necessity of a professional army, and the superiority of offensive over defensive warfare. In the West Point class of 1837, Bragg ranked fifth among fifty graduates.[5]

His first major assignment was in the Florida Seminole wars. Bragg saw few Indians and little action. As regimental adjutant of the 3rd U.S. Artillery, he learned much about organization and routine— and the need for strict discipline in both. Worse for Bragg, he quickly discovered in Florida how susceptible he was to sickness and disease. He was in the field less than a year when he was sent home to recover his health.

Migraine headaches, dyspepsia, rheumatism, boils, and diarrhea not only impaired Bragg's physical stamina; the steady discomforts left him irritable and contentious most of the time. Even as a young lieutenant, Bragg demonstrated that he was an authoritarian who resented superiors' authority. He was unable to see more than his side of a question.

For months, whether on duty or on sick leave, he waged a running battle of letters with officers up to—and including—the army's adjutant general. Impertinence and disrespect brought an 1844 court-martial and official reprimand. By then, he was widely regarded as "the most cantankerous man in the army."[6] Interestingly, his closest friend in those tumultuous years was fellow lieutenant William T. Sherman.

War with Mexico temporarily lifted the cloud of negativism surrounding Bragg. He went to Mexico at the head of an artillery battery. His service was exemplary. Supposedly, in the final and futile Mexican attack at Buena Vista, Gen. Zachary Taylor rode up to Bragg's guns, surveyed the scene, and shouted: "A little more grape, Captain Bragg!"[7]

People in general, and the press in particular, tend to romanticize war. The dramatic moment, the catchy phrase, were ideal newspaper copy. That the incident probably never happened did not dim the story. Bragg became an instant headliner. His high standards of discipline and efficiency, plus three brevet promotions for gallantry, were heralded across America. Bragg came home to a hero's welcome.

Then the irascible temper and almost pathological contentiousness returned. U. S. Grant related a story that is at least allegorically true. Bragg was stationed at a small Western outpost where he served as both company captain and post quartermaster. He once submitted a list of company requisitions: the quartermaster (Bragg, himself) denied the request; the company captain (also Bragg, himself) persisted. A heated exchange of letters passed between the man and his two offices. When no solution seemed forthcoming, Bragg forwarded all of the paperwork to the post commander. The officer looked at the pile of communiqués and exclaimed: "My God, Mr. Bragg! You have quarreled with every officer in the army, and now you are quarreling with yourself!"[8]

He *was* a quarreler, and in the years that followed Bragg had no hesitation in waging a verbal war with even the general-in-chief.[9]

In 1849 he married Eliza Ellis, a rich and beautiful heiress to a Louisiana sugar plantation. "Elise" became the love of Bragg's life—his refuge from outside barbs as well as an inner source of strength and confidence.

Bragg and Jefferson Davis had served side by side in the Mexican War. They may have been friends, but relations between the two became strained after Davis's 1854 appointment as secretary of war. When Davis proposed to station artillery at army garrisons in the West, Bragg objected. He thought it a waste of time for men and horses "to chase Indians with six-pounders."[10]

Resentment also boiled in Bragg when he and his new wife had to spend months of cruel life on the Western frontier. Bragg blamed Davis for the situation and asked for a transfer. The secretary refused. On the last day of 1855, Bragg submitted his resignation from the army. Davis accepted it without hesitation.[11]

The embittered Bragg purchased a 1,600-acre sugar plantation near his wife's family home at Thibodaux. For five years he was a Louisiana planter who organized and ran his estate like a military establishment. Bragg was a leader in founding a nearby military school, which elected William T. Sherman as first president. At one point, Bragg even had the school declared a state arsenal in order to get a substantial salary raise for his old army friend.[12]

He watched war clouds gather with a mixture of concern and contempt. Two days before South Carolina led the exodus of states from the Union, Bragg wrote Sherman: "The Union is already dissolved. The only question now is, can we reconstruct the government without bloodshed?" Bragg felt that "a few old political hacks and barroom bullies are leading public sentiment. . . . They can easily pull down a government, but when another is to be built, who will confide in them?"[13]

When the secession movement reached Louisiana, however, Bragg moved decisively. On January, 11, 1861, he led 500 volunteers who forced a peaceful surrender of the Federal arsenal at Baton Rouge. The state secession convention then established a Louisiana army and chose Bragg to be commander with the rank of major general. His military reputation was such that when the new Confederate government took shape the following month in Montgomery, Alabama, Bragg's name emerged as a possible secretary of war.[14]

A former nemesis had other ideas. In March, Bragg received appointment as a brigadier general in the Confederate army from Pres. Jefferson Davis ("your old comrade in arms"). Bragg was to take command of defenses at Pensacola, Florida.[15] Some evidence exists that Davis expected a war, if it came, to begin at Pensacola, one of the two most important Confederate ports at the time. The assignment of Bragg was therefore important to Davis, even though Bragg represented an unusual combination of proven high ability and potentially dangerous eccentricities.

Bragg established his headquarters at Fort Barrancas, nine miles west of Pensacola. A mile and a half across Pensacola Bay stood Fort Pickens and its federal garrison. In his first message to the War Department from Pensacola, Bragg painted as gloomy a picture as possible. He had three companies of "temporary volunteers," the old Regular Army officer stated. "This heterogeneous force, badly organized, undisciplined, and totally uninstructed, is scattered over a space of at least three miles. However good might be the raw material of which this force is composed, there can be no question of the ability of our opponents to place us at once in the position of the besieged should they desire it."[16]

Having pointed out all of the weaknesses confronting him, Bragg proceeded methodically to correct them. He was a professional soldier who favored professional armies. No attempt was made to conceal that bias. (Bragg once referred to a group of Louisiana volunteers as "the mere sweepings of the streets in New Orleans."[17]) Bragg organized eager recruits into a military framework. Officers who did not meet their challenges were removed. "An inefficient officer, especially a captain, renders his command a burden," Bragg warned.[18]

Constant drilling, parading, and exercising occurred, all under the stern supervision of the general. One of the few Civil War commanders with an eye to sanitation, Bragg ordered the army camps shifted to new sites every two weeks. The sale and use of alcohol among the men was forbidden under threat of severe punishment. Discipline was to be constant and blind.

Nor did Bragg waste time in idle conversation. A minister who went to the general with a request noted: "The promptness of his decision and the abrupt manner of his dismissal, not granting a moment of time to thank him, puts you in ill humor with yourself; you feel when you rush out of his presence that it would be a relief if somebody would fight you."[19]

By summer 1861, in spite of having close to 6,0000 volunteers at hand, Bragg saw the impracticality of taking Fort Pickens. He simply did not have the means or experienced ranks necessary to overwhelm the strong Federal garrison, Even if the fort surrendered, the Union naval blockade of Pensacola would continue. Moreover, measles and typhoid fever were raging out of control. Bragg reported "nearly 1000 men unfit for duty"—almost 20 percent of his command.[20]

In the autumn Bragg suggested a rather startling alternative to having well-prepared troops do nothing. He offered to exchange four of his best regiments for four newly organized ones. Secretary of War Judah P. Benjamin called the move "a noble and self-sacrificing spirit." Jefferson Davis was so impressed that Bragg shortly thereafter received promotion to major general and command of a military department encompassing western Florida and all of Alabama.[21]

Bragg was not satisfied. Command of New Orleans was the jewel he wanted. When the assignment went to a lesser officer, Bragg grumbled: "I am not surprised at the President, who, in his feeble condition, is entirely under the control of a miserable *petticoat* government as tyrannical as Lincoln's despotism." When Davis responded by offering Bragg command of the entire Trans-Mississippi region, the general declined the offer as "not enticing."[22]

By now the Bragg of history was taking final shape. He was in his mid-forties, but he looked older. A grizzled gray-black beard and bushy eyebrows surrounded what many people regarded as the face of a chimpanzee. Tall and thin, Bragg suffered for most of his adult life from several physical afflictions. These maladies soured his temper and enfeebled his being so that he appeared "haggard and austere" in the best of times.[23]

Richard Taylor, a fellow Confederate general, thought that Bragg "furnished a striking illustration of the necessity of a healthy body for a sound intellect."[24] Highly self-disciplined himself, Bragg valued self-discipline in others. He pushed himself and those under him hard.

This sometimes impaired his health, which in turn aggravated his quarrelsome disposition. And so the cycle would continue through the war years.

A change of assignment came to Bragg in February 1862, when Jefferson Davis finally saw the need to concentrate forces in the sprawling Western theater. Gen. A. Sidney Johnston was in charge of the huge Confederate department, with the "Hero of Sumter," Gen. P. G. T. Beauregard, as his second-in-command. A sick and depressed Beauregard urged Davis to send Bragg to the main army in Tennessee. "I will, when well enough," Beauregard asserted, "serve under him rather than not have him here." Davis issued the orders. He told Johnston: "General Bragg brings you disciplined troops, and you will find in him the highest administrative capacity."[25]

Bragg arrived at army headquarters in Corinth, Mississippi, with all the calmness of a hurricane. Although he would maintain cordial relations with Johnston, he found the Western army in wretched condition and said so. Some of his first observations hinted that Beauregard was responsible for the lack of discipline and habitual plundering by the raw recruits. Bragg began a fatal split with Gen. Leonidas Polk by personally accusing Polk of participating in the looting.[26] This was not the smoothest way to become part of the Confederacy's major army in the West.

Sidney Johnston overlooked such carping. On March 29, in announcing the organization of his forces, he named Bragg a corps commander as well as chief of staff.[27] The last-named position was interesting, since no such title existed in the Confederate military hierarchy. Johnston's move stemmed from two factors. Bragg's organizational skills were well-known, and making him chief of staff placed him in rank above the always untrustworthy Polk.

Bragg's first Civil War battle came April 6–7 at Shiloh. Beforehand, he thought the army too disorganized to engage the enemy, and the march to the Federal encampment was so chaotic that Bragg pled for postponement. Johnston would not be deterred. The attack began at dawn and caught the Union army by surprise.[28] Bragg's line stretched "thro a dense forest cut by ravines & creeks & bogs." His troops formed the center of Johnston's morning attack. Bragg had three horses killed under him and suffered a bruised leg in the fall from one.

Shifting his forces to the right in midmorning, Bragg spent five hours directing piecemeal assaults against Union lines in the

"Hornet's Nest." His mistake was in forgetting Professor Mahan's admonition against making frontal attacks against strong defenses. Bragg's efforts to overwhelm the enemy with bayonet charges failed.[29]

Johnston's death in the afternoon fighting put Beauregard in command. The Confederates were pushing forward slowly and bloodily. Bragg admitted that his troops were "greatly exhausted by twelve hours' incessant fighting, without food."[30] However, when Beauregard recalled the army near sundown, Bragg exploded in anger. He was confident that a final attack would have routed the Union army. Long after the war, he insisted that Beauregard's order cost the South a victory at Shiloh.[31]

The withdrawal to Corinth further triggered Bragg's rage. In his official report he stated with characteristic bluntness: "The want of proper organization and discipline, and the inferiority in many cases of our officers to the men they were expected to command, left us often without system or order."[32]

Steadfastness and determination made Bragg one of the few Confederate heroes of Shiloh. The governor of Alabama called him "a master genius;" Mississippi's chief executive asserted that he had more confidence in Bragg than in any "other military (or civil) man."[33] President Davis had to put the best face on an ugly defeat. Five days after the battle, Davis appointed Bragg a full general in the spot created by Johnston's death. The outspoken critic and stickler for discipline became the fifth-ranking general in Confederate service.

With Beauregard ill, secluded, and inaccessible, Bragg took charge of reviving the army. Such times brought out the best in Bragg. He could take shattered regiments and remold them into a better-disciplined, stronger organized army. This he did in midspring, 1862. He tightened discipline with "excessive severity," an inspector noted.[34] The army was not accustomed to it, and reactions were understandably negative.

Soon the story circulated that on the retreat from Shiloh, when stealth was necessary, Bragg had issued orders that no weapon be discharged. A drunken young soldier fired at a chicken along the road. Bragg had the man summarily shot. The incident had no factual basis, but it circulated throughout the entire Confederacy. Worse of all for Bragg, the men in the army actually believed the story to be true.[35]

As desertion increased in the months ahead, Bragg turned more frequently to firing squads—which, of course, gave more credence to the execution of the chicken-shooter. A Tennessee soldier was not exaggerating too much when he observed in late spring: "So far as patriotism was concerned, we had forgotten all about that, and did not now so much love our country as we feared Bragg."[36]

In mid-June, plagued still by sickness, Beauregard directed Bragg to take temporary charge of the army. Beauregard then left for home without permission or notifying Davis. The president interpreted this as blatant desertion. On June 20, Davis named Bragg to take immediate and permanent command of the army.

The general began an immediate rebuilding. In the face of desertion, lack of food, inadequate transportation, and poor communication with Richmond, Bragg applied his keen organizational skills. Rations increased, the water supply improved, troops secured rest and new clothing, good weather prevailed—all of which caused health and general spirits to rise to positive levels.

Rehabilitation of the army sparked the audacity inherent in Bragg. Only a month after taking command, he was ready to seize the offensive. Chattanooga was then the key city in Tennessee. Union general Don Carlos Buell was inching his way toward that supply depot as he repaired and garrisoned a railroad. Bragg left 15,000 troops to guard his rear and began an unprecedented transfer of 35,000 soldiers by rail from Tupelo, Mississippi, through Mobile, Alabama, to Chattanooga. The trip was 776 miles on six different lines. In "the most masterly movement of his career," Bragg occupied Chattanooga before Buell could get close. One authority called Bragg's move "the most spectacular railway operation of a war in which rails for the first time played a critical part."[37]

Not only did Bragg show a perceptive knowledge of the value of railroads. His movement exposed the flank and rear of Buell's forces, posed a threat to three other Union armies in Tennessee, and momentarily changed the direction of the war. After the big leap to Chattanooga, Bragg now had a chance to regain all that had been lost in the West.

Meanwhile, Confederate officials had convinced themselves that Kentucky fidgeted under Federal rule and would welcome Southern liberators. Jefferson Davis supported the idea in part because Kentucky was his home state. He approved Bragg's plan for an offensive northward into the Bluegrass State. The ranks of the army were now solid, the men well trained. Bragg's only concern was his high command. He was a good judge of military competence because he measured other men by his own rigid standards of duty. On the eve of the campaign, Bragg had real questions about the competence and the cooperation of corps and division commanders. He brought this "dead weight" to Davis's attention, to no avail.[38]

The Kentucky campaign failed as much because of Davis as of Bragg. Not only did the president refuse to transfer undermining officers such as Leonidas Polk and E. Kirby Smith; he also insisted on maintaining independent military departments. The original Confederate strategy called for Smith to move northwest from Cumberland Gap with his command; Bragg would lead his army north from Chattanooga; two other Southern forces would check Federal forces in northern Mississippi from becoming a menace. Davis believed that his generals would cooperate fully. Hence, no one was appointed to overall command of the operations. Almost inevitably, "the Confederate offensive degenerated into spastic, uncoordinated efforts."[39]

At first, however, all went well. Bragg left Chattanooga on August 28 with 27,000 men and moved steadily into Kentucky. Smith won a small fight at Richmond, Kentucky. In mid-September, Confederates under Gen. Simon Buckner captured a 4,000-man garrison at Munfordville. "My army is in high spirits and ready to go anywhere the 'old general' says," a happy Bragg wrote his wife. "We have made the most extraordinary campaign in military history."[40]

Then the multipronged Confederate advance began to stall. Kirby Smith, his ego "apparently inflated from the lavish praise" he received a year earlier at 1st Manassas, now proved "willful and headstrong."[41] Smith ignored Bragg's orders and led his force in a singular attempt to occupy Lexington. An unobstructed Buell surged ahead with his Union army and reinforced Louisville. Bragg then halted his movement to review the situation. He wasted time in inaugurating a powerless Confederate "governor" at Frankfort. Meanwhile, an officer observed, "I heard Bragg feelingly deplore the inaction of the state and the indifference of the people from whom he had been led to expect great efforts."[42]

By the first week of October, Bragg's enthusiasm had turned to confusion and indecision. He did not understand Kentucky terrain; and in trying to throw out a Confederate net across the state, he dispersed his forces and gave the Union army maneuverability and tactical advantage. His senior corps commander (Polk) disobeyed orders and displayed incredible foot-dragging when he did comply with orders. Perplexed by conflicting reports, Bragg blundered into battle on October 8 at Perryille.

He fought blindly and showed no talent for tactical innovations. The Confederates gained a limited success when total victory was within reach. Worst of all, immediately after the fighting ended at Perryville, Bragg ordered the whole army to retreat back to Tennessee.

Theretofore, Bragg had always denounced acts of pillage and plunder by Southern troops; but as his army trudged southward out of Kentucky, Bragg approved laying waste to a wide stretch of country south of the Green River. One inhabitant subsequently named the area the "Land of Sorrows."[43]

Bragg's failure in Kentucky sent shock waves through the Confederacy. The *Memphis Appeal* called Bragg's retreat "a sad finale" to a promising campaign. The *Daily Richmond Whig* termed the Confederate invasion from start to end "a brilliant blunder and a magnificent failure." Confederate general Henry Heth stated in his memoirs: "Bragg's management of this campaign was as faulty and badly managed as any other military operation of the war." After the army returned to Tennessee, Heth asserted: "I came to the conclusion that General Bragg had lost his mind."[44]

Commensurate with the public outcry against Bragg were complaints direct to Davis from subordinates in the army. Kirby Smith begged permission to come to Richmond to explain why he never wanted to serve under Bragg again. Then there was the suave and charming Leonidas Polk.

He and Davis had been together at West Point. Polk declined a military career to enter the ministry. When civil war began, he was Episcopal bishop of Louisiana. Davis somehow thought his friend would make a good major general in spite of his military inexperience. As a bishop, Polk knew how to lead, but as a soldier he never learned how to follow. He quickly became the core of dissension in the Western army. Following the Kentucky campaign, Polk convinced a number of fellow generals that he was responsible for the defeat not being a disaster. Meanwhile, Kentucky officers such as Simon Buckner and John C. Breckinridge resented Bragg for blaming lack of support from Kentucky people as a major cause of the failure of the campaign.

Bragg never ducked a fight. Once the army was back on home turf, he came out swinging. His relations with border state troops and their leaders had always been strained. The army chief began referring to Tennessee soldiers as "Polk's mob"; he openly regarded Kentuckians as cowards unworthy of liberation.[45]

Then Bragg got personal. Polk's shoddy performance in Kentucky included one instance when he refused to obey an order from the commanding general. Bragg wanted him cashiered. "Genl. Polk by education and habits is unfitted for executing the plans of others," Bragg wrote Davis. "He will convince himself his own are better and follow them without reflecting on the consequences."[46] Davis refused to intercede, thereby leaving Bragg to live with discord while rebuilding a morale-shattered army.

To his credit, Bragg's official report of the Kentucky campaign was surprisingly free of criticism save a statement that at Perryville, while all of his generals seemed "in ignorance that my orders were urgent and imperative for the attack," he "was within one hour's ride [of the action] and was not consulted or informed."[47]

One of Bragg's worst failings, however, was in denouncing officers he could not remove from command. Had he been more tolerant, he might have avoided more criticism. His snap judgments too often backfired. Bragg seemed incapable of realizing that his own generalship was often below the standards he sought to impose upon others. Throughout the autumn of 1862, the army seemed to dwell in a sense of pending doom. "The men wanted him gone. It was a deep-seated want, spilling upward from companies to . . . corps, hanging darkly in the air over headquarters."[48]

A Texas cavalryman (one of those frontiersmen Bragg disliked) reflected the army's feeling when he wrote: "I saw Gen. Bragg several times as he was passing backwards and forwards examining the fields. He is the ugliest man I ever saw. His ears would hafter be set back to make his mouth any bigger. He has got Eye Brows like Brush heaps."[49]

By December 1, the 37,000-man Confederate force encamped at Murfreesboro had received the permanent name Army of Tennessee. By then as well, Gen. William S. Rosecrans's Union army of 43,400 men was on its way from Nashville to do battle. It took Rosecrans thirty days to advance thirty miles. Bragg used Rosecrans's slowness to prepare an offensive of his own.

His men were on the west side of Stones River and facing northwest. Confederates were going to assail the Union right and use a wheeling movement in broken country to turn Rosecrans away from Nashville. Bragg's battle plan lacked any flexibility for success. Unless his first attack crushed the Union army, the Federals could fall back into a tighter and stronger position.

Things did not go well beforehand. Bragg's incredibly poor timing shown forth on December 26—the day after Christmas—when he executed a young Kentucky deserter despite pleas from the Kentucky officers. Feeling against Bragg was high with Bluegrass soldiers on the eve of battle.[50] Polk was also his usual uncooperative self, while William J. Hardee and other generals remained passive. One historian concluded: "Never had a general begun a campaign in the West with such little support from his lieutenants."[51]

Initial attacks by Polk and Hardee on December 31 caught Rosecrans by surprise. Yet the Federals soon rallied and fought fiercely for ten hours. The two armies then stared at each other in the cold darkness. Had Bragg's officers encouraged him with zeal and good advice, the battle might have continued to a Confederate success. Instead, the generals on whom he depended offered little that was useful. Throughout January 1, over 70,000 soldiers continued to man their positions and watch warily. Bragg confidently wired Davis: "The enemy has yielded his strong position and is falling back. We occupy the whole field and shall follow him[,] . . . God has granted us a happy new year."[52]

In truth, Bragg had lost his nerve. He appeared unsure what to do. The following day, Bragg ordered John C. Breckinridge to attack the strongly posted Union left. Bragg seemed unaware that entrenched troops supported by artillery could repulse twice their number, especially in a bayonet charge. Kentucky colonel Robert Trabue thought Bragg's orders "impractical madness." The Orphan Brigade commander, Roger Hanson, exclaimed that attacking the Union left was "absolutely murderous." Hanson then voiced a desire to go to army headquarters and kill Bragg.[53]

Breckinridge made a suicidal assault that Federals repulsed after bloody fighting. Late that night, Polk told Bragg: "I greatly fear the consequences of another engagement at this place with the enemy's army."[54] Hardee endorsed the feeling. Bragg convinced himself that reinforcements for Rosecrans were near at hand. At midnight in a driving rain, Confederates abandoned the field.

Bragg, the bold and aggressive attacker, became so hesitant and cautious a retreater that he did not know where to halt his withdrawal. Confederates did not stop until they reached Duck River, thirty miles from the battlefield. The Stones River defeat had cost Bragg almost a third of his command.

On January 8, Bragg telegraphed Davis: "We made a most gallant fight and so crippled the enemy that he had not dared to follow me."[55]

That statement was at least misleading and at most a cover-up. Stones River destroyed Bragg's usefulness as a field commander.

One of Bedford Forrest's cavalrymen stated matter-of-factly: "No one man, that ever lived, I don't believe ever had as much hatred expressed against him as Bragg." To one staff officer, Bragg possessed "the instincts of a drill sergeant but not the genius of a General." Southern newspapers raged that "Boomerang Bragg" had thrown away another victory.[56]

In Richmond a War Department clerk did not know how painfully accurate he was when he wrote after hearing of the Stones River defeat: "Bragg is said to have lost the confidence of his command completely. . . . Discontent inside the army has come to a head." If Bragg could irritate a friend, he could infuriate an enemy. Irascible and impatient, Bragg "never admitted to a fault, except to say that he had entrusted generals with tasks they were not good enough to perform."[57]

Bragg had retreated from Murfreesboro at the urging of his generals. In the face of overwhelming evidence to the contrary, he still believed that his lieutenants would support him in the dark postbattle hours. He sent each of them a note in which he asked if each had not in fact advised a retreat. If he had indeed acted without their advice and consent, Bragg added, he would resign at once as army commander.[58]

Polk, Hardee, their minions, and the Kentucky clique all saw their chance. While each admitted in his response to favoring withdrawal from Stones River, most of the officers stated bluntly that Bragg lacked the ability to command and should step down.[59] The foundation of rock that Bragg had sought had turned into quicksand. Bitterly angry over the generals' statements, Bragg told Louisiana senator Thomas J. Semmes that he was a martyr betrayed by a gang of Judases.[60]

Criticism was just as prevalent inside the ranks. "Bragg is the laughing stock of the whole army," a Tennessee soldier wrote his mother. "Many of the Tennessee troops will desert, and I can't say that they are to blame." Kentucky general William Preston declared: "No cheer salutes him as he passes. . . . No terror of his discipline or executions is felt by the brave soldiers he leads. We obey but do not tremble, and enter actions without hope of honor or renown and retreat with sullen indifference and discontent." By February, a popular story was circulating through the Army of Tennessee. Bragg died and went to Heaven. When St. Peter invited him to enter the gates, Bragg insisted first on falling back to reorganize.[61]

Jefferson Davis found himself in a no-win situation. In his view, Joseph E. Johnston had done nothing to deserve command of the major army in the West. Polk's seniority precluded promotion from within the army. Davis could make a public expression of error and recall the unpredictable Beauregard to command; he could take one of Robert E. Lee's best lieutenants from the Virginia army; or he could keep Bragg in the face of public outcry, internal dissatisfaction in the army, Bragg's quarrelsome nature, and Davis's growing doubts. The only real option, Davis concluded, was to retain Bragg and hope for the best.[62]

The cold winter months that followed were tough for Bragg. With generals working to undermine him, men in the ranks hating him, and Rosecrans waiting to strike again, illnesses both real and imaginary grew in intensity, Bragg seemed at the edge of a nervous and physical breakdown. A foreign visitor observed after meeting him: "This officer is in appearance the least prepossessing of the Confederate generals. He is very thin. He stoops, and has a sickly, cadaverous, haggard appearance."[63]

Migraine headaches, boils, diarrhea, and fatigue at times made Bragg beleaguered and befuddled.[64] Yet throughout those idle months of winter, he sniped at his subordinates. For example, after Breckinridge submitted his official reports of Stones River, Bragg added a long appendix highlighting "errors and misapprehensions" in Breckinridge's statements. Bragg omitted in his own report any mention of division commander Benjamin F. Cheatham. When asked why, Bragg replied: "Genl. Cheatham was drunk and unfitted for duty on [the] 31st of December. . . . I only overlooked it in consideration of his previous distinguished service."[65]

Spring began on a positive note. A religious revival swept through the Army of Tennessee. Chaplain Charles Quintard decided to venture where angels had feared to tread. He invited Bragg to be confirmed into the Episcopal Church. Bragg agreed, tears filling his eyes.[66]

In late June, Rosecrans moved on Bragg's position at the railroad junction of Tullahoma. Bragg left his sickbed and prepared to attack. Hardee's corps would block the Union advance while Polk's corps swung to the west and struck Rosecrans's flank. By then, relations between Bragg and his two corps commanders were so bad that communication between them was virtually nonexistent. Polk and Hardee were convinced that any movement Bragg ordered was potentially disastrous because Bragg ordered it. As a result, both corps commanders failed to carry out assignments. Rosecrans easily moved his whole army around the Confederate right. Bragg found it necessary to retreat all the way to Chattanooga.[67]

There the army sat for the better part of two months. A newspa-
perman described Bragg at the time: "Any afternoon you may see the
Commanding general, like a gray owl, on the front porch. To do Bragg
justice, he is not an Adonis. He is a long, dismal looking man—
ungraceful . . . with painful wrinkles round his eyes and mouth—a
man without much knack or tact."[68]

Discouraged by the loss of Middle Tennessee and the endless hostility of his subordinates, Bragg had succumbed to numbing pes-
simism. He saw the defense of Chattanooga as hopeless. To one of the
few officers he trusted, Bragg whined: "It is said to be easy to defend a
mountainous country, but mountains hide your foe from you, while
they are full of gaps through which he can pounce upon you at any
time." Bragg felt this way because his cavalry leaders—Bedford Forrest and Joseph Wheeler—failed to keep him fully and accurately
informed of enemy movements.[69]

Rosecrans in early September moved his three corps over the Tennessee River and around Bragg's left flank. This advance so threatened Confederate communications that Bragg abandoned
Chattanooga and fell back to protect his railroad in northern Georgia.
This latest retreat alarmed Confederate officials. Gen. James Longstreet with two divisions was dispatched from Virginia to reinforce
Bragg. More troops were sent from other points.

Meanwhile, Rosecrans was elated at the bloodless success he had
gained at Chattanooga. The Union general started in pursuit of what
he considered a beaten foe. Rosecrans sent his three corps on widely
divergent paths through the mountain passes in hopes of delivering a
deathblow somewhere to the Army of Tennessee. This splitting of the
Union army gave Bragg an unbelievable opportunity to attack Rosecrans's army piece by piece. Bragg quickly prepared his army for
attack, but with a tinge of caution. "A mountain is like the wall of a
house full of rat-holes," he told an aide. "The rat lies hidden in his
hole, ready to pop out when no one is watching."[70]

Twice Bragg sought to launch assaults against segments of the
Union army. Each time, delays and simple refusals to obey orders
allowed Federals to escape. Historian Steven Woodworth wrote of the
Confederate army's situation in mid-September, 1863: "The fires of
contention and bickering within the top ranks . . . had . . . spread so far
and grown so hot that the entire command structure was warped and
almost useless. Despite the strategic insights of Bragg and the courage
of his troops, the army had become no longer a sharp weapon that

could strike fatal blows to the opposing army, but rather a blunt instrument fit only for the crudest sort of bludgeoning."[71]

Further, those reinforcements from Virginia would prove a Trojan horse for Bragg. Longstreet came west with immeasurable opinions of his command abilities. In fact, he had worked to get the transfer for ambitious reasons. He told a Confederate senator whose support he sought: "I hope that I may get west in time to save what there is left of us. I dislike to ask for anything and only do it [now] under the impression that if I do not our days will be numbered." One of Longstreet's division commanders was D. H. Hill, "bitter, sour, critical and contentious, ever ready to pick nits and find faults."[72]

Such was the situation on September 19, when Bragg unleashed an attack on Rosecrans along Chickamauga in the northwest corner of Georgia. Bragg's strategy again called for a grand pivot: a simple, heavy, pivotal attack intended to hammer the enemy back and to one side into a mountain cul-de-sac. Fighting was desperate. The Army of Tennessee gained some ground as Confederate generals concentrated for a change on fighting the enemy rather than themselves.

Nightfall momentarily stopped the contest. Longstreet's men arrived from Virginia. Bragg speedily reorganized his army into two wings—and resentments immediately began anew. His officers objected to changes. Altering the chain of command in the middle of a battle was madness, they argued. When fighting resumed the next morning, orders went astray. Polk did not attack promptly, while Hill—hopelessly lost during the night—was not ready for battle.

Suddenly, Federals materialized on a part of the field where they were not expected to be. Bragg lost his composure. He raged at Polk and Hill, yet he was unsure whether to follow his original plan or to try something else. Ultimately, he did neither. With assignments confused and execution of orders spotty, Bragg sent in troops at random and with vague instructions to attack the Federals where they found them. Hill later remarked: "It was the sparring of an amateur boxer and not the crushing blows of the trained pugilist."[73]

As much from luck as anything else, Longstreet made an attack that plowed through a large gap on the Union right. The breakthrough shattered Rosecrans's army. A final stand by Union general George Thomas on Snodgrass Hill held the Confederates in check until darkness. The remainder of the Union army was in wild flight back to Chattanooga. Bragg had gained "the most crushing victory ever inflicted on a Yankee army." In a telegram to Davis, Bragg exclaimed:

"It has pleased Almighty God to reward the valor and endurance of our troops by giving our arms a complete victory over the enemy's superior numbers. Thanks are due and are rendered unto Him who giveth not the battle to the strong."[74]

Perhaps it was the casualties: 17,000 Confederates, 14,440 Federals. Possibly Bragg refused to believe the sweeping success he had gained. (After all, he was not overly familiar with victories.) Or maybe indecisiveness and confusion still engulfed the general. In any event, Bragg made only a leisurely pursuit of the badly wounded Union army. This sapped a great deal from the victory. The thousands of casualties at Chickamauga seemed to become meaningless. In a letter home, a member of Longstreet's staff grumbled: "Bragg is so much afraid of doing something which would look like taking advantage of an enemy that he does nothing. He would not strike Rosecrans another blow until he had recovered his strength and announced himself ready. Our great victory has been turned to ashes."[75]

Bragg occupied the heights overlooking Chattanooga and began a siege of Rosecrans's army. Confederate forces stretched in a thin semicircle six miles across the high ground and the valleys. Bragg's intention was to starve the Federals into surrender by cutting Rosecrans's lines of communication and supply. To accomplish this was the work of the cavalry. As usual, the mounted units would fail Bragg.

The Federal army was not Bragg's primary concern after he posted his unhappy soldiers at Chattanooga. Nor was he bothered by such criticisms of his post-Chickamauga inactivity as: "There sits Bragg—a good dog howling on his hind legs before Chattanooga, a fortified town—and some Yankee Holdfast grinning at him[,] . . . Waste of time."[76]

With the worst internal crisis in a Civil War army brewing, Bragg decided that the time had come to purge the Army of Tennessee. The first, obvious target was Polk. His official report of Chickamauga did not sufficiently explain his failures to Bragg. The commander relieved Polk of his corps and banished him to Atlanta.[77] Division leader Thomas C. Hindman was sacked; Hill was censured for his insubordinate attitude—a clear warning that Hill's head would be the next to roll if something went wrong.

One general did not take punishment silently. When Bragg transferred Bedford Forrest to Joseph Wheeler's command, Forrest exploded. He forced his way into Bragg's office; pointing a bony forefinger and accentuating every word with stabbing motions, Forrest snarled in part: "I have stood your meanness as long as I intend to. You have played the part of a damned scoundrel, and if you were any part of a man I would slap your jaws. . . . You may as well not issue any orders to me, for I will not obey them, and . . . if you ever again try to interfere with me or cross my path, it will be at the peril of your life."[78]

Bragg's dissatisfaction with his generals was more than matched by their disapproval of him. Less than a week after Chickamauga, Longstreet declared to the secretary of war that the only right thing Bragg did in the battle was to order attacks on the second day (when, of course, Longstreet was on the field). "All other things that he has done ought not to have been done. I am convinced that nothing but the hand of God can save us or help us as long as we have our present commander." Other generals were sending similar messages to influential friends in the government.[79]

When Bragg began an ill-advised reorganization of the army, which separated men from old and admired commanders, that was the last straw. Early in October, twelve generals in the Army of Tennessee signed a petition calling for Bragg's removal. Other high-ranking officers doubtless would have signed the petition had they not been either under arrest by Bragg or—as in the case of Hardee—already transferred elsewhere. Davis became alarmed at the uproar in the West. He came to Tennessee to visit the army. At an October 9 meeting with an embarrassed Bragg in attendance, Davis listened to condemnations from one general after another.

In the end, the president did little but stir the fire. He sent Polk off to Mississippi, but he brought the responsibility-shunning Hardee back to the army. Personal animosity prevented Davis from putting either Johnston or Beauregard in command. The president did not regard Longstreet, for all of his bluster and self-acclamation, as competent for army command. Davis's high esteem for Bragg had long faded, but there was no one else of proven stature to place at the head of the army. Once again the president left Bragg to fend for himself.

The general got rid of the last major troublemaker early in November. Probably at Davis's suggestion, Bragg sent Longstreet and his division, along with Wheeler's cavalry, to Knoxville to attack Union forces there. "It was folly for Bragg to do this," one of his chief advisers wrote. Chattanooga, not Knoxville, was the key to controlling Tennessee. The detachment of Longstreet left Bragg with barely 25,000 men to "besiege" a force that outnumbered him four to one.[80]

By mid-November, Bragg was in a good mood for a change. He had removed the most rebellious of his lieutenants; he was satisfied to let the remaining disaffected generals grumble to their hearts' content; he apparently had secured anew the blessing of his commander in chief. Bragg was impervious to the fact that he had demoralized the troops by separating them from generals under whom they had served through many campaigns. The siege of Chattanooga was proceeding successfully (so Bragg thought).

The days passed with Bragg issuing orders pertaining to rations, furloughs, handling of reports, prohibiting general officers from communicating with newspapermen, tightening crime control—all of this minutiae occupying attention while a heavily reinforced Union army now under Gen. U. S. Grant was massing in his front. Bragg's friend, General Liddell, concluded that the army commander was "undecided what to do; . . . He had been successful up to this time and asked nobody's advice now."[81]

On November 24, Grant struck. His men easily swept the thin line of Confederates off Lookout Mountain on Bragg's left. While Bragg vacillated over this unexpected development, Union forces the next day charged up seemingly impregnable Missionary Ridge on Bragg's right and sent the entire Army of Tennessee into panicky flight down the east side of the mountain. "We made a perfect stampede," one Confederate admitted. "It was a disgraceful affair. . . . Such confusion and disorder I never beheld before amongst 'Rebels'; . . . [F]right was in the ascendant and no entreaty or threat could stem the current."[82]

Bragg sought single-handedly to rally the broken ranks. He took a flag and rode back and forth among the men shouting: "Stop! Don't disgrace yourself! Fight for your country! Here is your commander!" "And here's your mule!" a muscular private yelled as he grabbed Bragg around the waist and threw him aside. Bragg picked himself up in the realization of absolute defeat.[83]

Indignation throughout the South greeted news of the disaster. "The Confederates have sustained the most ignominious defeat of the whole war—a defeat for which there is but little excuse or palliation," one newspaper declared. A Richmond editor passed final judgment on Bragg with the caustic statement: "An army of asses led by a lion is better than an army of lions led by an ass."[84]

Bragg was unable to explain his failure. "No satisfactory excuse can possibly be given for the shameful conduct of the troops," he reported. On November 29, he asked the War Department to make an investigation into the whole Chattanooga campaign. Then, almost as an afterthought, Bragg added: "I deem it due to the cause and to myself to ask for relief from command." The following day, in a two-sentence communiqué, Adjt. Gen. Samuel Cooper directed Bragg to turn over his command to William J. Hardee.[85]

Emotions inside the army at Bragg's resignation were somewhat mixed. The majority of soldiers were happy to see him go, but a sizable minority came to his defense. Many "loved him and respected him while they feared him." A lieutenant wrote disgustingly: "Bragg has been hunted down by a discontented set of croakers who will in time be ready to cry down Hardee."[86]

Bragg spent the next several weeks at Warm Springs, Georgia, where, aided by his wife Elise, he nursed his wounded pride and rested his tired body. He continued to criticize his enemies in the army—Hardee, Cheatham, Cleburne, Buckner, and others—while acknowledging support from such allies as Joseph Wheeler and W. H. T. Walker. President Davis, meanwhile, was aware of Bragg's extraordinary organizational skills. Obviously unsuited by health and temperament for field service, Bragg was ideal for a high staff position. He could assist the president with paperwork and handle the constant and bothersome logistical problems. Hence, on February 23, 1864, while the Congress was out of session, Davis appointed Bragg as essentially general-in-chief of all Confederate armies.[87]

The assignment of a proven loser to a high supervising position defied logic. A Richmond newspaper stated sarcastically that when a man fails, it is natural to assume that his failure stemmed from "the inadequacy of the task to his capabilities." Another Richmond editor viewed Bragg's assignment as having all of the positive impact of "a bucket of water on a newly kindled grate." [88]

How Bragg felt about the new job is unknown. Certainly he was pleased to be back serving his country, and the high-ranking position was an honor—deserved or not. On the other hand, he was offering himself anew as a target for abuse. He and Davis shared the knowledge of being patriots widely damned by people in the country they served. Such gave them a mutual loyalty that never wavered.

Bragg approached his new position with characteristic intensity and purpose. In the next eight months, he oversaw inspections of field armies, looked at supply systems, investigated the prisoner of war network, and overhauled the quartermaster system and conscription bureau. His intrusions were usually traumatic. In his tactless manner,

Bragg removed department heads and paid little heed to personal feelings or conveniences. He proposed that a number of government agen-
cies be moved from Richmond without regard to families or facilities.
A Bureau of War official declared: "The idea was worthy of the hero
of Missionary Ridge."

That same government figure noted five months later: "Bragg gets
worse and worse, more and more mischievous. He resembles a chimpanzee as much in character as he does in appearance. . . . Prying,
indirections, vindictiveness, and insecurity are the repulsive traits
which mark Bragg's character, and of which together or separately I
see evidence almost daily."[89]

In July, Davis sent Bragg to Atlanta to confer with army commander Joseph Johnston. Union forces under William T. Sherman had
driven almost to the gates of the city, while Johnston appeared to do
nothing but retreat. Bragg and Johnston had long been friends. Now
Bragg put duty above friendship. His long report to Davis led directly
to Johnston's removal from command. Later, testifying before a congressional committee, a bitter Johnston asserted that Davis "tried to do
what God had failed to do. He tried to make a soldier of Braxton
Bragg and you know the result. It couldn't be done."[90]

October brought a change of venue. Bragg received orders from
Davis to leave at once for Wilmington, North Carolina, one of only two
Confederate ports left open on the Atlantic coast. Bragg was to replace
the popular W. H. C. Whiting and to "exercise immediate command
over the troops and defenses at Wilmington, and its approaches." That
meant promoting harmony with officers loyal to Whiting as well as
overseeing Fort Fisher and other defensive installations along the Cape
Fear River. Two months later, Bragg's command was broadened to
include all of North Carolina east of the mountains.[91]

Bragg's performance at Wilmington was the most shameful of his
career. He proved too cold and unpleasant to cordial relations with his
new subordinates. Bragg failed to prepare adequate defenses for the
safety of Wilmington, he refused to concentrate troops at points where
they were most needed, and he continually "indulged himself in his
favorite pastime—griping and carping."[92] Morale in the Wilmington
area went down almost from the day of Bragg's arrival, as predicted,
for a Richmond newspaper had announced at the outset: "Bragg has
been sent to Wilmington. Goodbye Wilmington!"[93]

A December assault by Union army and navy forces was unsuccessful primarily because of the ineptitude of Union general Benjamin

F. Butler. To Bragg, however, Fort Fisher's strong defenses had with-
stood the test. The garrison was quite capable of defending itself.
Three weeks later, a heavier, more concerted assault came against the
fort. Bragg remained in nearby Wilmington, wringing his hands in
uncertainty and paying no attention to frantic pleas from Fort Fisher
for reinforcements.

Fort Fisher surrendered, Wilmington had to be abandoned, and
Bragg began seeking scapegoats. His long official report of the cam-
paign has been called "a masterpiece of distortions and innuendoes
concocted to show that he could not be blamed" for the disaster. A
North Carolina planter's wife who had watched the course of Civil
War closely viewed the debacle in a different perspective. "Altho
Wilmington was swarming with troops & they had ample warning,
there were not men enough in the [Fort Fisher] garrison to resist the
onslaught upon them. So will it ever be where Bragg commands.
Bragg the Unlucky is a Millstone which Mr. Davis persists in tying
around our necks!"[94]

Later that month, Robert E. Lee officially became general-in-chief
of what was left of Confederate military forces. At the same time,
John C. Breckinridge—who hated Bragg—assumed the duties of secretary of war. That left Bragg with only his dwindling North Carolina
district. He became a subordinate to Johnston as the remnant of the
Army of Tennessee sought unsuccessfully to stop Sherman's advance
through the Carolinas. Being a subaltern in the army he more than any
man had created was the ultimate indignity.

Bragg joined Davis as members of the Confederate government
fled southward. On May 10, 1865, the general and his wife were captured near Concord, Georgia. Bragg signed his parole on the spot and
thereafter received no harassment from Federals.

The Bragg's Louisiana plantation was gone, so the couple settled
on his brother's estate near Lowndesboro, Alabama. Bragg thereafter
held a number of jobs, primarily with railroads. Almost without fail,
the positions were short-lived because of disputes Bragg had with his
superiors. In 1868 he assisted in the creation of the Southern Historical
Society in New Orleans and chaired its first meeting. Bragg actively
solicited papers for the society's journal. Yet he refused to contribute
any memoirs of his own. "I dare not tell the truth," he said, "and I dare
not tell lies."[95]

Bitterness always remained. In April 1869, Bragg learned that
Longstreet had joined the Republican Party and obtained a position

from President U. S. Grant as surveyor of customs at New Orleans. Longstreet, Bragg growled, is "utterly destitute of moral or mental capacity, courage or integrity—a Scalawag!"[96]

At 9 A.M., September 27, 1876, Bragg was walking with a friend to his office in Galveston, Texas, when he suddenly fell dead in the street. He was fifty-nine. A steamer took the remains to Mobile, where Bragg was buried in Magnolia Cemetery. His wife survived him by thirty-two years.

Bragg's many faults are well documented: the inability to inspire and motivate those around him, his lack of desire to cultivate—or tolerate—those with whom he disagreed, a distrust of volunteers (especially officers), the failure to win battles even when he appeared to have the upper hand, wretched health, vacillation, a tendency to evade responsibility at critical moments, an incapacity to learn from mistakes, and a personality that ranged from choleric to repulsive. Underneath the man, however, was occasionally a well-intentioned attribute.

Countless veterans of the Army of Tennessee carried hatred of Bragg with them to the grave. Some of them might have had at least a mild change of heart had they read the closing section of the general's report of the battle of Stones River. "To the private soldier a fair meed of praise is due. . . . Without the incentive or the motive which controls the officer, who hopes to live in history; without the hope of reward, and actuated only by a sense of duty and patriotism, he has, in this great contest, justly judged that the cause was his own, and gone into it with a determination to conquer or die; to be free or not to be at all. No encomium is too high, no honor too great for such a soldiery. However much of the credit and glory may be given, and probably justly given, to the leaders in our struggle, history will yet award the main honor where it is due—to the private soldier."[97]

NOTES

The writer expresses deep gratitude to Richard M. McMurry for his critique of the manuscript version of this essay.

1. Sam Watkins, *"Co. Aytch": Maury Grays: First Tennessee Regiment* (1882; reprint, Jackson, Tenn.: McCowat-Mercer, 1952), 71 (hereafter cited as Watkins, *"Co. Aytch"*).
2. David Donald, ed., *Why the North Won the Civil War* (Baton Rouge: Louisiana State University Press, 1960), 34; Clement A. Eaton, *A History of the Southern Confederacy* (New York: Macmillan, 1954), 119;

Thomas L. Connelly, *Army of the Heartland* (Baton Rouge: Louisiana State University Press, 1967), 206 (hereafter cited as Connelly, *Army of the Heartland*); Steven E. Woodworth, *The Art of Command in the Civil War* (Lincoln: University of Nebraska Press, 1998), 176.

3. Grady McWhiney, *Braxton Bragg and Confederate Defea*t, vol. 1 (New York: Columbia University Press, 1969) (hereafter cited as McWhiney, *Braxton Bragg*); Judith Lee Hallock, *Braxton Bragg and Confederate Defeat*, vol. 2 (University: University of Alabama Press, 1991) (hereafter cited as Hallock, *Braxton Bragg*).

4. McWhiney, *Braxton Bragg*, 10.

5. In that class were future Civil War generals Jubal A. Early, Arnold Elzey, William H. French, Joseph Hooker, John C. Pemberton, John Sedgwick, and W. H. T. Walker.

6. McWhiney, *Braxton Bragg*, 51.

7. K. Jack Bauer, *Zachary Taylor: Soldier, Planter, Statesman of the Old Southwest* (Baton Rouge: Louisiana State University Press, 1985), 204–5; McWhiney, *Braxton Bragg*, 90–92.

8. Ulysses S. Grant, *Personal Memoirs of U. S. Grant*, 2 vols. (New York: Webster, 1885–86), 2:86–87.

9. For example, see McWhiney, *Braxton Bragg*, 36, 96, 101.

10. Steven E. Woodworth, *Jefferson Davis and His Generals* (Lawrence: University Press of Kansas, 1990), 92.

11 Jefferson Davis, *The Papers of Jefferson Davis*, ed. Lynda Lasswell Crist and others, 11 vols. to date (Baton Rouge: Louisiana State University Press, 1971–2003), 6:389 (hereafter cited as Davis, *Papers*).

12. McWhiney, *Braxton Bragg*, 148–49.

13. Ibid., 150.

14. William C. Davis, *Jefferson Davis: The Man and The Hour* (New York: HarperCollins, 1990), 311 (hereafter cited as Davis, *Jefferson Davis*).

15. Ibid., 331.

16. Bragg to Maj. George Deas, March 10, 1861, Braxton Bragg Papers, 1833–79, roll 1, MSS 2000 Microfilm Edition, Western Reserve Historical Society, Cleveland, Ohio [hereafter cited as Bragg Papers].

17. Davis, *Jefferson Davis*, 333.

18. Bragg to War Department, April 22, 1861, roll 1, Bragg Papers. Bragg informed his wife at the time: "It comes now to be a long contest of hard knocks. . . . Our cause is just and must prevail, no matter how much individuals may suffer." (McWhiney, *Braxton Bragg*, 171.)

19. McWhiney, *Braxton Bragg*,179.

20. Bragg to War Department, July 28, 1861, roll 1, Bragg Papers.

21. Judah P. Benjamin to Bragg, October 8, 1861, ibid.; U.S. War Department, *The War of the Rebellion: A Compilation of the Official Records of the Union and Confederate Armies*, 127 vols., index, and atlas (Washington, D.C.: U.S. Government Printing Office, 1880–1901), I, 6:751

(set hereafter cited as *OR*, with all references to Series I; for volumes that appeared in more than one part [volume 6 is not one such], the part is shown in parentheses after the volume number).

22. Bragg to W. O. Moore, October 31, 1861, W. O. Moore Papers, Louisiana State University, Baton Rouge.

23. James Lee McDonough, *Chattanooga: A Death Grip on the Confederacy* (Knoxville: University of Tennessee Press, 1984), 23 (hereafter cited as McDonough, *Chattanooga*). See also McWhiney, *Braxton Bragg*, 179–80.

24. Richard Taylor, *Destruction and Reconstruction: Personal Experiences of the Late War* (New York: Appleton, 1879), 100.

25. *OR*, 7:258, 912.

26. Connelly, *Army of the Heartland*, 146.

27. *OR*, 10 (2):370–71; McWhiney, *Braxton Bragg*, 213–15.

28. Sherman was in command of the Federal forces Johnston struck. The Union general had been convinced that no attack was imminent; *OR*, 10 (2):93–94.

29. McWhiney, *Braxton Bragg*, 232, 240, 251.

30. *OR*, 10 (1):467.

31. St. John R. Liddell, *Liddell's Record*, ed. Nathaniel C. Hughes (Dayton, Ohio: Morningside, 1985), 67 (hereafter cited as Liddell, *Liddell's Record*; McWhiney, *Braxton Bragg*, 244.

32. *OR*, 10 (2):469. Whether criticizing Beauregard's slowness to advance or Grant's slowness to pursue, Bragg felt that a major lesson from Shiloh was the need for speed: "Never on a battlefield to lose a moment's time, but leaving the killed, wounded, and spoils to those whose special business it was to care for them, to press on with every available man, giving a panic-stricken and defeated foe no time to rally"; quoted in Allan Nevins, *The War for the Union*, 4 vols. (New York: Scribner's, 1959–71), 2:110 (hereafter cited as Nevins, *War for the Union*).

33. John Gill Shorter to Bragg, April 22, 1862, and Thomas C. Manning to Bragg, May 5, 1862, roll 1, Bragg Papers.

34. Davis, *Papers*, 8:256.

35. Peter Cozzens, *No Better Place to Die: The Battle of Stones River* (Urbana: University of Illinois Press, 1990), 4 (hereafter cited as Cozzens, *No Better Place to Die*); Larry J. Daniel, *Soldiering in the Army of Tennessee* (Chapel Hill: University of North Carolina Press, 1991), 110 (hereafter cited as Daniel, *Soldiering*); C. Vann Woodward, ed., *Mary Chesnut's Civil War* (New Haven, Conn.: Yale University Press, 1981), 413 (hereafter cited as Woodward, ed., *Mary Chesnut's Civil War*).

36. Watkins, *"Co. Aytch,"* 78.

37. Nevins, *War for the Union*, 2:169.

38. Steven E. Woodworth, *No Band of Brothers: Problems of the Rebel High Command* (Columbia: University of Missouri Press, 1999), 71 (hereafter cited as Woodworth, *No Band of Brothers*).

39. Richard M. McMurry, *Two Great Rebel Armies: An Essay in Confeder-ate Military History* (Chapel Hill: University of North Carolina Press, 1989), 62.

40. McWhiney, *Braxton Bragg*, 284.

41. Woodworth, *No Band of Brothers*, 52.

42. Liddell, *Liddell's Record*, 84.

43. Nevins, *War for the Union*, 2:295.

44. J. Cutler Andrews, *The South Reports the Civil War* (Princeton, N.J.: Princeton University Press, 1970), 248 (hereafter cited as Andrews, *The South Reports the Civil War*); Henry Heth, *The Memoirs of Henry Heth*, ed. James L. Morrison (Westport, Conn.: Greenwood, 1974), 168. See also Catherine Ann Devereux Edmondston, *"Journal of a Secesh Lady"*, ed. Beth Gilbert Crabtree and James W. Patton (Raleigh: North Carolina Division of Archives and History, 1979), 299 (hereafter cited as Edmon-ston, *"Journal of a Secesh Lady"*).

45. Thomas L. Connelly, *Autumn of Glory* (Baton Rouge: Louisiana State University Press, 1971), 19–20 (hereafter cited as Connelly, *Autumn of Glory*); Woodworth, *No Band of Brothers*, 73; Nevins, *War for the Union*, 2:407.

46. McWhiney, *Braxton Bragg*, 328–29. Later in the war, Davis stated in an unrelated case: "No officer has a right to stop troops moving under the orders of superior authority—if he assumes such power he does it at his hazard and must be justified by subsequent events rather than by good intentions." Yet Polk did precisely those things at Perryville and else-where. (Steven E. Woodworth, *Jefferson Davis and His Generals* [Lawrence: University Press of Kansas, 1990], 160 (hereafter cited as Woodworth, *Jefferson Davis and His Generals*).)

47. See *OR*, 16 (1):1088–94.

48. Frank E. Vandiver, *Their Tattered Flags: The Epic of the Confederacy* (New York: Harper's Magazine Press, 1970), 181.

49. Thomas H. Colman to parents, November 6, 1862, Colman-Hayter Fam-ily Papers, Western Historical Manuscript Collection, University of Mis-souri, Columbia.

50. Ed Porter Thompson, *History of the Orphan Brigade* (Louisville: L. N. Thompson, 1898), 201–2; A. D. Kirwan, ed., *Johnny Green of the Orphan Brigade* (Lexington: University of Kentucky Press, 1956), 59–61; *Confederate Veteran* 10 (February 1902):68. In stark contrast to Bragg's unbending treatment of deserters was a comment he allegedly made at the time to St. John Liddell: "General, I have no children. Hence, I look upon the soldiers of my army as my own—as *my* chil-dren." (Liddell, *Liddell's Record*, 106.)

51. Connelly, *Autumn of Glory*, 23.

52. *OR*, 52 (2):402.

53. William C. Davis, *The Orphan Brigade: The Kentucky Confederates Who Couldn't Go Home* (Garden City, N,Y.: Doubleday, 1980), 155.

54. Leonidas Polk to Bragg, January 3, 1863, roll 2, Bragg Papers.

55. Davis, *Papers*, 9:18.

56. McWhiney, *Braxton Bragg*, 375; Davis, *Jefferson Davis*, 490–91. See also Cozzens, *No Better Place to Die*, x. Bragg always had a distrust of the press. In time he barred reporters from battlefields and army headquarters. (Andrews, *The South Reports the Civil War*, 237, 259.)

57. Robert Garlick Hill Kean, *Inside the Confederate Government: The Diary of Robert Garlick Hill Kean*, ed. Edward Younger (New York: Oxford, 1957), 38, 42 (hereafter cited as Kean, *Inside the Confederate Government*); Connelly, *Autumn of Glory*, 70. Much later, Bragg insisted: "I shall still bear the burden of having failed, where I am confident a prompt execution of my orders would have secured to our arms the most brilliant results." (Bragg to Jefferson Davis, May 21, 1863, roll 3, Bragg Papers.)

58. *OR*, 20 (1):699. The letter, from one who no longer knew who his friends were, seemed little more than "a pathetic plea for love and understanding." (McWhiney, *Braxton Bragg*, 377–78.)

59. Typical was Breckinridge's response. In the opinion of his brigade commanders, the Kentuckian stated, "you do not possess the confidence of the Army to an extent which will enable you to be useful as its commander. In this opinion, I feel bound to state that I concur." (Breckinridge to Bragg, January 12, 1863, roll 2, Bragg Papers; see also Patrick R. Cleburne to Bragg, January 13, 1863, ibid.)

60. Joseph F. Stevens, *1863: The Rebirth of a Nation* (New York: Bantam, 1999), 64 (hereafter cited as Stevens, *1863*). A similar statement by Bragg is in *OR*, 52 (2):407.

61. *West Tennessee Historical Society Papers* 4 (1950):55; Cozzens, *No Better Place to Die*, 208; Charles P. Roland, *An American Iliad: The Story of the Civil War* (Lexington: University Press of Kentucky, 1991), 112.

62. Davis, *Jefferson Davis*, 493. Departmental commander Joseph E. Johnston agreed with the decision. (Johnston to Jefferson Davis, February 3, 1863, roll 2, Bragg Papers.)

63. A. J. L. Fremantle, *Three Months in the Confederate States, April-June, 1863* (London: W. Blackwood, 1863), 145.

64. See McWhiney, *Braxton Bragg*, 389; Connelly, *Autumn of Glory*, 71–72; *OR*, 53 (2):499.

65. Bragg to Samuel Cooper, March 3, April 9, 1863, roll 3, Bragg Papers.

66. Bell Irvin Wiley, *The Life of Johnny Reb: The Common Soldier of the Confederacy* (Indianapolis: Bobbs-Merrill, 1943), 181; Charles T. Quintard, *Doctor Quintard, Chaplain, C.S.A., and Second Bishop of Tennessee* (Sewanee, Tenn.: University Press, 1905), 78–79.

67. "Without a battle, Rosecrans had, in a little over a week, advanced four times as far as he had after his victory at Murfreesboro." (Richard E. Beringer et al., *Why The South Lost the Civil War* [Athens: University of Georgia Press, 1986], 259.)

68. Andrews, *The South Reports the Civil War*, 345. For Bragg's deteriorating relations with the press, see *West Tennessee Historical Society Papers* 21 (1957): 81, 90.
69. Robert Underwood Johnson and Clarence Clough Buel, eds., *Battles and Leaders of the Civil War*, 4 vols. (New York: Century, 1887–88), 3:641 [set hereafter cited as *B&L*]. At one point, Bragg blurted: "I have not a single general officer of cavalry fit for command!" (Liddell, *Liddell's Record*, 150-51.)
70. George Brent journal, roll 4, Bragg Papers.
71. Woodworth, *No Band of Brothers*, 78.
72. Hallock, *Braxton Bragg*, 79; Woodworth, *No Band of Brothers*, 78.
73. *B&L*, 3:650–51.
74. Davis, *Jefferson Davis*, 517; *OR*, 30 (2):22.
75. Charles M. Blackford III, ed., *Letters from Lee's Army, or Memoirs in and out of the Army in Virginia during the War between the States* (New York: Scribner's, 1947), 219.
76. Woodward, ed., *Mary Chesnut's Civil War*, 469.
77. Polk angrily sent a 2-$\frac{1}{2}$-page response, which Bragg dismissed as "an unsatisfactory written explanation [that] is but a repetition of the past." (Bragg to Jefferson Davis, October 1, 1863, roll 3, Bragg Papers.)
78. Robert Selph Henry, *"First with the Most" Forrest* (Indianapolis: Bobbs-Merrill, 1944), 199. Bragg took no direct action against Forrest for the outburst. The cavalry leader received independent command in Mississippi. Shortly after the incident, Bragg told one of his aides: "I have not a single officer of cavalry fit for command. . . . Look at Forrest; . . . [t]he man is ignorant, and does not know anything of cooperation. He is nothing more than a good raider." (Quoted in McDonough, *Chattanooga*, 32.)
79. *OR*, 30 (4):706; see also Davis, *Jefferson Davis*, 520; Edmondston, *"Journal of a Secesh Lady,"* 470; Andrews, *The South Reports the Civil War*, 364; Connelly, *Autumn of Glory*, 236–39.
80. Liddell, *Liddell's Record*, 157. Only Polk exceeded Longstreet in efforts to ruin Bragg. (See Hallock, *Braxton Bragg*, 108, 120–22.)
81. See roll 4, Bragg Papers, passim; Liddell, *Liddell's Record*, 148.
82. Hallock, *Braxton Bragg*, 140–41.
83. Ibid., 141; Stevens, *1863*, 392.
84. *Richmond Daily Dispatch*, December 4, 1863; *Daily Richmond Whig*, November 30, 1863.
85. *OR*, 31 (2):666, 682; Samuel Cooper to Bragg, November 30, 1863, roll 4, Bragg Papers.
86. Daniel, *Soldiering*, 136; see also Watkins, *"Co. Aytch,"* 131; Charles T. Jones, "Five Confederates: The Sons of Bolling Hall in the Civil War," *Alabama Historical Quarterly* 24 (1962): 190. In March 1864, the soldiers of two brigades sent Bragg "as a slight token of esteem" a sword with the inscription: "To him whose history shows, he loves his country

more than he loves himself." (Resolution of March 18, 1864, roll 4, Bragg Papers.)

87. He was to operate "under the direction of the President" and be in charge of "the conduct of military operations in the Armies of the Confederacy." (*OR*, 32 [2]:799.)

88. *Daily Richmond Whig*, February 25, 1864; *Richmond Examiner*, February 25, 1864.

89. Kean, *Inside the Confederate Government*, 145, 175. Bragg's strongest defender at present has written: "Davis's appointment of Bragg . . . was wise, but the president reduced the benefit that might have accrued from such an arrangement by failing, at times, to heed Bragg's generally excellent advice." (Woodworth, *Jefferson Davis and His Generals*, 302.)

90. *OR*, 39 (2):712–14; Hallock, *Braxton Bragg*, 196.

91. Jefferson Davis to Bragg, October 15, 1864, roll 5, Bragg Papers; *OR*, 42 (3):1209.

92. Hallock, *Braxton Bragg*, 232–33.

93. Rod Gragg, *Confederate Goliath: The Battle of Fort Fisher* (New York: HarperCollins, 1991), 27 (hereafter cited as Gragg, *Confederate Goliath*).

94. Hallock, *Braxton Bragg*, 238–39; Edmondston, *"Journal of a Secesh Lady,"* 657. For more on Bragg's official summary of the campaign, see Gragg, *Confederate Goliath*, 241–422. The manuscript report is in roll 5, Bragg Papers.

95. Hallock, *Braxton Bragg*, 264.

96. Bragg to Andrew Kellar, April 15, 1869, Historic New Orleans Collection, Confederate Memorial Hall, New Orleans.

97. *OR*, 20 (1):670–71.

General Samuel Cooper

William C. Davis

It is poor Samuel Cooper's fate to be remembered, if at all, as a recurrent question on Civil War trivia quizzes. "Who was the senior ranking general in the Confederate Army?" Many are still surprised that it was not Robert E. Lee. More have never even heard the name of the man who is the right answer. Once they do, they quickly forget, for he seems to have done so little else to make himself memorable. That he was charged with the task of administering the largest organizational bureaucracy in the Confederacy makes little difference. He never fought a battle, never commanded so much as a squad of soldiers, and apparently never even wore his uniform. His virtual anonymity makes it difficult to assess Samuel Cooper's deserved place in the Confederate galaxy, especially when so much of what survives in relation to him are the disgruntled complaints that almost always orbit around the bureaucrat. There is no case to be made that he was a military or organizational genius who helped keep the Confederacy alive longer than otherwise, nor is there merit in the opposite notion that he was so inept and ineffectual that he hampered the war effort. It is somewhere in between those poles that his proper position is to be found, if at all.

His great-grandfather emigrated from Dorset in England and settled in Massachusetts. His grandson Samuel Cooper, born in 1757, was eighteen years old when he stood with other rebels on the village green at Lexington in the first skirmish of the Revolution. He fought again at Breed's Hill, and later at Trenton, Brandywine, Monmouth, and other actions, serving in the 3rd Continental Artillery in Washington's army and rising to the rank of captain. Shortly after Independence he moved to New York, and in the 1780s he married Mary Horton of Dutchess County, settling at her family's estate at Hackensack on the Hudson River. They would have eight children there, including Samuel Cooper, born June 12, 1798.[1]

Young Samuel Cooper, aged still just fourteen, took the appointment to the Military Academy at West Point secured for him by his father, and entered the school on May 25, 1813. Thanks to a shorter course of instruction then than later, he graduated on December 10, 1815, in a class of forty, though at a time when class standings were not yet assigned, so his academic performance is hard to determine. The fact that with his commission as a brevet lieutenant he was assigned to the artillery suggests that he performed well, for the best graduates went to the engineers and artillery. Two years later, on November 15, 1817, when a vacancy came open to replace his brevet rank with a confirmed commission, he became second lieutenant in the 1st Artillery, then stationed at Boston. Four years later he got his first promotion, to first lieutenant, and reassignment to the vicinity of Washington with the 3d Artillery. In 1824 Washington reassigned him again, this time to the 4th Artillery stationed on the Virginia coastal defenses. It was as close to active field service as he would ever get.

In April 1827, in Washington, Lt. Samuel Cooper married Sarah Maria Mason, a granddaughter of Founding Father George Mason, and followed the nuptials with a three-day family frolic. His new wife was the sister of James M. Mason, then a budding local politician and attorney in Winchester, Virginia. That alone was a good connection for young Cooper, but probably better was the fact that his new wife's oldest brother John was married to the daughter of Gen. Alexander McComb, destined to become commanding officer of the U.S. Army the following year.[2] When McComb got the appointment, rumors circulated that the Masons had used their influence with Pres. John Quincy Adams to gain him the position, and that in return McComb agreed to appoint Cooper to his staff. That would keep the lieutenant safe in Washington, and keep his wife close to her family rather than seeing them possibly assigned to some remote outpost. Whether true or not, it could not have hurt that yet another Mason sister had married Adams's secretary of the treasury Benjamin Rush. Thus Cooper was launched upon a lifetime career as a desk soldier in the office of the adjutant general, serving as McComb's aid until 1836, but not before some brief service as an aide to General Winfield Scott, one of his tasks being to issue a furlough to young Lt. Jefferson Davis.[3] It may be significant that Scott was also an aspirant for the position given to McComb, and felt he had been cheated of his due. Thereafter he and Cooper would often find themselves on opposite sides of a question, and while there is no evidence of ill blood between the two, still the influence of such an alignment would be felt in years to come.

There was little for Cooper to do on his paperwork battlefield to distinguish himself in the years under McComb. Still, as an aide and assistant adjutant general now, he was given the brevet rank of captain in 1831, pending an opening that could be confirmed at the higher rank. In fact, for the next thirty years, all of his promotions would be brevet rank, but he would never actually rise above the confirmed rank of captain in the Regular Army. In 1835, however, he did get a chance to make a mark on the military when McComb asked him to edit and abridge Scott's translation of a French military manual for the use of U.S. soldiers. This again put Cooper and Scott somewhat at odds, as the latter objected strenuously to having the fruits of his labor reduced and—as he felt—diluted by a mere bureaucrat. The result was *A Concise System of Instructions and Regulations for the Militia and Volunteers of the United States, Comprehending the Exercises and Movements of The Infantry, Light Infantry, and Riflemen; Cavalry and Artillery: Together with The Manner of Doing Duty in Garrison and Camp, and the Forms of Parades, Reviews, and Inspections.* The ponderously titled work announced that it was "Prepared and Arranged by Brevet Captain S. Cooper," and published under McComb's supervision, but nowhere was credit given to Scott, who had done the initial translation.[4] This work, for all its heavy title, would become the standard manual of the military for the next generation until Cooper himself, serving another master, oversaw a new system of tactics by William J. Hardee that would dominate Civil War armies North and South.

Soon afterward Scott fell afoul of authorities, and went before a court of inquiry in Washington headed by Cooper, who was reassigned to the capital as judge advocate. Despite the fact that McComb and others antithetical to Scott sat on the court, it returned a finding in Scott's favor. A year later in July 1838 he got confirmation in his rank as captain and a promotion to the staff rank of brevet major—the army then making a distinction between staff and field ranks—and assignment as assistant adjutant general in the War Department directly under the adjutant general.[5] Cooper worked well with Secretary of War Joel R. Poinsett, and members of Congress who had concerns for constituents in the military also found Cooper easy to work with and obliging, among them Sen. Franklin Pierce of New Hampshire, who averred that whenever he wanted information on military matters, he went to Cooper rather than the secretary of war. One of the people whom Pierce introduced to Poinsett and Cooper in 1838 was a former Regular Army officer from Mississippi. Jefferson Davis came to Washington hoping to get back into the army with an appointment in a new infantry regiment that might be authorized by Congress. He did not get what he came for, but he left remembering the genial and cooperative assistant adjutant general.[6]

Cooper's court's exoneration of Scott perhaps worked in the major's favor in 1841 when McComb died and Scott finally became general-in-chief. Had he wished, Scott could have banished Cooper to the Western frontier somewhere, but instead kept him in the adjutant general's office. But then at the end of that year Poinsett resigned before the end of his term, and for a few months before the new administration took over, Cooper filled in as acting secretary. In that capacity, he was technically General Scott's superior, a change in relations that did not suit the proud Scott at all. Perhaps that explained Cooper's reassignment to a war zone when he was transferred to the staff of Gen. William Worth in Florida during the Seminole War in the early 1840s. But there, too, he was confined to staff work behind the lines, and though he may actually have been present for the small engagement at Pila-Kil-Kaha on April 19, 1842, he was not personally engaged.[7]

Returned to Washington, Cooper continued to please his civilian masters and continued his slow but steady rise, with another brevet to lieutenant colonel in 1847. Following the close of the war with Mexico in 1848, yet another promotion for his efficient performance as assistant adjutant general made him a brevet colonel—though still only a captain in Regular Army rank. Yet following Scott's return from field command in Mexico, now with the added prestige of being a victor and potential presidential candidate, the general wasted little time in banishing Cooper from his sight. He ordered him to go on an inspection survey of the nation's Western outposts, perhaps just to get rid of him for a time, but also with practical ends in sight. Cooper's full title was assistant adjutant and inspector general, and thus it was part of his job to gather information on conditions throughout the army. Cooper went first to New Orleans, then sailed to Galveston, and from there proceeded on horseback with a party that rode as far west as El Paso, Texas. From there he returned by riding the length of the Rio Grande and visiting each of the outposts facing a still unsettled Mexico on the other side. Turning north through San Antonio, he rode on into the then unorganized Indian territory—later to be Oklahoma—and on to the Missouri River at Westport and thence to Fort Leavenworth.

His inspection was only half done, however, for now he journeyed west to Fort Laramie, there to meet with delegates of some of the major Plains Indian tribes, and also to inspect conditions along some of the immigrant trails now exploding with westbound wagon trains headed for California and Oregon. By the time he returned to Fort Leavenworth in the summer of 1852, he had been on the road more than two years, and covered some 5,000 miles. It was on reaching Fort Leavenworth that he learned that the adjutant general of the U.S. Army had died suddenly, and that now Cooper would succeed to his position. He returned at once to Washington, filed his lengthy report of his inspection tour, and prepared to undertake on July 15, 1852, his now expanded duties as the senior ranking staff officer in the military, reporting directly to the secretary of war, in a position that carried with it the staff rank of brigadier general.[8]

Now an accidental juxtaposition of men and events came together to dictate Cooper's course in the crisis less than a decade away. He assumed his new office duties in the last days of the Millard Fillmore administration, but in March 1853 a new administration took over under Pres. Franklin Pierce. Cooper's new immediate superior as secretary of war would be that same Jefferson Davis he had met more than a decade before. Himself a West Point graduate, a man with several years of active frontier duty experience, and more recently a volunteer commander who emerged from Mexico as a true military hero, Davis had definite ideas about how the army should be run, and enough background to know how it worked. He also remembered Cooper, with whom he had some intermediate dealings during his brief terms in the House and Senate just before and after the Mexican War.

Cooper was Davis's kind of man, even-tempered, efficient, good at his paperwork, and obedient. They conferred almost daily, and Davis came away from their association convinced that Cooper was "a man of great native force, and had a supreme scorn for all that was mean." In a military establishment small and inbred enough to generate multiple layers of resentments and internal feuds, Davis remarked that "I never, in four years of constant consultation, saw Cooper manifest prejudice, or knew him to seek favors for a friend, or to withhold what was just from one to whom he bore reverse relations." The adjutant possessed, thought the secretary, "supremacy of judgment over feeling."[9] Davis may have thought so, and in the main he would be right about Cooper, but the Mississippian was a notoriously poor judge of character, and now and later Cooper would occasionally demonstrate that Davis rather idealized his attributes.

For the next four years Cooper worked almost daily with Davis, and though little is known of the details of their professional interaction, it must have been smooth and unruffled, for Davis's was not a personality that easily brooked challenge or controversy. As for Cooper, now aged fifty-five and with forty years service in the army, his was a position too high to jeopardize by breaking the habits of a lifetime by being anything other than subordinate. During Davis's tenure the old Scott-Cooper manual was completely revised under their direction by Hardee. Cooper played his role in the creation of new and more modern regiments of cavalry, and perhaps supported Davis's abortive efforts to revamp the fossilized seniority system

Meanwhile Cooper's office oversaw the editing and publication of Capt. George B. McClellan's report of his observations of the Crimean War in 1857, and the adjutant himself employed women friends in the city to do clerical work for his department on this and other reports. It is also apparent that, having had the example of the impact of family and friendship ties on his own career thus far, he did not shrink from using his own influence now to favor social friends with holiday furloughs for their sons in the army. Cooper was also a fixture on the social scene in Washington. He read widely and was often at the theater.[10] He and his wife held holiday receptions at their home, and regular attendees included Davis, the banker W. W. Corcoran, Cooper's brother-in-law Captain Sydney Smith Lee of the navy, and Captain Lee's brother Col. Robert E. Lee during his tenure as superintendent of the Military Academy at West Point. In 1857, in one of the most festive and well-remembered weddings of the decade in Washington, Cooper's daughter Maria married promising Lt. Frank Wheaton of Rhode Island, destined to become a major general in the Union army during the Civil War. The best man was Fitzhugh Lee, Robert E. Lee's nephew.[11]

As the sectional turmoil grew ever more dangerous, and despite his New York nativity and New England heritage, Cooper evidenced little inner turmoil over his course in the coming crisis. Some believed that he was swayed in his decision by friends like Davis and his brother-in-law James Mason, but there seems little reason to doubt that Cooper made the decision himself, and for his own reasons. He had married a Virginia woman and had ties to a distinguished Old Dominion heritage. As a longtime resident of Washington, a predominantly Southern city in its social caste, his associations had for decades been Southern. His own home "Cameron" was in Virginia, near Alexandria. He had lived there since 1839, and he was a slave owner, giving him common cause with the secessionists. In going South, he had to know that in any Northern invasion of the new Confederacy, his own property, almost within sight of the capital, would be among the first to fall to the Yankees, possibly forfeited forever if the revolution failed. In the face of the cost confronting him, the choice he made almost certainly came from conscience rather than self-interest. Just when he made the choice is unclear. Only one month before his resignation from the Army on March 7, 1861, he actually upbraided an officer for too easily yielding Federal property in Louisiana when that state seceded. It may have been a sign that he was as yet undecided, or it may just as likely have been the punctilious bureaucrat in him, determined to fulfill his sworn duty to the U.S. right to the moment he left its service.

Cooper resigned his commission a month before his adopted Virginia seceded, and went south to Montgomery, arriving March 14 to take a position already offered him in the new Confederate military by Davis.[12] Cooper was always Davis's choice for the post. In later years Davis intimated that Cooper might have asked for a field command, but self-sacrificingly offered merely to serve wherever he might be useful.[13] However, there would hardly have been any thought of putting him in the field. He was just a few months short of 63, and had never led so much as a squad in the field. Commissioned a brigadier general—then the highest rank in the incipient Southern forces—Cooper first lodged at Montgomery Hall, one of the principal hotels in the new Confederate capital, but he soon tired of the cramped conditions and joined with Abraham Myers, David De Leon, Lt. Col. George Deas, and other War Department officials, in renting a house.

Christened "the Ranche," their home soon became a destination for arriving officers seeking assignment. Its front porch attracted much of Montgomery's new military and political society as Cooper and the others smoked cigars and read the latest press. The grouping required something of a rapprochement, since it was Myers with whom Cooper went through the brief contretemps when Cooper officially censured him for turning over that property in New Orleans. Myers retorted that Cooper's remarks betrayed "a splenetic spirit and contain[ed] offensive language from a source personally irresponsible."[14] That seemed to be forgotten now, however, showing that Cooper was not necessarily the slave to grudges that the new president would become. Instead, at the Ranche not a little conversation turned on the future, of campaigns yet unfought, and predictions of eventual victory.[15] When not there or in his office, he was often seen huddled with Davis and other generals over a table at the Exchange Hotel, mixing their meals with anxious discussion.[16] And when news came in by telegraph of the surrender of Fort Sumter on April 13, Cooper himself ordered a fifteen-gun salute as the capital celebrated.

Personally many people liked Cooper, even if they did not find him very dynamic. Charles E. L. Stuart of the War and later Postmaster's Departments, a chronic faultfinder with almost all of the high officials in the government, looked rather fondly on the old general. "The mild creature has some spunk," said Stuart. "A fine old soldier is he." Cooper was slim, tall, and bore himself with a certain stateliness befitting his age and position.[17] Apparently Cooper rarely wore a uniform in spite of being the senior ranking general in the army.[18] His professional experience and habits being those of a bureaucrat and bookkeeper, he dressed as one. Even then he seems never to have been entirely comfortable. He fidgeted almost constantly with his stiff shirt collar, sticking a finger into it and pulling at it while twisting his neck seeking a better fit. He did it so much that it was more probably an unconscious habit than an indication of genuine discomfort, and Stuart observed that in general Cooper was "nervous in his motions."[19]

Cooper was also accessible, more so than some of his subordinates, and generally more agreeable and less officious, though he could be "quick and often querulous in his words," found Stuart, who also thought him tactful, and certainly very knowledgeable on matters of military organization. "He is not, however, the 'I am' of the Department," said Stuart, "nor is he a whit more useful than when he was more docile." In the end Stuart conceived perhaps the briefest and most apt description of Cooper's place in the government firmament, when he said that "the Adjutant and Inspector General of Dixie's armies was really the great functionary of the War Office."[20]

The duties of that office were the preparation and promulgation of all official orders emanating from the War Department to the field commands of the Confederacy, maintenance of army records, oversight of military installations, and the inspection of those installations and personnel. Duties did not include planning strategy, but Cooper could certainly expect to be consulted on the appointments and promotions exercised by the president. Indeed, Davis often asked for Cooper's opinion when it came to giving commissions to dignitaries wanting to be generals, recalling the political sensitivity Cooper had shown during the Pierce administration.[21] Some, mainly friends, thought the old soldier the ideal man for the job. According to the adoring Fitzhugh Lee, hardly an impartial observer, Cooper possessed "the master mind, the perfect knowledge and vast experience, necessary to put the intricate machinery into successful operation."[22] In a way Lee was right, for no one save perhaps Davis himself had, through such long experience, as thorough an understanding of the necessary organization and operation of the bookkeeping department of an army. Nevertheless, complaints about Cooper would emerge early, and often.

When the Congress voted to move the capital to Richmond, Virginia, at the end of May, Cooper ordered that all future correspondence received there should be forwarded on to Richmond and then boarded a train with Davis and a few others on May 26 and began the journey eastward.[23] On his arrival in the new capital, Cooper came with enhanced rank and the beginning of a bitter controversy in which he was not himself directly involved; for ten days before leaving Montgomery, acting on new congressional legislation creating a top rank of full general in the new army, Davis gave the senior spot to Cooper by virtue of his seniority among officers of the old army who had come over to the new cause. He was thus the top ranking general in the Confederate army.

Cooper's only command, however, was the small army of clerks numbering up to eighty or more who occupied the right half of the first floor of the Virginia Mechanics Institute at 9th and Franklin Streets in Richmond. Everyone seemed to comment on the busy atmosphere and the number of staff in Cooper's department.[24] George Morgan of Georgia visited Richmond in December 1862 seeking an appointment and was ushered to the War Department. "There was a multitude of clerks—old men and boys," he found. Visitors were allowed to remain as long as they pleased, but Cooper enforced a strict gag rule on conversation, and questions could only be asked that pertained to the caller's business.[25] Cooper's own private office was right next to that of the secretary of war, but Robert Garlick Hill Kean, chief of the Bureau of War, complained that Cooper was rarely there, a charge not echoed by others in the department.[26]

Indeed, Cooper was often to be found working late at night after others in the department had gone home.[27] That was especially the case at critical times. He was closeted for long hours with Davis, chief adviser Robert E. Lee, and others on July 14 when Gen. P. G. T. Beauregard presented a foolish plan for an attack on Washington that all rejected. They decided to stand on the defensive and allow a Yankee advance known to be coming to meet them on their own ground. Indeed, it appears that at this stage of the new conflict Cooper exercised more influence in counsels with Davis and Lee than at any other time.[28] When initial reports came into Richmond on July 19, 1861, that forces commanded by Beauregard had repulsed the foe and enjoyed a substantial success in action at Blackburn's Ford—a prelude to the 1st Battle of Bull Run on July 21—Cooper beamed in relief. Even while sticking a finger in his collar and pulling it away from his neck, he congratulated Beauregard's supporters that their man had "done a capital thing."[29] Two months later, after Secretary of War Leroy Pope Walker resigned, there was a little talk of Cooper perhaps replacing him. "He is an efficient and good man," said Gen. Robert Toombs, formerly the first Confederate secretary of state. Moreover Davis trusted him and, Toombs presumed, would let Cooper do his duties in office rather than using him as a mere clerk as he had Walker.[30]

Nevertheless, a few like Kean groused that even when Cooper was at his desk he did little. "There is not one paper a week which bears evidence of his personal examination," said Kean. "He never decides anything, rarely ever *reports* upon a question, and when he does the report is very thin." Sarcastically, Kean added that "he is said to be in frequent consultation (!) with the President."[31] One of the most frequent complaints against Cooper was that his office did not keep adequate records. John B. Jones, a clerk in the War Department, complained in June 1862 that Cooper did not know how many regiments there were in the army that Lee then commanded in Virginia, or where they were stationed. That created problems when officers or men returned from furlough while the army was on the move, and applied in vain to the adjutant general's office to find out where to rejoin their regiments.[32] A year later on July 28, 1863, Kean grumbled in his diary:

As *Inspector General* one would suppose that the offic[er] highest in rank, the official keeper of the rolls whose specific duty it is to *know* the state of the army and *compel* proper returns, would in two and a half years have got some complete returns. Yet it is notorious that the returns are not complete even from the nearest and most stationary army, while of the Trans-Mississippi forces, they have almost no account whatever. There has never been a time when the A. I. General could give even a tolerably close *guess* of the whole force on the rolls of the army, still less of the *effective* force.[33]

In fact, Cooper's office did produce, over his signature, at least one comprehensive report of total enlisted and serving forces of the Confederacy on March 1, 1862, including militia. Within it regiments were even broken down according to terms of service, though not by assignment. It is probably the only such report his office ever produced.[34] Still, Gen. Isaac Trimble recalled in 1909 that during the war Cooper told him that there were some 21,000 Marylanders in Confederate service, suggesting that the adjutant general himself was not entirely unaware of army statistics. Trimble's recollection was vastly inflated, however, for only a fraction of that number served in actual Maryland units in gray (many more Marylanders certainly enlisted in regiments from other states, but Cooper's office did not maintain statistics of that kind).[35] Important is simply the fact that Cooper was able to give Trimble a figure, whatever it was at the time.

Contrary to complaints like Kean's and Jones's, at least in the Army of Northern Virginia few if any such criticisms of want of information emerged during the war. If Cooper's office was culpable for anything, it was more likely in not vigorously encouraging and requiring tardy commanders to submit timely data. Still, that there was occasional confusion in the adjutant general's office is evident in cases like the withdrawal of regiments from vital duty guarding bridges in the line of retreat of the Army of Tennessee in January 1863 during active campaigning, and their shift to protect Richmond shortly after Lee's great victory at Fredericksburg, which negated any Yankee threat to the capital for months to come. "Gen. Cooper is *old* in office, and should have known better," complained war clerk Jones. Had the Tennessee army suffered a severe defeat—as in fact it had at that very moment, unbeknownst to Jones—and found its line of withdrawal cut off at those bridges, it could have meant disaster.[36] In May 1864

Cooper actually ordered two regiments to leave their posts at prisoner of war camps and join the Army of Tennessee, then immediately afterward ordered them to Richmond, apparently having forgotten his own previous order, and in the process got the number of one of the units incorrect, though whether the confusion was his own or a clerk's is unclear. Still, it was his responsibility to ensure that such confusion did not happen.[37]

Cooper did at least once personally exercise his mandate—indeed, obligation—to perform as an inspector, when in June 1862 he made a visit to Charleston, South Carolina, to inspect its defenses, which he toured in the middle of that month. It may have been the only time he ever left Richmond to perform such an inspection, and this one he cut short on June 24 in order to join Gen. Wade Hampton and Sen. James Chesnut on a hasty train trip back to Richmond to be in the capital then under threat from the advance of a Union army that the next day would commence the Seven Days battles.[38] Meanwhile, his department conducted quite a number of inspections by lesser officers of posts, armies, and prison camps, and there is little basis to complain that the War Department was not well aware of the condition of its outposts at any time in the war until the last year, and of course in territory west of the Mississippi after the Federals took control of the river in July 1863 and virtually cut off the Western Confederacy.

In his relations with the several secretaries of war to whom he reported, Cooper appears to have been uniformly courteous and subordinate, at least to their faces. He made no secret of his contempt for the inefficiency of Davis's first appointment, the Alabama lawyer Leroy P. Walker, who remained in office too short a time for them to clash seriously. He thought little more of Walker's replacement, Judah P. Benjamin, a man clearly high in the president's esteem, who did much harm to good military order and morale in his brief tenure. But as Benjamin was a favorite with Davis, Cooper stayed on good terms with him. Cooper actually liked Gen. Gustavus W. Smith, who followed Benjamin for a few days on an interim basis, but then came George W. Randolph.[39] Cooper quickly read the presidential mood when Randolph showed an inclination to exercise too much independence, and in November 1862 some in the War Department believed that Cooper encouraged and played on Davis's feelings to magnify a small disagreement over Randolph's assigning troops on his own authority, turning it into an issue that led to Randolph's essentially forced resignation.[40]

Certainly Cooper jealously guarded the president's prerogatives when it came to movements of troops or assignment of officers. Under the next secretary of war, James Seddon, Cooper at least once short-circuited Seddon's assignment of a general without prior consultation with the president, directing Seddon to see Davis first.[41] He also circumvented Seddon on his own, and in the summer of 1864 apparently made an attempt to persuade Seddon to resign by leaking to him the news—probably as yet untrue—that Davis wanted the secretary to resign.[42] When Seddon did finally resign in January 1865 and John C. Breckinridge took over, the cause was already lost, and the interaction between Breckinridge and Cooper would be aimed almost solely at preparing for the evacuation of Richmond. Besides, Breckinridge, after more than three years in uniform, had heard more than enough of the calumny heaped upon the adjutant general, not to be wary of him.

The criticism of Cooper's capacity for his office came from several quarters. Not surprisingly, many found him suspect simply by virtue of his New York birth, adding this to what was perceived as a penchant of the president's to give high office to Yankee natives.[43] At least once this prejudice was thrown directly in his face, in March 1862, when Cooper was introduced to the wife of South Carolina's governor Francis Pickens. In the course of drawing-room conversation she began to complain that the president was always sending Yankee-born men to command in Charleston, and this just as Cooper himself was on the verge of leaving for his inspection tour of South Carolina. Cooper stayed quiet, just fiddling with his finger in his collar, and stared blankly through his spectacles, while someone whispered to Mrs. Pickens that Cooper himself was from New York, followed by an embarrassing silence.[44] Some—no doubt unfairly—believed that Cooper retaliated for this suspicion with a deliberate insult to Virginia in December 1862. When Cooper temporarily put Gen. Arnold Elzey—a Maryland native—in immediate command of the defenses of Richmond during the absence of Virginia-born Robert E. Lee, critics accused Cooper of deliberately insulting the capital of the Confederacy by placing it in the care of someone not native born to the Old Dominion.[45]

More telling complaint came from within the War Department. Kean thought him completely incompetent. "It is so manifest that nothing but the irrepressible *West Pointism* of the President, and that other peculiarity of preferring accommodating, civil-spoken persons of small capacity about him, can account for his retention," Kean grumbled in July 1863.[46] Maj. Samuel W. Melton, assistant adjutant general in Cooper's department itself, found the frustration of dealing with his superior almost too much by summer of 1863. "He is getting old & childish—Says one thing to-day and another to-morrow; and just as apt as not he will put me to trouble about it," Melton complained to his wife in July. "Every day in our business he annoys me more and more, with this indecision, changefulness and freakfulness."[47] Much of this complaint can be put down to the perennial discontent among subordinates in any office setting, as well as to the resentment of the young like Kean and Melton for the old. But that there was sometimes inefficiency, delay, and confusion, in the adjutant general's office, went beyond question.

Perhaps the most common charge leveled at Cooper was that he was essentially a cipher, venturing no opinions, merely letting himself be used as a glorified clerk by Davis, who made all decisions, even to such minor things as the appointments of low-grade officers. Kean believed that Cooper avoided even trying to make decisions, but simply ran to Davis on every little matter.[48] It was a charge of some substance. In February 1864 rumors circulated in Richmond that Gen. Braxton Bragg, virtually forced to resign his command of the Army of Tennessee after the loss of Chattanooga the previous fall, might be brought to the capital by his patron Davis and installed in Cooper's place. Given the low regard in which both were held, it was "no matter" said one society matron. Besides, she added, "it will be years before that slow coach Cooper finds it out."[49] Davis made Bragg chief of staff instead.

Like all functionaries, Cooper also came under fire for being a "red tapist," a hidebound bureaucrat slavishly tied to rules and regulations. That charge, in the main, held true, but then part of Cooper's job was to ensure that such regulations were obeyed.[50] One of the few times on record when observers saw him "in high dudgeon," as Jones described it, was in July 1864 when he became enraged that documents referred to him from other War Department bureaus were being sent signed by underlings rather than by the heads of the bureaus. Cooper took his protest to the president, who took time out from attention to the critical situation around Atlanta to pen an admonition to Seddon that his subordinates observe proper protocol with the adjutant general. "Thus," lamented Jones, "important affairs wait upon 'red tape.'"[51] In December 1864 Cooper spent hours closeted with Davis and Seddon on the hardly vital task of combining some

Mississippi companies and battalions in order to make a skeleton regiment for an unoccupied colonel to command, a job that should have been beneath Cooper's priorities, and certainly the president's.[52] The sad fact was that Davis and Cooper were brothers under the skin when it came to love of paperwork.

Certainly Cooper lived up to Kean's sarcastic remark about spending a lot of time in consultation with Davis. The president turned to Cooper and a small coterie of other advisers, including the sitting secretary of war, during every military crisis, as when Cooper was closeted with him for long periods when news first arrived of the fall of Vicksburg and the defeat at Gettysburg in early July 1863, or later that year during the battle of Chickamauga.[53] Cooper was also believed to be withholding bad news from the front on occasion, and in one instance even apparently withheld a much-expected report from the president.[54]

As he had in the old U.S. Army—and contrary to Davis's later assertion that Cooper never took counsel of his own prejudices—the adjutant general was willing to use his access to the president to assist the ambitions of friends and favorites. He apparently shared Davis's generally wise—though controversial—penchant for favoring West Point graduates over nonprofessional soldiers when it came to promotions and important commands, the very "West Pointism" that so outraged Kean. It was a policy that made sense, of course, but not in every instance, as in June 1861 when Cooper used what influence he had with Davis to undermine Gen. Gideon Pillow, then commanding in west Tennessee, and make him subordinate to West Point graduate General Leonidas Polk, who had no actual experience in uniform and nothing to recommend him for such an important command other than his friendship with Davis.[55]

In March 1864 Cooper would go farther when he helped get Gen. Martin L. Smith assigned chief of the department's Engineer Bureau by making a recommendation for the assignment himself and then taking it directly to Davis, bypassing the secretary of war who was known to oppose such an appointment. Seddon only found out about it after the fact, and it was not the first time that Cooper used his friendship with the chief executive to get around his own immediate superior.[56] Earlier in the war officials had perceived that rather few orders went out of the War Department signed "by command of the secretary of war." Most were simply signed "by order," the assumption being that they came from the president through Cooper, often without even consulting or informing Randolph.[57]

Oddly enough, given that people, especially in the War Department, knew how jealously Davis guarded his prerogatives of commissioning and assigning general officers, sometimes Cooper's critics charged him instead with such unfortunate choices, as when Gen. John W. Frazer surrendered Cumberland Gap, Tennessee, almost without a fight in September 1863. "Where did Gen. Cooper find him?" complained Jones.[58] The perception was far more common throughout the War Department and elsewhere in the government that while Davis often consulted Cooper about campaign policy or the assignment or replacement of officers in the field, in the main the president did not ask his advice on matters outside Cooper's mandate. Even when such advice was sought, as Stuart observed, "it was seldom acted on."[59] Cooper could be forcefully reminded from time to time that if he had the president's ear, he still did not command enough influence in the executive mansion to persuade Davis to change his mind. Occasionally people approached him with ideas that they hoped he would espouse to Davis, as when Col. William Preston Johnston— one of Davis's most trusted aides—conceived the idea early in 1862 to start a buildup for a campaign to take Kentucky from the Yankees. He approached Cooper, and the adjutant general was won over, but it took more than just Cooper's endorsement before Davis finally assented to the idea months later.[60] Gen. Roswell S. Ripley, commanding officer in the Charleston defenses in 1864, was notorious for his excess drinking, and numerous complaints came to the War Department. In October 1864 Ripley apparently offered some insult or indecent remark to a Charleston lady, and that was enough for Cooper to go to Davis along with Seddon to plead that he be relieved of his command.[61] Instead, Davis retained Ripley in Charleston until the city itself fell to the Federals the following February. And despite Cooper's strenuous objections in February 1865 to giving a brigadier's commission to the governor of South Carolina, Milledge L. Bonham, one of the politicians Cooper so disdained, Davis went ahead and did it.[62]

Thus reminded of his essential powerlessness to influence important decisions, Cooper—while retaining excellent relations with Davis—retreated into the confines of his own department "and gradually came to act only as he was regarded," thought Stuart: "an excellent Adjutant, who had not a word to say beyond the routine of his office."[63]

Meanwhile, as he could, Cooper tried to stay out of the numerous controversies between feuding general officers. When such a disagreement arose, his preference was to keep official correspondence and battle reports out of the press. Still on more than one occasion his office was dragged into the melee unwittingly, as in Braxton Bragg's vendetta against some of his subordinates, including Breckinridge, in 1863.[64]

Not that Cooper did not let his frustration with difficult officers show. Early in the war—and often later—he was the target of the ire of disappointed aspirants for office, or of men who thought their commissions beneath them. In Montgomery in 1861 one such malcontent stormed into Cooper's office, vented his rage and tore up his commission in front of the adjutant general's eyes, threw the bits on the floor, and stomped out again.[65] In Richmond later in the war, asked to take a statement for a pending court of inquiry from a general officer whom he particularly disliked, Cooper rose from his desk in anger, threw his arms in the air, and declared "I cannot do it, sir!" Cooling rapidly, he went on to explain with a smile that "life is too short to talk to that gentleman."[66]

The adjutant general was also capable of striking out occasionally, showing his own frustration at being taken for granted by some, and ridiculed by others, especially when someone stepped on his own prerogatives, few as they were. In late 1862 John A. Campbell was appointed assistant secretary of war, and soon became a powerful presence in the War Department, and one much resented for imperiousness—even corruption—by some of its employees. From the outset he began issuing peremptory orders to Cooper on his own authority, and without consideration for the adjutant general's own position. Cooper responded by issuing an order creating—without requisite congressional action—the office of acting assistant secretary of war and assigning Lt. Col. George A. Deas to the post, thus giving Cooper a man of his own in the secretary's office.[67]

"I am not simply a bureau [officer] as some view me," Cooper complained to Davis in July 1864, and the president had to step in to remind the secretary of war that as "Chief of Staff of the whole army," Cooper was more than merely "an organ for the transmission of the instructions and inquiries."[68] That was fine, but in practice Cooper rarely rose in the estimation of others to anything more than a rubber stamp. Even Davis hardly ever acted on his advice, thought one department clerk. Instead, according to Charles E. L. Stuart, who actually liked Cooper, the senior general in the army was "left severely at his own specialty and gradually came to act only as he was regarded—an excellent adjutant who had not a word to say beyond the routine of his office."[69]

He could also take more direct action against those whom he disliked or distrusted. Often they were simply guilty of not being West Point educated, but a few won his enmity by other means, notably Gen. Henry A. Wise, former governor of Virginia. After Wise was defeated severely and his own son killed in a foolish engagement at Roanoke Island, North Carolina, in February 1862, the irascible Wise conducted a ceaseless campaign of condemnation against those in the War Department whom he deemed responsible, chiefly Benjamin. Even if he did not directly name Cooper, still Wise's denunciations included the adjutant general by association, and thus when Wise got into a controversy with the quartermaster general, Abraham C. Myers, Cooper sided with Myers and simply buried Wise's complaint by filing it without putting it before the president or the secretary of war.[70] It was a bureaucrat's revenge. In a petty move—if intentional—Cooper even assigned Wise's other remaining son, then serving on his father's staff, to another command entirely.[71]

In an equally petty move—if true—Cooper was accused of intentionally failing to build the division of Maj. Gen. John C. Breckinridge up to full strength prior to the heavy losses it took in the September 1863 battle of Chickamauga. The reason, according to the not unprejudiced clerk Jones, was that Breckinridge had not gone to West Point, like Wise, and the adjutant general had "no desire to replenish the dilapidated command of an aspiring 'political general.'"[72] In December 1863 Cooper struck at another of the nonprofessional "politicals" when he recommended to the president that the conscription bureau charged with enforcing the draft in the Western theater be closed after a career of excess and inefficiency. Not coincidentally, it had been under the command of Pillow, and Cooper took seeming delight in telling Davis that this was a "convenient opportunity" to relieve Pillow. Within a few months Cooper would be attacking the conscription process itself, and with good cause in view of its excesses and inequities.[73] Even in the extremity of February 1865, with collapse imminent, Cooper managed to use his influence to delay giving another command to Pillow. "*Gen. Cooper* must be consulted to throw obstacles in the way!" grumbled Jones. It was another example of the triumph of Cooper and what Jones called the "red tapists."[74]

Much as he tried to stay out of the internal squabbles among the generals in the field, he could not remain aloof from the feuds involving the president and his generals, especially those with Joseph E. Johnston and P. G. T. Beauregard. With Johnston it all started over a matter of rank. In May 1861 when the Congress authorized the new rank of full general, Cooper was the first and only man so appointed, on May 16. Thereafter as others were raised to that rank, Davis's rationale for the order of seniority in the dating of their commissions was the congressional provision when the first rank of brigadier had been created that officers appointed should mark seniority from the date of their promotion to the highest rank held in the old U.S. Army. That preserved in the new order the seniority of the old. It was assumed that this was fair, and would also obviate jealousy and disagreement among men who got their Confederate commissions on the same day.

As the men joined the Confederacy, Davis bestowed full general's rank on Albert Sidney Johnston, then Robert E. Lee, and in July on Joseph E. Johnston. The last immediately bristled. When he left the old U.S. Army, he had been quartermaster general with the staff rank of brigadier. Cooper had held staff rank only as a colonel, and if they were to compare actual confirmed field ranks, Cooper was only a captain and Johnston had been a lieutenant colonel. In fact, Johnston's sights were not set on Cooper. His concern was that he felt he ought to outrank the other Johnston and Lee as the senior field officer of the army. The feud with Davis erupted in the summer of 1861, and as quickly abated, but relations between the two were never wholly cordial again, and would get worse after 1863; and Cooper naturally sided with the president.

Then shortly after the victory at 1st Manassas, Beauregard began a feud with Davis that would last the rest of their lives. The general complained about lack of support from Richmond, contacted politicians behind the president's back, retreated into piqued fits when higher authorities turned down his impractical invasions of the North, and started a side feud with Benjamin when he became secretary of war. Capping it all, Beauregard delayed his official report of the Manassas fight for almost three months. When it arrived in the War Department on October 15, Cooper and Benjamin certainly saw it but did not pass it on to Davis, perhaps because they saw that it insinuated that only Davis prevented victorious Confederates from following up their victory with a march on Washington, whereas the fact was that Davis could not get Beauregard and Johnston to agree to try to do so. Cooper and Benjamin may have held up the report, knowing that the president would bristle at the unjust criticism, but then someone— Beauregard denied doing it and suspected Benjamin—sent an abstract of the report to the press, and Davis first learned of it when he read it in the newspaper on October 29. He exploded, Beauregard immediately backed down; Benjamin had made a point against the general with Cooper's tacit compliance, and relations between Davis and Beauregard would never get better again.

Cooper often had to be involved in delicate, not to say explosive, issues that required tact and judgment, and his seems generally to have been sound, if not very forcefully expressed. In late February 1864, when the abortive Kilpatrick-Dahlgren Raid foundered in the environs of Richmond, and papers were captured on Dahlgren's body suggesting that his intent had been the capture or death of the president and his cabinet, Fitzhugh Lee took them to Davis, who then directed that they be turned over to Cooper. The adjutant general filed them in his office, having charge of perhaps the most explosive captured correspondence of the war.[75]

A few months later in August 1864, when one of Cooper's own inspectors produced a report on conditions at Camp Sumter prison at Andersonville, Georgia, it showed appalling suffering, however unintentional. Cooper's office passed it on to the secretary of war with the endorsement that "the condition of the prison at Andersonville is a reproach to us as a nation." Even though Cooper himself did not sign the endorsement, it must be assumed that the assistant adjutant general who wrote it did not do so contrary to his superior's views, and that the same has to be said for the assistant's following up the condemnation with an endorsement of the report's recommendation that Gen. John H. Winder be replaced in charge of the post by someone competent and energetic enough to redress the evils of the place. The result was Winder's eventual reassignment. That Cooper did not actually author and sign the endorsement himself may have been because Winder had been an acquaintance—perhaps friend—of some years standing, and he did not have the heart to endorse embarrassment for a general nearly as old as himself—Winder was sixty-four—and known to be in ill health.

The report caused considerable stir in the War Department, and angry repudiation from Winder himself, yet Cooper apparently remained silent during the controversy. Nevertheless, if he agreed with the assessment of Winder's performance at Camp Sumter, Cooper ought to have objected strongly three months later when instead of removing Winder, Cooper's own order placed him in command of all Confederate prison camps east of the Mississippi. The fact that in

October it was known that Cooper recommended Gen. Mansfield Lovell to Davis for the position Winder got is evidence that Cooper felt Winder was not up to the job, regardless of his public protestations then and later of complete confidence in Winder.[76] Experience, or his own weakness, apparently had shown Cooper that he had little to gain from making an energetic case for his own views before the president.

Whatever else was said of him, no accusations appeared of Cooper being involved in corruption of any sort, which could not have been said of Campbell, Kean, and some of the secretaries like Randolph. Still, there was a rumor in the War Department that Cooper and a few others had declined to take their salaries in Confederate treasury notes like everyone else, seemingly working for nothing, and letting the government build up indebtedness to them. The suspicion was that they expected that once independence and financial stability were secured, they would be able to draw their back pay then in hard specie rather than deflated and worthless scrip.[77] That, too, was untrue, but the fact remained that Cooper had to support his family in Richmond largely from his own dwindling resources.

Just as he had in Washington, Cooper and his wife enjoyed a rather active social life in the Confederate capital, such as wartime restrictions allowed. He attended the Episcopal Church, either St. James's or St. Paul's, the same one attended by Davis.[78] Cooper's younger daughter Jenny became popular in social circles, and there were many rumors about her suitors, including gossip of a romance with the family's friend—and now general—Fitzhugh Lee.[79] Her brother Capt. Samuel Cooper kept more to himself, and was kept in Richmond by his father.[80] In the days after the first battle at Bull Run in July 1861, Cooper's wife Sarah often risked arousing the ire of her fellow Richmond matrons by visiting wounded Union officers captured in the action. Perhaps it was the knowledge that her own son-in-law Wheaton, who also fought at 1st Manassas, might have been among them. As often as she could she called and brought little comforts to the men, and secured cooking utensils for them so they could make their own meals. To those already inclined to criticize General Cooper for his Yankee birth, his wife's actions only aroused even more prejudice.[81]

The Coopers made social calls on prominent families, their talk sometimes turning to Mrs. Cooper's distinguished ancestry, and Cooper himself revealed an occasional aptitude for bantering pleasantry, sometimes with a bite. When he attended a dinner party at which an army physician consoled a teenage girl that not all the fine young men would be killed in the war, and there would be plenty of them left afterward to make husbands, Cooper responded to the flippant remark with a cutting one of his own. "Let us wait awhile, be in no hurry," he said after the doctor. "Those fine fellows down there, see how they are being killed and cut up. Arms and legs flying right and left. Now the young surgeons who have taken care of their [own] well-made bodies—preserved them free from harm—will bring a good price after the war." The doctor himself did not even realize the insult until it was pointed out to him.[82]

In mid-October, 1864, with the crisis in manpower rising, Cooper revoked all details in order to force able-bodied men into the front lines, though he probably acted at Davis's order rather than on his own initiative, of which by this time he had almost none remaining.[83] A month later, in response to increasing demand that able-bodied government clerks be denied exemption from military service, Cooper released one fourth of his eighty-man clerical staff and, following his practice in Washington, began employing female clerks in their place.[84] He of all people should have been able to see what was coming in the new year, and perhaps he did, but if so, as usual, he kept it to himself. Certainly he did not object in February 1865, when it became clear to many, especially the new secretary of war Breckinridge, that Lee could not protect Richmond for long, when the secretary put the entire War Department to work in preparing for an evacuation. Cooper oversaw the work in his offices, and even as late as Saturday, April 1, he was still personally completing the final packing of his archives. That afternoon he joined Breckinridge and others in the office of Secretary of State Benjamin. Cooper openly expressed outrage at Benjamin's flippant manner in the crisis. "Nero fiddled while Rome burned," he chided Benjamin, who only continued singing and whistling until Cooper left the room in disgust.[85] On April 2 Cooper was sitting in a service at St. Paul's Episcopal Church when he saw a messenger call President Davis away, and soon thereafter another brought Cooper word from Breckinridge that the moment had come, and Lee advised that he could hold out no longer.[86]

That evening the adjutant general boarded the train loaded with most of the cabinet, and along with his clerks, books, and records set off for Danville.[87] Once there, Davis ordered Cooper to get his department in operation as quickly as possible in some temporary housing. Cooper found quarters in a onetime girls' school on Wilson Street, and by the next day he was actually transacting business, handling the appointments and assignments that had built up in the unanswered mail brought out from Richmond.[88] Soon the surrender of Lee at Appomattox forced them to move on south, and the government repacked and headed to Greensboro, North Carolina, where inhospitable citizens offered them no housing and they were forced to live on their railroad cars, about which an increasingly unwell Cooper grumbled ceaselessly.[89] Still he guarded the essential record books and papers necessary to continue operating his department, and from railroad car, temporary lodging, and soon wagon bed, he and a few of his clerks kept the red tape coming.[90]

When the government had to abandon Greensboro and keep moving, the rails could no longer take them, and wagons were made available for the officials. Cooper was about to get into his, pulled by a fine healthy team, when a brigadier general got to the seat first and, obliging as usual, Cooper agreed to take another wagon, only to discover that his traveling companion would be Benjamin, with whom he had never enjoyed warm relations. Cooper may already have been ailing when they left Richmond, but travel was not improving his condition. Now with Benjamin, Attorney General George Davis, and the president's secretary Burton Harrison, he discovered that their conveyance rocked behind broken-down animals. Rains turned the roads into mires, and at times even Cooper had to get out and wade in the mud to help push the wagon through the slop. Once when the horses gave out altogether, Cooper was heard to complain that he was in this mess through the impudence of an officer who was "only a brigadier-general, Sir." It was the only time during the war that he was known to complain about improper deference to his rank. Cooper's consolation came that evening when they stopped at a house for the night. The owner's slave man somehow mistook Cooper for the president, and escorted him to the best bedroom, meaning that when Davis himself arrived shortly afterward, the adjutant general was already fast asleep and for once the president had to make do with second best. Happily his wagon got a fresh team the next morning for the trip to Charlotte.[91]

Still Cooper tried to continue his bookkeeping, actually ordering his head of the Ordnance Bureau to convene an examining board to test an infantry cadet being considered for a commission, as if it mattered at all now.[92] But on April 26, when Davis announced in a cabinet meeting that they would have to move south again, and it was generally assumed that Joseph E. Johnston was about to surrender the only other substantial army east of the Mississippi, Cooper finally spoke up to say that he was too ill to go farther, a decision the president had no choice but to accept. In meetings with Breckinridge it was decided that Cooper would remain there in charge of the archives of the War Department, so carefully packed and preserved during the trip. When the Federals arrived, as they must, Cooper was then to turn the archives over to them, Breckinridge stressing that these records were "essential to the history of the struggle." Breckinridge also had Cooper issue an order to some remaining Virginia officers cut off from their commands that they should go home.[93] When Cooper and Davis took their farewell of each other that afternoon as the government moved on, it was an emotional moment for both.[94]

On May 1 Cooper was still in Charlotte, in a city no longer very hospitable to the remnants of the Confederate high command. Even though Johnston had surrendered his army two weeks before, Cooper still apparently acted on Davis's intention to regroup and concentrate Confederate remnants in Georgia in or around Augusta. Meanwhile he used what troops remained under orders to guard commissary and quartermaster stores and to protect private citizens from public disorder, not to mention restraining soldiers themselves who were on the verge of desertion and plunder. The next day, however, soldiers there learned that they were covered by the terms of Johnston's surrender, and that ended the matter. Cooper, of course, by the nature of his position, was not covered in the surrender. However, there was nowhere for him to go. That evening Yankee soldiers came into Charlotte to begin the process of paroling the soldiers the next day, and Cooper gave his own parole on May 3 and prepared to leave by train for Danville, Virginia, with a small escort. Three days later he reached Danville, his war over at last.[95]

Cooper spent the first year of peace living in Mecklenburg County before he finally returned to Alexandria, where he found his house in ruins and a federal wartime earthwork erected in its place. Fortunately his son-in-law Wheaton, recently a major general in the Union army, persuaded the pro-Southern Washington philanthropist W. W. Corcoran to buy the confiscated farm and return it to the Coopers. Corcoran well remembered his earlier friendship with the family, and also gave them enough money to enlarge a smaller overseer's house on the property to occupy. There Cooper spent his remaining years in almost constant financial straits, left almost penniless after the war.[96] In December 1867 when Robert E. Lee visited Richmond, he encountered the old adjutant, and found him looking "very thin."[97] By 1870 the rumors of Cooper's near destitution were so prevalent that General Lee took it upon himself, just two months before his own death, to raise some $400 among former army associates to send to their old friend to relieve his distress.[98]

On March 26, 1868, Cooper had been named along with Lee, and several other former high-ranking military officers in an indictment for treason, but following the decision of the United States not to prosecute Davis himself, the charges against Cooper and the rest were dismissed on February 15, 1869, and thereafter he lived unharassed by his former foes.[99] But in those last years Cooper had a few consolations. In 1869 his brother-in-law James Mason returned from exile in Canada and occupied a home next door to him. Thereafter the Coopers and Masons spent much time together, the old general and the aged diplomat often being seen outdoors puttering in their gardens and orchards. Sometimes they sat on crude three-legged stools in Cooper's corncrib, shucking ears and laughing over who had the biggest blisters and who had shucked the most corn.[100]

Cooper did not turn his back on his former Confederate associates, and after the war Cooper was ready to defend the actions of those in his department who came under criticism, especially if they were no longer living. Gen. John H. Winder, responsible for Confederate prisons, was especially execrated for the conditions that prevailed at Andersonville and elsewhere under his charge, but in 1871—and despite his tacit 1864 endorsement of Winder's removal from command—Cooper made a rare statement to endorse Winder's conduct and try to relieve his memory of calumny. Having known Winder for several years prior to the war, Cooper testified that he did his best for the prisoners, and then went on to contribute his mote to the defense of Davis himself on the same score.[101] Cooper also engaged in a fair bit of correspondence with others who were seeking details and numbers for their memoirs, and he also began the writing of his own recollections, perhaps hoping to provide some modest income for his family as did a number of his Confederate contemporaries. He had gotten only up to his return from the Western inspection tour in 1852, however, when age and his final illness stopped his pen.[102] He died December 3, 1876, and was buried in Alexandria's Christ Church Cemetery.

Jefferson Davis spoke glowingly of his old friend a few months later. "No one presents an example more worthy of emulation," said

Davis. "The many who measure the value of an officer's service by the conspicuous part he played upon the fields of battle, may not properly estimate the worth of Cooper's services in the war," he concluded, but those who understood the adjutant's efforts "will not fail to place him among those who contributed most to whatever was achieved."[103] Davis was surely hyperbolic in his appraisal, but surely some of the praise was due. Cooper, in his role as adjutant and inspector general, did what the job demanded of him. He was not supposed to frame strategy or lead troops. He was supposed to keep records of the army and maintain a watchful eye over the conditions of its installations. His office did the former perhaps as efficiently as could be expected under the difficult circumstances posed by shaky Confederate transportation and communications, and the accusations of his office being ignorant of army affairs were largely unfounded, though certainly there was occasional—and sometimes embarrassing—confusion. As for inspections, he may be more culpable. Certainly he made few himself, perhaps only the one visit to Charleston, but then personal inspections were not the duty of the adjutant and inspector general himself. His office did oversee rather thorough inspections of the military prisons, and Cooper inserted himself directly into administration and shifts of officers in the effort to supervise the camps efficiently and humanely. The steady contraction of Confederate lines in the field, however, made inspections more difficult and perhaps less worthwhile, since an installation inspected today might be in Yankee hands tomorrow.

When it came to his influence on appointments and promotions, it needs to be remembered that he did not have the authority to do either on his own. That rested with the president, who jealously guarded that prerogative. Cooper gave his advice when asked for it, as he was often, but if it had little impact in the face of a contrary opinion of Davis's, the adjutant general was hardly culpable for the president choosing to follow his own mind. Where Cooper may deserve censure, as so many complained, is that he seems not to have argued his own views with any force, but then that is an argument that presumes that Davis's mind could be changed, which history reveals seldom happened.

In the end, Samuel Cooper did a thankless job in an environment in which greater success might have been unattainable. He could not produce more men for the army where there were none to be had. He could not influence or direct campaigns that were outside his official prerogatives. And no one could change Jefferson Davis's mind, while those who tried lost favor—and their positions—in direct proportion to the earnestness with which they tried. There was nothing in Cooper's assigned mandate that required the heavy weight of rank that he bore as senior ranking general other than the fact that orders did come out of his office to the other full generals in the field, but since most of those were really by order of the president or secretary of war anyhow, no real rank was needed to be a simple conduit of information. In short, Cooper did not do what he could not, and cannot be blamed for that. What he could do he did, and generally competently, if not with flair. But then flair is the one quality that history has never demanded of a bureaucrat.

NOTES
Special thanks are due to Robert K. Krick, Michael Musick of the National Archives, and Lynda Crist, editor of the Jefferson Davis Papers, for assistance with this essay.

1. Fitzhugh Lee, "Sketch of the Late General S. Cooper (hereafter cited as Lee, "Sketch")," in *Southern Historical Society Papers*, ed. J. William Jones and others, 52 vols. and 3-vol. index (1877–1959; reprint, Wilmington, N.C.: Broadfoot, 1990–92), 3:271 (hereafter cited as *SHSP*).
2. Anne Hollingworth Wharton, *Social Life in the Early Republic* (Philadelphia: Lippincott, 1902), 225.
3. E. Rowland Dawson, "Gossip about Lieutenant Cooper," http://www.generalcooper.com; Lee, "Sketch," 271; Jefferson Davis, *The Papers of Jefferson Davis*, ed. Lynda Lasswell Crist and others, 11 vols. to date (Baton Rouge: Louisiana State University Press, 1971–2003), 1:106.
4. Philadelphia, 1836.
5. Lee, "Sketch," 272.
6. Jefferson Davis to Fitzhugh Lee, April 5, 1877, in Lee, "Sketch," 274–75; Varina Davis, *Jefferson Davis: A Memoir by His Wife*, 2 vols. (New York: Belford, 1890), 1:166–69; William C. Davis, *Jefferson Davis: The Man and His Hour* (New York: HarperCollins, 1991), 86–87 (hereafter cited as Davis, *Man and His Hour*).
7. Lee, "Sketch," 272.
8. Samuel Cooper reports, C 292, 293 (AGO) 1851, C 401 (AGO) 1851, Record Group 94, Records of the Adjutant General's Office, M567, National Archives, Washington, D.C. (repository hereafter cited as NA); Lee, "Sketch," 272.
9. Davis to Lee, April 5, 1877, Lee, "Sketch," 275.

10. Ibid.

11. Elizabeth Lindsay Lomax, *Leaves from an Old Washington Diary, 1854–1863* (New York: Dutton, 1943), passim; T. C. De Leon, *Belles, Beaux and Brains of the 60's* (New York: Dillingham, 1909), 109 (hereafted cited as De Leon, *Belles*).

12. Cooper to Charles C. Jones, May 27, 1871, copy in author's possession.

13. Davis to Lee, April 5, 1877, Lee, "Sketch," 276.

14. U.S. War Department, *War of the Rebellion: A Compilation of the Official Records of the Union and Confederate Armies*, 127 vols., index, and atlas (Washington, D.C.: U.S. Government Printing Office, 1880-1901), I, 1:459 (hereafter cited as *OR*, with all citations to Series I unless otherwise noted; for volumes that appeared in more than one part, the part is shown in parentheses after the volume number).

15. T. C. De Leon, *Four Years in Rebel Capitals* (Mobile: Gossip, 1892), 28.

16. *New York Citizen*, May 4, 1867; De Leon, *Belles*, 48; De Leon, *Four Years*, 24–25.

17. *New York Citizen*, July 20, 1867.

18. Edward D. C. Campbell, Jr., "The Fabric of Command: R. E. Lee, Confederate Insignia, and the Perception of Rank," *Virginia Magazine of History and Biography* 98 (April 1990):282.

19. *New York Citizen*, July 20, 1867.

20. Ibid.

21. Davis, *Man and His Hour*, 317; Davis to Lee, April 5, 1877, Lee, "Sketch," 275.

22. Lee, "Sketch," 273.

23. *Montgomery Weekly Advertiser*, May 29, 1861, *Charleston Mercury*, May 30, 1861.

24. *New York Citizen*, July 20, 1867.

25. George Hampton Morgan to Dear Ones at Home, January 12, 1863, in George Hampton Morgan, "Typical Letter of War Times," *Confederate Veteran* 16 (April 1908):156.

26. *New York Citizen*, July 20, 1867.

27. Lee, "Sketch," 274.

28. Davis, *Man and His Hour*, 345.

29. C. Vann Woodward, ed., *Mary Chesnut's Civil War* (New Haven, Conn.: Yale University Press, 1981), 100, 103 (entries for July 14, 19, 1861) (hereafted cited as Woodward, ed., *Mary Chesnut's Civil War*).

30. Robert Toombs to Alexander H. Stephens, September 22, 1861, in Ulrich B. Phillips, ed., *The Correspondence of Robert Toombs, Alexander H. Stephens, and Howell Cobb* (Washington: U.S. Government Printing Office, 1913), 576.

31. Robert Garlick Hill Kean, *Inside the Confederate Government: The Diary of Robert Garlick Hill Kean, Head of the Bureau of War*, ed. Edward Younger (New York: Oxford University Press, 1957), 88 (entry

for July 28, 1863) (hereafter cited as Kean, *Inside the Confederate Government*).

32. John B. Jones, *A Rebel War Clerk's Diary at the Confederate States Capital*, 2 vols. (Philadelphia: Lippincott, 1866), 1:135 (entry for June 24, 1862) (hereafted cited as Jones, *Diary*).

33. Kean, *Inside the Confederate Government*, 88-89.

34. *OR*, ser. IV, 1:962–64; Marcus J. Wright to *Richmond Dispatch*, September 9, 1891, "The Confederate Army," *SHSP* 19:254.

35. "Marylanders in the Confederate Army," *SHSP* 37:235.

36. Jones, *Diary*, 1:230 (entry for January 3, 1863).

37. *OR*, 36 (2):1011, 38 (4):704.

38. Carlos Tracy Diary, June 17, "Operations before Charleston in May and July, 1862," *SHSP* 8:546; Woodward, ed., *Mary Chesnut's Civil War*, 394 (entry for June 24).

39. *New York Citizen*, July 20, 1867.

40. Kean, *Inside the Confederate Government*, 30 (entry for November 25, 1862).

41. Ibid., 77 (entry for June 19, 1863).

42. Ibid., 171 (entry for August 20, 1864).

43. Jones, *Diary*, 1:166, 222 (entries for October 9, December 23, 1862); *New York Citizen*, July 20, 1867.

44. Woodward, ed., *Mary Chesnut's Civil War*, 316–17 (entry for March 20, 1862).

45. Jones, *Diary*, 1:222 (entry for December 23, 1862).

46. Kean, *Inside the Confederate Government*, 87 (entry for July 28, 1863).

47. Samuel Melton to his wife, July 29, 1863, Samuel Wickliff Melton Papers, South Caroliniana Library, University of South Carolina, Columbia.

48. Kean, *Inside the Confederate Government*, 100–101 (entry for August 23, 1863).

49. Woodward, ed., *Mary Chesnut's Civil War*, 572 (entry for February 20, 1864).

50. Jones, *Diary*, 1:263 (entry for February 23, 1863).

51. Ibid., 2:255 (entry for July 26, 1864).

52. Ibid., 2:359 (entry for December 20, 1864).

53. Ibid., 1:375, 2:49 (entries for July 8, September 21, 1863).

54. Ibid., 2:21 (entry for August 22, 1863).

55. Ibid., 1:53–54 (entry for June 21, 1861).

56. Kean, *Inside the Confederate Government*, 141 (entry for March 13, 1864).

57. Jones, *Diary*, 1:181 (entry for November 2, 1862).

58. Ibid., 2:48 (entry for September 19, 1863).

59. *New York Citizen*, July 20, 1867.

60. William Preston Johnston to William Preston, July 20, 1862, Mason Barret Collection, Tulane University, New Orleans.

61. Jones, *Diary*, 2:316 (entry for October 27, 1864).

62. Ibid., 2:414 (entry for February 9, 1865).

63. *New York Citizen*, July 20, 1867.

64. William C. Davis, *Breckinridge, Statesman, Soldier, Symbol* (Baton Rouge: Louisiana State University Press, 1974), 361.

65. George L. Crockett, *Two Centuries in East Texas* (Dallas: Southwest, 1932), n.p.

66. W. W. Porter, "Characteristics of Gen. Samuel Cooper," *Confederate Veteran* 14 (April 1906):186.

67. Jones, *Diary* 1:181 (entry for November 2, 1861).

68. Bradley Johnson to Samuel Cooper, July 23, 1864, and Jefferson Davis endorsement, July 26, 1864, Confederate Papers Relating to Army Officers, War Department Officials, and Other Individuals, Record Group 109, NA.

69. *New York Citizen*, July 20, 1867.

70. Jones, *Diary*, 1:203 (entry for December 4, 1862).

71. Ibid., 1:227 (entry for December 31, 1862).

72. Ibid., 2:51 (entry for September 23, 1863).

73. *OR*, IV, 2:1019–20; Jones, Diary 2:168 (entry for March 8, 1864).

74. Jones, *Diary*, 2:424–25 (entry for February 17, 1865).

75. J. William Jones, "The Kilpatrick-Dahlgren Raid Against Richmond," *SHSP* 13:553.

76. *OR*, ser. II, 7:550; Jones, Diary 2:315, 337, 345 (entries for October 25, November 23, December 2, 1864). Jefferson Davis, in *Rise and Fall of the Confederate Government*, 2 vols. (New York: Appleton, 1881), 2:598, said that Cooper and Winder had been classmates at West Point, and this could be interpreted as added cause for Cooper to withhold public censure of Winder's conduct. However, Davis was mistaken. Winder graduated from the Military Academy in 1820, five years after Cooper left in 1815.

77. Jones, *Diary*, 2:356 (entry for December 17, 1864).

78. Ibid., 1:42–43 (entry for May 26, 1861).

79. James L. Nichols, *General Fitzhugh Lee: A Biography* (Lynchburg, Va.: H. E. Howard, 1989), 95–96.

80. De Leon, *Belles*, 110.

81. Orlando B. Willcox, *Forgotten Valor: The Memoirs, Journals, & Civil War Letters of Orlando B. Willcox*, ed. Robert Garth Scott (Kent, Ohio: Kent State University Press 1999), 305.

82. Woodward, ed., *Mary Chesnut's Civil War*, 138, 317 (entries for August 8, 1861, March 20, 1862).

83. J. H. Lane to ———, October 23, 1864, "Glimpses of Army Life in 1864," *SHSP* 18:415.

84. Jones, *Diary*, 2:338 (entry for November 24, 1864).

85. W. H. Swallow, "Retreat of the Confederate Government from Richmond to the Gulf," *Magazine of American History* 15 (June 1886): 596–97 (hereafted cited as Swallow, "Retreat").

86. Jones, *Diary*, 2:465 (entry for April 2, 1865).

87. Stephen R. Mallory Recollections, Stephen R. Mallory Papers, Southern Historical Collection, University of North Carolina, Chapel Hill.

88. Ibid.; Swallow, "Retreat," 598.

89. Swallow, "Retreat," 600.

90. Davis to Lee, April 5, 1877, Lee, "Sketch," 276.

91. Fairfax Harrison, ed., *The Harrisons of Skimino* (N.p.: n.p., 1910), 235–41.

92. Josiah Gorgas, Extracts from My Notes Written Chiefly Soon after the Close of the War, ca. 1878, in Dunbar Rowland, ed., *Jefferson Davis Constitutionalist: His Life and Letters*, 10 vols. (Jackson: Mississippi Department of Archives and History, 1923), 8:332.

93. *OR*, 47 (3):842.

94. Davis to Lee, April 5, 1877, Lee, "Sketch," 276.

95. Harry C. Townsend Diary, May 1–7, 1865, "Townsend's Diary—January–May, 1865," *SHSP* 34:125–27.

96. http://www.generalcooper.com/dawsp.htm; Lee, "Sketch," 274.

97. Lee to Mary Lee, December 1, 1867, R. E. Lee, *Recollections and Letters of General Robert E. Lee by His Son* (Garden City, N.Y.: Doubleday, 1924), 291.

98. Lee to Cooper, August 4, 1870, in ibid., 420–21.

99. Charles M. Blackford, "The Trials and Trial of Jefferson Davis, *SHSP* 29:75, 80.

100. Virginia Mason, *The Public Life and Diplomatic Correspondence of James M. Mason: With Some Personal History by his Daughter* (Roanoke, Va.: Stone, 1903), 591–92.

101. Samuel Cooper to R. R. Stevenson, July 9, 1871, in Jefferson Davis, "Andersonville and Other War Prisons," *Confederate Veteran* 15 (March 1907):108.

102. http://www.generalcooper.com/dawsp.htm.

103. Davis to Lee, April 5, 1877, Lee, "Sketch," 274, 276.

"Thank God, He Has Rescued His Character": Albert Sidney Johnston, Southern Hamlet of the Confederacy

Stephen D. Engle

In early November 1861, a war correspondent to the *Nashville Republican Banner* came upon some Confederate commanders in Bowling Green, Kentucky. Among them was a rather tall and striking figure who wore the full general's stars. Despite his fifty-eight-years of age, he was "the very picture of good health . . . considerably above the medium size [for a man]," remarked this reporter and "heavy set, but not the least corpulent." He had dark hair with a slight curl and a "deep-set, dark and piercing eye." From his appearance, it was clear that he was "a prompt, decisive man, possessing an indomitable will and the greatest tenacity of purpose," and gave the impression of someone who was "self-reliant, bold, and dauntless, exhibiting the hero of leonine courage and unquailing energy."[1] Citizens who read the newspaper could now breathe a sigh of relief; Albert Sidney Johnston had arrived in Kentucky and with him the hopes of the Confederate war effort in the West.

Much was expected of Albert Sidney Johnston, because, like the editor's lionized assessment of him, many Americans came to believe that much could be expected from him. Southerners came to believe that Johnston was a soldier of many talents who possessed the skill, tenacity, resolve, and leadership to command successfully a large army in the Civil War. Zachary Taylor, who knew Johnston in the Mexican War, once remarked that Johnston was "the best soldier he had ever commanded." When he offered his services to Confederate provisional president Jefferson Davis in Richmond two months before arriving in Kentucky, the president "felt strengthened, knowing that a great support had thereby been added to the Confederate cause. . . . I hoped and expected that I had others who would prove generals," confided Davis, "but I knew I had one and that was Sidney Johnston."[2] Whether or not historians are satisfied that Davis's favorable assessment of Johnston's abilities was justified, Davis nonetheless believed it to be true, and his sentiment went a long way in convincing Southerners to think likewise.

Contrary to expectations, however, within seven short months Albert Sidney Johnston suffered the disabling effects of indecisiveness, which his critics claimed caused him to lose the war in the West early within the war's first year. Two of those critics were Ulysses S. Grant and John Pope, who had known Johnston before the Civil War. Grant remarked in his memoirs after the war that Johnston had impressed him as a man of "high character and ability." "His contemporaries at West Point, and officers generally who came to know him personally later and who remained on our side," Grant wrote, "expected him to prove the most formidable man to meet that the Confederacy would produce." And although neither Grant nor Pope questioned the personal courage of Johnston or his ability, after studying the orders and dispatches of Johnston years after the war, they changed their opinions. Grant wrote, "I am compelled to materially modify my views of that officer's qualifications as a soldier." "My judgement now," he remarked, "is that he was vacillating and undecided in his actions." "He did not win the distinction predicted for him by many of his friends," argued Grant, and instead proved he was "over-estimated." Pope agreed, remarking that while he was "more than willing to share with the most ardent of his admirers the conviction that he [Johnston] was a great general and military genius," he needed to "reconcile such a belief with the dictates of common sense and common experience."[3]

Albert Sidney Johnston commanded center stage among the *dramatis personae* of the Confederacy because he died on the battlefield of Shiloh. It was not that he died in combat, but that he died heroically leading a charge before the battle ended. Indeed, Thomas Connelly characterized him as the "Southern Hamlet of the Confederacy," as he epitomized the "ill-starred tragic hero, doomed to fail by uncontrollable forces and destined to be struck down at the height of success." Although it was Johnston's only battlefield experience in the war, the clash at Shiloh, April 6–7, 1862, was undeniably one of the war's greatest and most decisive battles. "Shiloh was the battle of the people," argues historian Frank Allen Dennis, "it was the one battle about which nearly everyone had an opinion." Thus, "as the legacy of Shiloh lives," Dennis contends, "so does its controversy." Even New Orleans author George Washington Cable wrote that "the South never smiled again after Shiloh." Such controversy prompted Larry Daniel to persuasively argue in a recent work that Shiloh was the battle "that changed the Civil War."[4]

Equally important to the battle's significance in the war was Johnston's prominence as a commander in the Confederacy. In the words of Albert Castel, Johnston's short-lived Civil War career has left an indelible mark in the minds of his contemporaries as one of "The Greatest Might-Have-Been's of the Civil War."[5] In his book *Articles of War*, Castel characterizes Johnston as a winner who became a loser. "Johnston's career," he argues, "first saw him emerge as a winner, then be branded a loser, in the end losing his life while—in the opinion then and since—winning a battle that, because of his death, also was lost."[6]

It may be the case that some early historians of the war, heavily influenced by those who fought the battle, heaped more acclaim on Johnston to emphasize the fact that his untimely death was another reason the Confederacy lost the war. Because his experience in the war was quite limited, the possible scenarios of his potential greatness and his ultimate demise will forever be the subject of continuing debate. Johnston's death, like that of Confederate commander Thomas J. "Stonewall" Jackson a year later at the battle of Chancellorsville, added to the postwar drama and speculative frenzy surrounding the Lost Cause. Because Johnston died so early in the war, Southerners could argue that because miracles were expected of him, his death was a turning point in the war and a significant loss to the Southern cause.[7]

Johnston did epitomize the quintessential Confederate general. His background was befitting a man of such military prominence. As a native Kentuckian born in 1803 whose father sought to educate him at one of the South's finest colleges, he enrolled in 1818, at Transylvania University in Lexington. After a brief respite from education, he returned to the university in the fall of 1821 to pursue a medical career. That year, among the university's 400 students, he met Jefferson Davis, also a native Kentuckian. The two students became friends and certainly made favorable and enduring impressions on one another that endured a lifetime. In 1822, Josiah Stoddard Johnston,

Sidney's eldest brother and prominent Louisiana lawyer and congressman, nominated his younger brother for the U.S. Military Academy at West Point. That same June, Johnston enrolled.[8]

Cadet life suited Johnston, and he found his true calling as a soldier. He was a competent student, and according to his biographer Charles Roland, once he adjusted to the military routine he made an excellent cadet. More than that, "his striking figure, sound judgement, and fine bearing quickly marked him as a leader." As a cadet of purpose and execution, he quickly earned the respect of his fellow cadets, including Leonidas Polk, Robert E. Lee, and his Transylvania colleague Jefferson Davis. He graduated eighth in his 1826 class, a well-cultivated second lieutenant in the infantry and a marked man of great promise, yet to be realized.[9]

When passing through Washington on furlough to meet his brother, the Louisiana congressman, the young and dashing officer made quite an impression in social circles about the nation's capital. Gen. Winfield Scott, the army's highest ranking officer, was instantly impressed by Johnston, so much so that he offered him a position on his staff as his aide-de-camp. The lure of field life, however, must have appeared more enticing to a young soldier than anything a staff position could offer him, and he politely turned it down. Training at the nation's elite military academy for four years certainly could not be wasted on such a staff position. Johnston wanted more personally satisfying assignments. After a brief posting with the U.S. 2nd Infantry, Lieutenant Johnston was ordered to St. Louis, Missouri, in April 1827 to join the 6th Infantry stationed at Jefferson Barracks.[10]

St. Louis was as far west as Johnston had ever been in his life. From the Missouri side of the Mississippi River, the U.S. Army launched military expeditions into the unorganized territory of the United States where a majority of Indian tribes had been relocated. It was at Jefferson Barracks that Johnston found himself at ease with his newfound responsibilities. Besides a few expeditions to subdue the Indians, Johnston spent the bulk of his early years in Missouri honing his skills as an officer, which earned him respect among his superiors. In 1829, he married Henrietta Preston, daughter of a well-respected and wealthy Louisville family. When troubles with the Sauk Indians erupted into an all-out war in 1832, Lieutenant Johnston served as an aide-de-camp and assistant adjutant to Gen. Henry Atkinson, commander of the 6th Infantry. It was from his experience in this first war that Johnston came to fully appreciate the hardships of real soldiering, routinely engaging in long fatiguing marches over inhospitable terrain and witnessing tactics unlike anything he read about as a cadet. Although he saw no significant combat, this experience was certainly not lost on Johnston. More than that, however, Johnston's performance was not lost on comrades such as Jefferson Davis, who also participated in the war and who came to know something of Johnston's personal character as a soldier.[11]

After the Black Hawk War, Johnston considered returning to civilian life as a Louisiana planter and possible political leader, like his eldest brother Josiah. Had it not been for the ill health of his wife and his growing family, which forced him to move to New Orleans for the medical benefits of the Southern weather, Johnston would never have resigned from the military in 1834. His wife's death the following year simply compounded his problems trying to make it as a farmer. At the age of thirty-three, he was a failed farmer with no wife and two small children. The tremendous grief of familial loss caused him great despair. Perhaps the only thing to look forward to was that his problems coincided with the Texans declaring their independence from the Mexicans. The ensuing hostilities inspired Johnston's return to the military—this time on a new frontier.[12]

The Lone Star Republic was just a few months old when Johnston arrived in Nacogdoches to offer his services in the summer of 1836. Standing over six feet tall and reflecting the seriousness of a soldier, his biographer wrote, "Johnston wore the look of command."[13] In need of qualified commanders and learning of Johnston's outstanding record and favorable military recommendation, the republic's provisional president, David G. Burnet, made him adjutant general with the rank of colonel. Within a year, Johnston would be promoted to brigadier general of the Army of Texas, a force he played a role in recruiting. But his fortunes turned in February 1837 when he was wounded in a duel with disgruntled Gen. Felix Huston, who felt Johnston had been promoted at Huston's expense and who demanded satisfaction. Even though Johnston lost the duel and would be bedridden for nearly a month, his decision to fight the duel earned him great admiration from those who knew the commander was not a great shot with a pistol, yet chose not to back down from a challenge. In the end, even his assailant came to respect him, and the two commanders would eventually become friends.[14]

Over the next few years, diplomatic relations waned between the two nations, but the expected war never came as neither the Mexicans nor the Texans under Pres. Sam Houston made good on their threats of invasion. When the United States recognized an independent Texas and moved toward annexation and eventual statehood, the army deteriorated as the soldiers grew frustrated and bored by inactivity and ill supervision. Johnston spent the next years battling his own frustration and demoralization with political and diplomatic affairs. His energy and sense of purpose were stifled by a disorganized Texas administration that was lacking a clear direction for the republic's future. Still, the administration and his officer comrades on the Texas frontier never lost faith that Johnston was a commander of high caliber more than suited to fulfill their expectations of him in military affairs.[15]

Over the next years, Johnston's association with the Texas problems grew into an involvement that transcended military life. He was becoming a Texas planter and was investing considerable time and energy thinking about the state's fate and how to secure its future from Indians and Mexicans. Moreover, he gave thought to how the Texans could acquire recognition from the Mexicans and create an independent republic. This required him to work with the administration in a productive way that drew him briefly into politics as secretary of war and almost as a presidential candidate of the republic.[16]

Johnston left the Texas War Department in March 1840 and spent the next five years as a civilian living in Kentucky and Texas. During his trips to Kentucky to visit his children he met and married Eliza Griffin in 1843. In the spring of 1845, he moved with his second wife and children to Galveston, where he attempted again to cultivate his life as a Texas planter. Faring no better now at this occupation than he had some years before, he was elated to see that within weeks of his arrival events between the Mexicans and Americans turned to war. Johnston welcomed the recent turn of events, for both financial and military reasons, and when Gen. Zachary Taylor personally invited him to join forces, the soldier in him prevailed. His attempt to gain rank in the U.S. Regular Army failed, but the volunteers of the 1st Texas Regiment elected him colonel, and Johnston was back in command.[17]

From the look of things to Johnston, it was obvious that despite years of precipitating a war with Mexico, when it actually commenced the Texans were wholly unprepared. After several weeks of training the men, Johnston was ordered to support General Taylor's 6,000-man advance up the Rio Grande to attack the city of Monterrey, a key objective in Taylor's northern Mexico campaign. By the time the army actually moved, however, many of the soldiers in Johnston's command were about to leave the army as their enlistment period expired. As a consequence, Johnston was the ranking officer of a regiment that simply left before it even saw combat. As a result, Taylor appointed Johnston to Gen. William O. Butler's division of volunteers as a staff officer.[18]

Johnston saw considerable combat in the battle of Monterrey, which lasted five days, September 20–25, 1846, and the young commander managed to distinguish himself on the field. When General Butler was wounded, Johnston demonstrated the kind of bravery and leadership that would distinguish him as a leader in combat. At one point during the battle, Johnston became separated from his commander. Seeing that the frightened and chaotic volunteers were without direction, Johnston rode up and ordered them to take positions and fire. Capt. Joseph Hooker was with Johnston throughout the combat and remarked later that Johnston was the outstanding officer of the entire division. "It was through [Johnston's] agency, mainly, that our division was saved from a cruel slaughter," wrote Hooker; "the coolness and magnificent presence [that he] displayed on this field . . . left an impression on my mind that I have never forgotten."[19]

Interestingly enough, just as soon as Johnston entered the Mexican War, he exited almost as quickly—a possible foreboding of things to come. At the peak of his military career, Johnston was not assigned to other commands, a curious turn in his career as he had certainly impressed his superiors and was expecting a new assignment. Nonetheless, he returned to the planter life on his Texas plantation and raised his family. Although tilling the soil reconnected him with the Southern way of life, he maintained a relatively modest lifestyle and remained virtually destitute. When Zachary Taylor became the president of the United States in 1848, he offered his old military warrior the responsibilities as paymaster of the frontier Texas forts, which Johnston accepted out of financial necessity. For the next six years, Johnston traversed the Texas landscape in this capacity. In 1855, his old friend Jefferson Davis, then secretary of war under the Franklin Pierce administration, appointed him colonel of the newly created 2nd Cavalry Regiment, ordered to protect the Texas frontier against the invasions of the Comanche Indians. Here he came to know Robert E. Lee and other commanders who went on to distinguish themselves in the Civil War.[20]

In the summer of 1857, Johnston was appointed commander of the U.S. force that was to march to the Utah territory to suppress the threatened rebellion by the Mormons and establish federal authority. For nearly three years, Johnston was the commander of an expedition that did little more than occupy the region of the Great Plains and the Rocky Mountains. Still, he proved more than capable in seeing to the army's survival in the inhospitable terrain and weather. The aging commander demonstrated outstanding leadership by guiding his men through the harsh winters of the region and by seeing to every detail of his command. Stretching his supplies, maintaining morale in the ranks, and handling the political aspects of his force uniformly impressed the nearly 2,000 soldiers of his command as well as the administration. "Nothing escapes his notice," wrote one officer, and his efforts earned him the promotion to brevet brigadier general.[21]

Johnston's handling of the Mormon expedition earned him respect from his superiors. He was allowed an extended leave of absence from the army in the spring of 1860. In November of the same year, Johnston was appointed commander of the army's Department of the Pacific, and he and his family journeyed west. He had hardly arrived in San Francisco and assumed his new duties when the Civil War broke out. The fact that he was an officer in the U.S. Army and had fought for three decades against the Indians, Mexicans, and Mormons, and that his adoptive state of Texas seceded February 1, 1861, made his tenure in the military suspect.[22]

Johnston's military career reflected his devout nationalism; his patriotism to the United States was without question. Not only had he developed a keen sense of honor and loyalty to his military calling and to the nation it supported, he came to believe in the strength of the Union. Still, his Union was one that the people of the seceded states had apparently come to believe could not endure under Republican leadership. His belief, like that of hundreds of thousands of Southerners, was that the Republican Party had simply refused to concede anything to Southerners for the sake of the Union. When he learned that Texas had seceded from the Union, he resigned his commission in the army just days before the firing on Fort Sumter. "I felt, as soon as I learned the course adopted by my State," wrote Johnston, "that it was my duty to conform to her will."[23] He had plenty of time to contemplate his next move. After making arrangements to have his family and pregnant wife travel by ship and rail to Texas, Johnston departed California and headed overland on an 800-mile journey to Texas.[24]

Eliza Gilpin, Johnston's sister, wrote from her Philadelphia home to her nephew, William Preston Johnston, urging him to convince his father not to resign. She did acknowledge that he had always been the "soul of honor," and thus she respected his decision.[25] Honor, however, did not support a family, and Johnston knew it. Although he was torn between remaining out of the conflict and offering his services to the Confederacy, after a month of "soul searching," Johnston cast his lot with the Confederacy. "It seems like fate," he wrote to his sister-in-law, "that Texas has made me a Rebel twice."[26]

Johnston reached Texas in late July and from there he headed toward the Confederate capital in Virginia. Despite his fifty-eight years of age, the war veteran was still the embodiment of a rugged, stout commander with an assured step and bearing that he had had when he graduated from the Academy. No wonder that Pres. Jefferson Davis was relieved to hear a familiar step in the Confederate White House when Johnston arrived at the end of the second week in September. Davis held Johnston in the highest esteem. As cadets, young officers, honorable combat veterans, and devoted loyalists to the notion of states' rights, the two men had come to appreciate the other's talents firsthand. Davis admired in Johnston the commander whom he firmly believed possessed tremendous military skill. Because he expected much from the Texan he gave him a task equal to those expectations. He appointed him a full general and named him commander of Department Number Two—the Confederacy's largest military department, which comprised parts of Mississippi, Alabama, Louisiana, Tennessee, and Arkansas, as well as military operations in Kentucky, Missouri, Kansas, and the Indian Territory. It was a vast responsibility indeed; Davis believed Johnston was "the only man who seemed equal to it."[27]

If Johnston was the match for the Confederacy's Western command, and if his superiors, his soldiers, as well as the public, expected much of him, it was because Jefferson Davis created about the commander an aura of success in which people came to believe. Johnston certainly wore the look of command, and he now had the departmental responsibilities that would test his merit as a commander of the highest rank. John Pope, who knew Johnston before the war, remarked that "a more noble, generous man and altogether honorable gentleman never wore the uniform of a soldier." "His engaging manners, his gracious smile, his noble countenance and fine martial figure," Pope remarked, "captivated all who came near him," and "I do not wonder that men were devoted to him and more than anxious to invest him with every high quality of which man is capable." When he arrived at the department's headquarters in Nashville in mid-September, the Civil War was five months old and residents of the heartland had been preparing with dizzying speed for the inevitable scourge of war. Recognizing that because of its proximity, the war would certainly devastate the Blue-grass State, Kentuckians had attempted to remain neutral.[28]

This neutrality, of course, underscored the very complexity regarding the nature of war and forced commanders on both sides to come to grips with having to secure two very different aspects of war. First, both sought to occupy the heartland's rivers, cities, railroads. Second, both would have to maintain the support of the people in these regions, as Johnston told a crowd in Nashville. Though he had returned to his native state, the commander found himself in the midst of a very complex set of problems that had more to do with the relationship between loyalty and locality than simply defending the western Confederacy against invasion and securing the states of Kentucky and Missouri along the vital Mississippi and Ohio rivers. "The defenseless condition of this department," concluded Johnston, "was patent from the moment I arrived and had a hasty view of the field. The necessity for a strong and efficient army is present and pressing."[29]

More than any other obstacle to Johnston's success, his department contained the entire Confederacy's weaknesses—navigable rivers that stretched far into the heartland and a bitterly divided population settled among the nation's most vital resources for wartime materials. Besides the Mississippi and the Ohio, wrote Allan Nevins, "a mere glance at the map would seem to reveal that the Tennessee-Cumberland river system offered the North a heaven-sent opportunity to thrust a harpoon into the very bowels of the Confederacy."[30] Moreover, wrote Avery Craven, "there were at least three Tennessees with Knoxville, Nashville, and Memphis at their centers."[31] What gave the Confederate heartland added logistical and economic prominence was its standing as the South's primary source for the production of war materials. As Thomas Connelly keenly observed, "the entire Heartland seemed a maze of such small but critical installations."[32]

All of these problems were to be solved by a commander whose military prowess was certainly not matched by the resources at his disposal. According to Steven Woodworth, Johnston "faced a situation unprecedented in his experience or in that of any other living American." In his command were roughly 40,000 ill-equipped soldiers who had been dispersed to defend the Kentucky-Tennessee line. After conferring with Tennessee governor Isham Harris, Johnston concluded that Kentucky neutrality was a thing of the past. With Felix Zollicof-fer anchoring the right flank of his several-hundred-mile-long line and Leonidas Polk anchoring his left flank at Columbus on the Mississippi River, the only likely path of Union invasion was over the railroad from Louisville to Nashville. To seize Bowling Green, Kentucky, on the Louisville-Nashville Railroad, Johnston dispatched a force under Kentucky West Pointer, Brig. Gen. Simon Bolivar Buckner. On Sep-tember 22, the Confederate commander issued a formal proclamation that rationalized his decision to enter the Bluegrass State. He reasoned that the Confederate army was in Kentucky because of a prior inva-sion by the United States, and that Confederate government's army "shall be withdrawn from Kentucky as soon as there shall be satisfac-tory evidence of the existence and execution of a like intention on the part of the United States."[33]

The truth was that Johnston's forces had begun to strengthen their position in Kentucky, hoping to hold on long enough for Confederate authorities to send reinforcements and for pro-South leaders in the state to rally its citizens to the Confederate cause. Johnston learned a valu-able lesson about the keenly political nature of the war; wherever he fought he would need the support of the people to sustain his army's occupation of their soil. If not, the fighting was futile. Still, the great weakness of the Confederacy—the rivers—remained neglected.[34]

While Johnston waited, the sprawling Confederate line that stretched from the Appalachians to the western border of Arkansas was beginning to feel the weight of war. As the weeks of September passed into October and November, the importance of President Davis's previous instructions to Polk to defend both banks of the Mis-sissippi and the area extending to the Tennessee River, but not the area between the Tennessee and the Cumberland Rivers, became clear. Holding on to the Mississippi River proved the more crucial to Polk, and the commander left the twelve miles that separated the Tennessee and Cumberland Rivers virtually unattended. When Johnston assumed command of the department, he understood that the Union forces could campaign on the rivers. He thought Polk was responsible for evaluating the strategic significance of the positions and fortifying them. Convinced that Fort Henry and Fort Donelson were fine as established, Polk decided simply to complete and fortify their con-struction and remained focused on securing Columbus. Although he was aware of the forts' vulnerability, Polk did little to change the situation. Though concerned about the situation with the river forts,

Johnston, nonetheless, failed to impress upon Polk their strategic importance. In November, the War Department placed Brig. Gen. Lloyd Tilghman in command of overseeing the construction of Forts Henry and Donelson, with the expectation that he could get the job done quickly.[35]

Polk's and Tilghman's neglect was not the only reason the forts remained incomplete and undermanned; Johnston had allowed his subordinates too much independence of judgment. In hindsight, it is easy to conclude that Johnston failed to see that the situation required considerable oversight of his department and its commanders. According to Steven Woodworth, not only did much depend on Johnston's ability "to adapt and adjust to the new situation as it pertained to not only the size of the conflict and the resources at his disposal but also a hodgepodge of inexpert and uncooperative subordinates." Whatever the faults, the cumulative impact of the Confederates' failure to secure the forts was ultimately Johnston's responsibility. Certainly he had more alarming reports suggesting the Union command would come from overland, but Johnston also had convincing evidence that the forts needed attention. In mid-January, however, Union commander Ulysses S. Grant found the weakness of the Confederacy in the West, and while Johnston hastened Tilghman to occupy the heights opposite Fort Henry, it was evident that this was the weak point in the entire Confederate line.[36]

Johnston was also considerably preoccupied with events elsewhere in his vast domain. The fact that Union commander Don Carlos Buell had amassed a large army in Louisville and was surely about to depart south to Bowling Green and then Nashville, and that his counterpart in Missouri, Henry Halleck, might head down the Mississippi River from St. Louis, kept Johnston focused on what he considered the more ominous routes of invasion. More than that, however, Johnston desperately needed an army equal to his huge responsibility and support from a president who appreciated and understood this urgency. While Johnston attempted to strengthen his forces by seeking volunteers, he also tried to convince Davis that the war in the Mississippi Valley was most important at the moment. Fears of Union advances on Richmond subordinated Davis's concerns relative to the dangers of a broad Federal invasion in the West. Johnston, however, had seen the strategic importance of the heartland since coming to Bowling Green, but the region remained neglected. He alerted Secretary of War Judah P. Benjamin that an 80,000-man Federal army was about to invade the Confederacy through central Kentucky. "They have justly comprehended that the seat of vitality of the Confederacy, if to be reached at all, is by this route," Johnston asserted, adding that "it is now palpable that all the resources of that Government will, if necessary, be employed to assure success on this line." "No doubt the strongest attack the enemy is capable of making will be made against this place," he proclaimed, "and we ought not surely to put in jeopardy the result by failing to meet it with a force sufficient to place success beyond hazard."[37]

But the Confederate government never provided Johnston with the sufficient force, and the frustrated commander attempted to concentrate his scattered troops to hold the Kentucky line and to make it appear as though his defensive line was stronger than it actually was. However, in this defensive mentality, Confederate governors sought to guard every corner of the Confederacy. Thus, neither Davis nor Johnston was able to concentrate effectively the Confederate forces to be successful in any one place. Still, Johnston requested reinforcements from Davis that he assumed would help focus the attention of political leaders on points of weakness. He displayed a passive attitude toward pressing the government for the things needed in his command, and consequently his department and army suffered. Perhaps such requests would have made him appear weak and not suited for the task. Nonetheless, he suggested to the president that units in departments not threatened by the enemy might be transferred to his command. His passive strategy changed in mid-January when he bypassed the chain of command and dispatched Col. St. John R. Liddell to Richmond to ask Davis in person for troops from Virginia, Charleston, Savannah, Pensacola, and New Orleans. A frustrated Davis lashed out that he had neither troops nor arms to spare. "Tell my friend, General Johnston," he told Liddell, "that I can do nothing for him." As much as he admired and respected his old friend, Davis could not be shaken from his apathy regarding the situation in the West.[38]

Johnston knew that Buell and Halleck were aware of his lack of strength, which gave the Federals considerable leverage in determining when and where they would strike at his defensive line. Grant's January demonstration on the Tennessee River had frozen the Confederates. The Union victory at Mill Springs, Kentucky, was Johnston's first defeat in his department and resulted partly because Felix Zollicoffer was overly aggressive. It came also because Johnston gave the area of eastern Kentucky, as he had done in western Tennessee, to an

untried subordinate. Allowing commanders such as Polk and Zollicof-
fer considerable independence was partially the result of Johnston's
inexperience in directing a large army on a broad, exposed defensive
line. With the Confederate defeat, Johnston stepped up his pleas for
reinforcements with more vigor, but Davis was unmoved.[39]

Throughout the fall and early winter, Johnston had concealed his
army's weaknesses by staging a series of raids along the entire front,
especially in the East, while he strove to create an army behind this
screen. Still, he was more successful in masking his weaknesses than
overcoming them largely because commanders such as Buell spent
considerable time anticipating Johnston's moves and reacting to the
fear of them rather than acting aggressively. Grant, on the other hand,
had probed the Confederate line and found the weakness. What Johnston could not mask was the obvious fact that the Tennessee and Cumberland Rivers flooded every winter, and this year would be no
different. As the sole Confederate obstacle in the path into northern
Mississippi and Alabama, Fort Henry would certainly succumb to
flooding, but if not, the Federals would be there soon enough.[40]

On February 6, Fort Henry fell to the Union gunboats of Andrew
Foote. The Confederate commander at the fort, Tilghman, surrendered
the Tennessee River fort, but not before his forces escaped and headed
to Fort Donelson, twelve miles east on the Cumberland River. In the
words of Confederate provisional governor of Kentucky, George W.
Johnson, the fall of Fort Henry "waked up" the South, but little could
be done to wake up Richmond authorities fast enough to prevent the
same fate for Fort Donelson. Embarrassing though it was to Davis's
administration, it was hardly unexpected. Johnston had bemoaned
his lack of resources to hold vital points for weeks. Recognizing
that an attack on Fort Donelson was imminent, Johnston reasoned
to Confederate authorities that given the Union penetration on the
rivers, he was contemplating concentrating his forces somewhere
below Nashville. This of course had political as well as military
ramifications, because it meant either diminishing or eliminating the
positions in central Kentucky and eastern Tennessee. Furthermore,
he had to consider Columbus and Bowling Green on the southern
bank of the Green River. Johnston continued to believe that Grant
would follow up his expedition with a move on Columbus. At a
time when Confederate leadership could not afford disarray, the
war in the West caused serious problems in deciding where to concentrate resources.[41]

The departure of Grant's army from Fort Henry toward Fort Donelson was a significant turn in the Western Theater of war. It forced the Confederate high command to make consequential strategic decisions and make them fast. Yet in a council of war on February 7, Johnston was unable to get a consensus among his commanders about the next move, and the disagreement reflected the fate of a deteriorating leadership. Newly arrived from Virginia, P. G. T. Beauregard favored abandoning Bowling Green and concentrating on the rivers, but Johnston remained fearful of Buell's threat on Nashville. Recognizing the vulnerability of Fort Donelson and the Kentucky-Tennessee line, the commanders decided not to concentrate there but instead fall back to Nashville. Still, knowing that Donelson was untenable, Johnston committed more men to go to the fort and defend it than he could afford to lose. He also assumed that if he retreated to Nashville, his subordinates could at least maintain delaying actions to hold off the bulk of the Union army until Confederate forces could assemble elsewhere. Johnston would entrust Fort Donelson, to John Bell Floyd, and he decided not to make a trip to the fort to determine what could be done. "When [Johnston] shunned the Donelson responsibility," concluded Thomas Connelly, "he gave indication that he was losing command of himself and of the Army."[42] For some reason, according to T. Harry Williams, Johnston "seemed obsessed with the idea that he personally had to conduct the column at Bowling Green to safety."[43]

When Floyd arrived at Donelson with the remnants of his brigade and assumed command, it brought total troop strength of the garrison to roughly 17,000 men. Over the next few days, the Confederate high command experienced even more indecision. While some advocated fighting at Donelson, others agreed that falling back toward Clarksville and Nashville was the only hope for the soldiers. Nonetheless, the Union amphibious expedition advanced across the Tennessee landscape and up the Cumberland River. By February 12-13, the Federals, who had practically encircled the fort, began their assault by land and were waiting on Union boats to advance closer before launching an all-out assault.[44]

On February 16, Fort Donelson fell to the Union forces. Whether Johnston did or did not make a trip to inspect the fort became irrelevant in light of the fact that his army was not large enough to defend both the river and land routes of invasion in the West. He was forced to choose between losing some strategic points and saving, in his estimation, more vital ones. Beauregard echoed this sentiment in his remarks to Confederate congressman Roger A. Pryor. "We must give up some minor points, and concentrate our forces to save the most important one," argued Beauregard, "or we will lose all of them in succession." Indeed, the Creole confessed that he was "taking the helm when the ship is already in the breakers and with but few sailors to man it."[45] Still, in Johnston's view Nashville was more important than Fort Donelson, and no doubt the residents of that city helped inform his decision on this matter. Even Beauregard admitted that Johnston was doing the best he could under the circumstances, "but what can he do against such tremendous odds?" Still, the loss of Fort Donelson would, in Beauregard's estimation, "be followed by consequences too lamentable to be now alluded to."[46]

When Simon Bolivar Buckner surrendered the Confederate fort to Ulysses S. Grant, the South had lost the line of the Tennessee and Cumberland Rivers and with it perhaps the whole defensive line in the West. The heartland now was open to Union penetration by land and sea. Soon, Confederate officials worried, the very backbone (the Memphis and Charleston Railroad) of the Confederacy would be next, and there were no troops to defend it. "The people will abandon the country to the occupation of the enemy," wrote Leroy P. Walker, former Confederate secretary of war, to Judah P. Benjamin.[47]

The Southern people placed the blame for the loss of Donelson squarely on the shoulders of Albert Sidney Johnston. No longer was the Confederate commander the lion of the West, as newspapermen had previously editorialized. The blunders in mid-February had relocated the war from Kentucky to Tennessee, and Nashville was directly in the path of Don Carlos Buell's strong army heading south. As a sense of urgency fell upon the residents of the Tennessee capital, angry mobs rioted, and at one point a group forced its way into Johnston's headquarters demanding an explanation for the defeat and his plans for the next campaign. Kentuckians shared this fear, as the Union penetration meant occupation. Provisional governor George W. Johnson wrote his wife, "the time of our severest afflictions has now come—our state is about to be abandoned by our armies."[48]

Political animosity followed closely behind public opinion. Tennessee congressmen sent a delegation to President Davis in the second week in March calling for Johnston's removal, claiming that "confidence is no longer felt in the military skill of Gen. A. S. Johnston."[49] Some representatives declared that Johnston had inexcusably lost the Mississippi Valley and demanded that Congress vote to investigate his conduct in the recent losses. At first, the president thought of going to the West, not to replace Johnston but rather to reassure the people there that all was not lost. Johnston encouraged the president to make the trip. Indeed, Davis was concerned about these disasters, citing them on February 22 as he officially accepted the presidency of the Confederate States of America. Though an unpopular move at the time, Davis stood by his trusted friend and kept him in command. "If [Johnston] is a not a general," Davis remarked, "we had better give up the war, for we have no general."[50] Critics then turned on Davis for his refusal to dismiss Johnston, arguing that the president himself should come to the West and take command, which was, they believed, the only way to revitalize what many came to believe was a thoroughly demoralized army.[51]

Had the military defeat not gone beyond the borders of the Kentucky, the criticism might have waned. But Middle Tennesseans now contemplated Yankee occupation of their rivers and their communities. The defeat cut into the social fabric of the Upper South society and economy. Though he refused to respond to the unforgiving criticism, the complaints of the people were not lost on Johnston. He kept his composure and exhibited a quiet dignity of character that had earlier won him supporters. He would later write privately to Davis that "[the] test of merit in my profession with the people, is success. It is a hard rule, but I think it right."[52] Indeed, it was a hard rule he learned, so much so that he vowed never to repeat his mistake—perhaps a foreshadowing of his urge to make something striking happen at Shiloh.[53]

Though Davis's support for Johnston was unchanged by the loss at Donelson, Johnston's strategic dilemma remained the same. The vastness of the area he had been charged to defend still dwarfed the few resources he had been allowed by an administration blinded by the war nearer Richmond. More to the point, the Union forces were on the move south in Middle Tennessee and the Mississippi Valley, and Johnston had to decide quickly which area would get his full attention. Clarksville fell on February 20, as did Nashville a week later. In Johnston's mind, without the ability to concentrate his forces quickly, the city was untenable. Besides his soldiers were thoroughly disheartened, and to remain in the capital city might prove worse to the morale of his command. Still, the loss of Nashville, at a time when Southern papers had reported that Johnston would make a stand to save the city at all costs, stunned the infant nation. With the Tennessee capital gone, Johnston lost his logistical and industrial base. Confederate authorities were concerned that Kentuckians and Tennesseans sympathetic to the South would not be able to endure long in a region occupied by the Union armies. More than that, Johnston needed to return his forces to the region and reassert Confederate control.[54]

Johnston had his army fall back to Murfreesboro, and from there it would move west as commanders would attempt to gather their forces at Corinth, Mississippi, a strategic railroad junction. Thomas Connelly argued that Johnston's army was severely dissatisfied with him, and that as a result he allowed Beauregard to assume conceptual superiority in designing the Confederate army's next move. While Connelly paints Beauregard as formidable and conniving in this situation, Charles Roland and Steven Woodworth perceived Johnston to still be in control of the army and Beauregard's actions the result of a "very genuine and sincere panic and state of virtual nervous collapse." Perhaps more significant was that Jefferson Davis refused to assert his own authority in making decisions for either of them.[55]

Still, once Beauregard found his prominence in the Confederate command in the West, he never relinquished his authority—in part because, as James McDonough argues, "Johnston seemed unable to grasp the total command picture of his department." In fact, McDonough contends that the correspondence during this time between Johnston and Beauregard "would leave an unknowing reader with the certain impression that it was Beauregard, rather than Johnston, who was in command." To stir public support for reinforcements to be sent to Mississippi, it was Beauregard, not Johnston, who addressed a confidential circular to the governors of Louisiana, Mississippi, Tennessee, and Alabama to supply vital troops to strengthen the army. Although there was little response from the governors, Davis consented to allow the Confederate concentration in the West at the expense of giving up some other regions. The War Department not only ordered Maj. Gen. Braxton Bragg north from the Gulf Coast to Corinth but also ordered Maj. Gen. Edmund Kirby Smith and his small command of East Tennesseans to cooperate with Johnston.[56]

Despite writing to Davis on March 7 that he considered the "tone of the troops" to be restored, Johnston must have been aware of the demoralized state of his men, particularly his subordinates, who now looked to Beauregard to restore the Confederate hopes that Johnston had diminished. An early biographer of Beauregard, Hamilton Basso, characterized Johnston at this time as depressed by the fact that he knew he had lost the confidence of the men, which compelled him to consider offering the command to Beauregard. Although lacking the official authority to form the newly arriving troops into a large army, Beauregard and Bragg would soon take charge of them anyway and do, according to T. Harry Williams, "what Johnston should have done."[57] The Texan still controlled the army, but Beauregard and Bragg were constructing it. They restored a faith in the men that a better fortune awaited them.[58]

The spring rains played havoc with the gathering of Confederate forces. The inhospitable weather and the failure to make effective use of railroads hampered road travel, and it would take nearly a month for Johnston to concentrate his army at Corinth. In the meantime, Davis, at the receiving end of numerous letters critical of Johnston, broke his month-long silence about the Donelson fiasco and wrote to the commander. The very importance of February's events began to dawn on the Confederate president. "We have suffered great anxiety because of recent events in Ky & Tenn," he confided, "and I have been not a little disturbed by the repetitions of reflections upon yourself. You have been held responsible for the fall of Donelson and the capture of Nashville, [and] a full development of the truth is necessary for future success." The Confederate president closed by supposing that the "Tenn. or Miss. rivers will be the object of the enemy's next campaign, and I trust you will be able to concentrate a force which will defeat either attempt."[59]

Davis still had confidence in Johnston, but these words were not lost on the melancholy commander as he rode into Corinth on the night of March 22. Over the next two weeks, Corinth would mirror the insufficiency of his command. After a few days and considerable reflection upon the situation, he surprised Beauregard by offering him command, an acknowledgment that his soldiers and the Southern public had lost confidence in him. More than that, Johnston had lost confidence in himself. Beauregard recalled after the war that Johnston "gravely and impressively declared, with visible emotion, that with my consent he would turn over to me the direct command of all the troops now collected at Corinth," and that "in his [Johnston's] opinion, the adoption of such a course would instill renewed confidence in the people, and even in the army, and eventually benefit the success of our cause." Johnston's offer to Beauregard certainly embarrassed him more than surprised him. Although the Creole appreciated Johnston's motives and gesture, he was not enthusiastic about leading the army

and instead agreed to be named second-in-command. Still, it was
Beauregard who drew up the plan to reorganize the army. Johnston's
biographer, Charles Roland, provides an insightful assessment of
Johnston's rationale for offering Beauregard the command, agreeing
with the Creole that Johnston had come to believe that "the army and
the people no longer trusted his leadership and that the Confederate
cause would be better served with Beauregard in command." In Johnston's mind, it was the honorable thing to do, and Beauregard agreed.
When Beauregard declined the command, he essentially returned the
honorable gesture, and Johnston knew he had another opportunity to
"retrieve his reputation as a general."[60]

In the days following Johnston's attempt to relieve himself from
overall command, he received one of his last dispatches from President
Davis. The president confided to the disheartened commander that "my
confidence in you has never wavered, and I hope the public will soon
give me credit for judgement rather than arraign me for obstinacy." He
closed by saying that it would be "worse than useless to point out to you
how much depends upon you." The point was well taken. By early
April, Johnston determined that his army must hit the Federals commanded by Brig. Gen. William T. Sherman encamped at Pittsburg Landing before Buell's army arrived from Nashville and gave the Union a
significant numerical advantage before heading south to Corinth. If the
Union soldiers expected great fortunes in Mississippi, it was in Tennessee where a better fate awaited the Confederates, or so they hoped.
Moreover, the impending battle was vital to Johnston's place in the
Confederate command, and Davis pointed out as much when he dispatched perhaps his last message to the Southern commander on April
5. It reads: "I hope you will be able to close with the enemy before his
two columns unite." More starkly to the point, Johnston recognized, was
the line that followed: "I anticipate victory."[61]

From his tent near Pittsburg Landing on the night of April 5, Johnston was painfully aware that he needed victory in the looming battle.
Win or lose, this would unquestionably be the turning point in his
career. Thus, for no other commanders, North or South, would the
next days play such a pivotal role in determining their worth to the
nations they served. Sidney Johnston's great crisis was near. When, in
the early Sunday morning hours of April 6 the crackling of musketry
could be heard in the distance from where Johnston and his men sat
eating breakfast, Johnston completely understood he had been given
new life when Beaurgeard declined his command. Now he must prove

his valor and live up to the expectations the president and the Southern populace had heaped on him. Rising to his feet, the towering commander remarked, "The battle has opened gentlemen; it is too late to change our dispositions." Mounting his thoroughbred, the general turned to his staff and, hoping to stir the soldiers, remarked "Tonight we will water our horses in the Tennessee River."[62]

As it soon became known by Southerners, the battle of Shiloh was the bloodiest clash on the North American continent up to that time. From the predawn hours until sun appeared overhead, Sherman's men fought valiantly to prevent succumbing to the surprise attack the Southerners had achieved. The complete failure of the Union commanders to prepare for such an attack astounded Southern commanders, who pressed their advantage throughout the morning. By midday on April 6, more Americans had fallen in combat at this unknown Tennessee landscape than had fallen in the war thus far. Johnston had encouraged his soldiers all morning, and at about 2 P.M. the commander took charge of a demoralized Tennessee regiment and persuaded it to make another advance in the face of overwhelming odds. More than that, he decided personally to lead the men in a charge on the Union lines. As he rode in front of the men, rallying them on, Johnston had perhaps made peace with the fact that he was either going to lead these men to victory or die trying. The fact that he rode with these men within easy range of the enemy's musket fire provided credible evidence that he hoped to redeem himself at Shiloh. James McDonough argued that Johnston's battlefield action marked the end of his authority as the army's commander. Rather than "acting as supreme commander of an army," observed McDonough, "Johnston was playing the role of a gallant combat leader," which caused him to be mortally wounded. He was shot in the leg and bled to death. When he expired roughly a half an hour later on the battlefield, Beauregard took command of the army. When the day's fighting ended and night fell, Buell's 25,000-man army arrived, and reinforced Grant's battered army. The following day, the combined Union army overwhelmed the Confederates, forcing them to retreat back to Corinth.[63]

The battle of Shiloh ended in Confederate defeat. More significantly, it ended in defeat after the death of Johnston. This, of course, allowed contemporaries and historians to raise the issue of whether the Confederate army would have won the battle had he lived. Several prominent newspapers carried the story of Johnston's death for months after the battle, arguing that Johnston was convinced he was

winning the battle when he led the charge and that his death brought
defeat. The *Southern Illustrated News* was representative of this kind
of editorializing, commenting that Johnston "fell where heroes love to
fall—in the arms of victory upon the battlefield." Like Thomas Connelly and T. Harry Williams before him, Albert Castel argues convincingly that while it is conceivable that had Johnston remained in
command "he might have provided the will and found the means to
defeat the Union forces on April 6," the greater likelihood is that Johnston "would have done essentially the same as Beauregard did, for the
same reasons, and with the same outcome." "To contend otherwise, as
some of his advocates do," Castel declares, "is to credit him with powers of leadership bordering on the incredible and to claim he would
have achieved what no other commander, Union or Confederate,
achieved during the whole Civil War: Total battlefield victory over a
major, still potent enemy army."[64] If Johnston's army had overwhelmed Grant's army on the first day of the battle, Castel insists that
"his own army would have been too depleted, exhausted, and disorganized to follow up its triumph by defeating Buell."[65]

Interestingly enough Castel raises another important issue relative
to the role Johnston played in the West compared with the role that
Robert E. Lee played in the East. He did possess the "aggressiveness,
willingness to take great risks, resolution and persistence in overcoming great obstacles, composure and decisiveness when faced with a
crisis, and an intellect and personal character that inspired trust, even
devotion, in others," as Castel asserts. But he lacked the competent
supporting cast of subordinates and, frankly, was compelled to operate
and defend a region of the country that would surely have pressed
even Robert E. Lee. Still, Thomas Connelly argued that in the mythology that appeared after the war, Sidney Johnston's role and death at
Shiloh surpassed Lee as the epitome of the "what-might-have-been"
syndrome. To conclude otherwise would force Johnston's advocates to
believe that there were some flaws in his leadership and thus some
imperfections in their idol.[66]

But there is more to Johnston than the battle of Shiloh. The circumstances of his death and the posturing of postwar what if's and
Lost Cause mythology created a Johnston mystique. "No figure had
such a unique hold on the South," concluded Connelly; "he represented two powerful currents of both the wartime and the postwar
Confederate mind." Thus, Johnston's role as a Confederate general
must be seen in the larger context of the issues surrounding the entire

political, social, and military situation in the war in the West in the early part of 1862. Given the vastness of his department and the fact it included a populace of bitterly divided loyalties, Johnston's responsibility was greater and far more complex than anyone could have anticipated, certainly greater than the Confederate government understood. Still, at the time of his entrance into the war, his contemporaries came to believe he could bring about the success they expected, whether historians believed this to be true years later or not. And although contemporaries believed the war was to be fought primarily in the East for the seizure of capital cities, it was in the West, and in the great Confederate heartland, where the war was ultimately won. The nationalistic sentiment that characterized postwar narratives and remembrances of the Confederacy made the war in the West more significant to the Lost Cause; therefore, the loss of Johnston so early in the war was all the more critical to the Confederate cause. Braxton Bragg, Leonidas Polk, William Hardee, Richard Taylor, Basil Duke, Jefferson Davis, and a host of other political and civil leaders expressed an inflated representation of Johnston to the Confederacy after his death at Shiloh. Bragg, for example, remarked that nothing "contributed so largely to our loss of time—which was the loss of success—as the fall of the commanding general." Davis argued years after the war that Johnston's death was the "fall of the great pillar of the Southern Confederacy."[67]

Whether or not historians believe Johnston was deserving of the high praise and public investment of hopes in him in the war in the West when he came to Nashville in September 1861, the fact remains that the people at the time came to believe he was the savior of the Confederacy. The criticism was so severe of him after the fall of Donelson precisely because of the enormity of the situation. Historians have been fruitful in passing judgments on his military ability, his worthiness of high praise as a commander of the West, and the significance of his role and death at Shiloh. "Had Sidney Johnston lived," argued Wiley Sword, "the course of the war in the West might have followed a different track." Had Johnston lost the battle of Shiloh and lived, as Steven Woodworth boldy contends, he "might have changed the course of the war."[68]

In the final analysis, whether historians of the war judged him to be a commander worthy of high praise when he came to the West or not, and whether or not the events of Fort Henry and Fort Donelson soon disproved what Southerners wanted to believe about him, his death at Shiloh, Southerners believed, constituted a turning point in the war. They judged him to be of incalculable value to the Southern cause. As a result, Johnston and his significance to the Southern effort continues to attract scholarly attention. In the end, Johnston himself, "a capable and resolute officer with excellent strategic and tactical abilities and exceptional leadership qualities" as Woodworth argues, who appreciated that the test of merit for a commanding general was success, would have a good case to argue that the circumstances in the West in 1862 "required of him an extreme quickness in learning and exacted a high price for mistakes already made."[69]

No wonder then that when Johnston died, at least one perceptive Southern editor remarked, "Thank God, he has rescued his character." No doubt this editor, of the *Natchez Weekly Courier* writing on April 8, 1862, recognized the controversy that was to come in the postwar years. Because the Southern populace had invested so many hopes in a Confederate general from whom they wanted to believe great things could be expected, the circumstances of his death eclipsed the imperfections of their Southern idol. Provided with the opportunity to once again inflate his character and elevate his status, they exhalting one of the war's what-might-have-been's. In doing so, Southerners could now argue, they thought convincingly, that by dying on the battlefield Johnston had rescued his character. [70]

NOTES

I am grateful to T. Michael Parrish for assisting me with this essay.

1. J. Cutler Andrews, *The South Reports the Civil War* (Princeton, N.J.: Princeton University Press, 1970), 120.

2. Charles P. Roland, *Albert Sidney Johnston: Soldier of Three Republics* (Austin: University of Texas Press, 1964), 260 (hereafter cited as Roland, *Albert Sidney Johnston*); Steven E. Woodworth, "When the Test of Merit Was Not Enough: Albert Sidney Johnston and Confederate Defeat in the West, 1862," in Steven E. Woodworth, *Civil War Generals in Defeat* (Lawrence: University Press of Kansas, 1999), 9 (hereafter cited as Woodworth, *Civil War Generals in Defeat*); Hudson Strode, *Jefferson Davis: Confederate President* (New York: Harcourt, Brace, 1959), 153–55 (hereafter cited as Strode, *Jefferson Davis*); William Preston Johnston, *The Life of General Albert Sidney Johnston* (New York: D. Appleton and Company, 1878), 291 (hereafter cited as Johnston, *Life of Albert Sidney Johnston*); Jefferson Davis, *The Rise and Fall of the Confederate Government*, 2 vols. (New York: Appleton, 1881), 1:309, 2:67 (hereafter cited as Davis, *Rise and Fall of the Confederate Government*).

3. Ulysses S. Grant, *Personal Memoirs of U. S. Grant* (2 vols., 1885; reprint in one volume, New York: Penguin, 1999), 187–95; John Pope, *The Military Memoirs of John Pope*, ed. Peter Cozzens and Robert I. Giradi (Chapel Hill: University of North Carolina Press, 1998), 77–78 (hereafter cited as Pope, *Military Memoirs*); Brooks D. Simpson, "Continuous Hammering and Mere Attrition: Lost Cause Critics and the Military Reputation of Ulysses S. Grant," in Gary W. Gallagher and Alan T. Nolan, eds., *The Myth of the Lost Cause and Civil War History* (Bloomington: Indiana University Press, 2000), 161–63. In later years, historians James Lee McDonough and Thomas Connelly argued that Johnston was not worthy of the fame heaped on him by contemporaries who considered him brilliant. See McDonough, *Shiloh: In Hell before Night* (Knoxville: University of Tennessee Press, 1977), 31–32 (hereafter cited as McDonough, *Shiloh*); and Connelly, *Army of the Heartland: The Army of Tennessee, 1861–1862* (Baton Rouge: Louisiana State University Press, 1976), 60 (hereafter cited as Connelly, *Army of the Heartland*). Union commander John Pope, who knew Johnston before the war, argued after the war that it was Jefferson Davis who created the inflated impression of Johnston's military skills. Pope argues that Johnston had relatively little combat experience before the Civil War and that his "military appointments and the impression of his military ability are based solely on Mr. Jefferson Davis. Except in Texas," Pope contends, "he was substantially an unknown man and the belief in his ability and his fitness for high military office was confined mainly to Mr. Jefferson Davis."

4. Thomas L. Connelly, *The Marble Man: Robert E. Lee and His Image in American Society* (New York: Knopf, 1977), 23 (hereafter cited as Connelly, *Marble Man*); Frank Allen Dennis, "Beauregard and Johnston at Shiloh: Some Historiographical Aspects," in *Southern Miscellany: Essays in Honor of Glover Moore* (Jackson: University Press of Mississippi, 1981), 98–99; McDonough, *Shiloh*, 225 (hereafter cited as Dennis, "Beauregard and Johnston at Shiloh"); Larry Daniel, *Shiloh: The Battle that Changed the Civil War* (New York: Simon and Schuster, 1997), 13 (hereafter cited as Daniel, *Shiloh*).

5. Albert Castel, *Articles of War: Winners, Losers, and Some Who Were Both during the Civil War* (Mechanicsburg, Pa.: Stackpole, 2001), 139–45 (hereafter cited as Castel, *Articles of War*); Albert Castel, "Dead on Arrival: The Life and Death of General Albert Sidney Johnston," *Civil War Times Illustrated* 36 (March 1997):30–37. See also Castel, "Savior of the South: Was Albert Sidney Johnston the 'Robert E. Lee of the West': The Missing Ingredient for Southern Victory," *Civil War Times Illustrated* 36 (March 1997):38–40.

6. Castel, *Articles of War*, 134.

7. Dennis, "Beauregard and Johnston at Shiloh," 101.

8. Roland, *Albert Sidney Johnston*, 10–13; William J. Cooper, *Jefferson Davis, American* (New York: Knopf, 2000), 25–28 (hereafter cited as Cooper, *Jefferson Davis*); Ralph W. Wooster, *Lone Star Generals in Gray* (Austin: Eakin, 2000), 23 (hereafter cited as Wooster, *Lone Star Generals in Gray*).

9. Roland, *Albert Sidney Johnston*, 13–19; Wooster, *Lone Star Generals in Gray*, 23–24.

10. Roland, *Albert Sidney Johnston*, 13–21; Wooster, *Lone Star Generals in Gray*, 23–24.

11. Roland, *Albert Sidney Johnston*, 21–46; Johnston, *Life of Albert Sidney Johnston*, 19–55; Wooster, *Lone Star Generals in Gray*, 25.

12. Roland, *Albert Sidney Johnston*, 46–54; Wooster, *Lone Star Generals in Gray*, 25.

13. Roland, *Albert Sidney Johnston*, 56.

14. Roland, *Albert Sidney Johnston*, 59–63; Wooster, *Lone Star Generals in Gray*, 25–26.

15. Roland, *Albert Sidney Johnston*, 64–72; Wooster, *Lone Star Generals in Gray*, 25–26.

16. Roland, *Albert Sidney Johnston*, 89–105; Wooster, *Lone Star Generals in Gray*, 26–27.

17. Roland, *Albert Sidney Johnston*, 106–24; Wooster, *Lone Star Generals in Gray*, 26.

18. Roland, *Albert Sidney Johnston*, 125–39; Wooster, *Lone Star Generals in Gray*, 26; K. Jack Bauer, *The Mexican War, 1846–1848* (New York: Macmillan, 1974), 90–96; K. Jack Bauer, *Zachary Taylor: Soldier, Planter, Statesman of the Old Southwest* (Baton Rouge: Louisiana State University Press, 1985), 175–81.

19. As quoted in Roland, *Albert Sidney Johnston*, 134–36.

20. Roland, *Albert Sidney Johnston*, 185–214; Wooster, *Lone Star Generals in Gray*, 26–28; Nathaniel C. Hughes Jr. and Thomas Clayton Ware, *Theodore O' Hara: Poet-Soldier of the Old South* (Knoxville: University of Tennessee Press, 1998), 86.

21. Roland, *Albert Sidney Johnston*, 194–236 (quotation from 201); Wooster, *Lone Star Generals in Gray*, 27–28.

22. Roland, *Albert Sidney Johnston*, 185–237; Wooster, *Lone Star Generals in Gray*, 29–30; U.S. War Department, *War of the Rebellion: A Compilation of the Official Records of the Union and Confederate Armies*, 127 vols., index, and atlas (Washington: U.S. Government Printing Office, 1880–1901), I, 50:433 (hereafter cited as *OR*, with all citations to Series I; for volumes that appeared in more than one part, the part is shown in parentheses after the volume number).

23. Johnston, *Life of Albert Sidney Johnston*, 271–72: *OR*, 50:463–64.

24. Roland, *Albert Sidney Johnston*, 252

25. Johnston, *Life of Albert Sidney Johnston*, 274; Roland, *Albert Sidney Johnston*, 248–67.

26. As quoted in Roland, *Albert Sidney Johnston*, 251–52.

27. Cooper, *Jefferson Davis*, 358–59; Roland, *Albert Sidney Johnston*, 258–61; *OR*, 3:687–88, 4:405; Dunbar Rowland, ed., *Jefferson Davis, Constitutionalist: His Letters, Papers, and Speeches*, 10 vols. (Jackson: Mississippi Department of Archives and History, 1923), 9:206–07.

28. Quote from Pope, *Military Memoirs*, 77–78; Steven E. Woodworth, "The Indeterminate Quantities: Jefferson Davis, Leonidas Polk, and the End of Kentucky Neutrality, September 1861," *Civil War History* 38 (December 1992):289–97 (hereafter cited as Woodworth, "Indeterminate Quantities").

29. Roland, *Albert Sidney Johnston*, 262–69; *OR*, 4:421–22.

30. Allen Nevins, *The War for the Union: War Becomes Revolution* (New York: Charles Scribner's Sons, 1960), 14–15; Stephen D. Engle, *Struggle for the Heartland: The Campaigns From Fort Henry to Corinth* (Lincoln: University of Nebraska Press, 2001), 1 (hereafter cited as Engle, *Struggle for the Heartland*). See also Benjamin Franklin Cooling, *Forts Henry and Donelson: The Key to the Confederate Heartland* (Knoxville: University of Tennessee Press, 1987), 1–10 (hereafter cited as Cooling, *Forts Henry and Donelson*).

31. Avery Craven, *The Growth of Southern Nationalism, 1848–1861* (Baton Rouge: Louisiana State University Press, 1953), 8; Engle, *Struggle for the Heartland*, 1–8.

32. Connelly, *Army of the Heartland*, 3–10.

33. Woodworth, *Civil War Generals in Defeat*, 4, 9–10; Engle, *Struggle for the Heartland*, 17–18; Woodworth, "Indeterminate Quantities," 289–97; *OR*, 4:420–21; Roland, *Albert Sidney Johnston*, 263.

34. *OR*, 4:420–21; Connelly, *Army of the Heartland*, 63–65; Woodworth, *Civil War Generals in Defeat*, 15; Engle, *Struggle for the Heartland*, 17–18.

35. Peter Franklin Walker, "Command Failure: The Fall of Forts Henry and Donelson," *Tennessee Historical Quarterly* 16 (December 1957):335–38 (hereafter cited as Walker, "Command Failure"); Cooling, *Forts Henry and Donelson*, 44–61, 83–84; Engle, *Struggle for the Heartland*, 44–46; Woodworth, *Civil War Generals in Defeat*, 15–17; Connelly, *Army of the Heartland*, 63–83; William C. Davis, *Jefferson Davis: The Man and His Hour* (New York: HarperCollins, 1991), 395–96 (hereafter cited as Davis, *Jefferson Davis*); Steven E. Woodworth, *Jefferson Davis and His Generals: The Failure of Confederate Command in the West* (Lawrence: University Press of Kansas, 1990), 57–58 (hereafter cited as Woodworth, *Jefferson Davis and His Generals*); Kendall D. Gott, *Where the South Lost the War: An Analysis of the Fort Henry-Fort Donelson Campaign, February 1862* (Mechanicsburg: Stackpole, 2003), 48–57 (hereafter cited as Gott, *Where the South Lost the War*).

36. Woodworth, *Civil War Generals in Defeat*, 4; Roland, *Albert Sidney Johnston*, 263–77; Robert Underwood Johnson and Clarence Clough

Buel, eds., *Battles and Leaders of the Civil War*, 4 vols. (New York: Century, 1887), 1:368–70 (hereafter cited as *B&L*); Engle, *Struggle for the Heartland*, 46; Cooling, *Forts Henry and Donelson*, 84–85; Woodworth, *Davis and His Generals*, 71; Gott, *Where the South Lost the War*, 48–57.

37. *OR*, 7:824–25; Roland, *Albert Sidney Johnston*, 276–77; Davis, *Jefferson Davis*, 395–96; Woodworth, *Davis and His Generals*, 54–60.

38. St. John R. Liddell, "Liddell's Record of the Civil War," *Southern Bivouac* 1 (December 1885):417–19; St. John R. Liddell, *Liddell's Record*, ed. Nathaniel C. Hughes (Dayton, Ohio: Morningside, 1985), 41–43; Connelly, *Army of the Heartland*, 92–93; Roland, *Albert Sidney Johnston*, 276–78; Davis, *Jefferson Davis*, 396–97; Cooper, *Jefferson Davis*, 376; Woodworth, *Civil War Generals in Defeat*, 13–15; Gott, *Where the South Lost the War*, 59–74.

39. Cooling, *Forts Henry and Donelson*, 81–82; Roland, *Albert Sidney Johnston*, 281–84.

40. Woodworth, *Davis and His Generals*, 56–57; Engle, *Struggle for the Heartland*, 48–49; Stephen D. Engle, *Don Carlos Buell: Most Promising of All* (Chapel Hill: University of North Carolina Press, 1999), 147–61 (hereafter cited as Engle, *Don Carlos Buell*).

41. Cooling, *Forts Henry and Donelson*, 86–109; George W. Johnson to wife, February 15, 1862, George W. Johnson Papers, State Historical Society of Kentucky, Archives, Frankfort (repository hereafter cited as SHSK); *OR*, 7:590, 860–864; Roland, *Albert Sidney Johnston*, 287–88; Woodworth, *Davis and His Generals*, 79–80; Engle, *Struggle for the Heartland*, 59–60; Woodworth, *Civil War Generals in Defeat*, 16–18; Gott, *Where the South Lost the War*, 75–114; Peter Cozzens, ed., *Battles and Leaders of the Civil War* (Urbana: University of Illinois Press, 2003), 5:234–35 (hereafter cited as Cozzens, *Battles and Leaders*).

42. Connelly, *Army of the Heartland*, 112; T. Harry Williams, *P. G. T. Beauregard: Napoleon in Gray* (Baton Rouge: Louisiana State University Press, 1955), 116–19 (hereafter cited as Williams, *P. G. T. Beauregard*); Cooling, *Forts Henry and Donelson*, 123–27; Roland, *Albert Sidney Johnston*, 289–90; Engle, *Struggle for the Heartland*, 63–66; Gott, *Where the South Lost the War*, 115–43; Cozzens, *Battles and Leaders*, 235–37.

43. Williams, *P. G. T. Beauregard*, 119

44. Cooling, *Forts Henry and Donelson*, 137–43, 164–65; James J. Hamilton, *The Battle of Fort Donelson* (New York: Yoseloff, 1968), 83–85; Walker, "Command Failure," 347–48; Connelly, *Army of the Heartland*, 115–121; *OR*, 7:52, 271–72, 183–224, 263, 285–86, 330; Gott, *Where the South Lost the War*, 143–70; Arnt M. Stickles, *Simon Bolivar Buckner: Borderland Knight* (Chapel Hill: University of North Carolina Press, 1940), 140–41; Nathaniel C. Hughes Jr. and Roy P. Stonesifer, *The Life and Wars of Gideon J. Pillow* (Chapel Hill: University of North Carolina Press, 1993), 222–24.

45. *OR*, 7:880; Williams, *P. G. T. Beauregard*, 120; Roland, *Albert Sidney Johnston*, 290–95; Gott, *Where the South Lost the War*, 171–272.

46. *OR*, 7:880; Williams, *P. G. T. Beauregard*, 120; Roland, *Albert Sidney Johnston*, 290–95; Cozzens, *Battles and Leaders*, 235–39.

47. *OR*, 7:889; Engle, *Struggle for the Heartland*, 79–82; Herman Hattaway and Archer Jones, *How the North Won: A Military History of the Civil War* (Urbana: University of Illinois Press, 1983), 68–76. See also Herman Hattaway, *Shades of Blue and Gray: An Introductory Military History of the Civil War* (Columbia: University of Missouri Press, 1997), 65–68.

48. George W. Johnson to Wife, February 15, 1862, George W. Johnson Papers, SHSK; *OR*, 7:257–61; Walter T. Durham, *Nashville: The Occupied City* (Nashville: Tennessee Historical Society, 1985), 14–18; *Harpers Weekly*, April 12, 15, 1862; John M. McKee, *The Great Panic, Being Connected with Two Weeks of the War in Tennessee* (Nashville: Johnson and Whiting, 1862), 8–11; Roland, *Albert Sidney Johnston*, 298–99; Stanley F. Horn, *The Army of Tennessee* (Norman: University of Oklahoma Press, 1955), 100–101 (hereafter cited as Horn, *Army of Tennessee*); Larry J. Daniel, "'The Assaults of the Demagogues in Congress': General Albert Sidney Johnston and the Politics of Command," *Civil War History* 37 (December 1991):328–35.

49. Jefferson Davis, *The Papers of Jefferson Davis*, ed. Lynda Lasswell Crist and others, 11 vols. to date (Baton Rouge: Louisiana State University Press, 1971–2003), 8:58–62, 87–89 (hereafter cited as Davis, *Papers*); Johnston, *Life of Albert Sidney Johnston*, 496–500; Roland, *Albert Sidney Johnston*, 299–300; *Richmond Enquirer*, February 18, 1862; *Richmond Examiner*, February 19, 1862; Horn, *Army of Tennessee*, 100–104; Davis, *Jefferson Davis*, 398–400; Strode, *Jefferson Davis*, 221; Davis, *Rise and Fall of the Confederate Government*, 2:30–31, 38; Benjamin F. Cooling, *Fort Donelson's Legacy: War and Society in Kentucky and Tennessee, 1861–1863* (Knoxville: University of Tennessee Press, 1997), 7–10 (hereafter cited as Cooling, *Fort Donelson's Legacy*).

50. Roland, *Albert Sidney Johnston*, 299; Strode, *Jefferson Davis*, 221; Davis, *Papers*, 8:58–62, 87–89; Davis, *Jefferson Davis*, 398–400; Johnston, *Life of Albert Sidney Johnston*, 496–500; *OR*, 7:260–61, 10 (2):365. Davis wrote to Johnston at this time "my confidence in you has never wavered, and I hope the public will soon give me credit for judgement rather than continue to arraign me for obstinancy."

51. Davis, *Jefferson Davis*, 398–400.

52. *OR*, 7:258–61; *B&L*, 1:399; Roland, *Albert Sidney Johnston*, 307; Cooling, *Fort Donelson's Legacy*, 7–10. See also Stephen V. Ash, *Middle Tennessee Society Transformed, 1860–1870* (Baton Rouge: Louisiana State University Press, 1988); and *When the Yankees Came: Conflict and Chaos in the Occupied South, 1861–1865* (Chapel Hill: University of North Carolina Press, 1995).

53. Dennis, "Beauregard and Johnston at Shiloh," 121. Dennis argues that at Shiloh "Johnston's personality changed dramatically." "With uncharacteristic bravado," Dennis contends, "Johnston intoned such phrases as 'I would fight them tonight if they were a million' and 'Tonight we will water our horses in the Tennessee River.'" Finally, Dennis contends that "perhaps Johnston tried to redeem his reputation by going to the front of the battle with something of a death wish." (Engle, *Struggle for the Heartland*, 84–87.)

54. Engle, *Struggle for the Heartland*, 86–108; Roland, *Albert Sidney Johnston*, 299–301.

55. Woodworth, *Davis and His Generals*, 332; Connelly, *Army of the Heartland*, 138–42; Daniel, *Shiloh*, 47–48; Engle, *Struggle for the Heartland*, 108–109; Roland, *Albert Sidney Johnston*, 300–301; Williams, *P. G. T. Beauregard*, 121–24; Horn, *Army of Tennessee*, 107–108; Thomas Connelly and Archer Jones, *The Politics of Command: Factions and Ideas in the Confederate Strategy* (Baton Rouge: Louisiana State University Press, 1973), 98–101.

56. McDonough, *Shiloh*, 35, 67; *OR*, 7:899; Connelly, *Army of the Heartland*, 139–40; Williams, *P. G. T. Beauregard*, 121–24; Horn, *Army of the Tennessee*, 111–12; Roland, *Albert Sidney Johnston*, 302–3; Davis, *Jefferson Davis*, 400; Cozzens, *Battles and Leaders*, 237–47.

57. *OR*, 10 (2): 302; Williams, *P. G. T. Beauregard*, 121–24; Connelly, *Army of the Heartland*, 140–41; Roland, *Albert Sidney Johnston*, 302–3; Engle, *Struggle for the Heartland*, 110–11; Dennis, "Beauregard and Johnston at Shiloh," 103–104; Hamilton Basso, *Beauregard: The Great Creole* (New York: Scribner's, 1933), 176 (hereafter cited as Basso, *Beauregard*).

58. Roland, *Albert Sidney Johnston*, 302–3; Williams, *P. G. T. Beauregard*, 121–24; Connelly, *Army of the Heartland*, 140–41.

59. Davis, *Papers*, 8:92–94; *OR*, 7:257–58; Roland, *Albert Sidney Johnston*, 309–10; Daniel, *Shiloh*, 89; Engle, *Struggle for the Heartland*, 119–20.

60. Cozzens, *Battles and Leaders*, 246–47; Connelly, *Army of the Heartland*, 147–51; Roland, *Albert Sidney Johnston*, 311–15; Grady McWhiney, *Braxton Bragg and Confederate Defeat* (New York: Columbia University Press, 1969), 208–17 (hereafter cited as McWhiney, *Braxton Bragg*); Williams, *P. G. T. Beauregard*, 125; Daniel, *Shiloh*, 90–96; Alfred D. Roman, *The Military Operations of General Beauregard in the War Between the States*, 2 vols. (New York: Harper, 1884), 1:267–68; Wiley Sword, *Shiloh: Bloody April* (New York: Morrow, 1974), 85; *B&L*, 1:578–79; Dennis, "Beauregard and Johnston at Shiloh," 103–105; Basso, *Beauregard*, 176.

61. *OR*, 10 (2):365, 394; Roland, *Albert Sidney Johnston*, 309–12.

62. *OR,* 10 (2):365; *B&L*, 1:556–57; and Cozzens, *Battles and Leaders*, 246–48; Roland, *Albert Sidney Johnston*, 326; Williams, *P. G. T. Beauregard*, 134; McWhiney, *Braxton Bragg*, 228

63. McDonough, *Shiloh*, 96–152; Daniel, *Shiloh*, 147–230; Roland, *Albert Sidney Johnston*, 331–37; Dennis, "Beauregard and Johnston at Shiloh," 108–9; Engle, *Don Carlos Buell*, 226–33.

64. *Southern Illustrated News*, January 31, 1863; *New Orleans Daily Delta*, April 8, 1862; Castel, *Articles of War*, 145–47; Dennis, "Beauregard and Johnston at Shiloh," 110–15.

65. Castel, *Articles of War*, 148.

66. Castel, *Articles of War*, 134–49; Connelly, *The Marble Man*, 23.

67. Connelly, *Marble Man*, 23; *OR*, 10:405, 469; *B&L*, 1:568; Johnston, *Life of Albert Sidney Johnston*, viii; Dennis, "Beauregard and Johnston at Shiloh," 110–15; Davis, *Rise and Fall of the Confederate Government*, 2:67–69; William Preston Johnston, "The Army of Tennessee," *Southern Historical Society Papers*, ed. J. William Jones and others, 52 vols. and 3-vol. index (1877–1959; reprint, Wilmington, N.C.: Broadfoot, 1990–92), 5:141 (set hereafter cited as *SHSP*); Richard Taylor, "Advance Sheets of 'Reminiscences of Secession, War, and Reconstruction,'"*SHSP* 5:138–40; Basil W. Duke, "The Confederate Career of General Albert Sidney Johnston," *SHSP* 5:140–41.

68. Wiley Sword, *Shiloh: Bloody April* (1974; rev, ed., Dayton, Ohio: Morningside, 2001), 448; Woodworth, *Davis and His Generals*, 101; Dennis, "Beauregard and Johnston at Shiloh," 110–15.

69. Woodworth, *Civil War Generals in Defeat*, 27; Dennis, "Beauregard and Johnston at Shiloh," 110–21; Davis, *Rise and Fall of the Confederate Government*, 2:67–69.

70. *Natchez Weekly Courier*, April 8, 1862.

"Snarl and Sneer and Quarrel": General Joseph E. Johnston and an Obsession with Rank

Robert K. Krick

Richard Washington Corbin came from an old Virginia family, but lived in Paris in 1861. When he returned to Virginia to serve on Gen. Charles W. Field's staff, young Corbin eagerly solicited opinions in the army about famous Confederates. Gen. Joseph E. Johnston "carried prudence to an excess," Corbin heard. "It was facetiously said that he intended to establish his base in the Gulf of Mexico, and . . . throw pontoons across to Cuba, preparatory to a retrograde movement to the land of fragrant weeds."[1]

Joe Johnston directed some notable campaigns, commanded large armies at crucial moments, and held the highest military rank the Confederacy could bestow. He was the only man who commanded both of that short-lived country's most prominent field armies. Johnston's historical persona, however, reflects two attributes that resonate above all else: prudence to, or perhaps beyond, the threshold of timorousness; and an ineradicable inability to get along with President Davis and the government at Richmond, based in large part on snarling about minute issues of rank.

When eighteen-year-old Joe Johnston matriculated at West Point in the summer of 1825, he was carrying forward a family military tradition. His father Peter (1763–1831) had served during the Revolution in the command of Henry "Light-Horse Harry" Lee, the father of Robert E. Lee, then as a youthful commissioned officer under General Nathanael Greene. Peter proudly carried the title "general," based on post-Revolution militia rank in Virginia. For a decade and a half, Peter Johnston served in the Virginia legislature, a portion of the time as Speaker of the House. Peter's wife, Mary Wood, was a niece of Patrick Henry.[2]

Mary Wood Johnston delivered Joseph Eggleston Johnston at "Cherry Grove," near Farmville, Virginia, on February 3, 1807, and named him for one of her husband's Revolutionary War comrades. The family moved in 1811 to Abingdon, where Peter Johnston occupied a judicial bench. The Johnstons called their home on the outskirts of the town "Panicello." Young Joe attended school at the Abingdon Academy, then in 1825 matriculated at the U.S. Military Academy.[3]

Joe Johnston arrived at West Point at the same time as a young Virginian destined to earn more fame than would fall Johnston's share, in fact as much renown as any soldier in American history. Robert E. Lee and Joe Johnston apparently got along well as cadets, and subsequently in the U.S. Army, but it is impossible to avoid the suspicion that Johnston's attitude during the Civil War included more than a tincture of jealousy. Perhaps it began in the 1820s, when Lee steadily stood above Johnston each year without fail. At the end of their first year, Lee ranked third among eighty-seven cadets who completed the session; Johnston stood thirty-fifth. In conduct, Lee came in sixth, Johnston twenty-sixth. The graduating class at the end of Johnston's first year included Albert Sidney Johnston and Samuel P. Heintzelman.[4]

For the year ending in June 1827, Johnston climbed to seventeenth rank; Lee ranked second. Graduates that year included Leonidas Polk and Philip St. George Cooke. At the end of their third year, Johnston and Lee ranked identically to their academic showings in 1827. No 1828 graduate earned wide military distinction during the Civil War, but that class included a young Mississippian who would grow into Johnston's most steadfast enemy on earth, Jefferson Davis.[5]

Lee graduated second in 1829; Johnston thirteenth. For their final year, Lee stood fifth in conduct, Johnston forty-fifth. Among their classmates, only Theophilus H. Holmes became a familiar Civil War name, and he barely. Cadets in later classes who attended during Johnston's tenure at West Point included William Nelson Pendleton, John B. Magruder, and Lucius B. Northrop.[6]

Joe Johnston's West Point years inevitably shaped him in fundamental ways. He learned a good bit about engineering, and somewhat less about military science; met some young men who would play major roles in his life; and generally stayed out of serious difficulties of either behavior or health, despite problems with his eyes.[7] Two episodes that may have affected the future unfolded not in the classroom or on the drill field, but rather in connection with an off-limits barroom.

Not many weeks after Johnston reached West Point, several cadets fell into serious trouble at Benny Havens's tavern outside the post. An officer caught them there drinking what they claimed was cider and he said was liquor. One of the thirsty lads, Jefferson Davis, defended himself successfully in barracks lawyer fashion by insisting that the rules against frequenting places that served liquor had not been adequately promulgated to the cadets. Furthermore, was wine really a "spiritous liquor?" Undaunted by this narrow escape, Davis continued to frequent the alluring taproom, in one instance escaping the notice of some officers by hurling himself down a roadside cliff and earning a months-long hospital stay in the process. Subsequently Davis skated on the edge of disaster when he played a ringleader's role in a drunken party that left a score of cadets dismissed. A rumor circulated that Joe Johnston and Jeff Davis engaged in a fistfight over the attentions of saloonkeeper Havens's daughter.[8]

More than thirty years later Pres. Jefferson Davis and Gen. Joseph E. Johnston would stand starkly at loggerheads, spewing venomous mistrust to the detriment of their joint cause. By then Davis had become an inflexible, cold figure who impressed some as austerely self-righteous. When trading accusations with Davis during the 1860s and beyond, did Johnston remember the time in their late-adolescent years when his enemy had squirmed around the edges of the truth, split hairs, evidently lied about his behavior, and then hidden behind legalisms? Apparently Johnston never said so, but it is easy to imagine that recollection spanning the decades.

In the summer of 1829, Joe Johnston became a very junior artillery officer. Several men later famous during the Civil War served before the war as artillerists. Thomas J. Jackson, for instance, won three brevets during the Mexican War commanding a section of guns. Johnston spent the first seven years of his army career assigned to an artillery company, but the long arm did not become a permanent part of his familiar image. The absence of exciting field duty, and a steady diet of detached assignments, probably account for that result.

Brevet 2nd Lt. Joseph E. Johnston first appeared on the rolls of the 4th United States Artillery in August 1829, but "unattached, furloughed to 1st Nov." The newly minted officer and gentleman finally reported to his regiment on the last day of 1829. From his arrival through all of 1830 and on to August of 1831, Johnston remained unassigned to any company, on supernumerary duty. Regimental clerks often casually misspelled the green youngster's surname as "Johnson." After two full years on the rolls of the 4th, Johnston received promotion to second lieutenant—free from the brevet stipulation—on September 23, 1831. At the same time he was assigned as the junior officer with the regiment's Company C.[9]

Johnston's superiors in the 4th Artillery did not include names widely familiar in the army's lore. No role models stand out on the regimental rosters. Captain Patrick Henry Galt, Lieutenant Johnston's company commander for years, had been an army officer for two decades. As a fellow Virginian, and named for Johnston's famous great-uncle, Galt may have been a congenial superior, but he had had no opportunity for military distinction. The 4th's commander, Col. John R. Fenwick, had joined the U.S. Marine Corps in the eighteenth century, then as an army officer won commendations on the Canadian frontier during the War of 1812.[10] These grizzled veterans doubtless afforded Lieutenant Johnston plentiful examples of military bureaucracy in full gear, if little of innovation and initiative in field operations.

Two men of future importance to Johnston served in the 4th with him. Lt. Samuel Cooper belonged to the regiment during all of Johnston's service. Already displaying a lifelong predilection for staff duty, Cooper remained steadily assigned as a general's aide-de-camp, so he and Johnston cannot have been regularly in each other's company. As adjutant and inspector general of the Confederacy, Cooper would become a béte noire to the rank-sensitive Johnston. Lt. Benjamin S. Ewell also served with Johnston in the 4th Artillery. Ewell came to the regiment from West Point in August 1832, and resigned four years later at the same time that Johnston left. During the 1860s, Ewell served as chief of staff to Gen. Joseph E. Johnston. Their relationship bore far more friendly fruit than that of Johnston and Cooper.[11]

Duty in the 4th Artillery afforded Lieutenant Johnston considerable experience with the movement of troops, and the resultant logistical entanglements. His Company C opened 1832 at Fort Monroe, Virginia, but beginning that June it moved regularly and far. The company headed for Chicago on June 19 and reached that frontier town on July 10, on the fringes of what became known as the Black Hawk War. At the end of September the artillerists camped on the Mississippi River opposite St. Louis. Their return trek reached Waynesboro, Virginia, by the end of October, and Fort Monroe on November 7. Joe Johnston served on a court-martial later that month, then two days before Christmas the company embarked for Fort Moultrie in Charleston Harbor (in reaction to the nullification crisis).[12] This military seasoning cannot have done much to prepare Johnston to face McClellan at Richmond or Sherman near Atlanta, but it surely exposed him to the rudiments of a soldier's trade. Perhaps the court-martial duty served as an early chapter in a life full of devotion to, even reliance upon, military red tape.

Lieutenant Johnston first went to war in Florida. In November 1833 the 4th Artillery detailed him to special duty as adjutant of a battalion of three companies headed for Alabama and then Florida in response to burgeoning conflict with the Seminole Indians. The temporary battalion returned to Virginia overland, reaching Fort Monroe on April 19, 1834. After more court-martial duty that spring, Johnston left the regiment on what was called temporary duty, but he never returned. The 4th carried him on its rolls, detached for duty with the army's Topographical Service, until the summer of 1836.[13]

Gen. Winfield Scott arrived in Florida in 1836 to assume command of the suppression of the Seminoles. On February 22, Johnston joined Scott's staff as an aide-de-camp. A few weeks later the lieutenant put his engineering training to work to prepare a sketch he entitled "Battle Ground of Major Dade, 28 Dec. 1835." Francis L. Dade (a fellow Virginian) and all but one of his detachment of more than 100 officers and men had been killed in the Seminole War's most famous event. Among Dade's dead was a lieutenant with whom Joe Johnston had attended West Point. If Johnston had occasion to reflect on the battlefield consequences of rashness as he prepared the sketch, he left no record of it.[14]

Winfield Scott's record in the War of 1812 and in Mexico warrant his designation as one of the greatest officers in American history. Scott's abilities did not extend to irregular warfare, however, and his time in Florida generated more disgruntlement than success. The general's bitterly quarrelsome relations with other officers, and his boundless distaste for militia troops (a well-grounded but impolitic position), made his Florida interlude a disaster.

Lieutenant Johnston's service on General Scott's staff only lasted for three months, ending on May 21, 1836. One year later the lieutenant resigned his commission in disgust over slow promotion, especially because some of his peers had advanced beyond him in rank. "Many of my juniors," he explained to a relative, had "by luck got before me on the army list." The green-eyed monster lurking in Joe Johnston's soul simply could not tolerate that kind of thing, in 1837 or in 1861. Ironically, his own promotion to first lieutenant had come through only a few months before the resignation.[15] Virtually the only civil engineers in the United States were graduates of the Military Academy, and civil engineers earned far more money than the pittance Congress allowed to junior officers.

The civilian Joe Johnston saw hotter action in Florida than he had as junior lieutenant. Under contract as a civilian engineer, he accompanied a small polyglot detachment—sailors and soldiers and volunteers, some black and some white—under Lt. Levi N. Powell, U.S. Navy, on a scout on Florida's southeast coast. John B. Magruder, a contemporary of Johnston's at West Point and later of some Confederate renown, led one detachment. In December 1837, Powell and his force explored the St. Lucie River. As they swung back east on January 15, 1838, near the head of Jupiter Inlet, they came upon a considerable body of Seminoles. Powell's eighty men drove the Indians to the edge of a dense cypress swamp, then stalled in the face of a galling fire. As darkness gathered, the soldiers and sailors fell back under steady pressure. Bullets hit five officers, including Powell, and the retirement turned frantic. Joe Johnston, civilian though he was, took control of the rear guard and covered the retreat until desperate men reached their boats, one-third of the force having been hit. A Seminole round had creased Johnston's skull, and he claimed to have found thirty bullet holes in his clothing.[16]

The gallantry and skill that Johnston displayed at Jupiter Inlet received warm and wide attention. His performance would clearly have warranted brevet promotion, the system then widely in use for such recognition, had he been a serving officer. On July 7 Lieutenant Johnston resumed his commission in the Regular Army, and on the same date received brevet promotion to captain for Jupiter Inlet. Eventually someone noticed the impropriety inherent in the brevet: how could a civilian be awarded with rank in an army to which he had not then belonged? For the first of many times during his career in (and in this instance out of) a series of armies, Joe Johnston's uncertain rank came under scrutiny and debate. A decade later, someone asked the adjutant general to rule on how Johnston's rank could be based on actions "when he held no commission in the army?" The adjutant general examined the matter and agreed that Johnston received the brevet for "services . . . performed in January 1838, when he did not belong to the Army but was employed in a Civil Capacity . . . and altho he well merited the brevet had he been an officer at the time . . . yet being a civilian, the Conferring [of] it . . . was without precedent and . . . without the authority of law."[17]

Despite the judgment from Washington about the unlawful brevet, no one undertook the actual reduction of Johnston's rank. By the time of the adjutant general's ruling, its subject had earned more brevet promotions, once again under peculiar circumstances that generated further barracks lawyering.

During the eight years between his return to the army and the Mexican War, Brevet Captain (or was he rightfully still a lieutenant?) Johnston served across the country on engineering assignments: improving the Black River in New York; surveying the Sault St. Marie; surveying the boundary between the new Republic of Texas and the United States; improving harbors on Lake Erie; in the Topographical Bureau in Washington; back to the Florida frontier; surveying the Canadian boundary; and on the Coast Survey.[18] Did all of that precise staff duty turn Joe Johnston into a cautious drone, lulled by all of its calipers and right angles and rigid rules that always worked out to a pretty arithmetic solution? A psychobabbler might build a thesis from such stuff, but in fact Robert E. Lee, engineer in the U.S. Army, spent the same years doing almost identical things, and no one accuses Lee of a shortage of audacity.

In 1845, Joe Johnston made one of the best decisions of his life. On July 10 he married Lydia McLane of Baltimore, fifteen years his junior and a daughter of the much- distinguished Louis McLane. Lydia's brother Robert, a West Point-educated army officer (later a congressman, governor, and diplomat), had known Johnston in Florida. Her father had served in both houses of Congress, as ambassador to England, and as secretary of state. In 1845, Louis McLane was president of the Baltimore and Ohio Railroad. Lydia's sweet nature, and Joe's warm devotion to her, resonate from their correspondence and the observations of contemporaries.[19]

Most Civil War leaders who brought battle experience to their duties in 1861 had earned it in Mexico in 1846 and 1847. Joe Johnston matched that pedigree, earning distinction at the cost of a wound in battle. He received orders on December 11, 1846, to report to Point Isabel, Texas, for duty with General Winfield Scott, of Florida acquaintance. Johnston accepted a commission as lieutenant colonel of the temporary Voltigeurs Regiment the next April and fought with that unit to Mexico City. In operations during the late summer of 1847, Johnston displayed a degree of aggressiveness all out of proportion to his later reputation. On August 20, he successfully led a detachment against a Mexican "intrenched position"—adding the word "intrenched" to his report as an afterthought, above the line.[20]

As the army approached Mexico City in early September, Lieutenant Colonel Johnston fought in some of the preliminary actions "under heavy fire" with great personal bravery, earning mention for being "active and efficient." Johnston's own report of his role in the battle of Chapultepec describes the action of the left wing of the Voltigeurs Regiment, with which he covered the advance of the storming party that clawed its desperate way into "the Halls of Montezuma" (some U.S. Marines participated, whence comes the line in the song that corps so loves). Although he did not take part in the main assault, Johnston performed credibly. His meticulous report teems with actions full of energy and aggression, expressed in language in the same robust vein. The early Mexican War history by Roswell S. Ripley, who would become a Confederate general himself, repeatedly describes Johnston's performance in glowing terms. Because Ripley wrote at a time when none of his subjects had yet become famous (in fact he steadily misspelled the surname as Johnstone), his perspective carries added significance.[21]

The unmistakable success with which Johnston fought in Mexico won him official plaudits and brevet promotions—but at the same time niggling questions of chronology and precedence interrupted the paean. The Florida brevet had come into question because of Johnston's civilian status. Now the Mexican War awards became bemired in matters of relative timing, and of differences between ranking in a temporary regiment as opposed to the Regular Army.

Johnston characteristically appealed decisions contrary to his own interpretation, and fumed when his appeals failed. As late as 1860, the matter of Johnston's brevet ranks prompted an intricate six-page letter by Secretary of War John B. Floyd. Johnston had been given a brevet colonelcy on April 12, 1847, based on his rank as lieutenant colonel of the Voltigeurs. In March 1849, after his return to Regular-Army status with the Topographical Engineers, Johnston received brevet promotions to the lower regular ranks of major (also to date from April 12, 1847) and lieutenant colonel (to date from September 13, 1847).

Should the earlier colonelcy, stapled atop a nonregular rank of lieutenant colonel and for the same event that won him a regular major's brevet, be added to the brevets—of later date—at lower regular ranks? Floyd (a cousin of Johnston's by marriage) noted dryly the prevalence of "whatever may appear anomalies" in this tangled business. He also concluded that the colonel's brevet was granted under a law "imperfectly valid in itself."[22]

Despite all of the gingerly worded equivocation, all the "anomalies" and "imperfectly valid" aspects, Floyd allowed the rank to stand. After years of grumbling about the matter, Johnston finally had his way. Most of his colleagues looked askance at a result won by political leverage after a succession of rejections stretching across more than a decade. Two colonels formally protested the matter to Jefferson Davis, senator from Mississippi and one of the earlier rejecting officials during his term as secretary of war. The colonels pointed out the incongruity of one Mexican War brevet, carried over past the "disbandment of a temporary corps." Robert E. Lee, never prone to carping about his fellows, wrote brusquely in a letter to his son that "it must be evident" even to Johnston "that it never was the intention of Congress to advance him" to that level. His friend's scrambling for rank, Lee concluded, created "injustice" and "has thrown more discredit than ever on the system of favoritism and making brevets."[23] Not many months later Davis would be dealing with a fractious Joe Johnston in the same vain vein in a brand-new army, and Lee would be looking on sorrowfully.

An inscription on the plinth that supports a large sculpture outside the entrance to the National Archives quotes the Bard: "What is Past is Prologue." Joseph E. Johnston's convoluted experiences with rank in the U.S. Army certainly served as prologue to his deadly obsession with like matters in the army of the Confederate States.

For more than a decade after he left Mexico, Johnston followed his profession through a succession of postings, at first focused on engineering: "Chief Top. Engineer of the Department of Texas," 1848–1853; and "in charge of Western River Improvements," 1853–1855. On March 3, 1855, Johnston received promotion to the regular rank of lieutenant colonel, and a much-coveted billet as second-in-command of the 1st Cavalry. With his distinguished regiment, Johnston's last half-decade before the Civil War included these assignments: Jefferson Barracks, Missouri; recruiting service; Fort Leavenworth, Kansas; quelling the Kansas troubles in 1856; surveying the

southern boundary of Kansas; the Utah Expedition of 1858; and Fort
Riley, Kansas.[24]

Starting in September 1858, Johnston spent two years in Washington on detached duty. He served in 1859 on a board studying cavalry organization and functions. The assignment at headquarters, away
from onerous frontier duty, gave Johnston opportunity to indulge a
passion for professional study. He also corresponded with fellow officers observing the Crimean War. Dabney Maury of Fredericksburg,
who knew Johnston at this period, could not imagine that "any man in
our country" had more thoroughly "studied the histories and biographies of wars and warriors." Johnston earnestly enjoined a congressional commission examining the status of the Military Academy to
ensure that cadets learned "habits of judicious reading" instead of
focusing on "abstruse sciences." He disdained the use of Jomini's
work and "especially recommend[ed] . . . three little works by Frederick the Great" as essential literature for military students.[25]

As a byproduct of Johnston's attention to military history and
affairs, he also sought to improve his army's structure. In a thoughtful
letter, Lieutenant Colonel Johnston urged the secretary of war to "put
an end to the inconvenience to the Service produced by *two* authorized
systems of infantry tactics." Johnston thought both antiquated, and
urged a new regime. Even more impressively, he repeated "a suggestion several times made by me, in relation to the establishment of a
course of instruction for our recruits." Novice soldiers, Johnston
insisted, must reach a "standard of proficiency"—including skill with
firearms—before entering the ranks. Such essential training, routine in
later years, was almost universally ignored in the mid-nineteenth-cen-
tury army, in part because of prevalence of much fond wishful nonsense about citizen soldiers being ready to leap into action in a
twinkling. Johnston deserves strong credit for recognizing these needs
and promoting a solution.[26]

Joe Johnston signed on June 30, 1860, a document that led to
tremendous difficulties in the Confederate era. His commission of that
date, replete with a regal eagle clutching lightning bolts in its talons,
made Johnston the quartermaster general of the U.S. Army. The post
carried with it the automatic rank of brigadier general—of staff. He
had been lieutenant colonel of the line, and now bypassed the rank of
colonel to reach brigadier, but only as "Brig.-Gen. Staff," in the wording of an official roster. Johnston's subsequent insistence on the application of that rank, staff instead of line though it was, as a means of

gaining precedence over Old Army colonels of the line, lay at the root of much of the squabbling about his relative position on Confederate rosters.[27]

The bureaucratic toils attendant on his new duty may well have suited Johnston, as they brought across his desk an array of minutiae soluble by reference to a host of rules and regulations. His first three signatures as Quartermaster General on correspondence, all dated on July 2, proved to be typical of what the next ten months would bring. He delivered a labyrinthine explanation of mileage reimbursement applicable to a noncommissioned officer newly promoted to lieutenant and sent to a different post. He also signed a report addressed to 169 officers who had accounts due with the quartermaster department. The next day Johnston adjudicated a dispute about what kinds of collateral duty warranted government-supplied stationery for officers. On July 9, Johnston added $168 to the quartermaster's account at Barrancas Banks, Florida. On September 21, he denied advanced mileage to a lieutenant on orders to New Mexico, leaving him to his own devices to get to that distant frontier.

Johnston did not rush to leave his post as quartermaster general as the sectional crisis erupted into war. On April 12, 1861, as Fort Sumter came under fire, he signed a letter regarding the lease of land at Fort Union, New Mexico. His last signature on an official document from the department came on April 21, as Virginia was seceding. It concerned 500 barrels of pork "detained in Philadelphia," perhaps to avoid shipment south into what rapidly was turning into enemy country.[28]

>⸱⟶⸱O⸱⟵⸱<

On April 22, Johnston delivered his resignation to the secretary of war. Four days later, he held rank in the forces of Virginia. Within a fortnight Johnston headed to Montgomery, Alabama, hoping for a Confederate rank instead of one issued by Virginia. On May 15 he accepted a commission as brigadier general in the Confederate army, and a week later he headed back for Virginia with orders to assume command at Harpers Ferry, on the Potomac River and on the military frontier.[29]

A visitor to Harpers Ferry can readily grasp the difficulties of defending the place. The importance of the village came from the arms manufactory there, from the strategically significant confluence of the Potomac and Shenandoah Rivers at the mouth of the crucial Shenandoah Valley breadbasket; and from a situation on the frontier between the two countries, north of the latitude of Washington. The rivers might aid a defender to some degree, but they also had carved the landscape into a bowl, with high ground dominating the village.

Bolder men than Joe Johnston would recognize the near impossibility of holding Harpers Ferry against a determined assailant. Federals who tried that in 1862 fell into the hands of Stonewall Jackson, losing 12,000 men and scores of cannon. A boisterously confident Confederate public, however, would brook no talk of retreat in the spring of 1861, nor listen to considerations of strategic advantages to be gained by withdrawals. If Johnston's postwar memoir can be believed (always an uncertain proposition), both Jefferson Davis and Robert E. Lee "had informed me distinctly that they regarded" Harpers Ferry "as a natural fortress."[30]

The force at Harpers Ferry included several officers destined for great fame. Johnston superseded Thomas J. Jackson in command, and the assembled Confederates included troops under J. E. B. Stuart and A. P. Hill. Joe Johnston had been a soldier for two-thirds of his life, since late adolescence, but he never had led more troops in action than one wing of the Voltigeurs Regiment in Mexico. Although the regiments gathered at Harpers Ferry did not seem to be nearly enough to achieve the protection of the town, they numbered twenty times as many troops as Johnston ever had led. A few weeks later, beyond the Blue Ridge Mountains, Johnston would find himself in command of an army larger than the American armies that had won the Revolutionary War and the Mexican War. He had amply demonstrated physical courage under fire in Florida and Mexico. Would he possess the far dearer commodity, moral courage, when faced with hard decisions? Commanding a few companies of Voltigeurs provided nothing at all by way of preparation for that.

Within hours of his arrival at Harpers Ferry, Johnston launched the first of what would become a barrage of messages to Richmond urging abandonment of the post he had been assigned to defend. On May 26 he wrote, "Our force is too small . . . to prevent invasion. . . . This position can be turned easily and effectively." Two days later: "The position cannot be defended by such a force. . . . An army will be necessary."[31]

On May 31, Johnston wrote further in the same tenor to Lee: "This place cannot be held." Lee responded with the plaintive hope that "you may probably hold your position." On June 5, Johnston recounted anew the litany of difficulties he faced and challenged Lee's emphasis on the importance of standing firm. "You say that 'the abandonment of Harper's Ferry would be depressing to the cause.' Would not the loss of five or six thousand men be more so?"[32] This communication, and many others Johnston wrote, displayed a deep yearning to be told what to do—to be ordered to do the only thing Johnston could imagine doing: abandon Harpers Ferry. Lee and Davis always responded with general guidance, instead of the "instructions" that Johnston solicited. For thirty-six years, people had been telling Joe Johnston how to act. Now that discretion was thrust upon him, he gave little indication of wanting to embrace it.

Explosions in Harpers Ferry on June 14 heralded Johnston's abandonment of the village. He blew up the bridge, wrecked the armory and the immobile portions of its invaluable machinery, and pushed railroad gear into the river. "Nothing worth removing was left," the general boasted.[33] This initial Confederate venture under Johnston's direction became the first step in a minuet that he would execute all across the Southern Confederacy: complain bitterly about strength and circumstances; seek orders to do the one thing palatable, retreat; when no one in Richmond would take that responsibility, retreat on his own discretion; and destroy far more precious matériel than seemed appropriate to officials of the overtaxed Confederate supply establishment.

The final element in what became a recognizable formula for Johnston was hypersensitivity, turning into bitterness after the fact, about credit and, more typically, blame. Adjutant and Inspector General Samuel Cooper had sent a long letter on June 13, reiterating the field commander's discretion. It of course did not reach Johnston until after he had abandoned Harpers Ferry. Cooper noted reasonably that "the movements of the enemy could not be foreseen, so it was impossible to give you specific directions." Based on everything Johnston had written, Cooper concluded that "you seem to desire . . . that the responsibility of the retirement should be assumed here." In a statesmanlike phrase, one Joe Johnston could never have written, or at least meant, Cooper cheerfully suggested that he had "no reluctance . . . to bear any burden which the public interests require." That was too blunt for Johnston. He responded coldly that "nothing in my correspondence" meant "that the responsibility of my official acts should be borne by any other person than myself."[34] It is impossible to read Johnston's repeated pleas to Richmond without seeing precisely what Cooper meant.

That Joe Johnston was entirely correct in his assertions about Harpers Ferry's vulnerability surely must have exacerbated the bad feelings he nurtured. That certainty perhaps gave him increased determination in later instances when Richmond refused to see things his way. The town in fact could not have been defended permanently without a very strong force. Johnston surely could have—should have—held it substantially longer, defying a Federal commander at least as uncertain as he was himself. Falling back eventually under direct duress would have played far better with the Southern populace from whom his troops were drawn; but Johnston never recognized the political aspects of warfare in a democracy. Holding Harpers Ferry longer also would have allowed for more thorough and systematic removal of supplies and equipment; but Johnston seemed never to afford logistical concerns their warranted gravity.

For the month after leaving Harpers Ferry, General Johnston made Winchester his headquarters. Federal movements, most of them feints, kept the Confederate force on the *qui vive*. The alarms resulted in a modest skirmish on July 2, but war's klaxon blared shrilly for the first time in Virginia on July 18. Early that morning a telegram from Richmond announced that the Confederate army around Manassas Junction under Gen. P. G. T. Beauregard faced an attack by Federals advancing from the outskirts of Washington, and ordered that Johnston hurry to its aid.

The dash to Manassas stands as one of Joe Johnston's best moments during the entire war. Responding briskly to a crisis, and aggressively employing railroad transport (one of the first significant military moves by that means), the general pushed his force eastward. With atypical energy and forcefulness, he accomplished a brilliant strategic movement. The result was that most difficult achievement, infrequently realized, of combining divergent columns upon a battlefield. Most of Johnston's regiments reached Manassas in time to participate in the battle of July 21, some of them playing crucial roles.

Who would command the Confederate amalgam, Johnston or Beauregard? Johnston inquired in a telegram to the president. Davis answered on July 20 with stimulating news: "You are a general in the Confederate Army, possessed of the power attaching to that rank. You will know how to . . . [use] the exact knowledge of Brigadier-General Beauregard." In fact, Johnston's promotion to full general took rank from July 4, but was not confirmed until August 31, so Davis's assurance did not carry the full weight of law.[35] Johnston would have scorned a colleague's rank encumbered by a similar anomaly, and muttered of conspiracies and persecution, but of course accepted the preliminary status without qualms in his own case. His delight at promotion to full general would turn into seething outrage a few weeks later when he saw the ordering of the names on the promotion sheet.

>-+-‹›-+-O-+-‹›-+-‹

To his credit, and in the face of his customary obsession with rank, Johnston left tactical arrangements at Manassas to Beauregard. A heavy majority of the troops to be engaged belonged to Beauregard's army. The Louisianian also knew the rolling, stream-cut, thickly wooded ground. Might Johnston's discomfort with making hard decisions have contributed to his willingness to give leeway to the general on the ground? The question is unanswerable, but provocative.

Johnston performed ably when the battle opened, probably as well as he did on any field during the war. "War is always a far worse muddle than anything you can produce in peace," a twentieth-century general has aptly said. Manassas exceeded that chaotic norm, as untrained mobs swayed and grappled across the field. The fighting writhed independently, defying anything like tight central coordination. When the roar of musketry from Henry House Hill prompted Johnston and Beauregard to ride to that crucial spot, Beauregard remained near the front. Johnston headed for the Lewis House, a spot from which he could vector reinforcements to the front. [36]

Hard-pressed Southern infantry outlasted their foe and won the war's first major battle. Johnston deserved what credit accrued to a commander—but the popular press, and the public influenced by that medium, counted Beauregard the conqueror of the day. The hero of the nonbattle at Fort Sumter stood high already in Southern consciousness. He had an exotic French aspect that played well in an era of Zouaves and Napoleonic military ardor. As late as November 1861, a Virginia soldier in a public letter declared that Johnston stood second with the army in affection and regard for military prowess.[37] Americans prefer something quixotic or eccentric—ivory-handled pistols, for instance, or fondness for lemons—in conjuring popular heroes.

In a peevish postwar article, ostensibly about Manassas although full of puling about subsequent rank issues, Johnston showed how much the attention paid to Beauregard displeased him. "An opinion seems to prevail," he wrote, "that important plans of General Beauregard were executed by him. It is a mistake. . . . The battle was made by me."[38] Johnston was right. An officer with an eye firmly affixed to the public service, however, would not have become nearly as obsessed with the matter

Most humans of all walks and pedigrees guard their prerogatives jealously, but some military officers seem to be more stridently prickly than the average. Perhaps their stressful and violent profession heightens the sense of perceived injustice when recognition falters; or maybe their public profiles simply make a near-universal trait more visible. Striving to defend a nascent country in dire circumstances does nothing to moderate the unseemly tendency. "There is as much pulling and hauling, about rank and pay, as if we had been accustomed to a military establishment here 150 years," a politician complained. "I am wearied to Death with the Wrangles between military officers," one of his colleagues grumbled. "They worry one another like Mastiffs. Scrambling for Rank and Pay like Apes for Nutts." The two frustrated men were delegates to the Continental Congress, writing not in 1861 but in 1777, expressing a disgust by no means limited to their revolutionary epoch.[39] Joe Johnston did far more than his share of similar pulling and hauling, worrying and wrangling, nearly a century later.

The volcanic bubbling about rank, never far submerged in General Johnston, began to overflow immediately after the battle of Manassas. On July 24 he wrote to Richmond about his rank "compared with that of other officers of the C. S. Army." On the twenty-ninth, he snarled that routine orders forwarded to him from Robert E. Lee, acting on behalf of the president, "I cannot regard, because they are illegal." This interference with his prerogatives from something "purporting" to be "the 'Headquarters of the Forces,'" simply could not be borne.[40] By Johnston's reckoning, his old rival at West Point and in the prewar army must not be allowed to harbor the delusion that he could issue orders. Although the official rankings had not been released, Johnston accepted as an article of faith that he would outrank everyone else.

Jefferson Davis had been patient with Johnston's complaints from Harpers Ferry and during the early summer. "I wish you would write whenever your convenience will permit, and give me fully both information and suggestions," the president had written on June 22. Davis closed the letter "With earnest wishes for your welfare and happiness . . . your friend." On August 31, 1861, any warmth between the two vanished forever. That date, with no (Northern) enemy in view, must be adjudged, amazingly and tragically, as the most important day of the war for Joe Johnston. On that day the Confederate Congress confirmed five full generals. On the list, Robert E. Lee stood third, Joseph E. Johnston fourth. Nothing that happened in the next four years obscured Johnston's focus on that intolerable moment. With the highest rank his army could bestow, and on the earliest promotion list to that rank, Johnston could never be outranked by more than three men in the entire Confederate nation; but one of those was Robert E. Lee.[41]

>—+◆>—○—<◆+—◁

Johnston could not bear the shame of it, and railed in a formal letter against the dark conspiracy of the government, unmistakably "aimed at me only." The brazen assault on his honor damaged his reputation, ignored his wounds in Florida and Mexico, insulted his father, and besmirched his father's sword, "delivered to me from his venerated hand without a stain. . . . Its blade is still unblemished. . . . I drew it in the war, not for rank or fame, but to defend the sacred soil, the homes and hearths, the women and children."[42] This remarkably paranoid and fatuous letter must have stunned those who read it, none of whom had thought much about Peter Johnston's sword theretofore. How could a savage, hyperbolic missive, athrob over narrow questions of rank, claim in so many words to be immune to "rank or fame"?

An adept response from the president might have been something on the order of a sizzling answer once sent to Davis himself by Winfield Scott: "Compassion is always due to an enraged imbecile." Instead Davis sent a crisp but reasonably calm brief reply. Johnston's letter, the chief executive wrote, was couched in "unusual" language, "its arguments and statements utterly one-sided and its insinuations as unfounded as they are unbecoming."[43]

Did Johnston's position, viewed legalistically, have more credibility than Davis's? The Byzantine intricacies of the question leave a modern auditor uncertain—and generally unwilling to care at all. Johnston unquestionably viewed his position as sacred and inviolable; only an enemy of the darkest hue, a veritable incarnation of evil, could disagree. His whole premise, however, rested upon wispy foundations: the brevet a quarter-century earlier in Florida, improperly awarded to a civilian; one of three brevets in Mexico given when in non-Regular service, and succeeded chronologically by two at lower rank; and finally an 1860 promotion to a staff rank, not line. For many years he had lost appeals, until a friendly politician tardily gave him what he wanted.

Even had he been proved wrong, Davis probably had the power in 1861 to revise the law as necessary, had he been inclined. He had helped to frame it in the first place, and now someone insisted that he did not know what he had meant to accomplish. Furthermore, the whole business could not possibly matter in any practical sense, as the government would not assign either of the two officers listed ahead of Johnston to the same field army. The tempest raged only on the pettiest of stages, within Joe Johnston's perfervid self-image. Reasonable people, then and now, might quarrel over just how to interpret the tangle. Joe Johnston's frantic obsession with the matter, however, to the vast disservice of his public duty, surely must be adjudged a character flaw of monumental proportions. To convince himself that he had launched the hubbub without thought of "rank or fame" indicated a disturbing capacity for self-delusion.[44]

For eight months after the battle of Manassas, Joe Johnston fumed about Jefferson Davis, but almost never fought the Yankees. By mid-September he was grumbling of his mistreatment in correspondence with a casual female acquaintance, who wrote in her diary reasonably enough that it was all about "rank."[45] Minor engagements at Ball's Bluff and Dranesville during the fall of 1861 seemed more significant than they actually were to a country not yet inured to warfare. During most of the long *sitzkrieg*, troops encamped on a broad arc across northern Virginia drilled, built huts in unhealthful circumstances, and died by the hundreds of disease.

Much of the army had grown fond of its general. His impressive military carriage and his demeanor suited their ideas of how an important officer should behave. A Georgian described the general in detail in December 1861: "he is about 45 yrs old, 5 ft 9 in h[e]ight, skin dark with dark grey beard & hair. He will weigh about 145 or 150 lbs, very erect in his walk." Some observers thought the general a little "rotund," or "round." An Alabama soldier admired Johnston's "clear cut, military air" and thought that his "military goatee with side whiskers . . . contributed largely to his soldierly appearance." The combination created "the impression that he was a man of quick perception and thoroughly self possessed." A Mississippi chaplain pungently expressed the opposite view: "Johnston is too slow, his blood is too cold, he is not capable of anything brilliant or daring."[46]

One trait that endeared Johnston to his soldiers was a remarkable faculty for remembering names, even after only brief contact. His personal style, which included unfailing poise and courtesy, elicited virtually uniform loyalty from staff officers. Given the difficulty of fooling direct subordinates, the general's hold on his official family constitutes a strong endorsement of Johnston the man.[47]

Joe Johnston roused from his months-long desuetude in March 1862 not to take action, but to avoid it. Gen. George B. McClellan had marshaled a mighty host in the outskirts of Washington. As winter ended, he seemed to be nudging it southward, displaying even more caution, were that possible, than Johnston's accustomed demeanor. The disadvantages of operating against heavy odds, facing a foe who controlled every navigable waterway, daunted Johnston, as well they might. Yet the army he commanded, under leadership of diametrically opposite mien, would triumph on this very ground a few months later. Identical conundrums would face Johnston wherever he sought to deploy an army during this war. He never would come to grips with the obligation to struggle against them, instead of succumbing to them.

In mid-February, at a daylong meeting with Davis and his cabinet, General Johnston described the necessity of abandoning the Manassas line. He left "with the understanding . . . that the army was to fall back as soon as practicable." Predictably, Davis had the different perception that Johnston was to hold on until circumstances made a withdrawal unavoidable. Johnston's unreserved loathing for Secretary of War Judah P. Benjamin ("that miserable little Jew," he called him) exacerbated the situation. So did the immemorial unreliability of politicians: before Johnston could reach his hotel from the meeting, a colonel on the street repeated the gist of the discussion to him; so did a country civilian miles away the next day.[48] If politicians could not keep their counsel, surely a soldier ought not to be frank with them.

On February 22, immediately upon his return to Manassas, Johnston ordered the removal of supplies from northern Virginia. On March 7 he started the army south. Four days later it rested on the right bank of the Rappahannock River. Ironically, forlornly, an uninformed president wrote to Johnston on the tenth, promising reinforcements "to enable you to maintain your position"—a position by then abandoned. On March 12, Johnston sent to Richmond the first official notification that he had truncated the Confederacy's territory by several hundred square miles. Davis responded with more sorrow than anger at the weeklong delay in notifying him of so momentous a change: "I was as much in the dark as to your purposes . . . as at the time of our conversation on the subject about a month since." The president had heard "many and alarming reports of great destruction of ammunition, camp equipage, and provisions, indicating precipitate retreat; but . . . was at a loss to believe it."[49]

Because McClellan's powerful Union force soon headed for Virginia's Peninsula, and would approach Richmond from that quarter, Johnston's retirement from the vicinity of Manassas was absolutely inevitable. As had been the case at Harpers Ferry, and would be again with numbing repetition, the question became whether he had retired too soon and without seeking an opportunity to damage his enemy. What, too, of the immense loss of stores and equipment, including heavy artillery and hundreds of tons of salt meat, so desperately needed in a struggling new country? The destruction vexed Davis and others mightily.[50]

Two weeks after Johnston's army relocated to the Rappahannock region, an armada carrying McClellan's Federal host appeared in the vicinity of Norfolk. When Davis sent Johnston to the Peninsula to face the dire threat, the general's first glance produced the same reaction he would have in virtually every circumstance. "Before nightfall," he wrote, "I was convinced that we could do no more on the Peninsula than delay." The only answer was to retire all the way to Richmond, call to his command all of the troops on the coast from Virginia to Georgia, and then be "almost certain to win."[51]

Faced with Davis's stubborn refusal to abandon most of the Atlantic littoral, Johnston had to stand, at least briefly, in McClellan's way near Yorktown. His eagerness to retire to Richmond would of course come to pass under his leadership, in the relentless manner of a self-fulfilling prophecy. Johnston calmly admitted his unswerving intention to follow his own preferences, rather than the president's orders, in a report written after he had done so. He quickly found that his own "opinion previously expressed was fully confirmed." He "determined, therefore, to hold the position as long as it could be done without exposing our troops to the fire" of McClellan's army. Lee told a subordinate: "Johnston should never have fallen back to Richmond . . . but should have delivered a general battle on the narrow isthmus at Williamsburg where McClellan's superior numbers would have been neutralized by the character of the ground."[52] George McClellan is widely adjudged as among the most timorous army commanders in American history. Against the wishes of his government, Joe Johnston contrived to outequivocate even McClellan.

Johnston's defense of the lower Peninsula lasted barely two weeks. It consisted exclusively of preparations to fall back. Some of his regiments began to retire on May 1. A desultory action in a steady rain at Williamsburg on May 5 protected the rear guard. Johnston, as usual, rode under the heaviest fire without flinching, in an unmistakable display of personal bravery. A South Carolinian who saw the general "under a storm of artillery fire . . . could not help admiring the courage and coolness of his bearing." By the time the army stopped retreating, it was within sight of the spires of Richmond.[53]

The hurried withdrawal might lose the Confederacy its capital, but meanwhile its immediate cost in matériel mounted far higher than had Johnston's earlier ill-managed experiments in abandonment at Harpers Ferry and Manassas. The tally included the naval base at Norfolk, unfinished vessels in the yards, the famed ironclad *Virginia* (née *Merrimack*), fifty-six large artillery pieces, and mountains of supplies. The guns and vessels could be replaced only laboriously, if at all. Only direct intervention by the new secretary of war, George Wythe Randolph, delayed the abandonment of Norfolk long enough to salvage some precious commodities. Otherwise Johnston's casual orders to abandon the city at once would have resulted in even greater loss.[54]

It is easy to suppose that Davis and Lee wondered anxiously whether Johnston would attempt to abandon Richmond, in continuance of his operations to date. A major in the army expressed the widespread concern a few months later, when Johnston had assumed command near Vicksburg. "I am afraid that the temptation to retreat from Vicksburg and burn his stores will be too strong . . . for as a participant therein I can never forget his 'masterly retreats' from Manassas, and Yorktown—and," had Johnston's wounding not intervened, "I verily believe he would have retreated from Richmond."[55]

The general did nothing to assuage the concerns of his superiors; in fact, he told them virtually nothing whatsoever of his intentions, despite being within a half-dozen miles of the capital. When a strong Federal column started south from Fredericksburg in late May, Johnston bestirred himself to launch an attack, on May 29, 1862, before the new enemies arrived. The weather gods conspired on his behalf. So did a nonchalant McClellan. Heavy rains flooded the boggy Chickahominy River Valley, across which the Federal army sprawled as it awaited the reinforcements. When the Fredericksburg column recoiled (in response to dashing maneuvers by Stonewall Jackson in the Shenandoah Valley), Johnston cancelled the attack. President Davis, excluded from Johnston's confidence, expectantly rode out on the twenty-ninth to follow the action and found nothing happening.

When Johnston's army finally moved forward on May 31, it launched the only major attack that Joe Johnston ever unleashed in Virginia. The simple, eminently workable plan, was to concentrate on Federals isolated south of the Chickahominy and defeat them in detail. In a remarkable display of intellectual sloth, Johnston failed either to issue detailed written orders or to communicate successfully the roles of his various columns. Gen. James Longstreet wound up moving on a sharp tangent away from where he was supposed to strike, in the process clogging the routes of other maneuver elements. The result was chaos of heroic proportions, unmatched in scope by any other major battle in the theater during the war. Johnston did nothing to unravel the ensuing mess, if in fact it could have been retrieved, and the rich opportunities of the day vanished. That evening, a musket ball and some artillery fragments hit Joe Johnston in the shoulder, chest, and thigh, causing moderately serious damage.[56]

The next day, Jefferson Davis named Robert E. Lee to lead the army. Joe Johnston would spend the rest of his Confederate career elsewhere. In 1864, faced with rounding the Army of Tennessee into shape, he would recall his former command in Virginia as "the truest army that ever fought or marched."[57]

The wounded general recovered without undue complications from his wounds, although he would be out of the field for nearly half a year. A letter dated June 7 reported him "improving every day. He sat up yesterday." Mrs. Johnston told a visitor on June 22 that her husband was "getting along very well, tho only strong enough to walk from one room to another." The convalescence proceeded steadily, although as late as November the general still reported "blistering myself" on doctor's orders.[58]

Johnston's final direct involvement with the army that would become so famous under Lee reflects badly upon his personal character. In reporting on Seven Pines, Johnston and Longstreet conspired to cover up the dreadful mistakes that had so altered the original plan. They cast the blame on Gen. Benjamin Huger, an apt scapegoat because of his own deficiencies, although in fact Huger had been the most adversely affected by Longstreet's errant march. Johnston's leading biographer suggests that the general collaborated with Longstreet's "absurd report" in part because "he was protecting Longstreet," and in part because Johnston "knew that he was himself partially, perhaps even fully, responsible for the misunderstanding." Johnston compounded the unlovely mess by directing another subordinate to alter his report as part of the cover-up.[59]

The notion that Johnston's wounding in the evening of May 31, 1862, proved fortunate for Confederate prospects gained wide circulation as Lee's fame grew. That perception was by no means a postwar phenomenon. In 1863, a Virginian commanding Alabama troops called Johnston's wounding "providential." When an engineer officer named Hinrichs, born on the Baltic coast, found himself assigned to Johnston early in 1862, the general promptly "made altogether a most favorable impression upon me." Hinrichs avidly absorbed the army's appraisal of the general, and recorded it with the careful wording of a second language. "There was always envy between him and Lee . . . Johnston got sore. . . . His injury during the battle of Seven Pines is considered a lucky happening for the State. The existing enmity between him and the Government seems to have been caused by his vanity and the fact, that he did not do anything." Hinrichs loyally called Johnston "a very brave man and has the strongest brain," but admitted in conclusion that "he has busied himself more with retreats than with anything else."[60]

Johnston's deep flaws as a commander made him a perilous choice for field assignment, yet a review of the slender alternatives clearly showed Jefferson Davis that he must be employed to fill one of the deficiencies across the Confederate frontier. The rift between the men had widened steadily during the six months of convalescence, as Johnston mingled steadily with the political camp that grew ever more hostile to the president. The antiadministration politicians and newspapers eagerly hymned Johnston's genius in *ex cathedra* pronouncements grounded solely on a timeless principle: an enemy of my enemy is my friend. Nonetheless, Davis recognized the desperate need for a new leader in the Western theater. He had not yet gotten over his inexplicable and mordant commitment to Gen. Braxton Bragg, so the Army of Tennessee must suffer further dire mismanagement. Accordingly, in late November 1862 Johnston headed west with a vague portfolio. He should supervise and coordinate somehow, but without any clear authority.

Jefferson Davis assigned Johnston to command, or at least some simulacrum of command, in the newly created Department of the West. The department sprawled across the South, covering all or parts of seven states. Two major armies operated within the department, under the spectacularly maladroit Braxton Bragg and the even worse, were it possible, John C. Pemberton. Those officers, and sometimes others, steadily corresponded directly with Richmond, rather than with the department commander. Logistical problems of nightmarish proportions bedeviled the region. What could Johnston do to effect change? The amorphous command situation of course stoked the general's ever-lurking paranoia. An officer functioning in a setting of mutual trust could have made little progress under the circumstances, and trust had no place in this frustrating equation.[61]

Everything that Johnston had done in Virginia foretold the course of events in his new theater of operations. Through the fall of 1862, the succeeding winter, and into the spring of 1863, Johnston sought in vain to coordinate—he could do no more with his limited status—operations across an enormous front. Pemberton's position seemed secure and Bragg's perilous; then the opposite circumstance prevailed; then the original again; eventually both Confederate armies staggered. In the aftermath of Bragg's bumbling at Murfreesboro, Davis instructed Johnston to visit the army and report on its condition. Although portions of Bragg's command structure seethed with mistrust of, and distaste for, its leader, Johnston astonishingly endorsed Bragg enthusiastically. The apparently disappointing operations at Murfreesboro, Johnston told Davis in February 1863, "evince[d] great vigor and skill." That he fully believed that stunningly unrealistic assessment is made obvious by a private comment to a political ally: "More effective fighting is not to be found in the history of modern battles."[62]

History surely cannot adjudge Murfreesboro matchlessly effective fighting, but far worse results loomed in the future of the department. Does the Confederate disaster at Vicksburg in the summer of 1863 fill a dark line on Joe Johnston's balance sheet? Little luster adhered to any Southern leader in connection with Vicksburg, but Johnston's role afforded limited opportunities to affect results. When he arrived near the Mississippi in mid-May, Federal combinations under Gen. U. S. Grant had overwhelmed the inept Pemberton. "I am too late," Johnston telegraphed to Richmond. For a time he hoped to combine his small relieving force with Pemberton's army somewhere east of Vicksburg, but Pemberton's intransigence and Johnston's characteristically imprecise and wishful orders stymied even that slender prospect. Saving the army and losing Vicksburg surely was preferable to losing both. "We must, if possible, save the troops," he wrote to Pemberton.[63]

Pemberton collapsed his force into works around the city and above the river and of course lost everything eventually. Time and again, before and after Vicksburg, Johnston's refrain ran the same: retreat and save the army. That doleful reiteration mounted up to proportions that overwhelm the general's reputation. In this instance, however, it is difficult to object to his analysis.

As the disaster at Vicksburg unfolded, Johnston had been needlessly secretive in dealing with Richmond, and artlessly hostile ("sharp captious . . . jejune and ice tempered," a War Department official noted) when he did communicate. The same Richmond official evaluated Johnston in early 1863 with remarkable prescience: "He is a *very little man*, has achieved nothing, full of himself . . . eaten up with morbid jealousy of Lee and of all his superiors in position, rank, or glory. I apprehend the gravest disasters from his command in the western department." Despite the general's unattractive behavior, however, his president deserves the most blame over Vicksburg. As the leading authority on the relationship has aptly observed, Davis "delegated responsibility without delegating authority and then refused to exercise the authority he withheld from the responsible commander."[64]

Less than three weeks after Vicksburg surrendered, the president restricted Johnston's aegis to a district that included none of the main theaters of operation. Outside Johnston's constricted area, Bragg's Army of Tennessee won a semblance of a great victory at Chickamauga in September, but Bragg quickly frittered away his advantage and wound up 1863 in northern Georgia, having lost his positions in Tennessee. For six months, Johnston exerted his primary energy— even more than usual—on his enemies in Richmond rather than his enemies in blue.[65]

The post-Vicksburg paper war included an unseemly degree of raw politics, outside the corridors of military discourse. Johnston's friend and patron in Congress, the bumptious and intemperate Louis T. Wigfall, showed the general's letters to other politicians and wrote scathing anti-Davis notes in reply. The president "should fall on his knees & thank God," Wigfall roared, that Johnston had "saved the blood of thousands in which [Davis] had wickedly intended to immerse his hands in order to cover up the disaster" brought on by Davis's "own big headedness & perverseness." The *Richmond Sentinel* summarized the opposing view about Johnston's performance as Vicksburg tottered, then fell: "Where was General JOHNSTON? . . . He made not a motion, he struck not a blow. . . . He sat down in sound of the conflict, and he fired not a gun. . . . He has done no more than to sit by and see Vicksburg fall, and send us the news."[66]

The quarrel between Johnston and Davis soon drew much of the government and the nation into its vortex. Mrs. Johnston and Mrs. Davis, once friends, now flung slurs at one another in sitting rooms filled with their acolytes. The coalescence of a steadily growing anti-Davis bloc behind Johnston solidified the schism. As newspapers chose sides, they of course did so based on their broad political views. Much of what respect Johnston's generalship enjoys today—and that perspective is not widely embraced—arises from the paeans to him in contemporary newspapers applauding the enemy of their own enemy. Every kudo to the general served simultaneously as a barb at the president. Johnston's biographer has concluded that Wigfall's fervid support, for instance, "was motivated as much by animosity toward Davis" as by friendship.[67]

The harm done by this quarrel reverberated across the country. As an early historian of the matter wrote, a "rift, in the nature of a serious and widely extended faction . . . centered in the person of Joseph Eggleston Johnston." A contemporary angrily described the damage early in 1864: "Johnston's disaffection has been the core round which all restless halfhearted disappointed people consolidated . . . like a dry rot. . . . It has served as an excuse for all selfishness, stay-at-home-ativeness, all languid patriotism." The dismayed Confederate called Johnston "A man who begins to snarl and sneer and quarrel at the very beginning because [of rank]."[68]

As fall turned to winter in 1863, observers must have been certain that Johnston would never again receive a major assignment from the president. The general surely believed that. The Confederacy's roster of generals, however, included so few options that Jefferson Davis, astonishingly, swallowed his pride and gave the Army of Tennessee to Johnston late in December. That sturdy army had fought magnificently under the hopelessly inept Braxton Bragg. Johnston's daunting task was to restore confidence to a command riven by factions; to find matériel to restore the army to reasonable efficiency; and to cope with a foe well led and in great strength. Those problems demanded a virtual miracle worker, not a man himself prone to factionalism, comfortable with slothful management, and unwilling to fight. Johnston probably would have failed in Georgia in 1864 had his crony Wigfall been president, doing everything possible to help him. In the atmosphere of harsh recrimination dominating his relationship with Richmond, Johnston's slender chance evaporated.

Although the administration cherished chimerical hopes of reclaiming part of Tennessee, the spring campaign actually would unleash Federals pushing toward Atlanta. The Army of Tennessee was ill-equipped to meet the threat in any number of ways. Johnston, never loath to announce his needs, bombarded Richmond with complaints.

After a single day in command, he damned the army's artillery as inadequate in every way, even though independent inspectors had certified its condition earlier in the month. In one short period, Johnston demanded 400 more horses, revised to 500, then 600, then 1,000, and the next day dropped back to 600—then convinced himself that he had been promised 1,000, and had been meanly betrayed when he did not get them.

Since horse supply bedeviled Confederate armies all across the country, Johnston's needs probably were legitimate in an absolute sense, although not relatively. An inspecting officer found the army's horses "quite serviceable," and comparable to "the average seen at this season" in other regions. Worse, Johnston's administrative indifference left him ignorant of the facts throughout his own command. Horses sent to the army had been misdirected to the use of staff officers and even clerks, and no one had bothered to establish any system for rehabilitating worn-down animals.[69]

Johnston's grappling with problems of administration and supply, repeated in countless other subthemes beyond horse replacement, paled by comparison with the inevitable question about operations in northern Georgia: would he fight? He would not.

In January, Johnston had written, amazingly, to the ever-aggressive Gen. J. E. B. Stuart in Virginia: "I agree with you to the utmost as to the principle of attacking when you fight." On the ground, as always, that principle rapidly evanesced. A general asked worriedly in March, "are we to hold still . . . in this position until" the enemy marshaled "his combined armies to drive us out?" In April, Gen. John B. Hood wrote of striving desperately "to induce" Johnston to advance, but "he will not consent." Confederate circumstances in 1864 surely would not offer many golden opportunities, and few good ones; that left as the only legitimate quest the search for the best possible terms of engagement. Seeking the textbook ideal would be in vain, yet nothing short of that could stir Joe Johnston to action. As Hood noted nervously and aptly, "When we are to be in a better condition to drive the enemy from our Country, I am not able to comprehend."[70]

When spring weather made campaigning possible, Gen. William T. Sherman grasped the initiative and moved his Federals against the Army of Tennessee. Johnston saw manifold defects in his army's situation, but in fact he enjoyed numerical odds notably more attractive than the Confederate norm. Davis had funneled troops from a broad region to Johnston in order to avoid the disastrous loss of the heart of

Georgia. Through the spring and early summer, the general sought to find precisely the right opportunity to assail his foe and thwart the Federal advance. No opportunity exactly fit his wishes; none ever would. Fighting rumbled sullenly, sometimes sharply, across the lines, swelling a dozen times into limited battle. Johnston won at least once in a limited tactical sense, achieved draws elsewhere, but steadily retreated toward Atlanta. Nothing ever approached a decisive initiative, as Johnston skillfully retired across north Georgia.[71]

The president and the government heard almost nothing from the sullenly incommunicative army commander, learning only tardily and with wrenching anxiety of the loss of position after position all the way to the outskirts of Atlanta. On July 17 the president relieved Johnston of command, and replaced him with Hood. The telegram tersely enunciated the government's position: "as you have failed to arrest the advance of the enemy to the vicinity of Atlanta, far in the interior of Georgia, and express no confidence that you can defeat or repel him, you are hereby relieved."[72]

For six months, as the Confederacy languished, General Johnston had no military role. He moved to a quiet corner of Georgia to work on his reports in defense of his record, then relocated through the Carolinas to avoid the Federal tide sweeping through the South. The Johnston position—martyrdom at the hands of Davis and Lee—solidified upon reflection. Maj. Richard J. Manning, a Johnston staff officer and intimate, doubtless spoke for his general when he "talked Joe Johnstonism run mad" in late July. "He coupled Lee and Davis and abused them with equal virulence. Lee was a solemn hypocrite. He used the garb of religion to mask his sins, but his iniquities were known." An amazed onlooker judged this outpouring a "mass of horror and wicked nonsense."[73]

>—+—+>—O—<+—+—<

In the final weeks of the Confederate nation, Johnston's quondam friend Robert E. Lee became general-in-chief of all the armies. Lee asked Davis to put Johnston in command of the Confederate remnants resisting in the Carolinas. When the president grudgingly agreed, Johnston admitted to "a most unchristian satisfaction" over Davis's discomfort. Even less charitably, Johnston convinced himself that "He was only put back to be the one to surrender."[74]

For two months, beginning on February 25, 1865, the general commanded the ragged detritus of the once-mighty Army of Tennessee in a forlorn hope. It fought with some success for Johnston at Bentonville on March 19, but on April 26 he faced the inevitable and surrendered its remnants to Sherman near Durham Station, North Carolina. U. S. Grant gave permission for Johnston to go to Canada, so long as he never returned "without first obtaining leave to do so." The surrendered general instead returned to Georgia.[75]

What was a defeated soldier nearing his sixtieth birthday to do for his livelihood in a shattered country? For some time Johnston used his engineering background as credentials for several positions with Southern railroads. Eventually he fell into a lucrative line when an English insurance company traded on his name to open an American branch. The resultant affluence gave Johnston the leisure he needed to write a detailed defense of his war record. For twenty years, until the general's death on March 21, 1891, he and Davis and other ex-Confederates waged a war with ink and paper that raged as warmly as ever the musketry had blazed.

>—◆—○—◆—◄

By almost any standard, Joe Johnston lost the battle of the books. His *Narrative of Military Operations* appeared in 1874 and ran to 602 pages, few of them well-balanced or graceful or even-tempered. The president's own memoir, in two thick volumes, appeared seven years later. It is a tedious, deadly dry, treatise, but relatively mild in tone toward Johnston and others. While the general thrashed violently about in print, flinging invective on every page, Davis played the statesman. When a subsequent series of articles by Johnston waxed even more virulent, a senator from Georgia wrote to Davis: "He has always had a respectable party of admirers in the South. He will have none now."[76]

The salient defects of *Narrative of Military Operations*, among many from which to choose, are dishonesty, excessive special pleading, and the absolute inability to imagine ever having erred. Given the species' universal ego's-eye view, every human narrative necessarily includes mild doses of the latter two shortcomings, but Johnston carried them to unseemly extremes. Paranoia and envy share the stage. In preparing to write of Seven Pines, for instance, Johnston convinced himself that his scorned rival Lee must have had about 125,000 men at the Seven Days. Powerful Federals, including Grant, Sherman, and McClellan, understandably loved Johnston and his writings, but few Confederates found much to praise. Even his friends blanched at portions of the book. A Johnston admirer from the staff of his bosom companion James Longstreet wrote in the margin of his copy of the memoir, "very Johnstonian, not worthy of Old Joe."[77]

Johnston's treatment at the hands of biographers and historians has followed the uneven path inevitable for a man so controversial. In the year of his death, hagiographic speeches and summaries appeared from nostalgic Confederates, as well as a lengthy (362 pages) biographical compendium by Gen. Bradley T. Johnson. Two years later Johnston's nephew R. M. Hughes wrote a large and adulatory biography. Amazingly, one publisher more attuned to marketing than historiography issued in 1891 a bound prospectus jointly advertising biographies of Johnston and Davis. Had the general still been alive, he surely would have delighted in the fact that his name came first on the cover, and only his visage appeared on it.[78]

Twentieth-century historians have not been overly kind to the general. Scholarly articles by Alfred P. James and Richard M. McMurry reached conclusions that range from unsympathetic to hostile. The 1956 biography by Gilbert E. Govan and James W. Livingood emphasized Johnston's problems and remained determinedly friendly. The standard work now is the fine 1992 book by Craig L. Symonds, which is frank and unblinking in criticism, though less than harsh. In a focused monograph, Jeffrey N. Lash's *Destroyer of the Iron Horse: General Joseph E. Johnston and Confederate Rail Transport, 1861–1865* (Kent: Kent State University Press, 1991) flails the general's indifference to rail facilities and equipment every bit as relentlessly as the title suggests. Lash makes a very strong case, but may be a bit more strident than the admittedly devastating evidence warrants.[79]

In 1868, Gen. Robert E. Lee discussed with an ex-Confederate colonel the impropriety of an officer's allowing "his own advantage or reputation to come into consideration" when defending his country. The example Lee used was "Gen. Joe. Johnston's sensitiveness on this score, and how wrong and unwise it was."[80] An examination of Johnston's record suggests that Lee's analysis was accurate.

>-+<>-O-<+-+-<

Joseph E. Johnston's own book, his ultimate autobiographical testimony, will remain the primary gauge of the man. The book, more apologia than history, surely does him more harm than good and constitutes a self-inflicted wound rather than a sturdy defense. Col.

Charles Marshall of Robert E. Lee's staff wrote a one-sentence depre-
cation of *Narrative of Military Operations* soon after its publication.
"If books as large as Genl J's 'Narrative' are to be written to explain
why things were *not* done," Marshall wondered, "what room will
be left in our libraries for the lives of those who actually did something deserving of record, and needing no apology or 'agility' of
explanation?"[81]

NOTES

1. Richard W. Corbin, *Letters of a Confederate Officer to His Family in
   Europe* (Paris: Neal's English Library, [1902]), 54–55.
2. Sketch of Peter Johnston in Dumas Malone, ed., *Dictionary of American
   Biography*, 20 vols. (New York: Charles Scribner's Sons, 1928–36),
   10:147–48 [set hereafter cited as Malone, ed., *DAB*]; Lewis P. Summers,
   History of Southwest Virginia (Richmond: J. L. Hill, 1903), 768–69
   (hereafter cited as Summers, *Southwest Virginia*). Summers includes a
   woodcut likeness of Peter Johnston. Late in life, Joseph E. Johnston
   claimed with some exaggeration that his father served as "adjutant" to
   "Light Horse Harry" Lee, (Johnston to J. William Jones, February 8,
   1875, offered for sale by RWA Auction, Wells, Maine, May 21, 2000.)
   For a brief but well-done biographical sketch, see *Peter Johnston,
   Junior: Virginia Soldier and Jurist* (Charlottesville: Historical Publishing, 1935).
3. Bradley T. Johnson, *A Memoir of the Life and Public Service of Joseph
   E. Johnston* (Baltimore: R. H. Woodward, 1891), 6–7 (hereafter cited as
   Bradley T. Johnson, *Memoir*); Summers, *Southwest Virginia*, 769;
   Robert M. Hughes, *General Johnston* (New York: Appleton, 1893),
   11–14 (hereafter cited as Hughes, *General Johnston*). Johnston's birth
   occurred two weeks and one day after that of Robert E. Lee, so he was
   behind his lifelong rival from the start.
4. *Register of the Officers and Cadets of the U.S. Military Academy, June
   1826* (West Point: U.S. Military Academy, 1884), 6–10, 19–22.
5. Ibid., *June 1827* (West Point: U.S. Military Academy, 1884), 6–9,
   19–20. The 1828 data come from the pamphlet of identical title for that
   year.
6. Ibid., *June 1829* (West Point: U. S. Military Academy, 1884), 6, 8–13,
   19.
7. The records of the cadet dispensary for this period are less substantial
   than those for the rest of the antebellum era. A single register (New York
   volume 600, in Record Group 94, entry 544, National Archives, Washington, D.C. (repository hereafter cited as NA) covers 1827–1833. It

does not record a single visit by Cadet Johnston. In Hughes, *General Johnston*, 16, that young kinsman of the general reported that Cadet Johnston suffered from an eye affliction while at West Point that included night blindness.

8. For these episodes and others from Jefferson Davis's frolicsome cadet years, see the excellent biography by William C. Davis, *Jefferson Davis: The Man and His Hour* (New York: HarperCollins, 1991), 30–38.

9. Returns of the 4th U.S. Artillery for August 1829 through September 1831, M727, "Returns from Regular Army Artillery Regiments," NA.

10. Francis B. Heitman, *Historical Register and Dictionary of the United States Army*, 2 vols. (Washington: U.S. Government Printing Office, 1903), 1:417, 444 (hereafter cited as Heitman, *Historical Register*). Galt died in 1851, having won some distinction in the Mexican War; Fenwick in 1842.

11. Returns of the 4th U.S. Artillery for January 1830 to July 1836, M727, "Returns from Regular Army Artillery Regiments," NA. Ewell became best known as a longtime professor at, then president of, the College of William and Mary. He was a brother of Confederate general Richard S. Ewell. Benjamin had been at West Point with Johnston, although three years behind.

12. Monthly and annual returns of the 4th U.S. Artillery for January 1832 to May 1833, M727, "Returns from Regular Army Artillery Regiments," NA.

13. Returns of the 4th U.S. Artillery for November 1833 to August 1836, M727, "Returns from Regular Army Artillery Regiments," NA.

14. George W. Cullum, *Biographical Register of the Officers and Graduates of the U. S. Military Academy, from 1802 to 1867*, 2 vols. (New York: James Miller, 1879), 1:343–44 (hereafter cited as Cullum, *Biographical Register*); Frank Laumer, *Dade's Last Command* (Gainesville: University Press of Florida, 1995), 219–20. Laumer reproduces the Johnston drawing, and another almost identical to it that accompanied an official report. Johnston apparently had not visited the massacre site when he prepared the sketch, perhaps based on someone else's field notes, since he showed the crude fortification as a square instead of a triangle. The schoolmate killed with Dade was Lt. William E. Basinger of Georgia.

15. Johnston to Beverly Johnston (his brother), June 13, 1837, Joseph E. Johnston Papers, Swem Library, College of William and Mary, Williamsburg, Virginia; Heitman, *Historical Register*, 1:578. Johnston's resignation took effect fourteen days before his letter to his brother.

16. George E. Buker, *Swamp Sailors in the Second Seminole War* (Gainesville: University Press of Florida, 1997), 59–65; John K. Mahon, *History of the Second Seminole War, 1835–1842* (Gainesville: University Press of Florida, 1967), 220, 232; Bradley T. Johnson, *Memoir*, 11.

17. R. C. Weightman to Adjutant General Roger Jones, June 23, 1848, document 163-J-1848, M567, "Letters Received by the Office of the Adjutant

General [Main Series]," NA; Adjutant General to Weightman, June 26, 1848, M565, "Letters Sent by the Office of the Adjutant General [Main Series]," NA.

18. Cullum, *Biographical Register*, 1:344.

19. Hughes, *General Johnston*, 22–23; Malone, ed., DAB, 12:113–16. For one apparent ripple in the domestic bliss, see a letter by Mark Twain, August 22, 1897, in Mark Twain, *The Selected Letters of Mark Twain*, ed. Charles Neider (New York: Harper & Row, 1982), 247. Many of the Johnstons' letters are at the Maryland Historical Society (repository hereafter cited as MHS).

20. Documents 273-A-1846, 493-T-1846, 97-J-1847, 111-J-1847, and 726-S-1847 (enclosure 37) in M567, "Letters Received by the Office of the Adjutant General [Main Series]," NA; Cullum, *Biographical Register*, 1:344.

21. Documents 345-A-1847 and 726-S-1847 (enclosure 104), M567, "Letters Received by the Office of the Adjutant General [Main Series]," NA; Roswell S. Ripley, *The War with Mexico*, 2 vols. (New York: Harper, 1849), 2:414–23. Johnston described his Mexican War experiences in a letter to Henry J. Hunt on January 16, 1870 (MS. 2382, Gilder-Lehrman Collection, Pierpont Morgan Library, New York [repository hereafter cited as G-L].

22. John B. Floyd letter, March 6, 1860, document 71-W-1860, filed for some reason at 47-J-1858, M567, "Letters Received by the Office of the Adjutant General [Main Series]," NA; see also 163-J-1848 in the same series.

23. Cols. Edmund B. Alexander and Philip St. George Cooke (J. E. B. Stuart's father-in-law), to Davis, March 15, 1860, in Jefferson Davis, *The Papers of Jefferson Davis*, ed. Lynda Lasswell Crist and others, 11 vols. to date (Baton Rouge: Louisiana State University Press, 1971–2003), 6:644–45; R. E. Lee to Custis Lee, April 16, 1860, in J. William Jones, ed., *Life and Letters of Robert Edward Lee: Soldier and Man* (New York and Washington: Neale, 1906), 113–14.

24. Cullum, *Biographical Register*, 1:344. A nice manuscript report by Johnston during the Mormon War, dated May 27, 1858, is MS. 4685, G-L. Because of surveying duty, Johnston missed his regiment's pitched battle with Cheyennes on July 29, 1857, one of the few frontier clashes that resembled the Hollywood notion of charging mounted lines (see William Y. Chalfant, *Cheyennes and Horse Soldiers: The 1857 Expedition and the Battle of Solomon's Fork* [Norman: University of Oklahoma Press, 1989]).

25. Dabney H. Maury, *Recollections of a Virginian in the Mexican, Indian, and Civil Wars* (New York: Scribner's, 1894), 146; *Report of the Commission Appointed under the . . . Act of Congress of June 21, 1860, to Examine into the Organization, System of Discipline, and Course of*

Instruction of the United States Military Academy at West Point (Washington: U.S. Senate), 189–90. Johnston also supported a five-year term at the Academy, thought the discipline "unnecessarily severe," and urged extensive instruction in fencing.

26. Johnston to secretary of war, January 24, 1860, document 9-J-1860 M567, "Letters Received by the Office of the Adjutant General [Main Series]," NA.

27. Cullum, *Biographical Register*, 1:344; the commission in M567, NA, document 69-J-1860. Cullum dates the staff rank from June 28, 1860, but the original is dated June 30.

28. All of the material in the paragraphs concerning Johnston's tenure as quartermaster general comes from the chronological file of correspondence of that office in M745, "Letters Sent by the Office of the Quartermaster General, Main Series, 1818-1870," NA. Roll 35 covers all of the period during which Johnston held that post. A series of letters by Johnston dealing with quartermaster quarrels, some of them over amazingly minute matters, is in M567, "Letters Received by the Office of the Adjutant General [Main Series]," in documents (all with 1860 appended at the end) 16-J, 69-J, 229-M, 18-Q, 23-Q, 363-S, and 71-W.

29. Joseph E. Johnston, *Narrative of Military Operations, Directed, During the Late War between the States* (New York: Appleton, 1874), 10–12 (hereafter cited as Johnston, *Narrative of Military Operations*); Johnston's official Compiled Service Record (hereafter cited as CSR), M331, "Compiled Service Records of Confederate General and Staff Officers, and Non-Regimental Enlisted Men," NA. A slip giving Johnston's date of appointment in the Virginia establishment as April 26, 1861, is in M347, "Unfiled Papers and Slips Belonging in Confederate Compiled Service Records," NA. In that useful and largely ignored source, the Johnsons and Johnstons are indiscriminately intermixed. The Confederate commission of May 15 took rank from the fourteenth. Students working on Johnston should be advised that M331 contains two distinct and separate files on Johnston, both on the same roll. A detailed eyewitness account of Johnston's resignation is in *Harper's Weekly*, September 14, 1872.

30. Johnston, *Narrative of Military Operations*, 17–18.

31. U. S. War Department, *The War of the Rebellion: A Compilation of the Official Records of the Union and Confederate Armies*, 127 vols., index, and atlas (Washington: U.S. Government Printing Office, 1880-1901), I, 2:880–81, 889 (set hereafter cited as OR, with all citations to Series I unless otherwise noted; for volumes that appeared in more than one part [volume 2 is not one such], the part is shown in parentheses after the volume number).

32. *OR*, 2:895–98, 907–8.

33. Johnston, *Narrative of Military Operations*, 23–29.

34. *OR*, 2:923–25, 929.
35. Ibid., 2:985; Johnston's CSR, M331, NA. The dates of rank and confirmation are from the general's official CSR. On one slip, the confirmation date of August 31, 1861, is crossed through and replaced above the line by April 23, 1863!
36. Sir A. P. Wavell in a 1933 training discourse, quoted in Robert D. Heinl, *Dictionary of Military and Naval Quotations* (Annapolis: U.S. Naval Institute, 1966), 64. An excellent, well-balanced history of the battle is William C. Davis, *Battle at Bull Run: A History of the First Major Campaign of the Civil War* (Garden City, N.Y.: Doubleday, 1977).
37. "Private," a member of the 1st Virginia Infantry, in *Richmond Dispatch*, November 14, 1861, 1. A letter in similar vein by another soldier appeared in the same journal on September 12, 1861, 1.
38. Joseph E. Johnston, "Responsibilities of the First Bull Run," in Robert Underwood Johnson and Clarence Clough Buel, eds., *Battles and Leaders of the Civil War*, 4 vols. (New York: Century, 1887–1888), 1:250–52. Another among the rich panoply of Davis-Johnston quarrels was a furor over pursuit of the fleeing enemy after the battle of July 21. One of Johnston's defenses in that regard appears in the same article.
39. Letters of James Lovell to William Whipple and John Adams to Abigail, July 7 and May 22, 1777, in Paul H. Smith, ed., *Letters of Delegates to Congress, 1774–1789*, 26 vols. (Washington: Library of Congress, 1976–2000), 7:317, 103.
40. *OR*, 2:1007.
41. Ibid., 2:945. After the war, Jefferson Davis referred to Johnston as "Lee's envious detractor" (Davis to J. William Jones, April 9, 1883, offered in Alexander Autographs Auction, Cos Cob, Connecticut, October 18, 2000).
42. *OR*, IV, 1: 605–8. The legislation upon which Johnston based his complaints is printed in this source on pages 163-64.
43. Dunbar Rowland, ed., *Jefferson Davis Constitutionalist: His Life and Letters*, 10 vols. (Jackson: Mississippi Department of Archives and History, 1923), 3:39; *OR*, IV, 1:611.
44. The obsession with rank is reminiscent of, among others, Douglas MacArthur. That general's leading biographer described his arrogant subject as "a pleader for special consideration and a sensitive, self-righteous protester against any infringements upon what he felt were his prerogatives" (D. Clayton James, *The Years of MacArthur*, 3 vols. [Boston: Houghton Mifflin Company, 1970–1985], 1:126).
45. Ida Powell Dulany diary September 24, 1861, copy in the author's possession.
46. John M. Tilley to wife, December 1, 1861, in Georgia Division United Daughters of the Confederacy, *Confederate Reminiscences and Letters, 1861–1865*, 15 vols. (Atlanta: United Daughters of the Confederacy,

1995–2000), 14:242; W. R. Houghton and M. B. Houghton, *Two Boys in the Civil War and After* (Montgomery, Alabama: Paragon, 1912), 53; T. D. Witherspoon letter, July 18 (?), 1861, sold by Siegel Auction Galleries, Atlanta, Georgia, May 28, 1994. Despite his short stature Johnston had a very large head, wearing a size $7^1/2$ hat (*The Letters of Major General James E. B. Stuart* [Richmond: The Stuart-Mosby Historical Society, 1990], 252).

47. For an example of Johnston's amazing memory, see John B. Beall, *In Barrack and Field* (Nashville: Publishing House of the M. E. Church, South, 1906), 311–12. The virtual unanimity of the general's staff in his support extends even beyond the expected norm in such circumstances.

48. Johnston, *Narrative of Military Operations*, 96–97. The comment about Benjamin is from a letter to Mrs. Johnston on February 13, 1862, quoted in Craig L. Symonds, *Joseph E. Johnston, A Civil War Biography* (New York: Norton, 1992), 137–38, 403 (hereafter cited as Symonds, *Joseph E. Johnston*. Benjamin's regime as secretary of war was about as unsuccessful as it could well have been. His meddling directly within outlying establishments, abetted by the detail-obsessed Davis, might serve as a model for how not to wage war.

49. Johnston, *Narrative of Military Operations*, 97–103; *OR*, 5:527–28, 1096.

50. Jefferson Davis, *The Rise and Fall of the Confederate Government*, 2 vols. (New York: Appleton, 1881), 1:466–69; *OR*, 51(2): 1073–74.

51. Johnston, *Narrative of Military Operations*, 109–13.

52. *OR*, 11(3): 275–76; John S. Mosby, *The Letters of John S. Mosby* (n.p.: Stuart-Mosby Historical Society, 1986), 77-78.

53. William C. Coker, "Incompleted History of Companies F&M, 8th Regiment, So. Ca. Volunteers," Darlington County Historical Commission, South Carolina. An exceptionally fine study of Williamsburg during the war, which includes a solid summary of the May 5 battle, is Carol Kettenburg Dubbs, *Defend This Old Town: Williamsburg during the Civil War* (Baton Rouge: Louisiana State University Press, 2001).

54. *OR*, 11(1): 337; Davis, *Rise and Fall*, 2:92–93.

55. Eugene Blackford to "My dear Mary," May 21, 1863, Gordon-Blackford Papers, MHS, Baltimore (hereafter cited as Gordon-Blackford Papers, MHS).

56. The best studies of Seven Pines are both by Steven H. Newton: *The Battle of Seven Pines* (Lynchburg, Va.: H. E. Howard, 1993) and *Joseph E. Johnston and the Defense of Richmond* (Lawrence: University Press of Kansas, 1998). Both are uncommonly well written, but neither has the bulk to be definitive on the battle.

57. Johnston to J. E. B. Stuart, January 21, 1864, Stuart Papers, Huntington Library, San Marino, California (repository hereafter cited as HL). The general's envy of Lee and of the army's post-Johnston success is

reflected in a remarkably disloyal letter to Johnston from James Long-street on October 5, 1862, for which see Robert K. Krick, *The Smooth-bore Volley that Doomed the Confederacy* (Baton Rouge: Louisiana State University Press, 2002), 60–61.

58. Letter printed in *The Sunny South* (Aberdeen, Mississippi), July 3, 1862, reporting on Johnston's condition by a young woman in the family party; Henry L. P. King diary, June 22, 1862, Southern Historical Collection, University of North Carolina, Chapel Hill; Johnston to "My Dear Lizzy," November 7, 1862, George F. Holmes Papers, Library of Congress.

59. Symonds, Joseph E. Johnston, 173. Longstreet's dishonest report is in *OR*, 11(1):939–41. This much-discussed affair is examined, among many other places, in Gustavus W. Smith, *The Battle of Seven Pines* (New York: C. G. Crawford, 1891) and George W. Mindil, *The Battle of Fair Oaks: A Reply to General Joseph W. Johnston* (Philadelphia: privately printed, 1874). Mindil's extensive correspondence with participants, which is interesting and important, survives at the post library, Fort Monmouth, New Jersey. The Mindil pamphlet and its supporting MSS constitute a strikingly underutilized resource on Seven Pines, not even cited in most works on the subject. Johnston's valedictory to his former army included determined attempts to make clear the immense reinforcements Lee received to make possible his subsequent success. See for example *Southern Historical Society Papers*, ed. J. William Jones et al., 52 vols. (Richmond, Va.: Southern Historical Society, 1876–1959), 1:89–90, 407–24.

60. Eugene Blackford to Mary, May 21, 1863, Gordon-Blackford Papers, MHS; journal of Lt. Oscar Hinrichs, 34–38, TS in the author's possession. Hinrichs (1835–1893) was assigned early in 1862 to Johnston and subsequently did engineer duty with Ewell and Jackson.

61. The best summary of Johnston's ordeal in the western theater is a masterful analysis by Richard M. McMurry, "'The *Enemy* at Richmond': Joseph E. Johnston and the Confederate Government," *Civil War History* 27 (March 1981):5–31 (hereafter cited as McMurry, "'The *Enemy* at Richmond'").

62. *OR*, 23(2): 613-14624, 631; Johnston to Louis T. Wigfall, February 14, 1863, as quoted in Symonds, *Joseph E. Johnston*, 197.

63. *OR*, 24(1): 215–16, 272.

64. Robert Garlick Hill Kean, *Inside the Confederate Government: The Diary of Robert Garlick Hill Kean*, ed. Edward Younger (New York: Oxford, 1957), 50; McMurry, "'The *Enemy* at Richmond,'" 12.

65. A superbly analytical and gracefully written study of the relationship between Johnston and Davis is Joseph T. Glatthaar, *Partners in Command: The Relationships between Leaders in the Civil War* (New York: Free Press, 1994), 95–134.

66. Wigfall to Johnston, August 1863, quoted in Symonds, Joseph E. Johnston, 223; *Richmond Sentinel*, July 9, 1863, 2.

67. Symonds, *Joseph E. Johnston*, 265. For an example of friendship between the two women into the fall of 1861, long after the first eruption over rank that summer, see the *Richmond Dispatch*, October 4–5, 1861 (page 2 both days), for a report of an accident during a joint carriage ride.

68. Alfred P. James, "General Joseph Eggleston Johnston: Storm Center of the Confederate Army," *Mississippi Valley Historical Review* 14 (1927): 359; C. Vann Woodward, ed., *Mary Chesnut's Civil War* (New Haven, Conn.: Yale University Press, 1981), 607–8.

69. The details of the astounding dithering about horses is summarized nicely in McMurry, "'The *Enemy* at Richmond,'" 22–24.

70. Johnston to J. E. B. Stuart, January 21, 1864, Stuart Papers, HL; A. P. Stewart and John B. Hood to Braxton Bragg in March and April 1864, quoted in McMurry, "'The *Enemy* at Richmond,'" 25.

71. Johnston, *Narrative of Military Operations*, 355–56, reported (far too conservatively) just under 10,000 casualties in his army during this campaign, one-third of them near Dalton and Resaca. He also compared his operations with Lee's concurrent efforts in Virginia, which were, he noted somewhat bitterly, "increasing his [Lee's] great fame." His contemporary autobiographical comparison of his own prowess with Lee's is in *OR*, 38(5):888.

72. *OR*, 38(5): 885. For the campaign, see Richard M. McMurry, *Atlanta, 1864: Last Chance for the Confederacy* (Lincoln: University of Nebraska Press, 2000) and Albert E. Castel, *Decision in the West: The Atlanta Campaign of 1864* (Lawrence: University Press of Kansas, 1992). Both books are very well written studies. Castel supplies far more operational detail (in three times as many pages), while McMurry concentrates on analysis.

73. Woodward, ed., *Mary Chesnut's Civil War*, 623. Congressman Jeremiah Morton reported an example of Johnston's similarly bitter envy toward Stonewall Jackson. Johnston told Morton that he did not consider Jackson a military genius, but "he was possessed with a sublime enthusiasm." (Morton as told to Jedediah Hotchkiss, recorded by Hotchkiss in 1864 in MS notes on blank pages of a printed 1857 catalog for Mossy Creek Academy, Alderman Library, University of Virginia.)

74. Symonds, *Joseph E. Johnston*, 343; Gilbert E. Govan and James W. Livingood, *A Different Valor: The Story of General Joseph E. Johnston, C.S.A.* (Indianapolis: Bobbs-Merrill, 1956), 347.

75. Grant to J. M. Schofield, May 22, 1865, in Johnston's CSR, M331, NA.

76. Symonds, *Joseph E. Johnston*, 365–71. The quote (p. 367) is from Sen. Benjamin H. Hill. The full citations for the Johnston and Davis memoirs appear in earlier notes. An editor who worked with Johnston in the 1880s called him "as dry as the remainder biscuit after a voyage," afflicted with "dogged obstinancy," and "quite irascible." (Robert

Underwood Johnson, *Remembered Yesterdays* [Boston: Little, Brown, 1923], 199–200.)

77. Johnston to Benjamin S. Ewell, June 7, 1872, in catalogue of Chapel Hill Rare Books, Chapel Hill, North Carolina, August 1997; manuscript marginalia in Osmun Latrobe's copy of Johnston's memoir, TS in the author's possession. The letter to Ewell insists that Johnston left 70,000 men to Lee, Jackson added 16,000, Holmes 15,000 more, and 22,000 men came up from the Atlantic coast. An obscure and interesting contemporary account of the warmth between Johnston and McClellan is in George B. McClellan Jr., "Reminiscences of Geo. B. McClellan and 'Stonewall' Jackson," *Blue and Gray* 1 (1893):30–31.

78. An example of the mortuary hagiography is Leigh Robinson, *Joseph E. Johnston: An Address Delivered before the Association of Ex-Confederate Soldiers and Sailors of Washington, D.C.* (Washington: R. O. Polkinhorn, 1891). Robinson, a veteran of the Richmond Howitzers in the Army of Northern Virginia, wrote extensively and well about his own experiences, but this published speech is shallow and entirely uncritical. The biographies by Johnson and Hughes have been cited repeatedly in earlier notes. The joint Johnston-Davis prospectus is in cloth bearing the cover title "Life and Reminiscences of Johnston and Davis"; an interior title page lists a variant publisher from the final Bradley Johnson book, but there is no title page for the Davis portion of the sample.

79. In two earlier articles, Lash examined the same subject in rich detail focused on specific periods: "Joseph E. Johnston and the Virginia Railways, 1861–1862," *Civil War History* 35 (March 1989):5–27; and "Joseph E. Johnston's Grenada Blunder," *Civil War History* 23 (June 1977):114–28. Ironically, the Richmond, Fredericksburg, and Potomac Railroad named a new locomotive the "Gen. Johnston" in late 1861 (*Richmond Dispatch*, September 23, 1861, 2, October 9, 1861, 2). Articles by James and McMurry (McMurry has written several, all good) have been cited in earlier notes, as have the books by Hughes, Johnson, Govan and Livingood, and Symonds.

80. Lee to William Allan, April 15, 1868, in Gary W. Gallagher, ed., *Lee the Soldier* (Lincoln: University of Nebraska Press, 1996), 15.

81. Charles Marshall to G. W. Mindil, April 26, 1875, original at the post library, Fort Monmouth, New Jersey.

Edmund Kirby Smith

Joseph T. Glatthaar

Among the full Confederate generals who commanded soldiers in the field, Edmund Kirby Smith is by far the most obscure. With the exception of Samuel Cooper, the adjutant and inspector general of the Confederacy who spent the entire war behind a desk, Smith was the only one who never led one of the two principal armies of the Confederacy. Instead, he headed the Department of the Trans-Mississippi, a region that had little impact on the ultimate outcome of the war and one of great importance only to those who either resided or had loved ones there.[1]

Because of the remote nature of his duty as full general—all Confederate territory west of the Mississippi River—Smith has generated comparatively little interest. Among those few who have voiced an opinion on his performance, however, sentiments have varied. Confederate President Jefferson Davis admired Smith's patriotism and sense of duty and demurred whenever others called for his removal, informing the general in late 1864, "Your various promotions and assignments to high and responsible duties furnish the best evidence of my confidence in your zeal and ability." The two retained a strong friendship for the remainder of their lives, even though some of Smith's closest friends loathed the ex-president. By contrast, Davis's former brother-in-law, the hot-tempered Richard Taylor, clashed frequently with Smith during his days of service under him, and his hostility abated little over the postwar years. In his memoirs, Taylor suggested that Smith's incompetence bordered on aiding and abetting the enemy. He accused the general of seeming "determined to throw a protective shield around the Federal army and fleet" and vituperated that Smith "had the power to destroy the last hope of the Confederate cause, and exercised it."[2]

Within the historian's ranks, two in particular, Joseph H. Parks and Robert L. Kerby, offer distinctly divergent portraits of Smith as a departmental commander. Parks, the author of the only modern biography of Smith, never provides an analysis or assessment of his tenure as commander of the Trans-Mississippi Department. Still, the supportive tone and uncritical exploration of his military career convey a very favorable impression to the reader. Kerby, whose classic volume *Kirby Smith's Confederacy* is by far the best treatment of the wartime region, rebukes Smith for his lack of leadership and poor judgment. Kerby suppresses any disdain for Smith; the author merely depicts him as incompetent to direct a department or to command large military units.[3]

What makes Smith so difficult to assess, though, is that his duties encompassed far greater variation than other army commander, with the exception of Gen. Robert E. Lee in the late stages of the war when the commander of the Army of Northern Virginia assumed the mantle of general-in-chief as well. With most army commanders, success or failure on the battlefield is the measuring stick by which they are evaluated. Smith's department—often referred to as Kirby Smithdom because of its vastness and his extensive powers to command it—literally extended over hundreds of thousands of square miles. It suffered from sundry unique problems: a frontier with active, hostile Indians to the west; a foreign country on its southern border; a massive river to the east, the Mississippi, which Federals dominated by mid-1863; a dearth of manufacturing, even by Confederate standards; prolonged slow and irregular communication with government officials in Richmond; and a limited transportation network. His concerns extended far beyond those of a single army, to include politics, diplomacy, economics, and civilian society. Severed from direct or speedy communications with Richmond officials after Federals seized control of the Mississippi River, Smith assumed responsibilities that authorities traditionally reserved for the political realm. The delicate boundaries between military command and political decision-making often blurred, as Smith searched for solutions to myriad problems, military and civil, with varying degrees of success.

Edmund was born in 1824, the fourth child in a family that hailed from Connecticut but resided in Florida. At the time of his birth, his oldest brother, Ephraim, was already attending the U.S. Military Academy at West Point. Ephraim, whom people often referred to as Kirby, graduated in 1826 and embarked on a military career. Edmund followed his brother's footsteps, entering West Point in the class of 1845. Unlike his brother, who was a poor student, Edmund—Ted to his family and "Seminole," in honor of his Florida upbringing, to his classmates—graduated in the middle of his class. Weak eyesight and a few too many demerits nearly sidelined young Smith. He shaped up his conduct just enough, and faculty came to his rescue after he failed his medical examination, so that he received, nonetheless, a commission as a brevet second lieutenant.

Unfortunately, as the youngest child, Smith had to deal with his parents' marital difficulties. His father, Joseph Lee Smith, was a lawyer who had attended the famed Litchfield Law School in Connecticut, probably the best in the nation. Somehow, however, his father never lived up to his potential. Although the Smiths were small-time slave owners, money was always tight, and this may have worsened the strain between husband and wife. In his later years, financial and professional frustration compounded, and Joseph became ever more cantankerous. His interference in Edmund's life was usually for the worse. In one instance, he wrote an intemperate letter to government officials about his son, which proved extremely embarrassing to both of them. Toward his wife, he was abusive verbally, and possibly physically as well.

Sadly, the burgeoning marital tensions, which culminated in separation, fell largely on Edmund's shoulders. Playing the role of parent and broker to the adults, his West Point correspondence home sought common ground for some type of reconciliation. At times, his letters exuded empathy; in other missives, he beseeched them to try work out matters. Ultimately, the inability to bring them together, to get his mother to return home to care for his aging father, evoked frustration in young Edmund.

At a time when his West Point peers worried about grades and sneaking off to Benny Havens's Tavern without getting caught, Edmund carried the burden of his parents' estrangement. The entire affair forced him to assume the role of adult at a very early age. The unfortunate experience, however, never destroyed his love for them. He continued to act as emotional caretaker, and after his father's death Edmund provided for his mother financially.[4]

Smith's first assignment was with the 5th Infantry Regiment under Brig. Gen. Zachary Taylor, headed for duty in Texas after annexation. Serving alongside his brother Ephraim, young Smith exhibited considerable courage under fire against Mexican forces at Palo Alto, Resaca de la Palma, and Monterrey. Promoted to second lieutenant and transferred to the 7th Infantry, Edmund participated in Maj. Gen. Winfield Scott's capture of Vera Cruz and the inland march on Mexico City. At the battle of Cerro Gordo, he distinguished himself again, earning a brevet promotion to first lieutenant. In the battles around and in Mexico City, Smith continued to fight boldly and somehow managed to escape injury. His brother Ephraim, though, was not so lucky. During a battalion attack at Chapultepec, a musket ball crashed through his eye and emerged near his ear. Several days later, Ephraim lapsed into a coma from which he never recovered. Despite his grief, Edmund finished out the campaign and the war.[5]

After a stint as mathematics professor at West Point, he returned to his regiment, now stationed back in Texas, to command a company of infantrymen. Duty consisted of extensive boredom, followed by lengthy scouts that might take them on a journey of six weeks, covering more than a thousand miles, and achieving little. Not only did they have to engage hostile Indians but troops had to battle the Texas elements as well. Assignment to escort a boundary commission broke the routine, and upon his return, some welcome news awaited him.[6]

The secretary of war was Jefferson Davis, a powerful Southern Democrat, a West Point graduate, and a hero in the war with Mexico. Davis convinced Congress to authorize the expansion of the Regular Army by four new regiments. Rather than fill these new vacancies by seniority, Davis pored over the service records of the officer corps and promoted individuals based on achievement. The War Department assigned Smith to the rank of captain in the 2nd Cavalry Regiment, a new command that Davis stacked with many of the very best officers in the army. Col. Albert Sidney Johnston commanded the regiment, with Lt. Col. Robert E. Lee as second-in-command. Majs. George H. Thomas and William J. Hardee, Capt. Earl Van Dorn, and Lts. John Bell Hood and Fitzhugh Lee were among the other officers. The infantryman had joined the elite cavalry.

Over the next five and a half years, Smith spent the bulk of his time in Texas campaigning against Indians. During his service with the infantry, he realized that manning outposts in an attempt to protect settlers and their property from Indian raids was a futile proposition.

Often the government built these fortifications on "some defenseless position for the purpose of being kept in check by the Indians," he commented wryly. With the cavalry, he learned that large expeditions accomplished little against nomadic peoples. "We travelled through the country, broke down our men, killed our horses and returned as ignorant, of the whereabouts of Mr Sanico [the prey], as when we started." Unless they were cornered, the Indians gave battle only on terms advantageous to themselves. Over time, he learned that campaigning on mules, fighting Indian style, offered them the best hope of victory. "T'is only by adopting their mode of life & assimilating ourselves whilst on scout to their habits," he explained, "that we can operate successfully against them." By seizing the initiative and campaigning in smaller, more mobile units, the army achieved its best results. Still, there were no assurances of success. Fighting in scouting parties also increased chances of disaster. In one raid in 1859, Smith suffered his first combat wound, a shot in the upper thigh—the projectile passing through flesh and muscle and barely missing an artery—from which he recovered quickly. A policy of active campaigning, with its long, tedious marches in inhospitable Texas summers, too, took its toll on men and animals. And while it might reap the greatest results, progress was sporadic. "With our utmost endeavour," he confessed in 1860, "we but occasionally meet with success."[7]

As Smith and his comrades battled Indians on the Texas frontier, the sectional conflict heated up with the approach of the presidential election that year. Despite service in the national army for fifteen years, he expressed his support for the slave states. "I am a southern man," he justified to his mother, "in all my feeling." Several weeks later, his mother reassured herself of her son's stance by pressing him, if the "North and South are arrayed against each other in *war* we feel assured which side you will take." Within two months, after his native state of Florida withdrew from the Union, her son resigned as a major in the U.S. Army and sought a commission as an officer for the Confederate States of America.[8]

Like virtually all Southern whites, Smith never challenged the righteousness of the "peculiar institution." He owned a literate slave named Aleck, whom his family had raised as a boy and trained to be the officer's personal servant, and he had no qualms about the "peculiar institution." To be sure, there were a few elements that upset him. A man who was sensitized to the breakup of families, he found the practice of separating slave families through sale reprehensible. When he learned a slave family whom he knew was dissolved through sale, he informed his mother, "I almost feel like voting for Lincoln when I see families broken up and children so completely separated from the parents." But it was the act and not the institution that bothered him. Smith grew up in a slave state, under a constitution that protected the rights of whites to own people of African ancestry, and he derived his moral compass from a divine book called the Bible, which apparently justified slavery. Since birth, his parents had raised him in a society that had taught and regularly reinforced the notion that the institution was both a necessary evil for slaveholders and a positive good for slaves. To challenge slavery on moral grounds was quite absurd. The North had embarked on a policy of threatening slavery, which undercut the compromises that the Founding Fathers had forged during the Constitutional debates. That Northern majority had elected a president whose party had openly vowed to erode Southern rights over slavery in the territories. Smith was a reluctant secessionist, one who regretted the dissolution of the Union, but he saw no alternative. He would join the Confederacy, use all his powers to see that it established its independence from the North, and place his trust in God. "We are in the hands of that Providence who knows the justice of our cause," he reassured his mother, "and has said he will listen to the prayers of the righteous." Edmund Kirby Smith never doubted the worthiness of the Confederate cause.[9]

Once Florida and then Texas seceded from the Union, Smith made up his mind to cast his lot with the Confederacy. He tidied up some military affairs, resigned his commission in early March, and headed for Montgomery, the seat of the Confederate government, to offer his services in this new army. By late April, he was destined for Virginia, a theater of operations that would change his life in several dramatic ways.

Smith's first assignment was to organize and equip volunteers who arrived in the railroad town of Lynchburg, Virginia. While on duty, Smith needed two new shirts, and a competitive joke circulated among the townspeople that the woman who sewed the best shirt would marry the eligible bachelor. Frontier Texas offered few opportunities to meet a woman who could appeal culturally and intellectually with a college-educated, well-traveled officer. On trips home, his mother and family members tried to set him up with eligible women. Nothing took. This time, Cassie Seldon, a young woman from a wealthy, slaveholding family, made the best shirt and ultimately claimed the prize. The two fell for one another quickly, and before the year was out, they married. Over the years, Cassie bore eleven children, which, as one historian has mentioned, "should give pause to any young lady volunteering to make shirts in wartime." She was, moreover, an emotional rock. When the two were separated, she handled affairs for the family skillfully. Most of the time, she willingly transported herself and the family to uncomfortable locations to be near her husband. The two were devoted, but beyond that, she acted as his confidante and greatest supporter, fortifying him in his blackest days.[10]

By the time Smith had arrived in Virginia, Robert E. Lee had assumed the task of commander of Virginia forces. Lee had been the superintendent at West Point when Smith instructed in mathematics, and the Virginian had served as lieutenant colonel in the 2nd Cavalry and head of the Department of Texas, with Smith as a subordinate. At the time the War Department formed the 2nd Cavalry, Smith pronounced Lee "the most accomplished officer and gentleman in the army." Sometime over the next six years, however, Smith soured on Lee. Certainly overlapping responsibilities between the C.S. Army and the Virginia forces caused a clash, but Smith's hostility and terse jabs at Lee indicate a deeper source. In mid-May 1861, he described Lee's appointment to head the Virginia forces as "unfortunate." The Floridian hoped Davis would assume control of operations personally, "or that [Joseph E.] Johnston or [P. G. T.] Beauregard will be assigned to the command." Several days later, he grumbled again about "the tardiness of Lee," an unwillingness to make decisions quickly enough to suit Smith. Lee simply was not up to the job of directing large forces, so Smith believed.[11]

About the same time that Smith took issue privately with Lee, he received an order that would dramatically alter his life: to report to Joseph E. Johnston for duty at Harpers Ferry. For Smith, the directive was a huge improvement over administrative tasks at Lynchburg. In Harpers Ferry, he would be at the front with one of the principal field commands in the Confederate service, virtually ensuring him of extensive combat and enhancing opportunities for advancement. What he did not anticipate, though, was the impact that Johnston would have on his military development and thinking.

Johnston had earned an excellent reputation as an officer in the U.S. Army. A West Point graduate and classmate of Lee's, Johnston fought valiantly in the War with Mexico and against various Indian nations, suffering numerous wounds in the process. When his home state of Virginia withdrew from the Union, he resigned as quartermaster general of the U.S. Army, with a rank of brigadier general. Charismatic, courageous, and intelligent, Johnston could be extremely competitive and hypersensitive.[12]

Johnston and Smith bonded immediately. Within days of his new assignment, Smith had decided that Johnston was "the first military man of the day—active, experienced and intelligent." Johnston assumed the role of both mentor and friend to Smith, and the Floridian absorbed Johnston's teachings and opinions and reciprocated that friendship.[13]

No doubt, Smith's negative opinions of Lee fed the burgeoning relationship. Whereas Lee saw Johnston as his dear friend, Johnston viewed Lee as both a friend and a competitor. Lee graduated second in their West Point class; Johnston ranked thirteenth. While Johnston earned an enviable reputation in Mexico, Lee emerged from that war as the army's rising star. Smith's own sentiments about Lee doubtless found favor with Johnston and helped solidify their relationship.[14]

Smith assumed the job of chief of staff to Johnston, usually the highest ranking and most trusted staff member. Three years later, Smith looked back fondly on those days, recalling that Johnston "lived with me at the opening of the war in the closest intimacy and friendship." Their relationship strengthened to the point that twenty-five years later, Johnston referred to Smith as "My dearest of Old friends." Laboring together side by side almost every day, wrestling with mobilization and defense issues, they shared opinions and confidences and discussed personnel and war matters frankly. "Johnson's brain," he once described, "soars above all that surrounds it." In time, Smith's respect and admiration for Johnston grew to the point that he completely absorbed his boss's opinions. When Johnston complained that Harpers Ferry was untenable, that authorities had botched its defenses and he would have to endure public criticism for the first Confederate retreat, Smith echoed those very words in his private correspondence. When Smith grumbled in personal letters about equipment shortages, inadequate arms, and widespread illnesses, Johnston relayed the same messages in official communications. Eventually, Smith came to see the war in much the same way as Johnston. While the Rebel president encouraged his generals to engage the enemy as close to the border as possible, to spare hardships on its citizenry, Johnston and Smith embraced an alternative doctrine. In their minds, a Fabian strategy, in which the nation yielded its own land and property to protect its troops, best suited the Confederacy.[15]

Just two months after Smith left to join Johnston at Harpers Ferry, another event occurred—the battle of 1st Manassas—that greatly shaped his wartime career. Johnston had received preparatory instructions to bring his troops to the aid of General Beauregard's command near Manassas Junction if the Federals approached that area in force. When the adjutant general signaled Johnston of the Union advance on July 18, he placed in operation a plan to slip away from the Union column in his front and shift his entire army to Beauregard's succor. With two regiments, Johnston embarked on a train for Manassas Junction; he left Smith behind to push additional forces eastward as rapidly as possible. After seeing off Thomas J. Jackson's brigade, Smith accompanied Arnold Elzey's brigade on the next train. As ranking officer, Smith assumed command, with Elzey as his second.

The battle opened in earnest early on the morning of July 21, with Federal troops crossing Bull Run to the west and turning the Confederate left flank. Throughout the morning, the Union maintained the initiative, pressing back the beleaguered defenders. Shortly after noon, the Confederate line began to hold, anchored around Jackson's brigade and the remnants of other troops from Johnston's command. Just as large numbers of Yankees gathered beyond the Rebel left flank, threatening to turn Johnston's line once again, a column of Confederates led by Smith raced toward the front. Hearing the sounds of battle, Smith had halted the train and disembarked the troops. At army headquarters, Johnston instructed Smith to attack on the left. Since Smith did not know the ground, he urged Johnston to lead them, and the army commander agreed. As Johnston and Smith ushered the brigade to the front, Col. J. B. Kershaw rode up to request that Smith extend the line to the left, to protect the flank of Kershaw's South Carolinians. Before Smith could respond, a lead ball crashed into him. Smith wavered and finally toppled from his horse. Although he attempted to resume command, the injury was too severe, and he was carried to the rear. He had been in combat barely a couple of minutes when a musket ball penetrated near the collarbone on the right shoulder and exited on the left side, narrowly missing the spine but striking no vital organs. Rumors circulated that he had been killed, and a month later he joked to his mother that he had "read my obituary with but little satisfaction." Attentive and sanitary care enabled him to recover quickly.[16]

Smith had brought up reinforcements at precisely the right time. And although he never had a chance to deploy them, those men were instrumental in turning the tide of the battle, and much of the credit went to him. The *Richmond Dispatch* called him "the Blucher in that glorious victory for the South," in reference to the Prussian field marshal who oversaw the defeat of Napoleon's army at Leipzig and Waterloo. The newspaper rejoiced that the "God of Battles" had "spared this noble and chivalric son of the South for future brilliant achievements." Under fire for just a few minutes, Smith emerged a Confederate hero.[17]

Even the recuperation time redounded to Smith's benefit. Once he could travel, he moved to Lynchburg, where the compassion and attention of Cassie Seldon improved his strength and solidified their relationship. They married, and then honeymooned in Florida, all the while keeping him from the army and some sticky matters. Johnston's relationship with Davis had begun to sour, and because Smith was absent, he could avoid taking sides and alienating one or the other. Upon his return to Virginia in October, Smith learned that in a reorganization of the army, he had been promoted to major general and would command a division in Beauregard's Potomac District, and under Johnston's overall direction. As he resumed command, details and responsibilities of running a division consumed his time, and a layer of authority removed him somewhat from Johnston. The two remained intimate friends, and he continued to work with and see Johnston often. Privately, too, Smith voiced concern for the relationship between the high command in Northern Virginia and officials in Richmond. "There is not that cordiality of feelings, that confidence & freedom of intercourse between our Generals in the field, and the President and authorities in Richmond, which should exist in the present critical state of the country," he informed his bride. But the new assignment took him away from headquarters, from daily and often hourly contact with Johnston, from the gossip, the side taking, and the politics of staffs, and this allowed him to retain his allegiance to both men, even while military and political factions were forming.[18]

Back in his days at West Point, the marital struggles between Smith's parents taught him how to preserve strong relationships with feuding parties. A regrettable experience, it nonetheless developed in him a valuable quality, a knack for getting along with people. Throughout the remainder of his life, Smith maintained good rapport with a wide range of personalities and egos. Even during the postwar years, when tensions among ex-Confederates bubbled to the surface, he managed to keep on good terms with most of the warring individuals.

Some personalities, like the prickly Dick Taylor, were the exception. Taylor turned on him during the war and criticized him severely in his postwar memoirs. Smith refused to fight back. It would only toss fuel on the fire. Better to remain silent publicly, and let the embers burn out, he believed.[19]

Those who saw or met Smith bore witness to the same characteristics and qualities. A Louisiana infantryman thought his division commander "looks as plain as some old farmer, but his keen eye and flashing countenance told of the sparkling intellect which lay hidden within." William Pitt Ballinger, a prominent Texas attorney and an unusually perceptive diarist, met with Smith in mid-1864 and depicted him as "not as tall as I supposed but carries himself well." After extensive conversations, Ballinger sized up Smith as "an educated man of quality rearing." What impressed the Texan most, though, was his delivery and demeanor. "He speaks calmly & deliberately & without pretension," Ballinger commented to a political friend. "I have the utmost confidence in his abilities & believe he will be of great service to our Cause."[20]

Smith fully grasped the gravity of his new appointment as division commander. "The fate of our Country, our very independence & existence," he informed his bride, "hangs upon the fate of this army." With Johnston and Maj. Gen. Gustavus W. Smith, he toured the Confederate defenses and concluded, "our position is not as strong as I had been led to believe." Throughout the winter months, Smith continued to work with his troops to enhance their defensive position. For the first time, his responsibilities as division commander compelled him to confront his mentor and friend, Johnston. The army commander clung to the notion that Union forces would advance during the winter, and he directed that his troops remain at their posts. Smith saw how the elements took their toll on his soldiers, and that if his men were to have good health and spirits in the spring, when campaign season commenced, they needed to go into winter quarters immediately. After extensive lobbying, he won Johnston's grudging consent.[21]

Smith loved his job as division commander, and it must have come as a jolt when in late February 1862, Davis appointed him the new commander of the troops in East Tennessee. Huge numbers of Unionists concentrated in East Tennessee, and pro-Confederate leaders from that region pleaded with Davis to send a Confederate general of ability and reputation to organize the Rebel troops there and to establish a Confederate presence that would stifle the unrest. Evidently, the Confederate president chose Smith because of his reputation as a hero at 1st Manassas, his sound judgment and administrative skills, and his unyielding commitment to the Confederacy. Most Confederate generals would have protested or sulked over the assignment to a backwater theater of operations. Smith, the good soldier, would undertake whatever his president called on him to do.[22]

To Smith's dismay, the situation in East Tennessee was worse than officials in Richmond had told him. The citizenry were "disloyal to the core" and the troops were "a disorganized mob without head or discipline." He considered operations more difficult to conduct there than if his command were in enemy territory. At least then he could assume that everyone was hostile toward him and his army. In the area of East Tennessee, Confederate soldiers had such strong personal and family ties to Unionists that he questioned their reliability. His solution called for a wholesale swap of his local troops with soldiers who served in some other region of the Confederacy. Once East Tennesseans left their family and friends, he believed they would serve conscientiously for the Rebel cause. And their replacements would have no ties to the local anti-Confederate elements. While the War Department mulled over the proposal and ultimately declined to act, Smith's loyal forces suffered regular harassment from pro-Union guerrillas, who viewed the Confederate troops as an unpopular occupying force and determined to rid the region of them.[23]

Without doubt, Smith achieved his most impressive work in East Tennessee. Lacking adequate resources in a third-tier department, he somehow managed to whip his forces into shape and deal intelligently with local partisans. By summertime, a stronger and more disciplined military presence had diminished the frequency of clashes with Unionists considerably. Here, too, as a commander in the field, he won his most stirring victory.[24]

In the late summer and fall, Smith joined with Gen. Braxton Bragg's army in an ill-defined strategy of raiding northward. The apparent purpose of the campaign was to recoup Confederate territorial losses in Kentucky and Tennessee, stir up Yankee resistance in that region, spur recruitment for the Confederate army, and draw supplies from a fertile area. Although plans shifted on an almost daily basis, the ultimate intention was for Bragg to swing around the Union army that was threatening Chattanooga and sever its communications and supply lines, while Smith sliced across from Knoxville, Tennessee, to the Cumberland Gap and linked with Bragg. They would then be in a position to deal with an easier target, a retreating Federal army. The original rendezvous point was Middle Tennessee. Later, that shifted to Kentucky, a destination that offered vastly superior results and better fulfilled the wishes of the Confederate president. Thus, they would join forces in Central Kentucky, but beyond that, Smith's superior Bragg had not decided whether to strike for Louisville or fight the retreating Yankee army on ground of his choosing.[25]

As his first step on the campaign, Bragg wanted Smith to seize the Cumberland Gap from the Federals, but the young Confederate general had other plans. Rather than strike a strongly fortified position, or lay siege in an area where supplies were scarce and time was short, Smith jumped at the real prize—an advance into Kentucky. Col. John Hunt Morgan had led a raid into central Kentucky and reported plentiful supplies and a huge outpouring of support for the Confederacy. If Smith could push into that region, gather foodstuffs for his hungry troops and recruit 25,000 or more soldiers for the Confederacy, as Morgan had described, he and Bragg would have the kind of force to hold Kentucky. Detaching part of his command under Maj. Gen. Carter Stevenson to keep tabs on the Union columns at Cumberland Gap, Smith took the rest of his force, some 10,000 after Maj. Gen. Patrick Cleburne had reinforced him, deep into the enemy rear. This penetration, in conjunction with Bragg's drive into central Tennessee and Kentucky, would not only compel the main Federal army to abandon this heartland, it would also force the evacuation of Cumberland Gap, which Stevenson could then occupy.[26]

On August 29, 1862, around Richmond, Kentucky, Smith's columns met their first resistance. At Mount Zion Church, White's Farm, and Richmond, Smith's Confederates fought skillfully and tenaciously, repulsing enemy flank attacks on them and executing their own version of fixing and then turning the enemy brilliantly. Although the Union troops occupied good defensive positions and Smith's men were tired from long marches, his infantry and artillery drove back the Federals each time. Smith had sent his cavalry well off to the enemy's rear, which impaired his ability to exploit the routs at Mount Zion Church and White's Farm. At the battle of Richmond, however, the plan reaped huge dividends. The Confederates stampeded the Yankees by crushing the flank and center, and the cavalry, some two miles in the rear, had positioned itself superbly to gathered up large numbers of prisoners. Even the Union commander admitted his troops fled in "utter disorder."[27]

Despite the fact that Smith had defeated third-rate Union generals who led a largely untried soldiery—many had only been in the service ten to twenty-five days, and few of those knew the manual of arms, let alone battalion drill—he won a complete victory around Richmond. Federals suffered over 200 dead and almost 850 wounded. The Rebels under Smith also captured some 4,300 Yankees, a total greater than all the casualties—killed, wounded, captured, and missing—that the Confederacy inflicted in the largest battle of the campaign, Perryville. By contrast, 78 Confederates were killed in action, 372 were wounded , and one was missing. Rebel troops seized nine artillery guns and nearly 10,000 small arms. And the triumph opened the door to a Confederate occupation of Lexington and Frankfort, where they picked up more artillery pieces and muskets. Some eighteen months afterward, the Confederate Congress offered a belated resolution of appreciation for this victory.[28]

With Smith's troops in Central Kentucky, and Bragg's columns closer to Louisville than Maj. Gen. Don Carlos Buell's Federals, the Confederacy was poised for a huge victory, one that could have dramatically reversed its western fortunes. The combination of Bragg's, Smith's, and other Rebel forces, along with its position astride the Yankee supply line, could have compelled the Union to fight a major battle on ground of Confederate choosing. Spirits in the Rebel ranks soared over combat victories and the skill with which their generals had outmaneuvered Federal leadership, breeding a confidence that was almost irrepressible among the men in gray.

It would have taken a colossal failure on the part of the Rebel commanders to snatch defeat from the jaws of victory, but somehow Bragg and Smith did it. Bragg's nerve vanished, and Smith lost the spirit of cooperation. Much to the dismay of Smith, whose aggressiveness had thus far provided the margin for his own command's success, Bragg yielded the initiative. He conjured weaknesses in his own army where none existed, and formed giants of the Yankees when they were mere mortals. Smith, for his part, exhibited little interest in abandoning fertile grounds of supply around Lexington to merge his columns with Bragg's army. When Bragg began to temporize, Smith neglected to urge the Rebel commander to attack. Whether the lack of popular support in terms of enlistment discouraged both Rebel generals, a peculiar malaise consumed them. Neither seemed to have an idea how to bring the campaign to a successful conclusion. By dawdling, they allowed Buell to march past Bragg's command and into Louisville, where Federals resupplied and received reinforcements.

The momentum quickly shifted over to the Union. Buell pressed down on Bragg's columns, and at the Battle of Perryville, his superior numbers struck part of Bragg's army. Although the Federals suffered heavier casualties, Bragg began falling back. Smith, who suddenly awakened and perceived a great opportunity slipping away, implored Bragg to stand and fight. For awhile, it looked like Smith's arguments held sway, but as the two armies closed for battle, Bragg backed down and ordered a retreat once more. The Kentucky Raid was over.[29]

Critics have split the blame for the failure in Kentucky among Davis, Bragg, and Smith. They hold Davis culpable for problems stemming from a muddled command structure, with commanders from two military departments participating in the same operation. In fairness to the Rebel president, Bragg and Smith actually had a reasonably effective partnership early in the campaign, as plans were evolving. Once the two forces entered Kentucky, Bragg, as ranking officer, should have assumed control and ordered Smith to join him. Bragg refused to assert himself and fill the power vacuum.

For his part, Smith lost faith in Bragg when the Rebel general offered no viable plan in Kentucky and allowed the initiative to lapse. Still, Smith proposed no scheme of his own. Evidently, he thought the lush area around Lexington provided the best staging ground for operations, but beyond that, he contributed nothing to the campaign once he settled in central Kentucky. Instead of joining Bragg to go after Buell, Smith was lured away in the wrong direction to pursue the Union command that had retreated from Cumberland Gap, a small prize, and one which he never caught.

Historians led by Thomas L. Connelly have cast blame for the campaign failure heavily on the shoulders of Smith, arguing that a runaway ambition prevented him from cooperating with Bragg and induced him to disobey his superior's orders. Connelly depicts Smith as a man thirsting for glory, an ego run amok, a quality that materialized only during the war and escaped recognition by his military peers. Other scholars have embraced this assessment uncritically.[30]

Unfortunately, Connelly bases his opinion on stretchy evidence and broad speculation from several passages in letters from Smith to his wife during the summer and fall of 1862. In one missive, Smith described his situation as "something like Cortéz." Connelly digs Smith by asserting, "On occasion he fancied himself as Cortéz burning his ships behind him." Three hundred years earlier, Cortés had burnt his ships and marched inland in Mexico; Smith's army marched northward into a mountainous region after cutting communications with his base. Neither had assurance where they would get supplies, or if locals would harass them, but both took the gamble—a perfectly innocuous historical reference.[31]

In another letter, Smith grumbled that Abraham Lincoln was converting the war into a struggle for abolitionism and reassured his wife that the Confederacy would prevail. "I have too much confidence in the justness and goodness of God to believe he will let us fail," he explained, "and but think that like the Egyptians of old he has hardened their hearts and blinded their eyes only to make their destruction more complete." To suggest that Smith viewed himself "as Moses leading the Israelites from Egypt," as Connelly asserts, is a huge stretch, especially for a deeply religious man like Smith. And if comparisons to biblical events were the bases for runaway ambition, then the bulk of all Civil War officers sported enormous egos.[32]

Finally, Connelly has seized on a statement by Smith that if the invasion of Kentucky were successful, it would be perceived as "a stroke of inspiration and genius." Connelly then omitted the next words, in which Smith urged in very Stonewall Jackson-esque terms, "pray for me darling wife . . . God is my dependence and earnest & devout prayers avail much with him." Smith saw God's guiding hand in all that he and the Confederacy did. Interestingly enough, had the Kentucky invasion worked effectively, we might very well compare it to Jackson's Valley campaign and depict it as a stroke of inspiration and genius. Braxton Bragg himself, who collaborated with Smith on the Kentucky campaign, described operations in much more hyperbolic terms. At one point, he wrote to his wife that this was "the most extraordinary campaign in military history." Thus far, Bragg has managed to escape accusations by historians of a runaway ambition.[33]

In reading all of Smith's letters, rather than a handful during the Kentucky campaign with passages removed from context, a different portrait of the man emerges. For the most part, the Smith who unfolds was a bright, sweet man who devoted himself wholly to his family and to the Rebel cause. Deep religious views and whole-hearted support from his wife centered Smith and sustained him through the war's tribulations. He could confide in his wife and, at times, in his mother, and trust in God's will to ensure the best outcome. In the candor of those missives, he exhibited no hypersensitivity or runaway ambition for promotion. On several occasions, he exaggerated his accomplishments confidentially to his bride, but these overstatements pale by comparison in both frequency and degree with many other officers, North and South. Nor did personal sentiments allow him to take some perverse pleasure in the failures of other Confederate generals. He wanted his comrades-in-arms to succeed, just as he personally hoped to triumph. When President Davis described him as an officer wholly devoted to the Rebel cause, he portrayed Smith accurately.[34]

At the end of the campaign, Smith fired off a heated letter to Davis, detailing his disgust with the way Bragg had run the campaign and insisting that he had no faith in him as an army commander. Davis, who liked both men and appreciated their services to the Confederacy, spoke directly to Bragg and reported that Bragg had a high opinion of Smith's performance. The president expected Smith, whom he elevated to lieutenant general for the Kentucky campaign, to cooperate with any effort on Bragg's part to advance into Middle Tennessee. He also asked Smith to come to Richmond for consultation. Exactly what occurred at that meeting, no one recorded, but neither Smith nor any of his staff criticized Bragg for the remainder of the war.[35]

Still, Davis realized that he had a problem, and his solution was to place Smith's dear friend, Joe Johnston, as overall commander of all Confederate forces from the Appalachian Mountains to the Mississippi River. On May 31, 1862, at the battle of Seven Pines, Johnston had sustained severe wounds, and first Gustavus W. Smith and then Lee had replaced him. By the time Johnston healed sufficiently to return to duty, Lee had built the Army of Northern Virginia into his own, and Davis sought a new position for an officer of Johnston's stature. The solution was to place him in overall control of Smith's, Bragg's, and John C. Pemberton's army in Mississippi.

Unfortunately for Smith, he had poisoned the well. He hoped to command a corps under Johnston, and his mentor would have approved the arrangement. But Davis wanted Bragg in command, which placed Smith in an awkward position. Over the course of a few months, the War Department dismembered Smith's command, which made him eligible for reassignment. This was no punishment for Smith; Davis liked and admired him. The president had other plans for the victor of the battle of Richmond, Kentucky.[36]

Having met with Davis and Bragg in December at Murfreesboro, Tennessee, Smith must have been surprised when the president summoned him to Richmond a month later. Rather than detracting from Smith's forces, this time Davis had a new job for him: commander of the Army of the Southwest. And a month afterward, long before Smith crossed the Mississippi River, Davis revised his responsibilities once more. Smith would command the Trans-Mississippi Department—all Confederate forces west of the Mississippi River.[37]

Clearly, Davis would not have entrusted Smith with such a major responsibility if he did not have faith in his abilities and judgment. Back in the days when Davis served as secretary of war, he had designated Smith as one of the bright young officers in the army by assigning him to the 2nd Cavalry. Up to that point in the war, the president had witnessed nothing that did not reinforce his earlier judgment. Smith had fallen in a heroic effort to reinforce the Confederate army at Manassas, one that may have turned the tide of the battle. A year later, he brought order to a chaotic mob of soldiers in East Tennessee and led them skillfully on a raid into central Kentucky. Although the campaign never lived up to its promise, the president had reason to believe that Smith did. He exhibited an ability to command independently, to think aggressively, and to fight successfully. The Union leadership against him may have been abysmal, and its troops neophytes to military service, but Davis either did not know this or did not let it detract from his assessment.

The president needed some bold leadership, someone who could function independently and transform disorder into military effectiveness. Davis sought a new departmental commander who had the administrative wherewithal to build armies and to fight them, but the individual also had to understand the complexities of partisan and raiding warfare in Missouri and Indian fighting in Texas. As Johnston's chief of staff early in the war, Smith had been an integral part of a team that assembled, trained, and equipped the victorious army at 1st Manassas. He possessed extensive prewar experience fighting Indians in Texas, and his service against Unionists in East Tennessee had taught him valuable lessons about partisan warfare. Smith was also a household name, not quite the stature of soldiers like Lee, Jackson, Johnston, Beauregard, or J. E. B. Stuart, but a rising star nonetheless. At first blush, then, Smith appeared to be an excellent selection.

The job of a successful commander of the Confederacy's largest military department, however, entailed talents above and beyond anything Smith had undertaken. The Department of East Tennessee did not compare in size, scope, or complexity with this new assignment. The job would test the depth and breadth of his administrative and military talents. While Smith had extensive combat experience, most of it was on the small-unit level. Because he was wounded literally within minutes of coming under fire at 1st Manassas, his battle experience rested primarily with company-level service in Mexico and prewar Texas. On the raid into Kentucky, Smith led a small corps, one that he commanded with tactical skill. During that expedition, Smith exhibited evidence that he conceived on the operational level—a campaign or major operations that seeks to attain strategic goals in a theater of war—but he never actually directed a large-scale, complicated military endeavor. Thus, Smith was short on senior-level command experience.

Compared with his previous assignments, Smith would have to function on a much higher plain than the tactical level in the Trans-Mississippi Department. He would have to demonstrate mastery of the operational and strategic art, which required distinct talents and sophisticated abstract thought. Previously, Smith had analyzed problems and sought solutions; this time, he must pull together various operational strands and synthesize them into a strategic whole, balancing ends, ways, and means. The job of commander in the Trans-Mississippi Department would also demand an assumption of responsibility for decision-making that tested every fiber of one's character. Absent that onus, many generals throughout history could make the right decisions—the infamous armchair commanders. Greatness has fallen to those who could formulate, adapt, and execute the proper plan when the pressure and burden of success or failure rested on their shoulders.

Even though his oversight of military operations would largely define him as a departmental commander, his duties encompassed an array of noncombat activities as well. The unusual distance to the West and the tenuous state of communications with Richmond officials would create a temporary power vacuum. As the ranking officer in that region during wartime, when the military establishment held unusual power and influence over society, Smith would be the most important representative of the national authority. This included extensive dealings with state and local politicians. In his role as the leading national official in the region, he represented the central government in various arrangements and negotiations with governmental officials. He must see that state and local organizations cooperated in the enforcement of national laws that affected the military.

His duties as departmental commander also brought him in contact with many of the most important businessmen, merchants, ranchers, and planters in the region. In comparative isolation, Smith had to build an administrative structure and draw from regional sources to sustain his armed forces. Those commands needed food, equipment, weapons, ammunition, horses and mules, wagons, shoes and clothing, medical supplies, and assorted other items, all of which citizens had to produce or obtain and bureaus and staff personnel had to procure and distribute. The two segments—civilian and military—had to operate hand in hand.

Technically, the Department of Trans-Mississippi embraced West Louisiana, Texas, Arkansas, Missouri, Indian Territory, and Arizona Territory, some 600,000 square miles. According to the 1860 census, there were approximately 2.6 million settled inhabitants in the area, nearly 2 million of whom were white. More than half of those white people, however, resided in Missouri, where Union forces dominated and guerrilla bands and occasional raiding elements challenged that power temporarily. Excluding Missouri, there were about half a million slaves. Nearly half of those chattels lived in West Louisiana, but as the war dragged on, the number of slaves in Texas grew astronomically, as slave owners took their property to what they considered the most secure area of the Confederacy. Along the western rim of the Confederacy, with frontier hardships aplenty, the Trans-Mississippi boasted little manufacturing outside Missouri. A poor transportation network hobbled travel and commerce, and the limited number and poor quality of the railroads did little to improve mobility, especially after two years of wartime wear and tear. Communication across the river had to go by boat, since the Confederacy had no telegraph lines that went under or over the Mississippi River.[38]

At the time Smith took over as commander of the Trans-Mississippi Department, he inherited a problem that could turn disastrous. Since late fall 1862, Union major general Ulysses S. Grant had attempted to crack the Rebel control of Vicksburg, Mississippi. If that city fell into Union hands, along with the smaller and less defensible position at Port Hudson, Louisiana, Federals would then have complete control of the Mississippi River. The loss would not only provide the Union with relatively easy movement of troops and goods up and down the river, it would virtually isolate the Trans-Mississippi as well. Delays in communications back and forth to Richmond would worsen, and large-scale movements of troops or supplies across the river would become extremely hazardous. For all intents and purposes, the Trans-Mississippi Department would become severed from the rest of the Confederacy. Davis had expressed his concern for the survival of Vicksburg—in fact, he had a personal attachment to the

area, residing not far from the city—and had instructed Smith to cooperate with the Confederate commander there, Lt. Gen. John C. Pemberton, and his boss, Johnston.[39]

Well before Smith had time to settle into his new job, crises struck.
Union major general Nathaniel P. Banks launched a raid into south-
western Louisiana, striking up toward Alexandria on the Red River.
With overwhelming numbers against him, Smith's best subordinate,
Richard Taylor, could only fall back and hope for the best. Meanwhile,
Grant shifted troops over to the west side of the Mississippi River,
marched them southward, and by the end of April 1863, the Union
general had shuttled them back to the east side for a campaign against
Vicksburg. Fortunately for Smith, the incompetent Banks dawdled and
then fell back for an attack on Port Hudson, taking much of his plunder
with him. This gave Smith an opening to assume the initiative and
assist the beleaguered Confederates along the eastern bank of the river.
At his disposal, Smith had Taylor's small force of three brigades; some
troops in Texas under a flamboyant, often erratic, yet sometimes skillful
commander named John Magruder; his strongest force of two small
divisions and a couple of brigades under Lt. Gen. Theophilus Holmes
in Arkansas; and a high-quality division under Maj. Gen. John G.
Walker, mired in the swampland of West Louisiana. According to Taylor, Smith had told him that "public opinion would condemn us if we
did not *try to do something*." Sadly, the something Smith did was woefully inadequate to the emergency.[40]

Once again, the long reach of Joe Johnston's influence may have
affected Smith, this time in part unintentionally. Before Smith headed
west, Davis had expressed his dissatisfaction with Holmes's performance, believing the old general focused too much on Arkansas, to the
detriment of the rest of the region west of the river. During that same
visit to Richmond, Smith had bumped into Louis T. Wigfall, a senator
from Texas and a charter member of the pro-Johnston, anti-Davis faction. To Wigfall, Smith vowed that he would consider any suggestion
from Johnston to have the force of an order. In mid-April, Johnston
had written Smith and casually asked Smith to pass along cordial
wishes to "Mrs. Smith—& to my old friend Gen l. Holmes." The message conveyed a sense of warmth toward Holmes, and it may have led
Smith to believe that as Johnston's close friend, Holmes merited a
level of independence and a respect for his judgment.[41]

During the Vicksburg campaign, Secretary of War James A. Seddon proposed to Johnston an operation against Helena, Arkansas, to

draw Federal forces from Grant's army. Unfortunately for the Confederates, a diversionary campaign can only work if the threatened target is of equal or greater importance to the enemy. In this case, the Federals would have gladly traded Helena for Vicksburg. In early June, as Vicksburg and Port Hudson lay besieged, Johnston endorsed the suggestion to take Helena, informing Smith that if it were "practicable," he thought "it is well worth doing." Following his commitment to support Johnston at all hazards and eschewing Davis's warning, Smith gave Holmes unfettered freedom to implement his own plan to relieve Vicksburg, an offensive against Helena. Acting without a sense of urgency that the crisis demanded, Holmes's attack did not take place until the day the garrison at Vicksburg surrendered. It was repulsed.[42]

Yet granting Holmes this independence of action was just one of Smith's fateful blunders. Instead of concentrating all his forces for a single, powerful thrust to disrupt the Union offensive that would isolate his department, he frittered away his strength in uncoordinated or meaningless actions. Taylor proposed to threaten New Orleans and compel Banks to break off his attack on Port Hudson, which in turn would have freed the garrison at Port Hudson to aid Pemberton. In order to accomplish this task, he needed additional manpower. Rather than combine forces for a mighty blow there or elsewhere, Smith followed Pemberton's suggestion and wasted Walker's fine division by having it "threaten" Vicksburg from the opposite side of the river and bar Grant's army from retreating the way it came.[43]

Perhaps Smith lacked the military strength to influence materially Grant's Vicksburg campaign or Banks's attack and siege on Port Hudson, but no one will ever know. While Smith generated nothing of significance, Grant implemented a brilliant campaign that hammered Pemberton's and Johnston's commands and squeezed the graycoats back into the defenses of Vicksburg. By early July, Pemberton surrendered to Grant, and shortly afterward, Port Hudson fell to Banks. If Taylor was off target, it was not by much when he described Smith's weak efforts to save either Rebel garrison as "absurd movements."[44]

With the capture of Vicksburg and Port Hudson, Federals had carved off Smith's Trans-Mississippi Department from the rest of the Confederacy. Patrolling vessels from the vast Yankee river fleet could impede troops and supplies from crossing over the river in significant numbers, and communications to authorities in Richmond would suffer even longer delays. The burden of formulating policies and plans and generating manpower and resources lapsed onto Smith's shoulders.

Immediately after the fall of Vicksburg and Port Hudson, Confederate president Davis wrote Smith a lengthy letter of advice. Absolving the new departmental commander of any blame for the twin defeats by suggesting that he "probably" did not receive Davis's instructions to cooperate before the disasters occurred, the commander in chief notified Smith, "You have not merely a military, but also a political problem involved in your command." Because Federals seized control of the Mississippi River, he would have to make his department self-sufficient. Smith would have to promote the development of ordnance works and gunpowder mills, protect vital agricultural areas, and encourage local production of cloth and other military and civilian necessities. By fulfilling both military and civilian needs, he would "encourage and sustain" public support for the war and enable more men to enter military service.[45]

As chief executive, Davis empowered Smith with unusual authority to establish an administrative apparatus for his isolated region. He directed the department commander to set up military bureaus to oversee the production and distribution of materiél, supplies, and food for his military forces. Since all this would entail the expenditure of vast sums of money, the Davis administration exhibited unusual flexibility in allowing Smith to direct Treasury officials in some of their duties and policies until the president could rule on them. Even in the area of appointments, the Confederate president bent to meet Smith's needs. Although he could not and would not grant Smith his constitutional power to appoint and promote individuals to offices, he agreed to allow Smith to assign them temporarily, until the president could rule on them permanently.[46]

Davis also offered some shrewd political advice. Smith's duties would inevitably blur the boundary with domestic affairs, and he would need the support of state officials to succeed. The president counseled his commander to inform governors of his plans to "prevent them from misconstruing your actions." By tendering this confidence, the president suggested, he often would co-opt them into endorsing his designs, without having yield any decision-making authority to them.[47]

The key element to Davis's initial guidance and supporting letters was a recognition that the situation in the Trans-Mississippi Department was different from anything else in the Confederacy. Contrary to some contemporary depictions of the president as rigid, unimaginative, and bureaucratic, Davis exhibited unusual flexibility and creativity with Smith. He pledged to support him with the powers that the

Confederate Constitution proscribed for the chief executive; he could do no more. And he sustained him to a remarkable level. The following spring, when Congress debated the idea of creating an assistant secretary of war for the region, Seddon voiced opposition on behalf of the president. Both Davis and his secretary of war feared that any diminishment of Smith's power could hurt the war effort in the Trans-Mississippi.[48]

Despite the overwhelming nature of his duties, Smith had an inkling of what was in store for him. To his friend Johnston, he privately disclosed that his job was a "herculean task." Essentially, the Trans-Mississippi Department had "No army, no means; an empire in extent; no system, no order; all to be done from the beginning." Yet he also confided to his old friend that he believed the department had the resources and could provide for its own needs. In his exchanges with Davis that first summer, Smith understood that his duties in the early days, weeks, and months "must be principally of an administrative character." It was in that area that he could contribute significantly. "The department has to be self-sustaining," he determined, "and its resources developed to that end." Before he could focus on military operations, he had to mobilize manpower and procure equipment, including arms and ammunition; secure sources of food and fodder for soldiers and animals and acquire medical supplies; and obtain reliable funding sources for pay and expenses.[49]

To his credit, Smith perceptively recognized that the critical element to developing a self-sustaining department was money. With a steady supply of funding, he could procure the necessary manpower and matériel to wage a good fight in the region. The difficult task was securing that flow of cash. Once the Union severed the Trans-Mississippi from the rest of the Confederacy, the movement of large sums of money from Richmond proved unreliable, and the defeat at Vicksburg shook confidence in the Rebel cause and further depreciated paper money and bonds. What Smith needed was a consistent flow of gold, silver, or British notes that would circulate competitively and retain their purchasing power over time at home and overseas. With money, he could buy goods and develop necessary industries at home for the long term; through importation, he could acquire manufacturing equipment to build those industries and obtain essential weapons for immediate use. Fortunately, his region possessed ample quantities of a fluffy white gold—cotton—which European and Northern mills demanded. A foreign country along his southern border would enable him to pass the cotton through Mexico and onto foreign ships without Union interference, and he could also import weapons and other war materials through the Mexican market.

Before Smith received Davis's suggestion to bring politicians into the loop, the Confederate commander had called a meeting with the governors and various other politicians in the region to discuss problems and to seek solutions. They gathered in Marshall, Texas, in August 1863, and among their recommendations was a proposal for the impressment of cotton. They suggested that the government take the cotton and in return pay the farmer in cotton bonds bearing 6 percent interest. Earlier that month, Smith had consolidated the work of agents who collected, purchased, and disposed of cotton for the government under the Cotton Bureau. With that recommendation as support, he embarked on a program of impressing cotton, largely in Texas, for government use by the Cotton Bureau.[50]

Prior to Smith's appointment, Confederate officials had attempted to seize cotton to finance military operations, but the program had been largely inefficient, as wartime turbulence badly disrupted the cotton industry. Growers near the path of invading Federal armies had their stockpiles destroyed by Rebel troops. Others preserved their cotton but had no way to ship it to market, since the Union controlled the waterways and New Orleans, and the overland trek through Texas was lengthy, expensive, and time-consuming. Despite the cost, larger producers generally could find ways of getting their cotton to market. It was the smaller growers, living independently and in relative isolation, who struggled to market their "white gold." Their economy of scale made shipping costs prohibitive.

These challenges lured speculators to purchase cotton at a mere fraction of its true value and incur the risks of shipping it to market. With so much money at stake, corruption abounded. In the meantime, cotton growers large and small grumbled to politicians about a fundamental problem for farmers in a market economy: Those who produced the crops reaped meager profits, while speculators harvested the real wealth. When politicians at Smith's conference saw an opportunity to appease constituents with a federal government program that softened the unfair burdens of impressment, checked rampant speculation and gouging, undercut corrupt practices, and solve the ticklish problem of transportation, they leaped at it. The government would impress the cotton, pay for it in bonds, transport it to Mexico, and oversee its sale in Europe. Cotton growers reaped all the financial benefits without middlemen or speculators taking a big cut, and they no longer had to worry about the difficulties of transporting their crops to market. The bonds would float at near par, because gold, silver, or British pounds would buttress them.[51]

On the surface, this appeared like an excellent solution. In fact, however, the creation of a Cotton Bureau and the expansion of impressment stirred up a hornet's nest for Smith. Just as Lee had feared when the Commissary Department urged him to seize food from Virginians for his army, widespread impressment smacked of arbitrary power and alienated the people from authority in the Trans-Mississippi Department. The army confiscated cotton, but it proved highly ineffective at hauling it to market. Meanwhile, the bonds that cotton growers received as compensation plummeted in value. Angry farmers did not receive adequate remuneration, and the army failed to obtain the equipment it needed. Others rushed huge quantities of cotton to market, to avoid compensated seizure, while the government barely got any of its cotton to market. Smith responded by demanding one-half of all cotton for his army's use, and the public balked even louder.[52]

Rather than provide order, the program instituted greater chaos. States' rights advocates rose up in hostility to Smith, claiming a gross abuse of his power and a violation of civilian control over the military. His program, moreover, placed the burden of responsibility for the purchase and transportation of cotton on the shoulders of the military. The shipment of cotton siphoned off manpower that hard-pressed, frontline units desperately needed, and it distracted the army from its critical mission of winning the war. By August 1864, the secretary of war notified Smith that the public and politicians had complained so vociferously that he was removing responsibility for cotton impressment from the army and turning over those duties to the Treasury Department.[53]

So flawed in design and execution was Smith's Cotton Bureau that Texas governor Pendleton Murrah offered a state alternate scheme that attracted Texas cotton farmers by the droves. The state of Texas agreed to pay fair market value for one half a farmer's cotton with state bonds, which drew interest at 7 percent. The state, however, would take claim to the entire crop and haul it to Mexico. Since the cotton was under control of the state military board, the state of Texas "owned" it, and the Cotton Bureau could not impress it. Once the cotton reached Mexico, the state turned over half the crop to the farmer, to dispose of it as he or she saw fit. By selling to the state, cotton farmers received higher prices, kept half their crop, and had secure passage to Mexico. Murrah's plan enticed so many Texas cotton growers that Confederate financing in the region nearly collapsed. After repeated efforts to suspend the state plan had failed, Smith finally sat down with Murrah in July 1864 to settle the dispute. What was said, no one knows, but Smith evidently made his case quite clearly. Murrah issued a decree in which accepted Smith's arguments fully. Meanwhile, much damage was done.[54]

A better policy would have been for Smith to request that Congress authorize an increase in the export tax. During Smith's honeymoon phase, which lasted through at least one legislative session, Smith could have requested Congress to increase the export tax on cotton from one-eighth cent per pound to something more reasonable, like five cents per pound. Such a very small tax would likely have generated support from both the Davis administration and Congress. Private enterprise and the profit motive would have ensured that large quantities of cotton bales crossed over into Mexico for trade, as they did throughout the war. Smith would not have committed the army to confiscation of a commodity like cotton, thereby preserving the army's reputation. Nor would he have to allocate valuable manpower and resources to a complex arrangement of seizing and transporting bulky bales of cotton to Mexico, which the army did with shocking inefficiency compared with the private sector. The Treasury Department would have collected the export tax at little expense to the government and generated huge returns for Smith's command. While surviving records are spotty, evidence indicates that between approximately 22,000 and 29,000 bales of Texas cotton per month passed from Reynosa to Piedas Negras in Mexico during 1863, and this did not include all cotton exported to Mexico. Still, that cotton alone would have generated $500,000 per month in specie from taxes, insufficient to cover all expenses, but enough to prevent the value of paper notes from collapsing and to meet the military's critical needs. Of course, it would not solve the problems of small farmers and speculation, but those were matters that the state and local governments, not the wartime military, could best handle.[55]

Just as Smith had suspected, tax revenues proved to be the linchpin of much of his duties. Without a steady supply of sound funds, Smith's soldiers suffered shortage after shortage. Thousands upon thousands of troops in his department carried substandard weapons, and some had none at all. He frequently complained to Davis and the secretary of war, "We are now embarrassed for the want of funds," which meant that soldiers and the war effort suffered. As the year of 1864 closed, Smith informed the president that he had last paid his troops in October 1863. During that time, the departmental debt had soared to $60 million, with vast consequences. Confederate monetary problems strained relations with the Mexican government and their trading agents there. Because the department lacked sound funds, it failed to import the proper machinery to manufacture war materials, and Smith never approached his goal of self-sufficiency. States' rightists, whose views Smith found antithetical to the Rebel cause, grumbled about inefficiency and abuse of power, and Rebels at home and in the ranks lost faith in the viability of the Confederate States of America. All in all, Smith's cotton plan was a bust, and the ripple effect damaged his credibility and nearly every aspect of his duty.[56]

As an administrator, Smith struggled to establish efficiency, largely because of financial difficulties. When he took over departmental command, there was no established process of communication and little of coordination between district headquarters. Smith promptly embarked on a program of systematization, created departments, and for the most part placed good personnel in these top posts. Without the resources to purchase food and other supplies, though, his administrators had to create large bureaucracies to secure what the army needed. At times, departmental personnel worked at cross-purposes with each other, outraging the civilian population and frustrating the designs of commanders. In one of his frequent outbursts against Smith, the crusty Taylor accused the departmental commander of creating a staff larger than the head of the Prussian General Staff in wartime.[57]

Invariably, policies that negatively affected civilians raised their ire, and complaints spilled out in conversations, letters to politicians, and newspaper articles. Historian Kerby has explained so insightfully that the severity of the war tended to camouflage divisions and frustrations east of the Mississippi, as the Confederate people largely pulled together to fend off an invader. In Kirby Smithdom, with its vast stretches of territory and no legitimate threat in many areas, people noticed the "symptoms of the country's interior corruption," and blame fell largely on Smith. Scrupulously honest himself, Smith shouldered much of the burden for the behavior of the occasional corrupt official, basic mismanagement, implementation of unpopular policies, unchecked speculation and greed of citizens—virtually anything that went wrong. As departmental head, he was an easy target. Caught up in the burden of command, Smith temporized, much like he had done during the Kentucky raid of 1862.[58]

In his policies with the Texas frontier, an area where Smith possessed vast expertise, the people and the Texas government lost faith. The prewar Indian troubles worsened somewhat as the war effort began to break down. Deserters, runaway slaves, and refugees—some of whom were Indians seeking sanctuary from the war—stirred an already bubbling cauldron of violence. As usual, settlers blamed the Indians for their woes and demanded that Smith increase troop strength in the region. Smith had allocated some 1,500 soldiers there, to buttress extensive fortifications and local reserves. And in fairness to the departmental commander, the casualties from Indian raids along the frontier totaled 400 for all four war years, a substantial number in peacetime, but not by Civil War standards. Nevertheless, frontiersmen demanded greater protection, and the Texas state legislature responded by creating a 4,000-man state frontier force at a time when the Confederate armies were desperate for manpower. Smith complained to Davis that the state had violated the conscription act and had allocated 3,000 more troops than were necessary to accomplish the mission. What Smith failed to grasp, though, was how this new policy reflected the waning confidence in him.[59]

Smith could have restored public faith in his leadership if his armies had performed extremely well in the field, but he neglected to adjust his strategy to meet the changing circumstances of the war. To Smith, a disciple of trading territory rather than giving battle except under the most optimum conditions, the Fabian doctrine offered certain advantages. Against much larger numbers, it enabled a retreating army a chance to search for an opportunity to strike or resist on better terms while the invading force stretched its supply line. Yet the Fabian approach possessed some serious drawbacks as well. In a nonparticipatory governmental system, a leader could direct armies to retreat, thereby uncovering the homes of its people and exposing farms and industry to destruction and confiscation. Since the will of the public played a small role in the conduct of the war, in many instances the practitioner of the Fabian policy would suffer only modest consequences. But in a democratic republic like the Confederacy, with its novel brand of capitalism, yielding territory exposed the families, homes, and private property of voters and soldiers to the mercy of the enemy. As a tactical approach, when an army fell back to secure a stronger position from which to defend or attack, it made sense. From the operational and especially the strategic perspective, it sacrificed valuable resources to the enemy, caused massive disruption on the home front, and sparked desertion as soldiers left the army to look after loved ones.

During the late summer and fall of 1863, Federals advanced from the north and the east. A Yankee column seized Little Rock, Arkansas, but proceeded in great force no farther, settling for limited gains. Maj. Gen. William B. Franklin directed another Union command westward toward Opelousas, Louisiana, which it occupied in October. As the Federals advanced, Smith advised his subordinate Taylor to act with caution. "The Fabian policy is now our true policy," he counseled, and a defeat would be disastrous to public support. "When you strike, you must do so only with strong hopes of success." In early November, Taylor had strong hopes of success. Exploiting his superior cavalry, Taylor obstructed and harassed the Federals, and then struck the attenuated Federals at Opelousas, delivering two powerful attacks that convinced Franklin to retreat. Despite the loss of Little Rock, Smith's forces had held the enemy at bay, and Davis rewarded him in February 1864, with a fourth star, the rank of full general.[60]

About the same time as Smith joined an elite group of officers who held the rank of full general, the Union launched a new campaign. Maj. Gen. Frederick Steele and 12,000 men struck out for Camden, Arkansas, and beyond, while Maj. Gen. Nathaniel P. Banks headed a column of 17,000 troops with Adm. David Dixon Porter's gunboats up the Red River, which would rendezvous at Alexandria with Maj. Gen. A. J. Smith's corps of 10,000 veterans from Maj. Gen. William T. Sherman's army. Despite the great distances between Steele and Banks, they had attempted to coordinate their campaigns, squeezing Smith's forces in the north and seizing Shreveport, Louisiana, where the Confederates had established valuable factories and depots.

Banks advanced first, and Taylor, with few troops at his disposal, obstructed the Yankee march as best he could, to allow Smith to concentrate his strength for a decisive engagement. Once Steele's columns began to move against Maj. Gen. Sterling Price, Smith decided to exploit his interior lines of communication. He would concentrate and defeat one Union command, then the other. But which one? Smith's initial inclination was to strike Banks first; then, he switched to Steele, only to revert to Banks as the target.

This sort of indecisiveness, and the loss of much of his beloved Louisiana, absolutely infuriated Taylor. While Taylor labored vigilantly to delay Banks's march with his vastly inferior Rebel numbers, Smith's promised reinforcements arrived in a trickle. Worse, the departmental commander held back 4,400 infantrymen under Brig. Gen. Thomas J. Churchill at Shreveport for days. Smith claimed that the troops needed a resupply of ammunition; in truth, Smith did not want to commit to an attack of either Banks or Steele just yet. After a face to face meeting with Taylor, Smith's intentions remained vague in Taylor's mind. Convinced that the departmental commander had no real plan and little intention of sparing the rest of Louisiana, the hot-tempered Taylor determined to fight with what little manpower he possessed.[61]

Wisely, he chose an area around Mansfield, where the road snaked far away from the river and well beyond the support of Union gunboats, to resist. One last time, Taylor warned Smith that circumstances were favorable and he would fight the next day unless Smith told him not to do so immediately. In Smith's written response, the departmental commander asked Taylor to let him know when he planned to fight, and Smith would come down to command in person. What Smith had in mind was the commanding general, swinging down with Churchill's men as reinforcements to inspire the troops and lead them to victory—a la 1st Manassas. For some bizarre reason, Smith replied by courier, instead of telegram, and the delay once more convinced Taylor that his commander could not make a decision. Taylor, then, would decide for both of them.[62]

That morning, April 8, Taylor laid plans to strike Banks's lead elements. In late afternoon, the Confederates attacked, and by evening they had won a resounding victory at Mansfield. With Banks's army knocked back on its heels, Taylor hoped to deliver a second crushing blow. Churchill's men, twenty miles to the rear at Keachie, rushed forward to catch up with Taylor's advancing command. The next day, having covered forty-five miles in some thirty-six hours, they joined fellow Confederates in a follow-up battle at Pleasant Hill. This time, Banks had on hand his best soldiers—men from A. J. Smith's command—and the Federals repulsed Taylor's attacks with substantial losses on both sides. Once again, Banks ordered his army to retreat.[63]

Smith arrived at the front late that night, and over the next few days he held several meetings with Taylor. Ultimately, he decided that Banks's army no longer posed a viable threat, and he stripped Taylor of troops to use with Price against Steele to the north. Thus far, Smith had performed poorly in the campaign. He had anticipated the Union advance along the Red River correctly and had adopted steps to defend against it, but when the campaign finally began, indecision plagued him. He could not choose which Union column posed a greater threat, and at the critical moment, he withheld valuable reinforcements from Taylor's army to fulfill some bizarre scheme to replay 1st Manassas. Because Churchill's men were so far to the rear, they missed the battle of Mansfield and were too exhausted to fight well at Pleasant Hill. A fresh 4,400 men may not have altered the outcome at Pleasant Hill, but no one will ever know for certain.[64]

Although his decision to shift forces northward against Steele made sense initially, by April 14, Smith learned that Steele had begun to retreat. Yet rather than try to punish and perhaps destroy Banks's command, he elected to leave Taylor with a handful of troops in charge in Louisiana and take the bulk of the troops personally into Arkansas to join Price and crush Steele's command. In late April at Poison Spring and again at Mark's Mill, portions of Smith's command drove off Union forces and captured large numbers of wagons, along with some guns, ammunition, and prisoners. Still, Steele's main column fell back toward Little Rock. Smith then lapsed into a series of blunders. He failed to give precise orders to his cavalry commander, Brig. Gen. James Fagan, to block Steele from seizing a bridgehead across the Saline River. He allowed Samuel Maxey to take his Indian troops home on the verge of the big fight. And when he finally caught up with the Federals along the Saline River at Jenkins' Ferry, Smith fought an amateurish battle. Rather than concentrating his troops for powerful blows, he threw his troops into the battlefield grinder piecemeal. Steele's bluecoats parried the weak blows and escaped over the river.[65]

Despite his inability to crush Steele's command, Smith proclaimed a great victory. "I have just passed through the most brilliant and successful campaign of the war," he crowed to his mother. In his announcement to officials in Richmond, he called it a "brilliant campaign" in which its fruits were "most glorious and satisfactory." His forces had repulsed not one but two enemy commands, inflicting far greater losses than they incurred, and compelling both Union columns to retreat rapidly.[66]

Taylor thought otherwise. In a series of heated letters, some of them so intemperate that they reached the point of gross insubordination, Taylor dismissed the campaign as an utter failure. He had punished Banks at Mansfield and Pleasant Hill and, had Smith left him with those troops, he would have destroyed the Federals along the Red River and captured Porter's gunboats. Instead, Smith stripped him of vital manpower in a quest for personal glory and suffered a defeat due to command incompetence at Jenkins' Ferry. Taylor doubtless could no longer restrain his nasty temper, perhaps believing that his strong combat record and personal relationship with Davis as his first wife's brother would shield him. Smith eventually removed Taylor, but the exchange went forward to Davis.[67]

Nor did Davis perceive the campaign as a significant Confederate victory. As Union forces under Grant, Sherman, and E. R. S. Canby concentrated their power and pressed the principal Confederate commands back toward Richmond, Atlanta, and Mobile that summer, Davis grew increasingly irritated with Smith's conduct that spring. Earlier in the war, repulsing enemy advances proved satisfactory. Smith genuinely believed that Steele could settle for nothing less than complete victory. "Retreat to him," Smith explained to a disbelieving Taylor, "is as disastrous as defeat."[68]

By the latter half of 1864, however, circumstances in the war had changed, and Smith had failed to adapt with them. The Confederacy needed its armed forces in secondary theaters of war, such as the Trans-Mississippi, to achieve such triumphs that they would influence Federal operations and strategy elsewhere. The Union had to suffer a disaster, and Smith, with his cautious and conservative Fabian approach, lacked the ability to achieve it. Even if Smith had crushed Steele's columns at Jenkins' Ferry, it would not have altered Federal activity east of the river significantly. Only the destruction of Banks's army and Porter's fleet would have compelled the Union to shift large numbers of troops to the west and eased the pressure on one of the three primary Yankee targets.[69]

Smith erred, too, when he left his most talented subordinate, Taylor, on the sidelines in the critical moment. With both Banks and Steele retreating, Smith had a choice of concentrating all his resources and exploiting the momentum of Banks's repulse or marching large numbers of infantry long distances in an effort to catch and destroy Steele. He could fight with the aggressive Taylor as his top subordinate or rely on the judgment and execution of the political general Price.

A year earlier, President Davis had confronted just such a dilemma. He could draw large numbers of troops from Lee's army and transport them over enormous distances to fight under Johnston in the unhealthy Mississippi climate, or he could place his trust in his best commander to reap big results with the most successful soldiers in the Confederacy. Davis let Lee and the Army of Northern Virginia raid Pennsylvania. Although the campaign ultimately failed, and the Confederacy lost Vicksburg, at least Davis could say that he placed his trust with the very best the army and nation had to offer. Smith could stake no such claim.[70]

During the summer of 1864, Smith hatched a plan to launch a raid into Missouri, but before it generated much momentum, Bragg as Davis's chief of staff directed Smith to shift large numbers of reinforcements east of the Mississippi River under Taylor. If Smith could not draw a substantial Union force over to the Trans-Mississippi and ease the pressure on Confederate commands to the east, then he must yield those soldiers to other hard-pressed areas. In a shocking display of neglectful incompetence, no one forced the issue. Taylor wanted to get away from Smith and secure another command, but he refused to throw himself into the work of moving soldiers—without artillery, horses, wagons, or many supplies—east of the Mississippi River. Because the directive would strip Smith of most of his available infantry, he unenthusiastically ordered Taylor to oversee the process and essentially washed his hands of the matter. Without anyone to push it, no one crossed the river.[71]

Like other departmental commanders, Smith had a tendency to focus on his own little world, to the exclusion of the greater needs of the Confederacy, a practice Davis well understood. "I have not failed to appreciate the tendency of a commander whose mind is properly concentrated upon the necessities of his own position to overlook the wants which may exist elsewhere, and the possibility of his supplying them," Davis counseled Smith. "We have one cause, one country, and the States have been confederated to unite their power for the defense of each." The Confederacy had to remain vigilant and to concentrate its power quickly to offset the Union superiority in manpower and resources. He expressed disappointment that Smith did not pin down large numbers of Federal forces by following up his April victories, or by transferring large numbers of his troops east of the river. Still, Davis would not replace him.[72]

All Smith did was authorize Price to launch a raid into Missouri with whatever the cavalry they could collect. For awhile that fall, Price's raid generated some uneasiness, especially in Missouri and Kansas. In the end, though, Price's mismanagement and poor decision making, combined with the Federals' ability to concentrate over-whelming strength, resulted in another Rebel failure. But for all Price's faults, at least he caused such a stir that he attracted large numbers of reinforcements. Had his raid lasted for several more weeks, he may have detained A. J. Smith's troops long enough to prevent them from reinforcing Maj. Gen. George H. Thomas's Federals in time to fight at the battle of Nashville—precisely the kind of contribution Davis hoped to obtain from the Trans-Mississippi Department.[73]

During those waning weeks and months of the Confederacy, Smith attempted to transport all his soldiers across the Mississippi River. Yet the Rebel collapse occurred so swiftly, and communication with Richmond traveled so slowly, that before Smith had transferred any troops, he learned the devastating news of Lee's surrender at Appomattox. He implored his soldiers to stand by their colors, but the capture of Lee and his army, followed by negotiations between Sherman and Johnston, cut out any of their remaining heart. Consultation with several of the governors yielded a recommendation to negotiate for honorable terms.[74]

Some later accused him of cowardice, or talked of arresting him and continuing the rebellion. His soldiers, however, voiced their opposition with their legs, accentuating the obvious futility of continued resistance. After initial discussions with Maj. Gen. John Pope broke down, he finally settled on terms similar to Grant and Lee. On June 2. 1865, off the coast of Galveston, Texas, on the USS *Andrew Jackson*, Smith signed the surrender agreement. The war was over.[75]

Unsure what punishment, if any, high-ranking Confederate officers would suffer, Smith fled across the border into Mexico and then made his way to Cuba, where he found quite a number of other Confederate military and political officials. Prolonged separation from Cassie and the children gnawed at him, until he finally decided to come home, regardless of the consequences. A letter from Grant reassured him of his status, and home he came. Once he took the oath of allegiance, Smith sought employment in a variety of areas. Eventually, he found permanent work teaching in Nashville and then Sewanee, Tennessee. Smith sired a massive brood and kept clear of most of the postwar debates. In 1893, just shy of seventy years of age, Smith died.[76]

All in all, Smith was an officer of some ability who had advanced beyond his capacity. A full general before the age of forty, Smith had risen in rank and responsibility too rapidly. He leaped from a staff officer to a corps commander and department head with little time in command. Prior to his assignment as commander of the Trans-Mississippi Department, his Civil War service leading men in battle consisted of a couple of minutes at 1st Manassas and the Kentucky raid of 1862. Lacking the necessary seasoning and judgment based on experience, he embraced an approach to war that clashed with the designs of the Confederate president and was unsuited to a revolution by a propertied democratic republic. Administratively honest, his political naïveté hurt his record of accomplishments and ultimately his reputation in the Trans-Mississippi Department. While he grasped the importance of generating a reliable source of sound currency, politicians induced him into an impractical and inefficient scheme of impressment of government sale of cotton. As furor rose in opposition to his approach, politicians, some of whom had endorsed his Cotton Bureau plan, condemned it and him. A more tested officer, wily in political ways, may have proven more adept at running this department. Whether the Trans-Mississippi could have altered the outcome of the war seems doubtful, but had a more talented officer commanded it, the department could have contributed more to the Confederate war effort and its administration improved the quality of life for those who resided there.

Gen. P. G. T. Beauregard assessed Smith's military talents in a postwar letter by writing, "He was an honest, intelligent & zealous officer—but with not much energy or force of character. He was a good subordinate commander, like Bragg, Longstreet, Hood & some others, but inferior as a com[man]der-in-chief. He had not the 'feu Sacre' [sacred fire] as Napoleon called it." Parks, Smith's biographer, dismissed the opinion as one given by a man who did not know Smith well. In fact, Beauregard may have possessed an uncanny understanding of the man.[77]

NOTES

1. See William C. Davis, Jr., *Jefferson Davis: The Man and His Hour* (New York: HarperCollins, 1991), 699.
2. Davis to Smith, December 24, 1864, in Dunbar Rowland, ed., *Jefferson Davis: Constitutionalist: His Letters, Papers, and Speeches* 10 vols., (Jackson, MS: Mississippi Department of Archives and History, 1923), 6:428; Richard Taylor, *Destruction and Reconstruction: Personal Experiences of the Late War*, Richard B. Harwell, ed. (New York: Longmans, Green and Co., 1955), 231 and 229 (hereafter cited as Taylor, *Destruction and Reconstruction*); William J. Cooper, Jr., *Jefferson Davis: American* (New York: Alfred A. Knopf, 2000), 399.

3. Joseph H. Parks, *General Edmund Kirby Smith, C.S.A.* (1954; reprint, Baton Rouge: Louisiana State University Press, 1982) (hereafter cited as Parks, *General Edmund Kirby Smith*); Robert L. Kerby, *Kirby Smith's Confederacy: The Trans-Mississippi South, 1863–1865* (New York: Columbia University Press, 1972), 112–13 and 129, for examples (hereafter cited as Kerby, *Kirby Smith's Confederacy*).

4. See Parks, *General Edmund Kirby Smith*, 7–40. His letters, especially during his West Point years, lay out his awkward situation; see reel 1, Edmund Kirby-Smith Papers, University of North Carolina Chapel Hill (repository hereafter cited as UNC).

5. See Parks, *General Edmund Kirby Smith*, 39–65.

6. Ibid., 66–87; Edmund Kirby Smith (hereafter EKS) to Mother, June 1, 1853, reel 1, Edmund Kirby-Smith Papers, UNC.

7. EKS to Mother, October 31, 1854; July 31, 1856; September 1, 1856; January 15, 1860; and January 2, 1859, reels 1–2, Edmund Kirby-Smith Papers, UNC.

8. EKS to Mother, November 10, 1860. Mother to Son, January 11, 1860, reel 2, Edmund Kirby-Smith Papers, UNC.

9. EKS to Mother, November 10, 1860 and June 2, 1861. Also see EKS to [Mother], January 28, 1860, reel 2, Edmund Kirby-Smith Papers, UNC.

10. Mark M. Boatner III, *The Civil War Dictionary* (New York: David McKay, 1959), 770. Also see Parks, *General Edmund Kirby Smith*, 119–26.

11. EKS to Mother, October 20, 1855, May 16, 1861, and May 21, 1861, reels 1–2, Edmund Kirby-Smith Papers, UNC.

12. See Robert K. Krick's essay in this volume and Joseph T. Glatthaar, *Partners in Command: The Relationships Between Leaders in the Civil War* (New York: The Free Press, 1994), 95–133 (hereafter cited as Glatthaar, *Partners in Command*).

13. EKS to Mother, June 2, 1861, reel 2, Edmund Kirby-Smith Papers, UNC.

14. For some interesting elements of the Johnston-Smith relationship, see Craig L. Symonds, *Joseph E. Johnston: A Civil War Biography* (New York: W.W. Norton, 1992) (hereafter cited as Symonds, *Joseph E. Johnston*); Parks, *General Edmund Kirby Smith*, 145.

15. EKS to Mother, August 17, 1864, reel 4; Johnston to EKS, March 14, 1887, reel 5, Edmund Kirby-Smith Papers, UNC; also see EKS to [?], May 29, 1861, reel 2, Edmund Kirby-Smith Papers, UNC; Glatthaar, *Partners in Command*, 99–101. (He spells it Johnson.)

16. EKS to Mother, August 16 and July 31, 1861, Henry Burst[?] to Mrs. Smith, July 22, 1861, reel 2, Edmund Kirby-Smith Papers, UNC; After Action Report (AAR) of Col. J.B. Kershaw, July 26, 1861, U.S. War Department. *War of the Rebellion: A Compilation of the Official Records of the Union and Confederate Armies*, 127 vols., index, and atlas (Wash-

ington: U.S. Government Printing Office, 1880–1901) I, 2:522 (set hereafter cited as *OR*, with all citations to Series I; for volumes that appear in more than one part, the part is shown in parenthesis after the volume number); Richard [Brindley] to my dear people, August 12, 1861, Bound Volume No. 111, Richmond National Battlefield Park Library; *Richmond Dispatch*, August 6, 1861, 3.

17. *Richmond Dispatch*, August 5, 1861, 2. Had the newspaper known that Blucher was a boorish illiterate, it might not have used the nickname with Smith.

18. EKS to wife, November 3, 1861, reel 2, Edmund Kirby-Smith Papers, UNC; also see General Orders, No. 15., Adjutant and Inspector General's Office (hereafter cited as A&IG), October 22, 1861, in *OR*, 5: 913-14; Parks, 137–43. For factionalism, see Thomas Lawrence Connelly and Archer Jones, *The Politics of Command: Factions and Ideas in Confederate Strategy* (Baton Rouge: Louisiana State University Press, 1973), 49–86.

19. See Taylor, *Destruction and Reconstruction*, 150–51 and 217;

20. Jolen M. Tilley to home, December 1, 1861. Georgia Division, United Daughters of the Confederacy, *Confederate Reminiscences and Letters, 1861–1865*, 14 vols. (Atlanta: United Daughters of the Confederacy, 2000), 14:242; Reuben Allen Pierson to Father, November 26, 1861, Thomas W. Cutrer and T. Michael Parrish, eds., *Brothers in Gray: The Civil War Letters of the Pierson Family* (Baton Rouge: Louisiana State University Press, 1997), 65–66; W. P. B[allinger] to Guy Bryan, June 30, 1864, Guy Bryan Papers, Center for American History, University of Texas at Austin.

21. EKS to Wife, October 25, November 1, and December 14, 16, and 18, 1861, reel 2, Edmund Kirby-Smith Papers, UNC; also see Parks, *General Edmund Kirby Smith*, 152–53.

22. See Special Orders, No. 45, A&IGO, February 25, 1862, in *OR*, 7: 908; Smith to Johnston, 4 June 1863, in *OR*, 24 (3):948.

23. EKS to Wife, March 13 and N.D., 1862, reel 2, Edmund Kirby-Smith Papers, UNC; EKS to Cooper, March 15, 1862, AAR of EKS, April 17 and 19, 1862, in *OR*, 10 (1): 20–1, 50, and 628.

24. This opinion is based on a survey of the *OR*.

25. See Bragg to Cooper, June 22, 1862. Bragg to EKS, June 22, 1862, EKS to Bragg, July 6, 1862, EKS to Davis, July 14, 1862, Morgan to EKS, July 16, 1862, EKS to Cooper, July 19, 1862, EKS to Bragg, July 20, 1862, EKS to Bragg, July 24, 1862, Bragg to Cooper, August 1, 1862, Bragg to EKS, August 8, 1862, EKS to Bragg, August 9, 1862, Bragg to EKS, August 10, 1862, EKS to Bragg, August 11, 1862, EKS to Davis, August 11, 1862, in *OR*, 16 (2): 701–02, 723, 726–27, 729–30, 733–35, 741, 745–46, 748–49, 752–53; Bragg to Beauregard, 22 July 1862, in *OR*, 17 (2): 330–31; EKS to wife, July 22, 1862, and August 13, 15, 21,

and 23, 1862, reel 3, Edmund Kirby-Smith Papers, UNC. Even Bragg's wife encouraged him to strike into Tennessee and Kentucky. See Elisse to Bragg, June 8, 1862, quoted in Grady McWhiney, *Braxton Bragg and Confederate Defeat* (New York: Columbia University Press, 1969), 268 (hereafter cited as McWhiney, *Braxton Bragg*). Missing from the *OR*, and perhaps causing some confusion is Bragg's telegram to EKS, dated June 26, 1862, and referred to in EKS to Davis, July 14, 1862. Bragg was at Tupelo and planned to move on Buell's rear. (*OR*, 16 [2]: 726–27.)

26. See Bragg to EKS, August 12, 1862, EKS to Bragg, August 13, 1862, EKS to Bragg, August 20, 1862, Bragg to EKS, August 24, 1862, in *OR*, 16 (2): 754–55, 760, 766–67, and 775.

27. AAR of W. Nelson, August 31, 1862; also see AAR of EKS, August 30, and September 3, 6, and 16, 1862, in *OR*, 16 (1): 908–09 and 931–36.

28. Table of Casualties. AAR of EKS, September 16, 1862. AAR of Mahlon D. Manson, September 10, 1862; Join to Resolution of Confederate Congress, Approved February 17, 1864, in *OR*, 16 (1): 909, 914–15, 935–36, and 1161–162.

29. See Parks, *General Edmund Kirby Smith*, 235–41. For information on Buell, see Stephen Engle, *Most Promising of All: Don Carlos Buell* (Chapel Hill: University of North Carolina Press, 1999).

30. See Thomas Lawrence Connelly, *Army of the Heartland: The Army of Tennessee, 1861–1862* (Baton Rouge: Louisiana State University Press, 1967), 192–93. Steven E. Woodworth, in his strong book, *Jefferson Davis and His Generals: The Failure of Confederate Command in the West* (Lawrence: University Press of Kansas, 1990), 126, repeats this claim and cites Connelly and Gary Donaldson, "Into Africa: Kirby Smith and Braxton Bragg's Invasion of Kentucky," *Filson Club Historical Quarterly*, 61, No. 4 (October 1987), 444–65 as the sources (hereafter cited as Donaldson, "Into Africa"). Donaldson's essay is chock-full of errors and misinterprets the source material, as does Connelly.

31. EKS to Wife, August 24, 1862, reel 3, Edmund-Kirby Smith Papers, UNC; Connelly, 193.

32. EKS to Wife, August 26 and 24, 1862, reel 3, Edmund-Kirby Smith Papers, UNC; Connelly, 193. The full quotation in Connelly also refers to Cortés. He writes: "On occasion he fancied himself as Cortez burning his ships behind him, and as Moses leading the Israelites from Egypt." Smith does not mention Moses in the letter! Woodworth, 138, states, "After comparing himself to Napoléon, Cortés, and Moses, he added, I care not what the world may say, I am not ambitious.'" He cites Donaldson, "Into Africa," 453.

33. EKS to Wife, 26 and 24 August 1862. Reel 3, Edmund-Kirby Smith Papers, UNC; Bragg to Elise, 18 September 1862, quoted in McWhiney, *Braxton Bragg*, 284. Other scholars have spun off on this theme with an equally loose use of evidence, such as Donaldson, "Into Africa," 453.

Donaldson states that Smith "described the march as a 'herculean undertaking,' a task `rivaling the passage of the Alps.'" These quotations come from two separate letters, and in both cases Smith was praising his troops. "We have had a rough time & have accomplished almost an hercularian undertaking in crossing the mountains. Our men have marched day and night and have carried their own subsistence in haversacks for five days-ragged, barefooted. They have climbed mountains born starvation and thirst without a murmur." (EKS to Wife, August 21, 1862.) In the other letter, dated two days later, Smith professes love for his wife and faith in God and the Confederacy for three pages. Then, he wrote: "we have crossed two ranges of rough and precipitous mountains and working day and night have been for six days pulling by hand wagons and artillery over rocks and precipices accomplishing a feat rivaling the passage of the Alps." In the succeeding sentences, he credited his troops with the achievement and discussed the hardships they endured and from where they came. (EKS to wife, August 23, 1862. Edmund Kirby-Smith Papers, UNC.) Donaldson uses both examples to suggest that Smith's huge ego led him to grossly inflate his achievements.

34. See Edmund Kirby-Smith Papers, UNC.
35. See Parks, *General Edmund Kirby Smith*, 244–45.
36. See Glatthaar, *Partners in Command*, 117–20; Symonds, *Joseph E. Johnston*, 171–203.
37. Special Orders, No. 11. A & IGO, January 14, 1863, in *OR*, 15: 948; Special Orders, No. 33. A & IGO, February 9, 1863, in *OR*, 22 (2): 787; General Orders, No. 1. Headquarters, Dept. Trans-Mississippi, in *OR*, 15: 1005.
38. See Kerby, *Kirby Smith's Confederacy*, 4 and 80.
39. William R. Boggs, *Military Reminiscences of Gen. Wm. R. Boggs, C.S.A.*, edited with William K. Boyd (Durham, N.C.: Seeman, 1913), 54 (hereafter cited as Boggs, *Military Reminiscences*.
40. Taylor, *Destruction and Reconstruction*, 165.
41. Johnston to Smith, April 18, 1863, reel 3, Edmund Kirby-Smith Papers, UNC; Boggs, 54-5.
42. Johnston to EKS, June 3, 1863, EKS to Gov. Reynolds, June 4, 1863, Holmes to Price, June 8, 1863, EKS to Davis, June 16, 1863, Schofield to Davidson, July 9, 1863, in *OR*, 22 (2): 914, 856, 863, 873, and 361; Holmes to EKS, June 15, 1863, EKS to Holmes, June 16, 1863, Blair to EKS, July 7, 1863, AAR of Holmes, August 14, 1863, in *OR*, 22 (1): 407–12.
43. Pemberton to EKS, May 9, 1863, in *OR*, 24 (3): 846; EKS to Gov. Reynolds, June 4, 1863, in *OR*, 22 (2): 855.
44. Taylor, *Destruction and Reconstruction*, 166; Boggs, *Military Reminiscences*, 54–5; Symonds, *Joseph E. Johnston*, 200; Kerby, *Kirby Smith's Confederacy*, 115. The quotation marks around "threaten" are mine.
45. Davis to EKS, July 14, 1863, in *OR*, 22 (2): 925–27.

46. Davis to EKS, July 14, 1863, Seddon to EKS, October 10, 1863, in *OR*, 22 (2): 925–27 and 1040–042; Davis Endsmt., October 2, 1863 of EKS to Seddon, September 12, 1863, Seddon to Davis, January 20, 1865, in *OR*, 53: 896 and 1036–038.

47. Davis to EKS, July 14, 1863, in *OR*, 22 (2): 926.

48. Davis to EKS, April 28, 1864, in *OR*, 53: 985–86; Kerby, *Kirby Smith's Confederacy*, 147–48.

49. EKS to Johnston, June 4, 1863, in *OR*, 24 (3): 948; EKS to Davis, June 16, 1863, in *OR*, 22 (2): 872.

50. Report of W. S. Oldham, Committee Chairman in Memorandum of F.R. Lubbock, August 18, 1863, General Orders, No. 35, Hdqrs. Trans-Mississippi Department, August 3, 1863, in *OR*, 22 (2): 1008–9 and 953. The committee suggested the government would pay the interest semi-annually in specie, so that cotton bonds would float near face value, but the group voted a tie on this clause.

51. Report of W. S. Oldham, Committee Chairman in Memorandum of F.R. Lubbock, August 18, 1863, in *OR*, 22 (2): 1008–009; W.S. Oldham to Davis, January 4, 1864, in *OR*, 34 (2): 820–21; Maj. Charles Russell to Maj. E.B. Pendleton, June 10, 1863, Maj. Charles Russell to Maj. B. Bloomfield, June 11, 1863, in *OR*, 26 (2): 92–4.

52. Maj. Charles Russell to Maj. E. B. Pendleton, June 10, 1863, Maj. Charles Russell to Maj. B. Bloomfield, June 11, 1863, in *OR*, 26 (2): 92–4; W.S. Oldham to Davis, January 4, 1864, in *OR*, 34 (2): 820–21; EKS to Citizens of the Trans-Mississippi Department, June 1, 1864, General Orders, No. 34, Hdqrs., Trans-Mississippi Department, June 1, 1864, in *OR*, 34 (4): 638–39; Kerby, *Kirby Smith's Confederacy*, 159.

53. Bee to Turner, August 24, 1863, in *OR*, 26 (2): 180–82; EKS to Davis, May 12, 1864, in *OR*, 34 (3): 821–22; William S. Oldham "Reminiscences," 356–57. William S. Oldham Papers, Center for American History, University of Texas.

54. See Kerby, *Kirby Smith's Confederacy*, 199–202; John Moretta, "Pendleton Murrah and States Rights in Civil War Texas," *Civil War History* 45, No. 2 (June 1999), 129–30 (cited hereafter as Moretta, "Pendleton Murrah").

55. The army struggled to ship cotton to market because of its more fundamental logistical demands, like feeding and equipping its troops in the field, which taxed its efforts in such an expansive region. See Kerby, *Kirby Smith's Confederacy*, 180. Mexico levied a 2.5 cent per pound import tax on cotton. One half of all vessel cargo spaces was restricted for Confederate Government use; see Seddon to EKS, June 11, 1864, in *OR*, 34 (4): 666.

56. EKS to Davis, January 20, 1864, in *OR*, 34 (2): 896; also see EKS to Davis, January 28, 1864, in *OR*, 34 (2): 920; EKS to Davis, December 13, 1864, in *OR*, 41 (4): 1109; EKS to Mother, June 2, 1861, R 2, Edmund Kirby-Smith Papers, UNC.

57. See Boggs, *Military Reminiscences*, 57; Taylor, *Destruction and Reconstruction*, 153 and 183.

58. Kerby, *Kirby Smith's Confederacy*, 57–8. Thanks to Dr. Patrick Kelly for pointing out the similarity of behavior between the Kentucky raid and his reaction in the Red River campaign.

59. See EKS to Davis, February 10, 1865, An Act to provide for the protection of the frontier and turning over the frontier regiment to C.S. service, Joint Resolution, State of Texas, November 22, 1864, Special Orders, No. 40, HQ, Bureau of Conscripts, Trans-Mississippi Department, March 12, 1864, C. S. West to Governor Murrah, October 19, 1864 and February 10, 1865, Murrah to West, November 23, 1864, Murrah to Smith, November 23, 1864, in *OR*, 48 (1): 1373–379; Moretta, "Pendleton Murrah," 129–30.

60. Smith to Taylor, October 20, 1863, in *OR*, 26 (2): 341–42. Also see AAR of EKS, November 14, 1863, in *OR*, 22 (1): 24–6; Kerby, *Kirby Smith's Confederarcy*, 242–48. Federals also attempted a move on Matagorda Bay and Brownsville, Texas.

61. See Ludwell H. Johnson, *Red River Campaign: Politics and Cotton in the Civil War* (Baltimore: The Johns Hopkins Press, 1958), 122–24 and 129–30 (hereafter cited as Johnson, *Red River Campaign*).

62. EKS to Davis, August 28, 1864, in *OR*, 34 (1): 485.

63. See Johnson, *Red River Campaign*, 154.

64. See EKS to Davis, April 12 and 16, 1864, in *OR*, 34 (1): 476.

65. Smith also allowed Samuel Maxey to withdraw his command in the middle of the campaign. See Edwin C. Bearss, *Steele's Retreat from Camden and the Battle of Jenkins' Ferry* (Little Rock: Pioneer Press, n.d. [1967]), for the best coverage of the campaign, and specifically 54, 78–9, 100, 136, 161–62; EKS to Cooper, May 4, 1864. EKS to Davis, June 11, 1864, in *OR*, 34 (1): 477 and 480–82.

66. EKS to Mother, May 5, 1864, reel 3, Edmond Kirby-Smith Papers, UNC; EKS to Cooper, May 4, 1864, in *OR*, 34 (1): 477.

67. See EKS to Taylor, June 5 and May 26, 1864, Taylor to EKS, April 28, May 24, and June 5, 1864, EKS to Davis, June 11, 1864, in *OR*, 34 (1): 538–48.

68. EKS to Taylor, April 22, 1864, in *OR*, 34 (1): 534.

69. See Davis to Smith, December 24, 1864, in *OR*, 41 (1): 123–24. Although Davis wrote this in late December, his annoyance with Smith's leadership was evident in messages dating back almost six months earlier. Smith's defensive message dated June 11, 1864 and another on August 28, 1864, indicates his fears that Davis was dissatisfied with his conduct and performance. Others, particularly people from Louisiana, had expressed their hostility toward Smith to Davis. (*OR*, 34 (1): 478–88.)

70. Some have criticized Davis for supporting this, but if Davis had attempted to shift substantial numbers of troops from Virginia to Missis-

sippi, or from Tennessee to Mississippi and Virginia to Tennessee, and they arrived too late or failed to prevent the loss of Vicksburg, he would have opened himself up to harsh criticism for that decision, too. At least Davis put his faith in his best commander and his most proven army. If they could not achieve, perhaps no one could.

71. See Cooper to EKS, July 18, 1864, S. D. Lee to Col. Golber, July 22, 1864, Butler to Bragg, August 22, 1864, Boggs to Buckner, August 22, 1864, Taylor to Buckner, August 25 and 27, 1864, Sale to EKS, October 3, 1864, Taylor to Bragg, August 25, 1864, Buckner to Boggs, September 3, 1864, Levy to Benjamin, September 15, 1864, Smith to Davis, October 8, 1864, Seddon to Smith in Seddon to Hardee, December 7, 1864, Davis to EKS, December 24, 1864, in *OR*, 41 (1): 117–24. He first considered it in mid-May. (EKS to Taylor, May 17, 1864, in *OR* 34 (1): 538.)

72. Davis to Smith, 24 December 1864, in *OR*, 41 (1): 123–24; EKS to Davis, 11 March 1865, in *OR*, 48, (1): 1418–419.

73. See EKS to Davis, 21 November 1864, in *OR*, 41 (4): 1068–069; EKS to Davis, 11 March 1865, in *OR*, 48 (1): 1418–419. The best account of Price's raid is Albert Castel, *General Sterling Price and the Civil War in the West* (Baton Rouge: Louisiana State University Press, 1968), 188–255.

74. Davis to EKS, January 31, 1865, in *OR*, 41 (1): 124; EKS to Davis, March 7 and 11, 1865, in *OR*, 48 (1): 1411–412 and 1418–419; EKS to Soldiers of the Trans-Mississippi Army, April 21, 1865, in *OR*, 48 (2): 1284; Memo from Governors Allen of Louisiana, Flanagin of Arkansas, Bryan for Murrah of Texas, and Reynolds of Missouri, May 15, 1865, in *OR*, 48 (1):190–91.

75. See Surrender Agreement, June 2, 1865, in *OR*, 48 (2): 600–02; Parks, *General Edmund Kirby Smith*, 460–68 and 478. Negotiations with Pope are in *OR*, 48 (1): 186–96. There was some confusion over disbanding the army. Canby, who signed the agreement, was not very clear in his communications with Grant, and the Union commander thought Smith had acted in bad faith, until Canby clarified matters.

76. See Parks, *General Edmund Kirby Smith*, 482–509.

77. Beauregard to Mrs. S. A. Dorsey, June 23, 1869, in Beauregard Papers, Duke University. (Quoted in Parks, *General Edmund Kirby Smith*, 443–44.)

"A Bold Fighter" Promoted beyond His Abilities: General John Bell Hood

Keith S. Bohannon

At noon on July 20, 1864, Southern newspaper correspondent Felix G. De Fontaine stood in front of the Army of Tennessee's headquarters on the outskirts of Atlanta. A bevy of high-ranking officers were nearby, including the army's commander, Gen. John Bell Hood, his chief of staff, Gen. William W. Mackall, Gen. Mansfield Lovell, and various staff officers and escorts. De Fontaine noted that Hood was "arrayed in full uniform, leaning on his crutch and stick" in the doorway. Hood's manner was calm, the reporter recorded, but his eyes flashed "with a strange, indescribable light, which gloams in them only in the hour of battle."

When Hood shook De Fontaine's hand, the general said "at once I attack the enemy. He has pressed our lines until he is within a short distance of Atlanta and I must fight or evacuate. I am going to fight." Hood admitted that "the odds are against us, but I leave the issue with the God of battles." Hood and his retinue then left to ride to the front lines. Later that afternoon, Confederate troops attacked the Federals in what became known as the battle of Peach Tree Creek.[1]

Hood had commanded the Confederate Army of Tennessee for less than three days when he spoke with De Fontaine. Hood was thirty-three years old at the time and handicapped by the loss of a leg and the use of an arm. He had the reputation of being a fierce fighter and a superb leader of men in battle. By the second half of 1863,

Hood was one of the Southern Confederacy's great heroes and a confidant of Pres. Jefferson Davis.

Hood inherited, in the words of Albert Castel, "a virtually impossible situation" when he took command of the Confederacy's Western army with Sherman's hosts on the very outskirts of Atlanta. Most historians agree that Hood had been promoted beyond his level of ability by this point. The downward turn that his military career took in 1864 was due in part to circumstances beyond his control, including bad luck, the superior generalship of his opponents, and his inability to have orders executed by subordinates. Hood also had his own critical weaknesses that probably prevented him from being an effective army commander, including inattention to staff work, reconnaissance, and the logistical needs of his troops. Hood's command lasted almost exactly six months and ultimately resulted in the near destruction of the Army of Tennessee in the battles of Franklin and Nashville.[2]

Hood was born on June 29, 1831, in Owingsville, Bath County, Kentucky, the son of Dr. John W. Hood and Theodosia French Hood. Dr. Hood, a plantation and slave owner in the eastern fringe of the Bluegrass region, wanted his son to follow him into medicine, even promising to pay for the youth to finish his studies in Europe. The son instead wanted to be a soldier and obtained an appointment to the U.S. Military Academy through the assistance of his uncle, Congressman Richard French.[3]

Hood graduated from West Point in the class of 1853 with a mediocre academic record. In almost every subject area, including infantry tactics and artillery, he ranked at the bottom of his class. At the time of his graduation, Hood's overall ranking was forty-fourth out of a class of fifty-two. Despite the poor record, the general milieu of West Point, including its authoritarian and military environment, markedly influenced the young Kentuckian. Hood internalized the professional military ethos of the Academy and saw the school's administrators and officers, especially Supt. Robert E. Lee, as models of professional conduct.[4]

Although Hood had hoped upon graduation to receive a commission in the cavalry, his low class standing resulted in him entering the service as a second lieutenant in the 4th U.S. Infantry Regiment. His first assignment was at Fort Jones, an isolated post in northern California, where he arrived in March 1854. Lieutenant Hood remained at Fort Jones for over a year, serving much of the time as post adjutant, before he heard that the War Department had authorized the creation of two new cavalry regiments to protect the frontier.[5]

Hood immediately attempted to gain a position in one of the cavalry regiments, trying at first to work through a family friend, former Congressman John C. Breckinridge. When Breckinridge apparently failed to urge Hood's appointment, Hood wrote directly to Secretary of War Jefferson Davis in late April 1855 asking that his application "be laid before the President." Hood apologized for having "violated the usual rule laid down in the Regulations for such applications," but explained that he feared the "delay in other departments which would cause this to reach you too late." Hood's willingness as a young lieutenant to write such a letter reveals what biographer Richard McMurry claimed was "a lifelong habit of corresponding unofficially with those in authority without going through channels."[6]

Hood's continued efforts to secure a transfer to the cavalry paid off in August 1855 when he received a promotion to second lieutenant and orders to report to Jefferson Barracks, Missouri, to join the 2nd U.S. Cavalry. From January 1856 through the spring of 1861, Hood served with that regiment, being absent only twice on lengthy furloughs. During his tenure with the 2nd, Hood renewed acquaintances with Robert E. Lee, the regiment's lieutenant colonel. The relationship, which Hood fondly remembered in his memoirs, only strengthened the respect Hood had gained for Lee at West Point.[7]

Lieutenant Hood spent most of his time in the 2nd Cavalry engaging in camp and post duties or patrolling the Texas frontier to protect it against Indians, Mexicans, and outlaws. He saw action only once, in July 1857 when he led a party of two dozen men on a patrol near Devils River that resulted in a small skirmish with hostile Indians.[8]

In 1860, Hood received an eight-month leave of absence from the 2nd Cavalry, which he took beginning in September of that year. During his journey back east, the lieutenant received orders to report to West Point to serve as an instructor of cavalry. Hood immediately went to Washington, where he told the U.S. adjutant general that he did not want the position, since he "feared war would soon be declared between the States, in which event I preferred to be in a situation to act with entire freedom." The surprised adjutant general granted Hood's request.[9]

Hood was two months shy of his thirtieth birthday when he resigned his commission as first lieutenant in the U.S. cavalry on April

16, 1861, to join the Confederate army, "seeing no hope of reconciliation or adjustment, but every indication of a fierce and bloody war." He entered Confederate service as a captain of cavalry on April 20, 1861, to rank from March 16, 1861. In late May 1861, Captain Hood received orders to act as an instructor of cavalry companies stationed on the Peninsula between the James and York Rivers. While there he engaged in scouting and picket duty, drawing the pay of a major beginning in June 1861.[10]

On September 30,1861, Hood received a promotion to the colonelcy of the 4th Texas Infantry Regiment. The appointment undoubtedly thrilled Hood since he had grown to admire the Lone Star state during his years of service there in the late 1850s. The state's "vast and undeveloped resources" had impressed the young officer and just prior to secession he had decided to make it his "home for life," possibly to reside on a ranch he owned on the Nueces River.[11]

Colonel Hood's West Point training, antebellum association with Texas, and demonstrated skill as a small unit commander made him an effective and popular commander in the 4th Texas. Hood told his men "no regiment . . . should ever be allowed to go forth upon the battle-field and return with more trophies of war than the Fourth Texas— that the number of colors and guns captured, and prisoners taken, constituted the true test of the work done by any command in any engagement." Similar statements in Hood's later orders to his corps in the Army of Tennessee reveal in part the measures by which he gauged success on the battlefield.[12]

The 4th Texas Infantry spent the winter of 1861-62 near the town of Dumfries in northern Virginia. While encamped there, Hood received a promotion to brigadier general on March 3, 1862. Shortly thereafter he took command of Gen. Louis T. Wigfall's brigade, known thereafter as Hood's Texas Brigade, composed of the 1st, 4th, and 5th Texas Regiments, the 18th Georgia, and later, the Hampton Legion Infantry of South Carolina.[13]

By the first week of April 1862, Hood's men were in the trenches at Yorktown, part of an army under Gen. Joseph E. Johnston facing Union troops that had landed on the southern end of the Peninsula. On May 3, Johnston's men began a retreat westward toward Richmond. During the withdrawal, Hood received orders to assist in preventing enemy landings on the York River, a development that might impede or even block the Confederate withdrawal. The Confederates learned on May 6 that Union troops had disembarked at Eltham's Landing on the Pamunkey River, one of two rivers that came together to form the York.

The next day, Hood's regiments attacked the Federals at Eltham's Landing. Hood took an active role in leading and directing his men during the fight, personally deploying companies of skirmishers. At one point, Hood recalled, a "corporal of the enemy drew down his musket upon me as I stood in front of my line." A private in the 4th Texas saved Hood's life by instantly shooting the Federal, who fell only a few feet from Hood. The action at Eltham's Landing ended with the Federals withdrawing to the Pamunkey. Hood's leadership in the contest elicited praise from his superiors, including his division commander Chase Whiting, who noted the Texas general's "conspicuous gallantry."[14]

Hood and his brigade gained even greater glory following the June 27, 1862, battle of Gaines's Mill, part of the Seven Days campaign. During the action at Gaines's Mill, the Federals occupied a strong line and managed to repulse numerous Confederate assaults early in the day. Realizing that the onset of darkness would allow for a Union withdrawal, Confederate army commander Robert E. Lee consulted with Generals Whiting and Hood about the possibility of their troops breaching the Federal line.

Fulfilling Lee's request would be a daunting task for Whiting's division. Hood's men would first have to cross several hundred yards of open slope leading to Boatswain's Creek, then cross the creek and charge up a steep hillside defended by multiple lines of Union troops. When the 4th Texas formed under fire to begin the charge, Hood reminded the men that he had promised to lead them in their first assault. Walking out in front of the regiment, Hood took off his hat, held aloft his sword, and shouted "Forward, Guide Right" in a voice that could "be heard in the storm of battle."[15]

Hood's men subsequently played a key role in breaking through three lines of Union infantry and capturing enemy cannon. Hood's Texas Brigade lost heavily in the charge, the 4th suffering approximately 50 percent casualties. The morning after the battle, Hood rode up in front of his old regiment and upon learning the extent of their casualties, "the strength of his attachment was seen developing itself in tears" on his cheeks. As the general rode off to hide the display of emotion from his men, "there was not a soldier in that line but what thought more of [him] . . . than ever before." Already popular among his men, Hood's performance at Gaines's Mill elevated his standing in the brigade and in the eyes of the Southern army's high command, including General Lee.[16]

Several weeks after the Seven Days Campaign, Hood's immediate superior, Chase Whiting, received a medical furlough and never returned to his division. As senior brigadier general in the division, Hood took command of Whiting's two brigades. In addition to the Texas Brigade, the division contained Col. Evander M. Law's "Old Third Brigade." Hood's first experience commanding the division in battle took place during the Second Manassas campaign.[17]

Hood's division, marching as the vanguard of Gen. James Longstreet's wing of Lee's Army, arrived on the Second Manassas battlefield in the early afternoon of August 29. Stonewall Jackson, who thought highly of Hood after the Seven Days Campaign, extended the Texan a "hearty welcome" as Hood's two brigades deployed facing eastward astride the Warrenton Turnpike. That evening, Hood received orders to conduct a reconnaissance in force to the east with his division. "If an opening was found" in the Federal lines "for an entering wedge," remembered Longstreet, the Confederates would "have all things in readiness" for a major attack the next morning. Hood's advance ended by 8:00 P.M., when it became in the words of one of Hood's colonels, "too dark to distinguish friend from foe at a distance of 20 paces."[18]

On the morning of August 30, Hood made one of his most valuable contributions to the Confederate victory at Second Manassas. When Col. Stephen D. Lee arrived on the field with his artillery battalion, he consulted with Hood and followed the general's suggestions to deploy the batteries on a "commanding ridge." Although Hood had not been the first person to recognize the importance of the position, his suggestions that Lee post his guns there proved fortuitous when the cannoneers contributed to breaking up Federal attacks against the positions of Stonewall Jackson to the north. [19]

At 4:00 P.M. on August 30, Hood galloped up in front of the Texas Brigade. In a few minutes, the men heard him shout, "Attention Texas Brigade, forward march." The Texans' advance was part of a massive assault ordered that afternoon by Robert E. Lee and Longstreet to envelop the Union left. A few minutes after the Texas Brigade began its advance, a messenger told Hood to ride back and report to Longstreet. Hood found the wing commander between a quarter and a half mile to the rear. Longstreet told Hood not to allow his division "to move so far forward as to throw itself beyond the prompt support of the troops he had ordered to the front." In Hood's absence, his troops did exactly that.[20]

When Hood rejoined the Texas Brigade that afternoon, he ordered the men to hold their ground. During the remainder of the battle, Hood assisted in coordinating attacks that drove Union troops off of Chinn Ridge and back beyond the Sudley Road. Hood's two brigades captured cannon, flags, and numerous other trophies at Second Manassas, being "true to their teaching," in Hood's words, but suffered heavy casualties in the process. [21]

Hood did not at first command his division in the subsequent invasion of Maryland, due to his having been placed under arrest by his superior, Gen. Nathan G. Evans. The dispute originated on August 30 when Hood assigned a number of captured ambulances to his men for the use of their sick and wounded. The next day, Hood received orders to turn over the ambulances to Evans's South Carolinians. Hood refused to obey, since his men had captured the ambulances and he considered them the rightful owners. Lee allowed Hood to march into Maryland with his division, but did not release the Texan from arrest. [22]

On September 14, 1862, Lee sent Hood's division into battle to assist in the defense of South Mountain. As the Texans passed Lee, they shouted "Give us Hood!" Lee asked Hood to apologize to Evans, but Hood refused, claiming that while it would afford him "pleasure to do anything that could please" the commanding general, he could not acquiesce "without any sacrifice of my personal honor." Lee "temporarily suspended" Hood's arrest in order for him to lead his division into battle at South Mountain, although nothing subsequently ever came of the matter.[23]

Hood's troops arrived at Sharpsburg, Maryland, on September 15, eventually being posted on the extreme left of Lee's line near the Dunker Church on the Hagerstown Pike. The next evening, Hood's command blunted a Federal attack before nightfall. Later on the sixteenth, Hood withdrew his famished men a short distance in order to prepare rations, with the understanding that they should go to the aid of Gen. Alexander Lawton's division on the front line if needed.[24]

Around 6:00 A.M. on September 17, one of Stonewall Jackson's staff officers came in great haste to Hood with the request that his men advance at once. "To arms was sounded," remembered Hood, "and in a few minutes I again moved out in line of battle" around the Dunker Church and north toward the Federals. After passing a wounded General Lawton being borne to the rear on a stretcher and encountering Gen. Harry T. Hays fighting with a remnant of his decimated brigade, Hood led his division into the struggle.

Ten days later, Hood wrote that his "two little giant brigades" had wrestled with a far larger enemy force at Antietam, losing hundreds of officers and men but driving the enemy back several hundred yards. Hood sent repeated requests during the battle to Generals Harvey Hill and Longstreet for troops to protect the left of his division. Hood received no assistance until his shattered brigades withdrew into the West Woods and the division of Gen. Lafayette McLaws entered the fighting. [25]

Hood was one of the Army of Northern Virginia's rising stars in the weeks following the Maryland campaign. In recommending Hood for promotion ten days after Sharpsburg, Stonewall Jackson commented on the Texan's "ability and zeal," stating that Hood was "one of the most promising officers of the army." An article in the *Richmond Enquirer* entitled "The Texas Brigade" referred glowingly to the Texans and their commander. Hood's "courage and genius" were unfailing, crowed the writer, and the general and his men had "won for themselves immortal honor." Several weeks later, Thomas J. Goree of Longstreet's staff wrote home that "it is very probable that Gen. Hood will be promoted to Major Genl. for his gallantry in these various contests. No man deserves it more. He is one of the finest young officers I ever saw." [26]

Goree's prediction about Hood's elevation in rank was correct. In the reorganization of Lee's army following the Maryland campaign, Hood received a promotion to major general, to take rank from October 11, 1862, and command of a division in Longstreet's I Corps. Hood's division included four brigades commanded by Gens. George T. Anderson, Jerome B. Robertson, Evander M. Law, and Robert Toombs (later Henry L. Benning). [27]

Shortly after Hood's promotion, Lee moved his army eastward into the Shenandoah Valley toward Fredericksburg. Longstreet's corps reached Culpeper Courthouse in early November and camped there for three weeks. On November 19, Longstreet's men marched to Fredericksburg to counter the Federal army massed on the opposite bank of the Rappahannock River from the Confederates. During the December 13, 1862, battle of Fredericksburg, Hood's division was on the right of Longstreet's Corps, connecting with Stonewall Jackson's corps to the south.

Early on the morning of December 13, Longstreet went to Hood and told him that the enemy would probably be attacking Jackson's line, and that "when an opportunity offered he [Hood] should move forward and attack the enemy's flank." Longstreet gave similar commands to Gen. George Pickett, one of his other division commanders. Ultimately only two regiments of Evander Law's Brigade of Hood's division advanced to skirmish with the Federals who broke through Jackson's line. When Pickett went to Hood with the suggestion that they assault the Union line, Hood decided instead to withdraw Law's regiments. [28]

Longstreet was deeply disappointed in Hood's performance at Fredericksburg. In 1868, Longstreet confided to Edward Porter Alexander that the victory at Fredericksburg was "so handsome that I did not care to mar the enjoyment of it by making official trouble." In retrospect, Longstreet claimed that he had "made a mistake in not bringing the delinquent [Hood] to trial." When Longstreet penned his memoirs many years later, he claimed that his reluctance to "push the matter" stemmed from Hood being in "high favor with the authorities." [29]

Hood spent the months after the battle of Fredericksburg attempting to increase the strength of his division. On February 6, 1863, he wrote Louis T. Wigfall that he would "like a Div of Texans, but I don't think I would like to leave this army, I am very fond of General Lee." In mid-February, Lee ordered Hood's brigades to Richmond in response to reports that Federals on the Peninsula were threatening Richmond and the main railroad leading south out of the city. [30]

Hood's division marched through Richmond on February 21 and camped south of the city, where it remained for several weeks. During that time, Hood ventured into the city where his medical director John T. Darby introduced the general to Col. James Chesnut, Jr, and his wife Mary Boykin Chesnut. Mary Chesnut became a confidant of Hood and her famous published "diary" is an important source on Hood's private life and romance with Sarah Buchanan Campbell Preston, known as "Buck." [31]

Hood met Preston, possibly for the first time, in the streets of Richmond on March 18, 1863, as his division moved through the city. Buck Preston was twenty years old and a member of an aristocratic and wealthy South Carolina family. Mary Chesnut described the ravishing Buck as having "a knack of being 'fallen in love with' at sight and of never being 'fallen out of love' with." [32]

By early April, Longstreet's command had moved toward Suffolk, Virginia, to drive away or besiege the city's Federal garrison so that Confederates could collect supplies in the region. Longstreet posted Hood's brigades on the left of the Southern siege lines along the Nansemond River. With the exception of an April 19, 1863, clash in which Union troops seized Fort Huger from a garrison that included some of Hood's men, the siege of Suffolk was uneventful. Hood was critical of the operation in his memoir, claiming that he "never could satisfactorily account for" Longstreet's move toward Suffolk. [33]

During the spring and early summer of 1863, Hood may have been torn between his loyalty toward Robert E. Lee and an apparent desire to serve in the Western Theater. On April 29, 1863, Hood wrote Lee from Suffolk saying that "when we leave here it is my desire to return to you. If any troops come to the Rappahannock please don't forget me." Earlier that month, Cadet A. D. C. Ethelbert B. Wade of Hood's staff told a friend that Hood was "very anxious to be sent to Tennessee." Hood may have believed that he could best serve the Confederacy in the West, where there would also be a possibility of being promoted to lieutenant general and receiving a corps command. [34]

Hood's burning ambition was obvious to the men who served under him. An officer in Anderson's brigade who interacted with Hood wrote home in April 1863 that the general "has his eyes fixed on other heights in rank to climb and he knows he has men to wing them for him." A man in the 5th Texas writing after the Chancellorsville campaign told his mother that the Texans had made Hood "what he is and he is saving us now for a Lt Gen.'s stars since [Stonewall] Jackson is gone." Although Lee did not replace Jackson with Hood, the army commander did tell Jefferson Davis that Hood was a "capital officer" who was improving and would make a good corps commander if necessary. [35]

Throughout the second half of June, Hood's division moved north along the Blue Ridge and across the Potomac River in Lee's second invasion of the North. On June 28, Hood encountered the Englishman Sir Arthur Fremantle, who described the Confederate officer as a "tall, thin, wiry-looking man, with a grave face and a light-colored beard." Fremantle also noted that Hood was "accounted one of the best and most promising officers in the army." [36]

While encamped in the vicinity of Carlisle, Pennsylvania, on July 1, Hood received orders to march toward Gettysburg, where Confederate troops had encountered the enemy. Hood's men arrived near

Gettysburg shortly before dawn on July 2. The general and his staff spent the early part of the morning with Lee, Longstreet, and others at Lee's headquarters on the western slope of Seminary Ridge observing the Federals to the east. Twelve years later, Hood remembered that Lee seemed eager for Longstreet to attack that morning, but the corps commander convinced Lee to wait until Pickett's division arrived. [37]

On the afternoon of July 2, Hood's and McLaws's divisions of Longstreet's corps marched southward to get into position to attack across the Emmitsburg Road and turn the left flank of the Union army. By about 4:00 P.M., Hood's men had reached the right flank of Lee's army. As the division deployed, Hood sent out scouts to ascertain the exact location of the enemy's left. [38]

Hood received reports from scouts and General Law that Federals did not occupy the Round Tops. Believing that a march around these elevations would place his men in the flank and rear of the enemy, Hood repeatedly sent staff officers to Longstreet requesting a modification of the attack orders as issued by Lee. In each instance, Longstreet responded that Lee's orders were to attack up the Emmitsburg Road. [39]

As Hood's troops began their advance, Longstreet rode up and conversed with the Texan. A Georgia private saw the two men "riding coolly up and down in front of us, seeming to examine every man." Hood for the last time expressed his regret at not being able to attack around Round Top, Longstreet replying that "we must obey the orders of General Lee." Hood then rode along his division's lines before stopping in front of the Texas Brigade, making a brief speech before ordering the men forward. [40]

When Hood rode into an orchard, probably one located just west of the Bushman farmhouse, a shell exploded over him sending fragments into his left arm. Artillerist John C. Haskell wrote that Hood "reeled and fell from his horse, utterly prostrated and almost fainting." Haskell remembered that the wound gave Hood "intense pain and utterly unnerved him, so that I could get no orders from him." Capt. Frederick M. Colston later saw Hood sitting in an ambulance near Pitzer's Schoolhouse, probably in shock. [41]

On the retreat south after Gettysburg, Arthur Fremantle once again encountered Hood, this time riding in a carriage. Hood "looked rather bad," noted Fremantle, "and has been suffering a great deal." By mid-July, Hood was in Staunton, Virginia, and by August 12 he had arrived in Richmond. Throughout August 1863, persistent rumors swirled through the Confederate capital and Lee's army that Hood would be promoted to lieutenant general and be given command of the Army of Northern Virginia's cavalry corps.[42]

While recuperating in Richmond, Hood "suffered himself to criticize very freely our operations in Pennsylvania," claimed Moxley Sorrel of Longstreet's staff. Hood's alleged criticism might have extended to his corps commander. Three decades after the war, Lafayette McLaws wrote that "Longstreet told me . . . that Hood had always pretended to be very friendly at his HdQrs when he frequently visited." On at least one occasion, Longstreet learned that Hood's "principal business" while on leave in Richmond had been abusing his corps commander. [43]

Hood's motives for criticizing Longstreet, if indeed he did at all, are unknown. Hood may have had misgivings about the Gettysburg campaign from its inception. E. P. Alexander remembered Hood saying in early June 1863 that the army was "taking a lot of chances" by marching north that summer. Hood might also have been critical of Longstreet's denying him permission on July 2, 1863, to execute a flank march around the Round Tops. In his memoirs, Hood wrote that the steep losses his division sustained at Gettysburg had often caused him "bitterly to regret" that he had not been allowed to "turn Round Top Mountain." [44]

When Hood's division passed through Richmond in mid-September 1863 en route to reinforce the Army of Tennessee in North Georgia, a number of officers appealed to the wounded Texan to join them. Although Hood's arm remained in a sling, he met his troops at the Richmond train station. A Georgia private noted that Hood told the men that "his Division was going west, and that he would bring up the rear in person and take command on its arrival out." Hood further remarked that he had heard it said that "the Yankees out West were of a different race from the Northern Yankees and were much harder to contend against," but that his division "could whip *any* Yankee Division, no matter where it was." [45]

Hood stopped in Petersburg while traveling to Georgia in order to propose to Buck Preston. He later told Mary Chesnut that Buck "half promised . . . to think about it." Hood left saying that he was engaged to Preston, but she said, "I am not engaged to you."[46]

When Hood arrived on the Chickamauga battlefield on the afternoon of September 18, he took command of troops attempting to force a crossing of West Chickamauga Creek. Hood's men pushed the Federals across the creek in the vicinity of Reed's Bridge and then advanced toward the southwest a short distance before nightfall.

During the fighting on September 19, Confederate army commander Braxton Bragg gave Hood command of his own division and those of Joseph Kershaw and Bushrod Johnson. While waiting for orders to advance on the morning of the nineteenth, the men saw Hood riding along, "his hat off in a token of salute, his left arm still in a sling, and his noble countenance still pale from the wound received at Gettysburg." Hood dissuaded his soldiers from cheering, lest it draw enemy artillery fire. "Boys, I am glad to see you," he said, "you must whip this battle here." In the subsequent fierce fighting that day, some of Hood's troops seized portions of the La Fayette Road, but they could not drive the Federals from the battlefield.[47]

That evening Hood rode to army headquarters, where Bragg instructed him to advance the next morning as soon as the troops on the Texan's right began attacking. On the morning of the twentieth, Hood met with Longstreet, who had taken command of the left wing of Bragg's army. Longstreet gave Hood command of the "main column of attack," which subsequently charged through a gap that had developed in the Union line near the Brotherton house. During the advance against the routed foe, Hood told Bushrod Johnson to "Go ahead, and keep ahead of everything."[48]

After seeing Johnson, Hood rode northward where he found the Texas Brigade falling back in confusion after a failed attack. A South Carolina officer in Kershaw's brigade saw Hood in the middle of the Dyer field "galloping on ahead" of the Texans trying to rally them. When the South Carolinians advanced, Hood asked their identity and told them they were "the very brigade he wanted to see." While cheering on the South Carolinians and trying to rally his Texans along a wood line, Hood reached out for the flag of one of his regiments. At that moment a ball struck the upper third of his right leg and an aide caught the wounded general "just as his crippled arm was about to be caught in the horn of his saddle."[49]

When Hood arrived at his division's field hospital at the Reed Farm, surgeons amputated his shattered leg at the thigh. A chaplain tending to the wounded at the hospital that day wrote in his diary that at some point Hood said "as long as I have a leg or an arm, and I can ride a horse, and command such men as I do, I will fight those Yankees." On September 21, a party of two dozen men accompanied Hood to the home of William Little in the Armuchee Valley.[50]

Hood's Chickamauga wound was so serious that stories circulated that he had died. On September 24, Longstreet wrote the Confederate adjutant general requesting that Hood be promoted to lieutenant general "for distinguished conduct and ability" on September 20. Longstreet claimed that Hood "handled his troops with the coolness and ability that I have rarely known by any officer on any field." Braxton Bragg agreed, and President Davis added that Hood's "character as a soldier & patriot are equal to any reward and justify the highest trust."[51]

By mid-October it seemed that Hood would recover from his wound and receive a promotion. The year between Sharpsburg and Chickamauga had clearly been the pinnacle of Hood's career. While Longstreet had written in support of Hood's elevation to lieutenant general, "Old Pete" might also have had other motives in mind in seeking his subordinate's elevation in rank. Lafayette McLaws, who disliked both Hood and Longstreet by the fall of 1863, claimed that "Longstreet wanted to get rid of Hood who was equally as unscrupulous as Longstreet and equally blind to his own demerits." McLaws claimed that Hood "was more of a politician & did not hesitate to denounce Longstreet's demerits."[52]

Hood's robust constitution sped his recovery to the point that by early November 1863 he moved to Atlanta, where he remained briefly before traveling to Richmond. By November 17, 1863, Hood was in Richmond. There he boarded in the home of his distant kinsman, Gen. Gustavus W. Smith.[53]

In late January 1864, Hood was eager to get back into active service. He appeared on Main Street in Richmond on horseback "groomed by a single servant, his lost limb supplied by an artificial one." As the crippled general rode along, crowds of people cheered and lifted their hats. A few days later, Hood wrote to Adj. Gen. Samuel Cooper, claiming that as soon as he got together staff members and purchased a small carriage for his use, he would "be ready for duty in the field."[54]

During his stay in Richmond, Hood persisted in his frustrating pursuit of Buck Preston. Hood told Mary Chesnut that after being wounded at Chickamauga, he had given up hope of becoming engaged to Buck, but upon his return to Richmond he had pressed his case. By mid-February 1864, Hood believed that Buck had consented to an engagement and said that he would speak to her parents. The aristocratic Prestons opposed the match, probably because they felt that Hood was not sophisticated and refined enough for their daughter. Word of the engagement nonetheless appeared in Southern newspapers.[55]

Hood also spent time with Jefferson Davis while in Richmond. Hood was clearly loyal to Davis; according to Mary Chesnut the Texan told the president "why don't you come and lead [the army] . . . yourself? I would follow you to the death." Such flattery raises the question of whether Hood praised Davis in order to win a promotion or whether the compliments were genuine. Richard McMurry's astute analysis concludes that because Hood was both "naïve and ambitious" his exact motives for praising the president are impossible to ascertain.[56]

Regardless of Hood's motives for praising the Confederate president, Jefferson Davis had good reason to recommend the Texan's promotion to the second highest grade in the Confederate army. Hood was one of the South's most experienced major generals by the winter of 1863–64, with an impressive record of contributing to decisive battlefield victories. On February 11, 1864, the Confederate Congress confirmed Hood's promotion to lieutenant general, to rank from September 20, 1863. Hood was given command of a corps in the Army of Tennessee, then encamped at Dalton, Georgia. While the Texan later claimed that while he was loath to leave Lee and the Army of Northern Virginia, he also agreed with Davis on the need for an "aggressive campaign" in the western theater.[57]

Hood arrived in Dalton to take command of his corps at the end of February 1864. Gen. Joseph E. Johnston, the Army of Tennessee's commander, welcomed Hood's arrival. On April 1, Johnston wrote to Louis Wigfall that Hood has been his "greatest comfort since getting here—indeed the only one in a military way."[58]

In March and April 1864, Hood began corresponding with President Davis, Secretary of War Seddon, and Braxton Bragg. The upshot of Hood's correspondence was that although the Army of Tennessee was in good condition it should be strengthened in order to go on the offensive in the rear of the enemy. Hood believed that a juncture of Johnston's army with troops under Leonidas Polk and William W. Loring in Mississippi and Longstreet's men in East Tennessee "should be sufficient to defeat and destroy all the Federals on this side of the Ohio River." Hood "never before felt that we had it so thoroughly in our power" to defeat the enemy.[59]

Hood's optimistic letters to Confederate officials differed from those of Joseph E. Johnston, who argued that his army's weaknesses made an offensive into Tennessee an unwise move. On April 13, Hood told Braxton Bragg that he had "done all in my power to induce General

Johnston to accept the proposition you made to move forward." Hood claimed that he regretted "this exceedingly, as my heart was fixed upon our going to the front and regaining Tennessee and Kentucky."[60]

Hood knew of Jefferson Davis's eagerness to take the offensive in the West and wanted the Confederate president to know that he shared this opinion. Such letters were a clear breach of military protocol, as Albert Castel points out, although Hood was not the only high-ranking officer in the Army of Tennessee to criticize Johnston or address letters directly to Confederate authorities in Richmond. Johnston undoubtedly did not know about these letters at the time they were written, because he and Hood remained on friendly terms throughout the first few weeks of the Atlanta campaign.[61]

Hood's corps of the Army of Tennessee consisted of three divisions commanded at the start of the Atlanta campaign by Gens. Thomas C. Hindman, Carter L. Stevenson, and Alexander P. Stewart. Hood attempted to instill confidence in his divisions by issuing numerous general orders, holding large reviews, and riding through the camps. On March 16, he held a corps review and a sham battle. A newspaper correspondent observed that during the mock battle, "all the Generals were seen urging forward the men, but conspicuous above all towers the manly form of the 'Sergeant,' the nickname given to Hood by his men. Hood's voice rang out "above even the roar of the artillery, and once more he is seen, as of yore, dashing through the lines." The observer claimed that when the "Sergeant" and his staff rode down the lines, "cheer after cheer greeted the new commander of the veteran corps."[62]

Hood also continued to assure people of his fitness to command. In a letter to a friend in Columbus, Georgia, that appeared in Southern newspapers, Hood addressed fears that he was in poor health, and "had to be tied or fastened on my saddle. . . . Since I came here," he continued, "I have been riding all over this country with Gen. Johnston and have been in the saddle every day enough to have fought two or three battles, without feeling any inconvenience." Hood claimed that he rode "with perfect comfort," and expected "to walk with a cane before long."[63]

When the Union armies under Gen. William T. Sherman began threatening Johnston's lines in the first week of May 1864, Johnston placed Hood's corps on the right of the Confederate Army. Hood's line stretched from Rocky Face Ridge at Mill Creek Gap across Crow Valley north of Dalton. During the ensuing Union demonstrations,

Sherman sent one of his armies to Snake Creek Gap south of Dalton to threaten Johnston's supply line, the Western and Atlantic Railroad, in the vicinity of Resaca, Georgia.

On May 9, Johnston ordered Hood to take three divisions and proceed to Resaca. Two days later, Johnston received reinforcements from Alabama and Mississippi that became a third corps of the Army of Tennessee, all under the command of general and Episcopal bishop Leonidas Polk. Hood knew Polk and apparently had asked about joining the Episcopal Church. At 12:30 A.M. on May 12, Polk administered the rites of baptism to Hood. Polk's son-in-law and staff officer noted in his diary that Hood "seemed much impressed" with the ceremony.[64]

Johnston deployed his entire army at Resaca on May 13, with Hood's corps on the right of the line. The next day, Federals launched an attack that fell in part on the left of Hood's corps, but the Confederates beat it back. At 4:00 P.M. on the fourteenth, Johnston ordered Hood to attack the Union left flank, overwhelm it, and then cut the road between Resaca and Snake Creek Gap. Hood's attack achieved some initial success, but Union reinforcements ultimately stemmed the Southern charge.[65]

The next afternoon, Johnston decided to send Hood forward again. Shortly before the attack was to start, the Confederate army commander learned that Federals were across the Oostanaula River and south of the Confederate position at Resaca. Johnston cancelled Hood's attack and ordered a retreat, but word reached Alexander P. Stewart after his division began its assault. Union troops repulsed Stewart's charge, and that night Johnston's men retreated across the Oostanaula.[66]

The Army of Tennessee had retreated to Adairsville by May 17, where Johnston came up with a plan to strike Sherman. Two roads led south from Adairsville. One went to Kingston and then east to Cassville, while the other led directly from Adairsville to Cassville. Johnston hoped that Sherman would divide his forces as they moved south from Adairsville, allowing the Confederates to strike the Union column marching on the road that went from Adairsville to Cassville.[67]

Sherman did what Johnston hoped, and the Confederate commander ordered Hood to assail the left flank of the two Union corps marching south from Adairsville to Cassville. When Hood's troops marched out to give battle on May 19, they moved a short distance before Hood saw a "body of the enemy," which he correctly perceived to be cavalrymen advancing against the rear of his corps. Hood canceled his attack and fell back to Johnston's main line. In the wake of this withdrawal, Johnston pulled his army back to a strong position on a ridge located one-half mile to the south and east of Cassville, Hood's corps forming the right of the new Confederate line.[68]

Johnston held a meeting on the night of May 19 at Polk's headquarters. Corps commanders Hood and Polk agreed that their positions would be rendered untenable the next day if Union batteries opened a cross fire against them. Sources conflict as to what happened next. Hood claimed in his memoirs (he did not discuss the meeting in his wartime report) that he and Polk urged Johnston to attack the next day. Johnston claimed that the two officers instead urged the army to retreat. Regardless of which version is true, Johnston decided to retreat when he received word that Union cavalrymen had crossed the Etowah River south of Kingston.[69]

Hood sent a volunteer aide, Col. Henry P. Brewster, to Jefferson Davis in Richmond on May 21. Hood told Davis that Brewster could provide "you an account of the operations of this army since the enemy made their appearance in our immediate front." It is unknown whether Brewster met with Davis, but Albert Castel surmises that if he did he probably criticized Johnston for not having a plan of attack at Dalton and for repeatedly retreating in the face of the enemy.[70]

After withdrawing across the Etowah River, Johnston halted his army in a strong position in the Allatoona Mountains, hoping that Sherman would attack the Confederates there. Instead, Sherman attempted to flank Johnston out of the position at Allatoona by ordering the Union army westward toward the town of Dallas. When Johnston learned of the Federal movement, he shifted the Army of Tennessee westward to block the enemy's advance.[71]

By May 25, Hood's corps was in position at New Hope Church, four miles east of Dallas. Union troops assaulted the center of Hood's line late that afternoon, in a battle that raged for several hours. The enemy were "repeatedly and handsomely repulsed at all points," wrote Hood. At some point that afternoon, Hood and Johnston had a narrow escape; while standing near New Hope Church, a Union shell "burst between them," but neither officer was hurt.[72]

Two days after the battle of New Hope Church, Hood received word from Gen. Joseph Wheeler that the Union army's left flank appeared to be "in the air." Hood went to Johnston and proposed to pull his corps out of line and swing around to attack the enemy's exposed flank. Johnston assented, but when Hood approached the Union position shortly before dawn on May 28, the Southern corps commander learned that the Federals had entrenched. Hood called off the attack and Johnston ordered him back into a defensive position.[73]

Johnston's and Sherman's armies shifted back eastward in the last days of May and the first two weeks of June 1864. On the night of June 18–19, the Confederates fell back to a position anchored on Kennesaw Mountain. By the evening of June 20, the movement of troops on Sherman's extreme right flank prompted Johnston to shift Hood's corps from east of Kennesaw Mountain to a position on the Powder Springs Road southwest of Marietta.[74]

When two Union regiments advanced as skirmishers against Hood's troops on June 22, the Confederate corps commander apparently took it for an enemy attack. Hood sent forward two divisions on his own initiative, apparently thinking that they would encounter little resistance and either turn the enemy's line or deliver a blow against an exposed flank. The ensuing battle of Kolb's Farm or Mt. Zion Church, was a bloody affair in which Union troops repulsed the Confederates with great slaughter.[75]

Throughout the last days of June and the first two weeks of July 1864, the Confederate army retreated to entrenched lincs at Smyrna and the Chattahoochee River. On July 9, Johnston pulled his troops back across the Chattahoochee after Union troops crossed the river north of the Confederate position. The Confederates then took up positions on the northern outskirts of Atlanta south of Peach Tree Creek.[76]

The relationship between Johnston and Hood had deteriorated during the month of June. While visiting James and Mary Chesnut in Columbia early that month, Hood's volunteer aide Colonel Brewster stated that the retreat in North Georgia was "breaking Hood's heart." Johnston, Brewster claimed, was "jealous of the favor shown Hood at Richmond."[77]

During the first two weeks of July, Jefferson Davis pondered what to do about the military situation in Georgia. Davis strongly disliked Joseph E. Johnston, a general who had abandoned Northwest Georgia, including the industrial city of Rome. Johnston seemingly did not have a strategy of keeping Sherman out of Atlanta, or if he did he did not communicate details of it to Davis.

Davis telegraphed Robert E. Lee on July 12 saying that it seemed necessary to relieve Johnston and asked Lee's opinion of Hood as a successor. Lee replied that while it was a "grievous thing to change commander of an army situated as is that of the Tennessee," that if it was necessary "it ought to be done." Hood was "a good fighter," Lee wrote, "very industrious on the battle field, careless off." Lee had not had an opportunity of judging Hood "when the whole responsibility rested on him," but had a high opinion of his "gallantry, earnestness & zeal."[78]

The Confederate president also sought advice from his advisor Braxton Bragg, who visited the Army of Tennessee in mid-July to assess the military situation. On July 15, Bragg wrote several telegrams and a letter to Davis stating that Hood "has been in favour of giving battle, & mentions to me numerous instances of opportunities lost." Johnston, Bragg continued, seemed to have no "more plan for the future than he has had in the past." Bragg recommended that if a change in the command of the Army of Tennessee was necessary, Hood "would give unlimited satisfaction." Hood was not "a man of genius or a great general," added Bragg, but was "far better in the present emergency than any one we have available."[79]

Bragg included in his July 15 letter to Davis one from Hood dated July 14. Hood wrote that during the campaign up to that point that there had been "several chances to strike the enemy a decisive blow." The army had failed to take advantage of these opportunities and had suffered 20,000 casualties. Its present position, Hood rightfully noted, was "a very difficult one." Hood asserted that Atlanta must be held and the enemy attacked, "even if we should have to recross the [Chattahoochee] River to do so." The Texan claimed that he had "so often urged that we should force the enemy to give us battle as to be almost regarded as reckless by the officers high in rank in this army, since their views have been so directly opposite."[80]

Most recent historians of the Atlanta campaign agree that Hood's July 14 letter was a bid to replace Johnston as commander of the Army of Tennessee. Hood's comment about "officers high in rank" opposing the offensive was probably an attempt to give Davis a false impression of the attitudes of William J. Hardee, the other main candidate being considered to succeed Johnston. (Hardee outranked Hood and thus technically should have succeeded Johnston.) While ambition undoubtedly motivated Hood, he might also have felt that he, not Hardee, had the determination and skill to save Atlanta from the Federals.[81]

Davis decided on July 17 to replace Johnston with Hood. Johnston, wrote Adjutant and Inspector General Cooper, had "failed to arrest the advance of the enemy to the vicinity of Atlanta" and expressed no confidence that he could can defeat or repel Sherman. Secretary of War Seddon told Hood that day that he had been "charged with a great trust" and must "test to the utmost your capacities to discharge it."[82]

Hood claimed in his memoirs that the order to assume command of the Army of Tennessee was "totally unexpected" and overwhelmed him with the sense of responsibility suddenly thrust upon him. He was certainly placed in an unenviable situation with an army far larger than his on Atlanta's doorstep. Hood's adjutant general, James W. Ratchford, recalled many years after the war that Hood seemed shaken when he learned of the change in command and asked Ratchford to "say nothing about it to anyone." On the morning of July 18, Hood joined with Generals Hardee and Stewart in sending a telegram to Jefferson Davis asking that the removal order be postponed until the fate of Atlanta had been decided. Davis refused to rescind the order.[83]

At the age of thirty-three, John Bell Hood became the last and youngest of the Confederacy's full generals. Davis and his government expected Hood to fight for Atlanta, and the Texan immediately determined to do so. Hood's plan called for Hardee's and Stewart's corps to attack several Federal corps located north of Atlanta and south of Peach Tree Creek. Hood hoped that these Union troops had not entrenched and that Confederate attacks would drive them north against the Chattahoochee and destroy them. The resulting battle of Peach Tree Creek, launched late in the afternoon of July 20, involved a number of badly coordinated Confederate attacks that failed to force back the Federals.

Historians have blamed the Southern defeat at Peach Tree Creek on both Hood and Hardee. Thomas Connelly and Richard McMurry claim that the Confederate attacks came too late in the day, not allowing enough time to enable the attacking troops to maneuver across difficult terrain. McMurry argues that Hood's failure to control the army on July 20 was probably due to "inexperience, physical handicaps, and impatience with an army commander's supervisory role.[84]

On July 21, Hood pulled his army back to a more compact entrenched line around Atlanta. He also issued orders for Hardee's corps to march south and then east around the rear of the Union Army

of the Tennessee, where the Confederates would attack on the morning of July 22. When Hardee's men drove back the flank of the Union
line, Gen. Benjamin F. Cheatham, commanding Hood's old corps,
would join the attack.

Hardee's divisions advanced around 11:00 A.M. on the twenty-
second, and some units succeeded in overrunning sections of the
Union line. Unfortunately for the Confederates, two Federal divisions
extended the left flank of the Union line, where they managed to
repulse Southern attacks. Later in the afternoon, Hood ordered forward
Cheatham's men, some of whom briefly broke through the Federal line
in desperate fighting. At the end of the day, the Confederates had suffered heavy casualties and captured a number of prisoners, cannon, and
flags, but their attacks had been only partially successful.[85]

On July 27, Hood learned that Sherman had shifted large numbers
of Union troops from east of Atlanta to west of the city. In order to
protect the junction of the Macon and Western and the Atlanta and
West Point Railroads at East Point, Hood ordered Gen. Stephen D.
Lee (newly appointed to command Hood's old corps) to seize on July
28 an important crossroads west of Atlanta at Ezra Church. The next
day, Gen. A. P. Stewart was to march another corps beyond Lee to the
west, then swing around and strike the Federal flank.

Lee found the Federals in possession of the Ezra Church crossroads on July 28 and decided without consulting Hood to attack the
entrenched Federals. The ensuing engagement, known as the battle of
Ezra Church, consisted of a series of uncoordinated assaults launched
by Lee and Stewart that failed to break the Union lines. When Hood
learned the results of the engagement, he canceled the plans for a
flank attack on July 29.[86]

Hood had clearly been willing to fight during his first week and a
half as commander of the Army of Tennessee. His overly ambitious
plans for the battles of Peach Tree Creek and Atlanta had not involved
his men charging headlong against entrenched Federals, but they had
both resulted in uncoordinated attacks that ended in bloody repulses.
The third engagement at Ezra Church had been precipitated without
orders from Hood. Although historians now assess the battles as tactical failures on the part of Confederates, in the summer of 1864 many
Southerners saw them as successful attempts to slow Sherman's
advance toward Atlanta.[87]

At the time of his transfer to the Army of Tennessee, Hood
claimed that he "was still under the influence of the teaching of Lee,

Jackson and Longstreet." In 1862, Robert E. Lee had been able to give his principal lieutenants, especially Stonewall Jackson, a great deal of leeway in achieving victory on the battlefield. Hood's subordinates in the Army of Tennessee in 1864, many of them relatively inexperienced in corps and division command, proved unable to win battlefield victories when he utilized the same command style.[88]

The siege of Atlanta commenced in the days following the battle of Ezra Church, the Confederates relying on the Macon and Western Railroad to supply the city. In an effort to lift the siege and drive the Federals out of North Georgia, Hood sent off his chief of cavalry Gen. Joseph Wheeler and half of his mounted force on a raid to disrupt Sherman's supply lines. Wheeler's men could do little to damage the railroads seriously due to improved techniques of defending and repairing the lines and the growing strength of Union cavalry forces.[89]

During the early stages of Wheeler's raid, the cavalry chief sent back reports that he had damaged and destroyed track on the Western and Atlantic Railroad at various points. This news, combined with reports from scouts on August 26 that the Union trenches north and east of Atlanta were empty, led Hood to conclude that the Federals had taken up a new line. The Confederate commander apparently believed that Sherman had shifted his lines so that Union troops could strike the railroads south of Atlanta.

On August 30, Hood called two of his corps commanders, Generals Hardee and Lee, to his headquarters and instructed Hardee to march two corps south to Jonesboro. Once Hardee's men arrived there, they were to attack a Federal force advancing toward the Macon and Western Railroad and drive it back west of the Flint River.

Hardee's attacks on August 31 were uncoordinated and bloody failures. In the late afternoon of the thirty-first, Hood instructed Hardee to send Lee's corps back to Atlanta and to deploy his remaining force so as to "protect Macon and communications in rear." Hood concluded his message to Hardee by incorrectly predicting that the enemy might "make an attempt upon Atlanta" the next day.[90]

Sherman's forces at Jonesboro attacked Hardee's corps on September 1 and temporarily breeched the Confederate line before the Southerners counterattacked and restored their position. Hardee then retreated southward from Jonesboro to Lovejoy's Station, leaving the Federals firmly in control of the Macon and Western Railroad. With the last Southern railroad leading into Atlanta in enemy hands and his army divided, Hood evacuated Atlanta and reunited his forces at

Lovejoy on September 3. In the wake of Atlanta's fall, Hood displayed an unwillingness to accept blame for recent Confederate defeats. Instead, he blamed his subordinate officers for mistakes and the men for failing to press home attacks at Jonesboro on August 31.[91]

Hood wrote Confederate secretary of war Seddon from Palmetto, Georgia, on September 21 outlining his plan for the fall. Hood hoped to cross the Chattahoochee River and march north against Sherman's supply line, the Western and Atlantic Railroad. Such a move, Hood claimed, "will force Sherman to give me battle or march upon Augusta or Macon, when I shall follow in his rear." In an extraordinary conclusion, Hood assured Seddon that the "army is anxious to take the offensive" and that he hoped the fall of Atlanta would "prove to be a benefit to us in lieu of a misfortune." When Jefferson Davis visited the Army of Tennessee a few days later, he approved of Hood's plan to strike at the Federal supply line.[92]

During the first two weeks of October 1864, elements of Hood's Army struck the Western and Atlantic at a number of points, capturing several small garrisons and destroying sections of track. From near Gaylesville, Alabama, in mid-October, Hood decided to move northward. He hoped to threaten Sherman's rail lines west of Chattanooga and possibly invade central Tennessee, seizing Nashville and continuing on into Kentucky. If blessed with victory in battle in Kentucky, Hood claimed that he would "send reinforcements to General Lee, in Virginia, or . . . march through the gaps in the Cumberland Mountains and attack Grant in the rear."[93]

Hood made his plans without first consulting his superiors. In his memoirs, he said that if he met his immediate superior, Gen. P. G. T. Beauregard (commander of the recently created Military Division of the West) he would submit his plans to him. When Beauregard did meet with Hood, he rightfully expressed concerns about possible logistical problems, but otherwise approved of the plan.[94]

The Army of Tennessee crossed the Tennessee River at Tuscumbia on November 18 and began marching north. After the war, Hood claimed that he entered Tennessee with the hopes of getting in the rear of Union forces under General John M. Schofield before they could cross the Duck River. Thomas Connelly convincingly argues, and Richard McMurry agrees, that Hood's plan when he entered Tennessee was simply to march against Nashville, capture the city, and then push on to the Ohio River.[95]

Hood's headquarters were in Mount Pleasant, Tennessee, by November 25, only eleven miles south of Columbia, where Schofield had placed his forces in a strong position. That afternoon Hood greeted Episcopal priest Charles Todd Quintard, who recorded in his diary that the Confederate army commander was "in the best of health and spirits, and full of hope as to the result of the present movements." Two days later, as Confederates skirmished with Federals in front of Columbia, Quintard recorded that Hood "expressed such an earnest trust in God and such deep religious feelings that I could plainly discern the Holy Spirit's work upon his heart."[96]

The Confederates awoke on the morning of November 28 to find that Schofield's troops had withdrawn from Columbia and crossed to the northern bank of the Duck River. Hood determined that he would march most of his army the next day to a ford on the Duck east of Columbia, cross the river, and then advance northwest toward Spring Hill, where his men could seize the Columbia-Spring Hill Pike. Such a move would interpose the Confederates between Schofield and a larger Union army in Nashville to the north.[97]

Hood was up at 3:00 A.M. on November 29. After Quintard prayed God's blessing upon the general, Hood told the chaplain that "the enemy must give me fight, or I will be at Nashville before tomorrow night." By 4:00 P.M., Hood's infantry had reached the vicinity of Spring Hill, where he gave orders for Gen. Patrick Cleburne's division to charge west and block the pike. Cleburne's troops drove back enemy infantrymen, but Union artillery fire stopped the Confederates before they could reach the road.[98]

Command confusion throughout the afternoon and evening in the Army of Tennessee resulted in the Confederate advance halting short of the Columbia-Spring Hill Pike. Throughout the night of November 29–30, Schofield's Federals escaped from a potential trap by marching northward along the pike only a few hundred yards from the encamped Confederates. On the morning of the thirtieth, Hood was "wrathy as a rattlesnake, striking at everything," claimed a staff officer. In a meeting with his subordinates, Hood blamed several of them (especially Cheatham) for the failure to block the pike on the previous day.[99]

Most recent historians place much of the blame for the Confederate fiasco at Spring Hill on Hood's shoulders. Richard McMurry points out that Hood did not closely supervise his corps commanders on November 29, something he should have done given their failure to execute his orders properly on battlefields around Atlanta. Hood's physical ailments, including fatigue, and the breakdown of his staff, probably contributed to his poor performance, notes McMurry, Connelly, and Wiley Sword.[100]

In the midafternoon of November 30, Hood's troops marched over Winstead Hill south of Franklin. From Winstead Hill, an open valley stretched northward to the Harpeth River, which surrounded the town of Franklin. When Hood reached the top of Winstead, he told several startled subordinates that he intended to order two corps of the army to launch a frontal attack against the entrenched Federals in Franklin.

Hood's motive for ordering this fateful attack has been a topic of great speculation. Hood claimed in his memoir that the army had been mortified and disappointed about the Spring Hill affair and that they were eager to retrieve a lost opportunity. In his official report of the 1864 Tennessee campaign, Hood claimed that it was "all important" to attack the Federals before they could retreat to Nashville.[101]

Thomas Connelly argued that Hood's anger and frustration over Spring Hill were partly to blame for ordering the assault. Connelly also claims that Hood might also have seen the frontal assault as "an exercise of discipline for the army." Hood certainly thought that while under Johnston's command the Army of Tennessee had been "so long habituated to security behind breastworks that they had become wedded to the 'timid defensive' policy." Both Connelly and Richard McMurry suggest that Hood might have been emulating Robert E. Lee's successful tactics of 1862, where frontal attacks won dramatic battlefield victories.[102]

Confederate prisoners taken during the battle of Franklin told of Hood riding along the lines as the men prepared to charge. He gave a similar speech at various points. "These lines must be broken boys," Hood said, "They are weak and cannot stand you." The general promised that if the men carried the Federal position, the campaign in Tennessee would be over, and "no enemy will exist who will dare to oppose your march to the Ohio."[103]

The five-hour battle at Franklin was a disaster for the Army of Tennessee, particularly so for the army's officer corps. Despite heavy casualties, Hood ordered the army to the southern outskirts of Nashville. When the Confederates arrived there on a frigid December 2, Hood apparently thought that at some point the enemy in the city would have to attack him in order to relieve smaller Union garrisons in Murfreesboro, Chattanooga, and Knoxville. Hood hoped that when the Federals sallied forth from Nashville his men could repulse them, thus gaining possession of the city and the abundant supplies stored there.[104]

The Federals in Nashville launched assaults against Hood's position on December 15. When the Confederate left flank collapsed, Hood pulled the army back to a shorter line two miles to the south. The Union army attacked again on December 16, seizing the key position of Shy's Hill and routing two of Hood's three corps. The shattered Army of Tennessee then began a long, painful retreat south.

At Columbia, Dr. Quintard encountered Hood again. The general, noted Quintard, "bears up with wonderful faith." During the night of December 19, Hood decided to leave Tennessee and recross the Tennessee River in northern Alabama, in part due to the advice of Gen. Nathan B. Forrest. By December 28, the entire Army of Tennessee was across the Tennessee River and marching toward Corinth, Mississippi, where the troops turned south toward Tupelo.[105]

Hood requested that he be relieved from command of the Army of Tennessee on January 14, 1865. (Mary Chesnut recorded that Hood's decision to resign stemmed from a resolution of the Virginia legislature to put Johnston back in command of the Western army, a move that Hood interpreted as a "vote of censure.") Hood telegraphed authorities in Richmond "that the campaigns to the Alabama line and into Tennessee were my own conception; [and] that I alone was responsible." On January 23, Hood formally turned command of the army over to Gen. Richard Taylor and departed for Richmond. Hood also reverted at this time from the temporary rank of full general to that of lieutenant general.[106]

En route to Richmond, Hood stopped in South Carolina to see Buck Preston, still intent on marrying her. Hood dreaded her family's opposition to the match, something he apparently faced from her parents, sister, and brother-in-law. Although the details are unclear, the Preston-Hood engagement apparently ended that spring.[107]

When Hood arrived in the Confederate capital, he spent several weeks writing his official report of the Atlanta and Tennessee campaigns. The completed document included a lengthy attack on Joseph E. Johnston for his conduct during the first part of the Atlanta campaign and criticisms of Hardee (for poor performances at Peach Tree Creek, Atlanta, and Jonesboro) and Cheatham (for his failure to obey orders at Spring Hill).[108]

During or immediately after the time that Hood compiled his official report, he submitted to Jefferson Davis a document entitled "Notes on the Spring Campaign of 1865." Hood predicted that by mid-April 1865, a "want of food, or the massed enemy, or both" would force the abandonment of Richmond. He therefore advocated that the three Confederate field armies concentrate in central Tennessee and Kentucky. Such a move was feasible from a logistical perspective, Hood claimed, and would maintain if not elevate the soldiers' morale.

Surrender to the enemy should not be an alternative, Hood argued. The terms would be "submission to hated ideas, and abandonment of national existence and national pride." "There is no instance in history," he continued, "of a hundred and twenty thousand men with arms in hand, begging for mercy on bended knee." Such a "sacrifice of manhood, and desertion of all that is prized among men," wrote Hood, "would make life intolerable in the land of our birth, and existence despised should we seek homes with other people." Robert E. Lee "attentively considered" Hood's remarks before returning them to Davis, but was far more skeptical than Hood of the likelihood of successfully concentrating the Confederacy's field armies in Tennessee or the value of such a move.[109]

On March 8, 1865, Hood requested that the War Department send him to the Trans-Mississippi Department to report on affairs and the practicability of transferring troops from there to Virginia. He apparently did not receive an immediate answer, for on March 21 he addressed Jefferson Davis, claiming that he "did not wish to appear impatient or restive," but wanted the Confederate president to know that he was "ever ready & willing to perform any duty which in your better judgment may seem best." Hood received orders to proceed to Texas and secure troops to return to Virginia.[110]

While en route to Texas, Hood had an exchange with Adjutant General Cooper and Joseph E. Johnston concerning his report of the Atlanta and Tennessee campaign. Angered at the report, Johnston sought to file charges against Hood. Hood responded by asking Cooper for a court of inquiry "to investigate and report" upon his official report. Cooper disposed of the matter by informing Hood that a court could not be convened and that he should proceed to Texas.[111]

Hood and his staff and escort journeyed to Natchez, Mississippi, learning along the way of the surrender of Lee's and Kirby Smith's armies. Although Hood talked with Gen. Richard Taylor sometime in late April or early May 1865 about the possibility of moving large numbers of troops across the Mississippi, the swollen conditions of the river made it impossible. On May 31, 1865, he surrendered in Natchez and received a parole.[112]

By the summer of 1866, Hood decided to settle in New Orleans, the city where he spent the rest of his life. He initially worked as a cotton factor and commission merchant with two other men, buying and selling cotton and other goods for a fee. An 1867 R. G. Dun & Company credit report of J. B. Hood and Co., Cotton Factors and Commission Merchants, noted that Hood and his partners were doing a moderate business, being "well spoken of as upright hon[ora]ble & relia[ble] men, but of lim[ited] means."

Hood's partnership had dissolved by the summer of 1868, but he continued doing business. He had very little means, good credit, and "strong and wealthy friends who help him." The next year he was "doing a sm[all] safe bus[iness]" with "many strong friends" and was worth an estimated five to eight thousand dollars. By 1870, he was out of the commission business, having acquired a position as president of the Louisiana Division of the Life Association of America. Hood probably remained in the insurance business until shortly before his death.[113]

On April 30, 1868, Hood married Anna Maria Hennen, the daughter of a prominent New Orleans attorney. The union ultimately produced eleven children in ten years, including three sets of twins. When the family traveled north in the summers, hotel employees would supposedly say "Here comes Hood's brigade."[114]

The limited extant source material on Hood's postbellum life makes it difficult to determine his true views on Reconstruction. The editor of the *Brownsville (Texas) Ranchero* claimed that in July 1866 interviews with Hood and Longstreet, both ex-generals stated that "the duty and safety of the South demanded submission on the part of the Southern people." Longstreet, however, was more emphatic in urging this course than Hood.[115]

In March 1867, the U.S. Congress passed a series of acts that ushered in "Radical" or Congressional Reconstruction. The acts divided the South into military districts and required the ex-Confederate states seeking readmission to the Union to draw up new constitutions that enfranchised freedmen and disfranchised many ex-Rebels. The editor of the *New Orleans Times* asked several prominent ex-Confederates in the city, including Longstreet and Hood, their views on the course that Southern whites should adopt.

Longstreet claimed many years later that he met with Hood to discuss the *Times* editorial shortly after it appeared in 1867. Longstreet believed that white Southerners, as a "conquered people," should submit to the terms of Radical Reconstruction. Hood claimed that everyone wished the return of constitutional government in the ex-Confederate states, but warned Longstreet that if he publicly supported the congressional program that "the Southern press and the Southern people will vilify you and abuse you." Longstreet claimed that while Hood "may have shared my sentiments he never trusted himself to public expression of them."[116]

Whether Hood truly sympathized with Longstreet's views on Reconstruction is unclear. In a July 1867 letter, Longstreet said that he had been disappointed by the harsh reaction to his views on Southern submission to Radical Reconstruction. "I believe now," wrote Longstreet, "as Gen. Hood says: 'They would crucify you!' but I think this number small and I am a little suspicious that he is one of them."[117]

Hood was clearly pleased at the so-called Compromise of 1877, which provided for the final "redemption" of the Southern states by providing for white Democratic rule. At a June 1877 reunion of the Texas Brigade, Hood told the veterans that he was "buoyant for the future, but had only become so within the past six months." Through the wisdom of the president, he continued, the last Federal troops had been withdrawn from South Carolina and Louisiana, a move that ushered in the collapse of the Republican governments in those states. The two states "were again free and prosperity was dawning on them," Hood announced.[118]

The appearance in 1874 of Joseph E. Johnston's *Narrative of Military Operations* spurred Hood to defend his actions as a corps and army commander in the Western Theater in 1864. Johnston's memoir claimed that Hood's inability and unwillingness to execute orders, combined with his constant advice to retreat, had been key to the loss of North Georgia during the Atlanta campaign. The disastrous outcome of the subsequent Tennessee campaign, claimed Johnston, was proof of Hood's ineptitude.[119]

Hood began in 1875 to compose a "Reply to Genl Johnston," defending his record against specific accusations made in Johnston's memoir. Over the next few years, Hood expanded the scope of his work to include a memoir of the Atlanta campaign and the 1864 Tennessee campaign, as well as a brief biographical section on his life up to the point of his promotion to lieutenant general in February 1864. The memoir appeared in print in 1880, one year after Hood's death, with the title *Advance and Retreat: Personal Experiences in the United States and Confederate Armies.*[120]

Sometime in 1878–79, Hood's business fortunes collapsed and his family fell into hard times. In hopes of making some money, Hood attempted to sell the papers he had collected while writing his memoirs to the U.S. government. While negotiating in Washington, D.C., over the amount he would get for the papers, Hood returned to New Orleans, possibly to handle business affairs.[121]

In August 1879, tragedy struck the Hood household. There had been a serious yellow fever epidemic in New Orleans the previous summer, and doctors warned Hood in the summer of 1879 to take his family out of the city. Hood failed to do so, probably for financial reasons. On August 24, 1879, the general's wife died from yellow fever and two days later his oldest daughter succumbed. General Hood also contracted the disease and died from it on the morning of August 30 at the age of forty-eight. He was buried in Lafayette Cemetery No. 1 in New Orleans and later reinterred in the Hennen family vault in Metairie Cemetery.[122]

NOTES

1. "Severe Fighting around Atlanta," Felix G. De Fontaine, *Mobile Advertiser and Register*, July 31, 1864.
2. Albert Castel, *Decision in the West: The Atlanta Campaign of 1864* (Lawrence: University Press of Kansas, 1992), 562 (hereafter cited as Castel, *Decision*); Herman Hattaway, "The General Whom the President Elevated Too High: Davis and John Bell Hood," in Gabor S. Boritt, ed., *Jefferson Davis's Generals* (New York: Oxford University Press, 1999), 85; Richard McMurry, *John Bell Hood and the War for Southern Independence* (Lexington: University Press of Kentucky, 1982), 190–91 (hereafter cited as McMurry, *Hood*).
3. McMurry, *Hood*, 2–6; John Bell Hood, *Advance and Retreat: Personal Experiences in the United States and Confederate States Armies* (1880; reprint: New York: Da Capo Press, 1993), 5 (hereafter cited as Hood, *Advance and Retreat*).
4. William B. Skelton, *An American Profession of Arms: The Army Officer Corps, 1784–1861* (Lawrence: University Press of Kansas, 1992), 167, 177, 179.
5. 4th United States Infantry, M 331, Returns from Regular Army Infantry Regiments, June 1821–December 1916, National Archives, Washington, D.C. (repository hereafter cited as NA); McMurry, *Hood*, 13–14.

6. John B. Hood to Jefferson Davis, April 25, 1855, RG 107, Records of the Secretary of War, Entry 262, Applications for Promotions from Regular Army Officers and for Commissions from Noncommissioned Officers, 1854–1862, NA.

7. McMurry, *Hood*, 16–22; Hood, *Advance and Retreat*, 8.

8. McMurry, *Hood*, 17–20.

9. Hood, *Advance and Retreat*, 15; Donald E. Everett, ed., *Chaplain Davis and Hood's Texas Brigade* (1863; reprint, Baton Rouge: Louisiana State University Press, 2000), 148 (hereafter cited as Everett, ed., *Chaplain Davis*).

10. McMurry, *Hood*, 25; Hood, *Advance and Retreat*, 18; Everett, ed., *Chaplain Davis*, 149. Hood's compiled service record in M 331 does not give the exact date of his promotion to major, but he signed requisitions at that rank as early as June 20, 1861, and as late as July 31, 1861. Hood claims in his memoir that he was promoted to the rank of lieutenant colonel while commanding cavalry on the Peninsula. (John B. Hood, General and Staff Compiled Service Record [hereafter cited as Hood, General and Staff CSR], M331, NA.)

11. Hood, General and Staff CSR, NA; Hood, *Advance and Retreat*, 16; John Marshall to Louis T. Wigfall, December 29, 1861, typescript letter in the personal collection of Robert K. Krick.

12. Hood, *Advance and Retreat*, 19.

13. Hood, General and Staff CSR, NA; McMurry, *Hood*, 35–36.

14. Hood, *Advance and Retreat*, 21; McMurry, *Hood*, 39–40.

15. Everett, ed., *Chaplain Davis*, 149; Robert E. L. Krick, "The Men Who Carried this Position Were Soldiers Indeed: The Decisive Charge of Whiting's Division at Gaines's Mill," in Gary W. Gallagher, ed., *The Richmond Campaign of 1862* (Chapel Hill: University of North Carolina Press, 2000), 191–92.

16. Everett, ed., *Chaplain Davis*, 91, McMurry, *Hood*, 49–50.

17. McMurry, *Hood*, 52.

18. Hood, *Advance and Retreat*, 33–35; U.S. War Department, *War of the Rebellion: A Compilation of the Official Records of the Union and Confederate Armies*, 127 vols., index, and atlas (Washington, D.C.: Government Printing Office, 1880–1901), I, 12 (2):612 (hereafter cited as as *OR*, with all references to Series I unless otherwise noted; for volumes that appeared in more than one part [volume 12 is one such], the part is shown in parentheses after the volume number); James Longstreet, *From Manassas to Appomattox: Memoirs of the Civil War in America* (Philadelphia: Lippincott, 1896), 183 (hereafter cited as Longstreet, *From Manassas to Appomattox*).

19. *OR*, 12 (2):577.

20. George Skoch and Mark W. Perkins, eds., *Lone Star Confederate: A Gallant and Good Soldier of the Fifth Texas Infantry* (College Station:

Texas A & M University Press, 2003), 73; Hood, *Advance and Retreat*, 37; *OR*, 19 (2):924.

21. *OR*, 12 (2):606; Hood, *Advance and Retreat*, 37.

22. Hood, *Advance and Retreat*, 38–39.

23. Hood, *Advance and Retreat*, 38–41; *OR*, 19 (2):609; R. W. York, "General Hood's Release from Arrest," *Our Living and Our Dead* 2 (June 1875):420–23.

24. John B. Hood to Ezra Carman, May 27, 1877, Civil War Collection, 1864–72, Huntington Library, San Marino, California (repository hereafter cited as HL).

25. Ibid.; *OR* 19 (1):923; Lafayette McLaws, *A Soldier's General: The Civil War Letters of Major General Lafayette McLaws*, ed. John C. Oeffinger (Chapel Hill: University of North Carolina Press, 2002), 182, 183, 275–77. In the spring of 1863, Lafayette McLaws became incensed over allegations in a book written by Chaplain Nicholas Davis of the Texas Brigade that McLaws's division had been slow in assisting Hood's men at Sharpsburg. Hood responded to an inquiry about the matter from McLaws by claiming that he had never read the book and regretted that it had been published. McLaws did not believe Hood's claim.

26. Hood, *Advance and Retreat*, 45–46; "Eyewitness" and "The Texas Brigade," *Richmond Enquirer*, September 13, 1862; Thomas J. Goree, *Longstreet's Aide: The Civil War Letters of Major Thomas J. Goree*, ed. Thomas W. Cutrer (Charlottesville: University Press of Virginia, 1995), 100.

27. Hood, General and Staff CSR, NA; McMurry, *Hood*, 61–62.

28. *OR*, 21:570, 621–22; James Longstreet to Edward Porter Alexander, January 19, 1868, James Longstreet Papers, Duke University, Durham, N.C. (repository hereafter cited as DU).

29. Longstreet to Alexander, January 19, 1868, DU; Longstreet, *From Manassas to Appomattox*, 317.

30. McMurry, *Hood*, 66–67.

31. Ibid., 68. The published Chesnut diary is actually part diary and part memoir.

32. John F. Dorman, *The Prestons of Smithfield and Greenfield in Virginia* (Louisville: General Printing Company, 1982), 210–13; C. Vann Woodward, ed., *Mary Chesnut's Civil War* (New Haven: Yale University Press, 1981), 430 (hereafter cited as Woodward, ed., *Mary Chesnut's Civil War*); McMurry, *Hood*, 29. Hood might have already met Preston, since earlier in the war she had been engaged to Maj. Bradfute Warwick of the 4th Texas, who was mortally wounded at Gaines's Mill.

33. Hood, *Advance and Retreat*, 51; McMurry, *Hood*, 69–70.

34. *OR*, 51 (2):697; Henry D. Jamison Jr., comp., *Letters and Recollections of a Confederate Soldier, 1860–65* (Nashville: n. p., 1964), 114. Ex-Con-

federate artillerist John C. Haskell wrote in 1906 that prior to Gettysburg Hood "expected to be sent to the Western Army." (John C. Haskell to John W. Daniel, May 12, 1906, John W. Daniel Papers, DU.)

35. Anita Sams, ed., *With Unabated Trust: Major Henry McDaniel's Love Letters* (Monroe: Walton, 1977), 165; Eddy R. Parker, ed., *Touched by Fire: Letters from Company D, 5th Texas Infantry* (Hillsboro, Tex.: Hill Junior College Press, 2000), 57; *OR*, 25 (2):811.

36. A. J. L. Fremantle, *Three Months in the Southern States, April-June 1863* (New York: John Bradburn, 1864), 242–43.

37. John B. Hood, "Letter from General John B. Hood," in *Southern Historical Society Papers*, ed. J. William Jones and others, 52 vols. and 3-vol. index (1877–1959; reprint, Wilmington, N.C.: Broadfoot, 1990–92), 4:147 (hereafter cited as Hood, "Letter from General John B. Hood"); Harry W. Pfanz, *Gettysburg: The Second Day* (Chapel Hill: University of North Carolina Press, 1987), 104–05 (hereafter cited as Pfanz, *Gettysburg*).

38. Pfanz, *Gettysburg*, 158–61.

39. Hood, "Letter from General John B. Hood," 148–49; Evander M. Law, "The Struggle for Little Round Top," in Robert U. Johnson and Clarence C. Buel, eds., *Battles and Leaders of the Civil War*, 4 vols. (New York: Century, 1887–88), 3:321.

40. Hood, "Letter from General John B. Hood," 150; William T. Fluker, "Graphic Account of the Battle of Round Top," *Atlanta Journal*, March 16, 1901; Pfanz, *Gettysburg*, 167.

41. Pfanz, *Gettysburg*, 172–73; John C. Haskell, *The Haskell Memoirs*, ed. Gilbert E. Govan and James W. Livingood (New York: Putnam, 1960), 49–50 (hereafter cited as Haskell, *Memoirs*); John C. Haskell to John W. Daniel, May 1, 1906, Daniel Papers, DU; F. M. Colston, "Gettysburg As We Saw It," *Confederate Veteran* 5:551–53.

42. McMurry, *Hood*, 75–76; *Richmond Sentinel*, August 12, 1863; "General J.E.B. Stuart," *Richmond Whig*, August 18, 1863; Jerome B. Robertson to Thomas H. Watts, August 18, 1863, Evander M. Law, General and Staff CSR, M 331, NA.

43. Gilbert Moxley Sorrel, *Recollections of a Confederate Staff Officer*, ed. Bell I. Wiley (1905; reprint, Jackson, Tenn.: McCowat-Mercer, 1959), 127–28; Lafayette McLaws to Thomas T. Munford, April 20, 1895, Munford-Ellis Papers, DU. The statements of McLaws should be viewed with some skepticism, since he harbored ill feelings toward both Longstreet and Hood during and after the Civil War.

44. Edward Porter Alexander, *Fighting for the Confederacy: The Personal Recollections of General Edward Porter Alexander*, ed. Gary W. Gallagher (Chapel Hill: University of North Carolina Press, 1989), 222; Hood, *Advance and Retreat*, 55, 60. Hood never wrote an official report of his division's participation in the Gettysburg campaign.

45. Hood, *Advance and Retreat*, 55; Charles F. Terrill to brother, September 13, 1863, original in possession of Steve Wade, Winterville, Georgia, ts. in possession of author.

46. Woodward, ed., *Mary Chesnut's Civil War*, 516.

47. Hood, *Advance and Retreat*, "Hood and His Men," *Huntsville (Ala.) Daily Confederate*, October 17, 1863.

48. *OR*, 30 (2):288, 458; Hood, *Advance and Retreat*, 62–63.

49. Captain James D. Williams to parents, September 24, 1863, *The Horse Soldier* (Gettysburg, Pa.) Catalog, January 2000, 67; "Battle of Chickamauga: The Confederate General Receiving His Wound," Frank Vizettelly Sketches, bMS Am 1585, Houghton Library, Harvard University, Cambridge, Mass.; Howell Carter, *A Cavalryman's Reminiscences of the Civil War* (New Orleans: American Print Company, 1900), 90–91; *OR*, 30 (2):512.

50. Jannelle J. McRee, comp., *Down on Cooter's Creek and Other Stories* (Atlanta: Cherokee, 1986), 134; Hood, *Advance and Retreat*, 65; Haskell, *Memoirs*, 49. Members of Hood's staff claimed that after being wounded at Chickamauga, the general "never lost his composure for a moment, and gave orders clearly and coolly before allowing himself to be taken from the field."

51. Hood, General and Staff CSR, NA.

52. Hood, General and Staff CSR, NA; Micah Jenkins, General and Staff CSR, M331, NA; Lafayette McLaws marginalia in James Longstreet to Lafayette McLaws, October 18, 1863, Lafayette McLaws Papers, Southern Historical Collection, University of North Carolina, Chapel Hill.

53. McMurry, *Hood*, 78–81.

54. Hood, General and Staff CSR, NA; "General Hood on Horseback," *Richmond Enquirer*, January 18, 1864.

55. McMurry, *Hood*, 89–92; Woodward, ed., *Mary Chesnut's Civil War*, 561–64.

56. McMurry, *Hood*, 87–88; Woodward, ed., *Mary Chesnut's Civil War*, 565; *OR*, 52 (2):555. Davis had decided as early as October 29, 1863, to promote Hood to lieutenant general, so Hood's flattery during the subsequent winter clearly had no real impact on his promotion.

57. McMurry, *Hood*, 88; Hood, *Advance and Retreat*, 67–68.

58. McMurry, *Hood*, 95; Thomas L. Connelly, *Autumn of Glory: The Army of Tennessee, 1862–1865* (Baton Rouge: Louisiana State University Press, 1971), 323 (hereafter cited as Connelly, *Autumn of Glory*). Connelly points out that even if officials in the Davis administration had not made a formal or informal arrangement with Hood to keep them informed about the state of affairs in the Army of Tennessee, no one discouraged his extensive correspondence with various individuals.

59. *OR*, 32 (3):606–07, 781; McMurry, *Hood*, 95–97.

60. McMurry, *Hood*, 96–97.

61. Castel, *Decision*, 76; McMurry, *Hood*, 97–98.

62. "Special," "A Gala Day at the Front," *Atlanta Southern Confederacy*, March 19, 1864.

63. "Gen. Hood in the Saddle," *Mobile Advertiser and Register*, March 25, 1864.

64. McMurry, *Hood*, 102–03.

65. Castel, *Decision*, 163; McMurry, *Hood*, 105.

66. Castel, *Decision*, 176–78.

67. McMurry, *Hood*, 107.

68. Castel, *Decision*, 201–203; McMurry, *Hood*, 108; Hood, *Advance and Retreat*, 100–03. Johnston claimed in his memoir that Hood's report of Federals being in his rear on May 19 was "manifestly untrue." Hood offered evidence to prove that there were indeed Union troops threatening his column. Historians have verified that Hood was right.

69. McMurry, *Hood*, 109; Hood, *Advance and Retreat*, 104–16.

70. Jefferson Davis, *The Papers of Jefferson Davis*, ed. Lynda Lasswell Crist and others, 11 vols. to date (Baton Rouge: Louisiana State University Press, 1971–2003), 10:434 (hereafter cited as Davis, *Papers*); Castel, *Decision*, 211.

71. McMurry, *Hood*, 110.

72. *OR*, 38 (3):761; "Special Correspondence of the Atlanta Intelligencer," *Atlanta Intelligencer*, June 1, 1864.

73. Hood, *Advance and Retreat*, 120-23; McMurry, *Hood*, 111.

74. McMurry, *Hood*, 111.

75. Castel, *Decision*, 293; McMurry, *Hood*, 113; *OR*, 38 (3):760, 762, 815. Hood apparently wrote little during or after the war about the June 22, 1864, action, so his motives for attacking are difficult to surmise.

76. McMurry, *Hood*, 114.

77. Woodward, ed. *Mary Chesnut's Civil War*, 616, 630. Hood openly broke with Johnston over Confederate strategy in a meeting with Sen. Benjamin H. Hill on July 1 at the Army of Tennessee's headquarters. For two different versions of this meeting by Hill, see *OR*, 52 (2):704–07; Jefferson Davis, *Rise and Fall of the Confederate Government*, 2 vols. (1881; reprint, New York: Yoseloff, 1958), 2: 557–59.

78. Robert E. Lee, *The Wartime Papers of Robert E. Lee*, ed. Clifford Dowdey and Louis H. Manarin (Boston: Little, Brown, 1961), 821–22.

79. Davis, *Papers*, 10:522–25; McMurry, *Hood*, 122–23. McMurry concludes that Bragg's July 15 letter to Davis and a July 14 letter from Hood to Bragg both probably arrived in Richmond too late to influence the Confederate president's decision to appoint Hood as Johnston's successor. Bragg's July 15 telegrams, however, probably helped convince Davis to choose Hood over Hardee as Johnston's successor.

80. *OR*, 38 (5):879–80.

81. Castel, *Decision*, 356–57; McMurry, *Hood*, 118–19; Stephen Davis, *Atlanta Will Fall: Sherman, Joe Johnston, and the Yankee Heavy Battalions* (Wilmington: Scholarly Resources, 2001), 112–13.

82. *OR*, 38 (5):885.

83. Hood, *Advance and Retreat*, 126; Evelyn Sieburg and James E. Hansen II, eds., *Memoirs of a Confederate Staff Officer* (Shippensburg: White Mane, 1998), 57; Davis, *Papers*, 10:539.

84. Connelly, *Autumn of Glory*, 443; McMurry, *Hood*, 129.

85. McMurry, *Hood*, 131–32.

86. Ibid., 133.

87. Ibid., 133–34.

88. Richard McMurry, *Atlanta 1864: Last Chance for the Confederacy* (Lincoln: University of Nebraska Press, 2000), 188–89; Hood, *Advance and Retreat*, 129.

89. McMurry, *Hood*, 144; Connelly, *Autumn of Glory*, 435.

90. McMurry, *Hood*, 147–149; *OR*, 38 (3):701.

91. McMurry, *Hood*, 148–149; Connelly, *Autumn of Glory*, 430.

92. John Bell Hood to James A. Seddon, September 21, 1864, in A. P. Mason, General and Staff CSR, NA; McMurry, *Hood*,157.

93. McMurry, *Hood*, 162; Hood, *Advance and Retreat*, 267; "General Hood: His Last Campaign in Tennessee," *New York Times*, November 2, 1865. Hood told a *Montreal Herald* reporter in the fall of 1865 that he also believed that the Army of Tennessee could gain large numbers of recruits and supplies in Kentucky.

94. McMurry, *Hood*, 162–63. For a fine critical analysis of Hood's logistical problems during the Atlanta and Tennessee campaigns, see Frank E. Vandiver, "General Hood as a Logistician," *Military Affairs* 16 (spring 1952):1 11.

95. Hood, *Advance and Retreat*, 281; Connelly, *Autumn of Glory*, 490–91; McMurry, *Hood*, 169.

96. Sam D. Elliott, ed., *Doctor Quintard, Chaplain C.S.A. and Second Bishop of Tennessee* (Baton Rouge: Louisiana State University Press, 2003), 181, 184 (hereafter cited as Elliott, ed., *Doctor Quintard*). Hood also told Quintard on the evening of the twenty-seventh of a plan to take the city of Nashville which apparently involved 700 volunteers who would "storm the Key of the works about the city."

97. McMurry, *Hood*, 170.

98. Elliott, ed., *Doctor Quintard*, 185; McMurry, *Hood*, 172–73.

99. Wiley Sword, *Embrace an Angry Wind* (New York: HarperCollins, 1992), 156–57; McMurry, *Hood*, 174–75.

100. McMurry, *Hood*, 174; Sword, *Embrace an Angry Wind*, 154–55; Connelly, *Autumn of Glory*, 501–2; Stephen Davis, "John Bell Hood's 'Addictions' in Civil War Literature," *Blue and Gray Magazine* 16

(October 1998):28–31. Some historians, including Connelly and Sword, have speculated that Hood might have taken a derivative of laudanum or imbibed alcohol on the evening of November 29 to ease his pain, resulting in clouded judgment. As Stephen Davis has pointed out, there is no solid historical evidence to support these conclusions.

101. Hood, *Advance and Retreat*, 292–329.

102. Connelly, *Autumn of Glory*, 503–04; Hood, *Advance and Retreat*, 162; McMurry, *Hood*, 174–75.

103. "Battle of Franklin," *Augusta Daily Constitutionalist*, December 16, 1864.

104. Hood, *Advance and Retreat*, 331; McMurry, *Hood*, 176–77.

105. Elliott, ed., *Doctor Quintard*, 199–201; Hood, *Advance and Retreat*, 332.

106. Hood, *Advance and Retreat*, 310; McMurry, *Hood*, 225; Woodward, ed., *Mary Chesnut's Civil War*, 708; Hood, General and Staff CSR, NA. McMurry points out that Hood's willingness to accept responsibility for the 1864 Tennessee Campaign was "a theme that he espoused for the rest of his life."

107. Woodward, ed., *Mary Chesnut's Civil War*, 658, 708, 769, 804–5.

108. Hood, *Advance and Retreat*, 317–37; McMurry, *Hood*, 185–86.

109. John Bell Hood [with March 23, 1865, endorsement of Robert E. Lee], "Notes on the Spring Campaign of 1865," Civil War Collection, Box 5, HL.

110. *OR*, 53:1047; John B. Hood to Jefferson Davis, March 21, 1865, Frederick Dearborn Collection, Houghton Library, Harvard University, Cambridge, Mass.; McMurry, *Hood*, 188.

111. *OR*, 38 (3): 637–638.

112. Hood, *Advance and Retreat*, 311; *OR*, 49 (2):1279.

113. Louisiana, Vol. 13 (New Orleans, Vol. 4), R.G. Dun & Co. Records, Baker Library, Harvard Graduate School of Business Administration, Cambridge, Mass.; McMurry, *Hood*, 194.

114. John P. Dyer, *The Gallant Hood* (Indianapolis: Bobbs-Merrill, 1950), 315 (hereafter cited as Dyer, *The Gallant Hood*).

115. Donald B. Sanger and Thomas R. Hay, *James Longstreet* (Baton Rouge: Louisiana State University Press, 1952), 329 (hereafter cited as Sanger and Hay, *Longstreet*).

116. "Gen. Longstreet," *New York Times*, June 8, 1890, 15; Dyer, *The Gallant Hood*, 314.

117. Sanger and Hay, *Longstreet*, 335.

118. F. B. Chilton, comp., *Unveiling and Dedication of Monument to Hood's Texas Brigade* (Houston: F.B. Chilton, 1911), 236.

119. McMurry, *Hood*, 198–99.

120. Richard McMurry introduction in Hood, *Advance and Retreat*, xv; "Gen. Hood. His Last Campaign in Tennessee," *New York Times*,

November 2, 1865. Hood had probably been collecting material on his career for years. As early as October 1865 Hood had told a reporter that he planned on compiling a memoir.

121. McMurry introduction in Hood, *Advance and Retreat*, xv–xvi. For an analysis of the papers Hood attempted to sell to the federal government, now kept in the National Archives, see Richard M. McMurry, "Disappointment in History: The Papers of John Bell Hood," *Prologue: The Journal of the National Archives* 4 (1974):161–64.

122. McMurry, *Hood*, 201–3, 227; Dyer, *The Gallant Hood*, 317.

INDEX